THE NAVY CROSS

The Navy Cross

The Navy Cross is awarded to a person who, while serving in any capacity with the Navy or Marine Corps, distinguishes himself by extraordinary heroism not justifying the award of the Medal of Honor —

(1) while engaged in an action against an enemy of the United States;
(2) while engaged in military operations involving conflict with an opposing foreign force; or
(3) while serving with friendly forces engaged in an armed conflict against an opposing armed force in which the United States is not a belligerent party.

To warrant this distinctive decoration, the act or the execution of duty must be performed in the presence of great danger or at great personal risk and must be performed in such a manner as to set the individual apart from his shipmates or fellow Marines. An accumulation of minor acts of heroism does not justify the award. The high standards demanded must be borne in mind when recommending the award.

Navy Cross is awarded to a person who, while
any capacity with the Navy or Marine Corps, distin-
self by extraordinary heroism not justifying the
Medal of Honor —

e engaged in an action against an enemy of the
ed States;

e engaged in military operations involving conflict
an opposing foreign force; or

serving with friendly forces engaged in an armed
ct against an opposing armed force in which the
d States is not a belligerent party.

nt this distinctive decoration, the act or the
ty must be performed in the presence of great
t personal risk and must be performed in such
et the individual apart from his shipmates or
An accumulation of minor acts of heroism
e award. The high standards demanded must
when recommending the award.

THE NAVY CROSS

Photo courtesy of The Department of Defense

The N

The N...
serving in a...
guishes him...
award of the...
  (1) whil...
   Unit...
  (2) while...
   with...
  (3) while...
   confli...
   United...
  To warra...
execution of du...
danger or at grea...
a manner as to s...
fellow Marines....
does not justify t...
be borne in mind...

The NAVY CROSS

VIETNAM

Citations of Awards to Men of
The United States Navy
and
The United States Marine Corps

1964 - 1973

Edited by Paul Drew Stevens

Sharp & Dunnigan

PUBLICATIONS

BOX 660 FOREST RANCH,
CALIFORNIA 95942 U.S.A.

May 1987
First Printing

Library of Congress Catalog Card Number 86-61999
Library of Congress Cataloging-in-Publication Data
The Navy Cross — Vietnam

  Includes index.
      1. Vietnamese Conflict, 1961-1975—Biography.
2. United States. Navy—Biography. 3. United States.
Marine Corps—Biography. 4. Navy Cross (Medal)
5. United States. Navy—History—Vietnamese Conflict,
1961-1975. 6. United States. Marine Corps—History—
Vietnamese Conflict, 1961-1975. I. Stevens, Paul
Drew. II. Sharp & Dunnigan Publications.
DS557.5.N38 1984 959.704'345'0922 [B] 86-61999
Sharp & Dunnigan Publications, Incorporated
Forest Ranch, California
95942 USA

ISBN 0-918495-15-6

The official records presented in this work were obtained
through U.S. Government sources and are as complete and
accurate as the records provided.

DEDICATION

This book is dedicated to those men of the United States Marine Corps and United States Navy who met the call of duty on land, on the sea, in the air, and on the deadly rivers of Southeast Asia. It is especially dedicated to those who defeated the enemy's purpose, even as their prisoner.

PRECEDENCE OF AWARDS

Military decorations take precedence over all other awards.
The precedence of Navy decorations is as follows:
Medal of Honor
Navy Cross
Defense Distinguished Service Medal*
Distinguished Service Medal
Silver Star Medal
Defense Superior Service Medal*
Legion of Merit
Distinguished Flying Cross
Navy and Marine Corps Medal
Bronze Star Medal
Purple Heart
Defense Meritorious Service Medal*
Meritorious Service Medal
Air Medal
Joint Service Commendation Medal*
Navy Commendation Medal
Joint Service Achievement Medal*
Navy Achievement Medal
Combat Action Ribbon

*Not a Navy medal but authorized if awarded by name and earned in joint service action.

ACKNOWLEDGEMENTS

The publishers would like to express their gratitude to Fred P. Anthony and the staff of the Medals and Decorations Section, Headquarters, United States Marine Corps; to Jeannie Kirk, Head of Awards and Special Projects Branch, Chief of Naval Operations; and the affable, able, Anna C. Urband, Media Services Division, Department of the Navy. We would also like to thank Danny J. Crawford, Head, Reference Section, History and Museums Division U.S. Marine Corps, and Colonel William V.H. (Bill) White, USMC (Retired), Editor, *Leatherneck Magazine*.

Harley S. Shane
Paul D. Stevens
Publishers

CONTENTS

THE SECRETARY OF THE NAVY
WASHINGTON

The President of the United States takes pride in presenting the
NAVY CROSS posthumously to

CAPTAIN JEB F. SEAGLE
UNITED STATES MARINE CORPS RESERVE

for service as set forth in the following

CITATION:

For extraordinary heroism while serving as an AH-1T (TOW)
Cobra Attack Helicopter Pilot with Marine Medium Helicopter
Squadron 261, 22nd Marine Amphibious Unit conducting combat operations on the Island of Grenada on 25 October 1983. While
conducting an armed reconnaissance mission in support of ground
forces, Captain Seagle's aircraft was hit by multiple antiaircraft artillery projectiles and forced down behind enemy lines.
Having been knocked out by the blast, Captain Seagle regained
consciousness after his fellow pilot had flown the aircraft to
impact and found that his aircraft was on fire and burning out of
control. As Captain Seagle exited the front cockpit of the Cobra,
he saw that the other pilot had been critically wounded and
remained helplessly trapped in the aircraft. With complete
disregard for his own safety, Captain Seagle courageously returned
to the aircraft which was now engulfed in flames and pulled him
out. As unexpended ordnance began to cook off all around them,
Captain Seagle carried the severely wounded pilot well clear of
the danger. Now exposed to heavy enemy small arms and machinegun
fire and faced with certain death or capture, Captain Seagle
ignored the danger and remained to attend the wounds of the
injured pilot by wrapping a tourniquet around his severely
bleeding arm. Realizing that enemy soldiers were approaching,
Captain Seagle fearlessly distracted them away from the helpless
pilot and ultimately sacrificed his own life in an effort to buy
time for the rescue helicopter to arrive. By his extraordinary
courage, uncommon valor, and loyal devotion to duty in the face of
danger, Captain Seagle ensured his brother-in-arms was rescued;
thereby reflecting great credit upon himself and upholding the
highest traditions of the Marine Corps and the United States Naval
Service.

For the President,

Secretary of the Navy

PREFACE

The citation reproduced here is for the posthumous award of the Navy Cross to Captain Jeb F. Seagle, United States Marine Corps Reserve, for action on 23 October 1983 on the Island of Grenada. Captain Seagle's award is the only Navy Cross that has been awarded for action since the close of U.S. involvement in the Vietnam War in 1973. The brave still serve.

Capt. Seagle's citation:
SEAGLE, JEB F.

For extraordinary heroism while serving as an AH-1T (TOW) Cobra Attack Helicopter Pilot with Marine Medium Helicopter Squadron 261, 22nd Marine Amphibious Unit conducting combat operations on the Island of Grenada on 25 October 1983. While conducting an armed reconnaissance mission in support of ground forces, Captain Seagle's aircraft was hit by multiple anti-aircraft artillery projectiles and forced down behind enemy lines. Having been knocked out by the blast, Captain Seagle regained consciousness after his fellow pilot had flown the aircraft to impact and found that his aircraft was on fire and burning out of control. As Captain Seagle exited the front cockpit of the Cobra, he saw that the other pilot had been critically wounded and remained helplessly trapped in the aircraft. With complete disregard for his own safety, Captain Seagle courageously returned to the aircraft which was now engulfed in flames and pulled him out. As unexpended ordnance began to cook off all around them, Captain Seagle carried the severely wounded pilot well clear of the danger. Now exposed to heavy enemy small arms and machinegun fire and faced with certain death or capture, Captain Seagle ignored the danger and remained to attend the wounds of the injured pilot by wrapping a tourniquet around his severely bleeding arm. Realizing that enemy soldiers were approaching, Captain Seagle fearlessly distracted them away from the helpless pilot and ultimately sacrificed his own life in an effort to buy time for the rescue helicopter to arrive. By his extraordinary courage, uncommon valor, and loyal devotion to duty in the face of danger, Captain Seagle ensured his brother-in-arms was rescued; thereby reflecting great credit upon himself and upholding the highest traditions of the Marine Corps and the United States Naval Service.

PART I

THE NAVY CROSS
HISTORICAL BACKGROUND

The Navy Cross was established on February 4, 1919 with the passage of Public Law 193 by the 65th Congress of the United States. Until then there was but one medal, the Medal of Honor, also known as the Congressional Medal of Honor because it is awarded in the name of Congress.

Established in 1861 the Medal of Honor was awarded "for gallantry in action and other seaman-like (soldier-like) qualities." With this broad criteria, two thousand six hundred twenty-five Medals of Honor were awarded between 1862 and 1916 when a permanent Medal of Honor Board was established as part of a sweeping review of the entire awards and decorations procedures of the military. Nine hundred ten awards of the Medal of Honor were recalled (eight hundred sixty-four of those recalled had been awarded to members of one regiment, the 27th Maine, by President Lincoln as inducement to continue guarding the capitol past the approaching end of their enlistment). No awards to Navy personnel were, or have since been, recalled.

1

It had become clear during the First World War that one medal alone could not effectively recognize the full range of exceptional service, including heroism. So the criteria of the Medal of Honor was elevated to be awarded to: "one who shall in action with an enemy, distinguish himself conspicuously by gallantry and intrepidity at the risk of his life above and beyond the call of duty." Stringent requirements for documentation were imposed, and new awards were created in a descending order of precedence.

The Navy Cross came into existence at this time along with the Navy Distinguished Service Medal, the Army Distinguished Service Cross and Service Medal, and the Silver Star Certificates (later to become the Silver Star Medals). These were the framework of a graduated system of recognition which did not exist before.

From their inception, distinction between the Navy Cross (originally intended for combat bravery only) and the Navy Distinguished Service Medal, became blurred. For many years the Navy Cross was ranked third in order of precedence below the Medal of Honor and Navy Distinguished Service Medal.

With the passage of Public Law 702 on August 7, 1942 the issue was resolved. This act clarified the criteria which now states that the award of the Navy Cross shall be to "any person while serving in any capacity with the Navy or Marine Corps who distinguishes himself with extraordinary heroism not justifying the award of the Medal of Honor — (1) while engaged in an action against an enemy of the United States; (2) while engaged in military operations involving conflict with an opposing foreign force; or (3) while serving with friendly foreign forces engaged in an armed conflict against an opposing armed force in which the United States is not a belligerent party. To warrant this distinctive decoration the act should involve risk of life so extraordinary as to set the person apart from his contemporaries. An accumulation of minor acts of heroism does not justify the award." Congress also specified that the Navy Cross was to rank (along with the Army Distinguished Service Cross and now the Air Force Cross) as the second highest honor the nation can bestow for combat heroism.

The Navy Cross, made of bronze, was designed by James Earle Fraser. It is a broad-faced cross patee with the ends of the arms rounded. The cross is one and one-half inches wide with a circle in the middle of the cross encompassing the design of a sailing vessel. Laurel leaves are represented at each joining of the arms about the center. In the center of the circle on the reverse side of the medal are crossed anchors and the letters "USN." The Navy Cross has not been numbered nor has it usually been engraved with the name of the recipient. The medal is suspended by a thin half inch ring from a one and three-quarter inch wide ribbon of navy blue moire silk with a quarter inch wide white center stripe. Through World War II the metal used was a dark bronze. Since then the cross has been made of a lighter, brighter colored metal.

The book *The Navy Cross — Vietnam* is, as its subtitle indicates, citations of awards to men of the United States Navy and the United States Marine Corps during the Vietnam era.

These are the official accounts of the acts of extraordinary heroism of 483 men who were awarded this high honor. Here are riflemen and riverboat patrolmen, machine gunners and medical corpsmen, SEALS, squad leaders and surgeons, infantry officers, pilots and prisoners of war. They served with honor, and these are the testimonials to the quality of their service.

PART II

CITATIONS OF AWARDS OF THE NAVY CROSS DURING THE VIETNAM ERA

[Asterisk (*) Indicates Posthumous Award]

*ABRAMS, LEWIS H.

Citation: For extraordinary heroism as Commanding Officer of Marine All Weather Attack Squadron 242 and as Pilot of an A6A Intruder aircraft in Vietnam. In the early morning hours of 25 October 1967, Colonel (then Lieutenant Colonel) Abrams, in the first Marine aircraft to strike at the heart of North Vietnam's Air Force, exhibited outstanding courage and presence of mind in the midst of violent combat action as he successfully completed a high-priority mission by bombing the principal military airfield in North Vietnam. A highly effective integrated complex of hundreds of radar-controlled antiaircraft weapons, barrage balloons with steel cables extending hundreds of feet into the air, two enemy airfields with MIG interceptor aircraft, and many active surface-to-air missile sites protected every approach to his target. Acting on an urgent fragmentary order, Colonel Abrams personally took charge of the preparations for a multiplane, multisquadron attack against the formidably defended Phuc Yen airfield. Barely six hours before takeoff time another

5

fragmentary order was received, modifying the previous plan and requiring Colonel Abrams to make extensive last-minute changes in navigation and attack procedures, which allowed no margin for error. With grim determination, he promptly made corrections in heading, altitude, and airspeed and accurately delivered his bombs on the runway at Phuc Yen. Under the most demanding conditions of degraded systems operation, low-level flight in mountainous terrain in darkness, and in the face of a vicious volume of antiaircraft and guided missile fire, Colonel Abrams courageously accomplished his mission of devastating the runway at Phuc Yen. His bravery and determination throughout the bitter action were an inspiration to all who were involved and were instrumental in accomplishing this crucial mission. By his intrepid fighting spirit, daring initiative, and unswerving devotion to duty, Colonel Abrams reflected great credit upon himself and the Marine Corps and upheld the highest traditions of the United States Naval Service.

ABSHIRE, BOBBY W.

Citation: For extraordinary heroism as Crew Chief of a UH-1E helicopter while serving with Marine Observation Squadron TWO during operations against the enemy in the vicinity of Danang, Vietnam on 21 May 1966. When a platoon from Company A, First Battalion, Ninth Marines was pinned down in an open rice paddy by heavily armed North Vietnamese and Viet Cong forces, Corporal Abshire's medical evacuation helicopter was assigned the mission of recovering the casualties, which included over half of the men of the platoon. Despite vicious incoming fire which damaged the helicopter, a successful landing was made on the second attempt. Since remnants of the platoon were too heavily committed to assist in the evacuation, Corporal Abshire jumped from the helicopter and gallantly carried two wounded Marines into the aircraft while enemy rounds struck all around him. When it became necessary to return to the home field to replace the battle-damaged helicopter, he quickly transferred equipment to a new aircraft and volunteered to return. On each of the eight trips by his aircraft into the besieged zone, Corporal Abshire ignored enemy fire to assist in loading wounded and dead Marines. On one occasion, he swiftly silenced an enemy machine gun with accurate fire from a grenade launcher. His fearless and determined efforts contributed in large measure to the success of the mission, in which twenty-three casualties were evacuated. His courage in the face of hostile fire and his compassion for his wounded comrades were an inspiration to all who observed him. By his daring actions and devotion to duty in spite of great personal risk, Corporal Abshire reflected great credit upon himself and upheld the highest traditions of the Marine Corps and the United States Naval Service.

*ABSHIRE, RICHARD F.

Citation: For extraordinary heroism while serving as a Platoon Sergeant with Company G, Second Battalion, Fourth Marines, Ninth Marine Amphibious Brigade in connection with operations against the enemy in the Republic of Vietnam on 2 May 1968. Sergeant Abshire's unit and a sister company were launched on a coordinated attack against a well entrenched North Vietnamese Army force occupying the village of Dinh To, Quang Tri Province. As the Marines entered the village, they were taken under devastating enemy small-arms and automatic weapons fire which inflicted numerous casualties and temporarily halted the lead platoon of each company. Directed to establish a defensive perimeter, Sergeant Abshire immediately deployed his men into advantageous firing positions and commenced directing a heavy volume of accurate fire into the enemy emplacements. As the enemy fire increased in volume and accuracy, it became apparent that the North Vietnamese force was preparing to launch a counterattack. Rapidly obtaining grenades from his fellow Marines, Sergeant Abshire boldly exposed himself to the full fury of the enemy fire and threw several grenades into the enemy's ranks, temporarily halting their assault. Returning to his unit, he moved from position to position, despite intense enemy fire, to pinpoint hostile targets and encourage his men. As their ammunition supply depleted, he ordered his men to withdraw across a river and resolutely provided covering fire, which enabled his men to reach positions of relative safety. After expending his ammunition, he was attempting to rejoin his unit when he was mortally wounded by enemy fire. By his superior leadership, intrepid fighting spirit and selfless devotion to duty, Sergeant Abshire inspired all who observed him and upheld the highest traditions of the Marine Corps and the United States Naval Service. He gallantly gave his life for his country.

*ADAMS, JOHN T.

Citation: For extraordinary heroism while serving with the First

Platoon, Company C, First Reconnaissance Battalion in Vietnam on 16 June 1966. Corporal Adams was a member of a reconnaissance team occupying an observation post on Hill 488, Quang Tin Province, deep in enemy controlled territory. During the early morning hours the platoon of eighteen men was subjected to an intense assault by an estimated North Vietnamese unit of battalion size. As the members of his team were withdrawing to a predesignated defensive perimeter, Corporal Adams braved the withering small-arms fire and returned accurate rifle fire which momentarily slowed the enemy assault force and enabled his companions to reach the relative safety of the defensive position. Firing all his ammunition, Corporal Adams fearlessly charged directly into the assaulting horde and, using his rifle as a club, killed two of the enemy soldiers before he was struck down by automatic weapons fire. Severely wounded, he once again engaged an enemy soldier in hand-to-hand combat and, in a final effort, killed his foe. As a result of his courageous action and fighting spirit, his comrades were able to rally and withstand the onslaught of the numerically superior enemy. Corporal Adams upheld the highest traditions of the Marine Corps and the United States Naval Service. He gallantly gave his life in the cause of freedom.

ADAMS, LAURENCE R., III

Citation: For extraordinary heroism on 12 January 1969 as a pilot in Medium Helicopter Squadron 165, Marine Aircraft Group 16, First Marine Aircraft Wing, in connection with combat operations against the enemy in the Republic of Vietnam. Assigned the emergency mission of extracting an eight-man reconnaissance team which had been engaged in combat with a numerically superior hostile force for twenty-four hours in a densely-jungled, mountainous area southwest of An Hoa, Captain Adams piloted his transport helicopter to the designated area and maintained his craft in a hover above tall trees while a cable ladder was lowered to the ground. Undaunted by the extremely heavy volume of enemy fire which caused extensive damage to his helicopter, he remained in this dangerously exposed position and then inadvertently lifted out of the hazardous area with only five of the eight members of the reconnaissance team on the ladder. Informed that three Marines still remained on the ground, Captain Adams resolutely elected to return to the perilous area after disembarking the five patrol members. Despite deteriorating weather conditions, approaching darkness, and a lack of adequate support from the helicopter gunships which had expended nearly all their ordnance, he established a hover on his third approach, after twice being driven back by the intense enemy fire, and succeeded in rescuing the three remaining Marines. A subsequent investigation revealed that his aircraft had sustained a total of twenty-three hits and over eighty grenade fragment holes from its extended exposure to the enemy fire. By his courage, superior airmanship, and dedication, captain Adams was directly instrumental in saving the lives of eight fellow Marines and upheld the highest traditions of the Marine Corps and of the United States Naval Service.

AJDUKOVICH, GEORGE

Citation: For extraordinary heroism on 7 October 1969 while serving as patrol officer of two river patrol boats in a night waterborne guardpost on the Muo Hai Canal, Republic of Vietnam. When an enemy grenade was thrown from the bank of the canal and landed on the craft in which Chief Petty Officer Ajdukovich was embarked, he immediately seized the grenade and clasped it to his body in an attempt to protect the lives of his fellow crewmen. Seconds later, when the deadly missile failed to explode, he hurled it into the canal where it detonated underwater almost instantly. With his two patrol boats now under a heavy concentration of automatic-weapons fire from four enemy positions on the river bank, Chief Petty Officer Ajdukovich requested air support and immediately directed a devastating barrage of suppressive fire while leading his units clear of the kill zone. Unable to make any further firing runs on the entrenched enemy force when one of the patrol boats became disabled, Chief Petty Officer Ajdukovich's patrol illuminated and mortared the hostile area until air cover arrived on the scene, and then continued illumination of the target area to help maximize the effects of the air strike. By his valiant fighting spirit, inspiring leadership, and selfless devotion to duty, Chief Petty Officer Ajdukovich was greatly instrumental in leading his patrol to safety without sustaining a single personnel casualty. His heroic initiative was in keeping with the highest traditions of the United States Naval Service.

ALFONSO, VINCENT

Citation: For extraordinary heroism with Company A, First Battalion, Third Marines in Vietnam. On 20 July 1966 near the Dong

Ha airstrip, during Operation HASTINGS, Private First Class Alfonso was serving as a machine gunner with a twelve man patrol when the squad was ambushed while taking on water at a small stream by a force of about sixty Viet Cong. In a matter of minutes enemy fire hit the group from three sides and the squad leader directed a move to key high ground in the right rear with Private First Class Alfonso designated to cover their move. Because his field of vision was extremely limited in the high grass and scrub, he courageously leaped to his feet and provided effective fire while his companions made their way to the new position. When the enemy augmented their fire with several mortar rounds, he again stood in full view of the enemy and displayed extraordinary aggressiveness and courage as he fired two hundred rounds from the hip directly into the hostile position. As armed helicopters arrived over the scene and forced the Viet Cong from cover, he continued to pour heavy and accurate fire at the enemy. When dangerously low ammunition supplies and a lack of communications forced the Marines to start withdrawing, he again displayed daring initiative and fearlessness as he exposed himself to the continuing hostile fire to cover the movement of his comrades. His valiant effort throughout was largely responsible for the toll of thirty Viet Cong killed, and enabled his unit to escape from the hazardous area without sustaining any casualties. By his extraordinary courage in the face of overwhelming odds, uncommon concern for others at great risk of his own life, and unwavering dedication to duty, Private First Class Alfonso reflected great credit upon himself and the Marine Corps and upheld the highest traditions of the United States Naval Service.

ALLEN, YALE G.

Citation: For extraordinary heroism while serving as a Fire Team Leader with Company C, First Battalion, Fourth Marines, Third Marine Division, in connection with operations against the enemy in the Republic of Vietnam. On 5 March 1969, Corporal Allen's company initiated an assault against a North Vietnamese Army regiment occupying nine well-fortified bunkers on top of a hill near Ca Lu in Quang Tri Province. During the initial moments of the attack, the third platoon was pinned down by a heavy volume of machine-gun fire from one of the enemy fortifications. With complete disregard for his own safety, Corporal Allen unhesitatingly left his relatively secure position on the opposite side of the hill and maneuvered up the steep slope. Although singled out by the enemy for concentrated fire, he skillfully utilized the scant available natural cover, attained his objective, and as he was throwing a hand grenade into a bunker he was knocked to the ground and seriously wounded by a barrage of mortar fire. After quickly regaining his footing, he climbed to the top of the emplacement and hurled another hand grenade inside. Completely exposing himself to the intense North Vietnamese fire, he then raced to the front of the fortification and sprayed the inside with rifle fire, thereby ensuring the destruction of the position and the death of the hostile soldiers occupying it. Ignoring his painful injuries, he rejoined his squad, and after steadfastly refusing medical attention, led his men in the final assault on the enemy force. His heroic and decisive actions inspired all who observed him and were instrumental in the subsequent rout of the North Vietnamese Army unit. By his courage, aggressive fighting spirit, and unwavering devotion to duty in the face of grave personal danger, Corporal Allen upheld the finest traditions of the Marine Corps and the United States Naval Service.

*ALMEIDA, RUSSELL V.

Citation: For extraordinary heroism while serving with Company "C", Third Engineer Battalion, Third Marine Division (Reinforced) in Vietnam on 20 December 1965. Lance Corporal Almeida was part of a combat engineer element assigned to Company "K", Third Battalion, Ninth Marines for anti-minewarfare and demolition support. While accompanying the Second Platoon, Company "K" through a hostile area in the vicinity of Duysen Son 2, Lance Corporal Almeida was called upon to neutralize an M-26 grenade booby trap device and to define a safe lane for passage of the infantry platoon. He fearlessly approached the booby trap device which was triggered when he was within a few feet of the grenade. Although Lance Corporal Almeida was aware that the grenade was armed and detonation was imminent, he, with total disregard for his own safety, turned toward the deadly device, stepping between it and his fellow Marines. As he reached for the grenade he was mortally wounded by its deadly explosion. His act of heroism and personal sacrifice saved several nearby Marines from certain injury and possible death. Lance Corporal Almeida's daring initiative, courageous actions and loyal devotion to duty reflected great credit upon himself and upheld the highest traditions of the Marine Corps and the United States Naval Service. He gallantly gave his life for his country.

ALSPAUGH, TIMOTHY D.

Citation: For extraordinary heroism during operations against an armed enemy in the Republic of Vietnam on 25 September 1969. Seaman Alspaugh was the after fifty-caliber machine gunner aboard River Patrol Boat 677, which had inserted in a night waterborne guard post on the north bank of the Cai Lon River in support of interdiction operations in Kien Giang Province. His boat was acting as cover boat and had taken a position about fifty yards astern of the patrol's lead boat, with its starboard side to a heavy growth of nipa palm along the river bank. Shortly past midnight, after several hours of waiting quietly in the darkness to detect enemy movement on the water, Seaman Alspaugh observed what he believed to be a sampan on the river upstream from his boat. Alerting his Boat Captain and bringing his machine gun to bear over the port quarter, he was concentrating on the barely visible craft when he was struck on his left side by an object which he instinctively recognized as a grenade thrown from the underbrush. He immediately shouted a warning to his fellow crewmembers, at the same time bending down to search for the grenade, which had come to rest on the pump covers on the far side of his gun mount. Despite the extreme darkness and the imminent danger of an explosion, Seaman Alspaugh succeeded in locating the grenade and quickly threw it back into the small clearing from which it had been thrown. Even before the grenade exploded near the enemy's position, he was firing his fifty-caliber machine gun into the brush, continuing until the boats were clear of the area. Because of Seaman Alspaugh's quick reaction and disregard for his own personal safety, the patrol escaped without casualty. His extraordinary courage and selfless devotion to duty reflected great credit upon himself and were in keeping with the finest traditions of the United States Naval Service.

AMBROSE, GERALD D.

Citation: For extraordinary heroism while serving as a Squad Leader with Company M, Third Battalion, First Marines, First Marine Division in connection with combat operations against the enemy in the Republic of Vietnam. On the night of 8 January 1970, Lance Corporal Ambrose was leading a ten-man joint combat patrol consisting of four United States Marines and six Republic of Vietnam Regional Forces soldiers when the unit came under a heavy volume of fire from approximately twenty-five enemy soldiers near the village of

Chau Son 1 in Quang Nam Province. Ignoring the hostile rounds and grenades impacting around him, Lance Corporal Ambrose quickly deployed his men and initiated an aggressive assault against the enemy positions. When a hand grenade exploded near him, he sustained several serious wounds but steadfastly refused medical attention. Shouting encouragement to his men, he relentlessly pressed the advance, personally accounting for five enemy killed. During the ensuing fierce fire fight, he repeatedly exposed himself to the hostile fusillade as he called directions to his companions and maintained the momentum of the attack until the enemy was forced to retreat, abandoning numerous weapons, documents containing information of intelligence value, and four troops who were captured. Although suffering intense pain and bleeding profusely, Lance Corporal Ambrose again refused medical assistance and, with his last remaining strength, led his unit and the four captured wounded enemy safely back over 1,200 meters of heavily booby-trapped enemy territory to a secure base. His heroic and resolute actions inspired all who observed him and were instrumental in defeating a determined numerically superior hostile force. By his courage, aggressive fighting spirit, and unwavering devotion to duty, Lance Corporal Ambrose contributed significantly to the accomplishment of his unit's mission and upheld the highest traditions of the Marine Corps and of the United States Naval Service.

*AMENDOLA, WILLET R.

Citation: For extraordinary heroism while serving as a Mortar Man with Company M, Second Platoon, Third Battalion, Seventh Marines, First Marine Division (Reinforced), in the Republic of Vietnam on the morning of 2 November 1967. The platoon-sized combat base, of which Corporal Amendola was part, was assaulted by an estimated 100 of the enemy. Maneuvering under the cover of darkness and a heavy mortar barrage, the insurgent forces were almost on the position before an effective defense could be established. Corporal Amendola, whose bunker was on the side of the perimeter which was being breached, fought with great tenacity and fearlessness, as he stoutly held his ground in the face of the oncoming enemy. He and the men in his bunker were holding their own, when Corporal Amendola left his position for scant seconds to give assistance at the 60mm mortar pit. In that brief time an undetected enemy threw a satchel charge, which demolished the bunker and Corporal

Amendola's weapon. Finding, then, that the mortar tube was in enemy possession, he bravely attempted to recover it. Unarmed and fortified with only sheer courage, he ran into the midst of the enemy. Shouting in their own language, he jumped into the pit and engaged the enemy forces in hand to hand combat. Grappling for the mortar tube, he succeeded in recapturing it, when another Viet Cong appeared and mortally wounded him with a burst of automatic fire. By his dauntless courage, initiative and indomitable fighting spirit, Corporal Amendola served to inspire all who observed him and upheld the highest traditions of the Marine Corps and the United States Naval Service. He gallantly gave his life for his country.

ANDERSON, JOHN J.

Citation: For extraordinary heroism while serving as Leader of a Rifle Squad in Company "I", Third Battalion, Ninth Marines, Third Marine Division (Reinforced), in combat operations in support of the Republic of Vietnam on 27 October 1965. Sergeant Anderson led his reinforced squad on a patrol and during the ensuing action, by his personal leadership and professional skill, maneuvered his squad and effected a successful ambush upon the advance guard of a numerically superior enemy. By exercising complete control of his squad, he allowed his men to open fire only when maximum surprise and shock effect could be attained. The first volley of fire killed seven guerrillas, and three more were killed by grenades. Sergeant Anderson then directed the withdrawal of his squad and personally covered the move by firing his M79, killing five more enemy. While continuously exposing himself to heavy enemy fire, he then called in and adjusted mortar fire for maximum effect upon the enemy. Noticing that one of his men was seriously wounded, he, without regard for his own personal safety, once again exposed himself to heavy enemy fire to rescue the wounded man and carry him upon his back while leading his squad to friendly lines. Sergeant Anderson's heroic conduct, inspiring leadership, and fearless devotion to duty reflected great credit upon himself and the Marine Corps and were in keeping with the highest traditions of the United States Naval Service.

*ARMSTRONG, PHILIP M., JR.

Citation: For extraordinary heroism on 8 June 1967 in connection with an armed attack on USS LIBERTY (AGTR-5) in the Eastern

Mediterranean. During the early afternoon hours, LIBERTY was attacked without warning by jet fighter aircraft and three motor torpedo boats. Subjected to intense incendiary, machine-gun, and rocket fire, and placed in extreme jeopardy by a torpedo hit below the waterline on the starboard side, LIBERTY sustained numerous personnel casualties and severe structural damage. Serving as Executive Officer, Lieutenant Commander Armstrong was on the bridge when the first strafing attack occurred. A large fire erupted in the vicinity of two 55-gallon gasoline drums, creating the grave danger that the drums might explode and cause a widespread conflagration. Lieutenant Commander Armstrong fearlessly exposed himself to overwhelmingly accurate rocket and machine-gun fire while proceeding to jettison the gasoline drums and organizing a party of men to extinguish the blazing lifeboats nearby. At this time, he received multiple injuries which proved to be fatal a few hours after the attack terminated. By his aggressiveness, composure under fire, and inspiring leadership, Lieutenant Commander Armstrong upheld the highest traditions of the United States Naval Service.

ARMSTRONG, RUSSELL P.

Citation: For extraordinary heroism while serving as a Platoon Commander with Company I, Third Battalion, Twenty-sixth Marines, Third Marine Division in the Republic of Vietnam on 7 and 8 September 1967. While moving toward the battalion perimeter near Con Thien, Company I came under a heavy volume of rocket, mortar and artillery fire supporting an attack by a reinforced North Vietnamese Army company which caused numerous casualties and separated the friendly unit into two groups. Rapidly assessing the situation, Staff Sergeant Armstrong fearlessly raced across the fire-swept terrain as he consolidated his position and organized a defensive perimeter. Shouting words of encouragement to his men and directing their suppressive fire against the enemy, he was supervising the movement of the more seriously wounded Marines to the center of the position when he was severely injured in both legs by a hostile mortar round impacting nearby. Unable to walk, he dragged himself across the hazardous area by the use of his arms alone and resolutely directed his platoon in successfully joining with the main body of the company. Although in great pain, Staff Sergeant Armstrong steadfastly refused medical evacuation and skillfully began coordinating artillery and mortar fire against the enemy soldiers, frequently adjusting the rounds to within 50 meters of friendly lines. Although periodically lapsing into unconsciousness, he continued his determined efforts throughout the night, crawling among his men to encourage them and ensure that every possible avenue of enemy approach was effectively covered by firepower. Upon the arrival of a relief force in the early hours of the following morning, he permitted himself to be evacuated only after ascertaining that all of his Marines were accounted for and the more seriously injured had been removed. His heroic and decisive actions were instrumental in his unit's accounting for over 60 of the enemy killed. By his courage, aggressive leadership and selfless devotion to duty, Staff Sergeant Armstrong upheld the highest traditions of the Marine Corps and the United States Naval Service.

*ARQUERO, ELPIDIO A.

Citation: For extraordinary heroism as Platoon Sergeant, First Platoon, Company B, Battalion Landing Team 1/3, in the Republic of Vietnam on 10 May 1967. While participating in Operation BEAVER CAGE in Tinh Quang Nam Province, Staff Sergeant Arquero's platoon was lead unit in a company search and destroy operation, when heavy contact was made with two companies of Viet Cong and North Vietnamese regular forces. His flank security began receiving heavy automatic weapons fire and sustained several casualties. He immediately made his way to its position through the hail of enemy fire and courageously directed effective return fire. In order to provide much needed time for his platoon to deploy, he organized an assault element from the remaining members of his flank security. By this time the enemy fire power had increased in severity and effectiveness, yet he daringly continued to expose himself. Without concern for his own safety, he rallied his brave assault force and charged directly into the entrenched enemy positions. This action, which cost him his life, halted the advance of the enemy long enough to allow his platoon time to extract its wounded and withdraw to a defensible position. As a result of his heroic conduct and fearless devotion to duty, Staff Sergeant Arquero undoubtedly saved the lives of many comrades, upholding the highest traditions of the Marine Corps and the United States Naval Service. He gallantly gave his life for his country.

*ASHBY, JAMES W.

Citation: For extraordinary heroism on 1 June 1967 while serving as a corpsman with Company "L", Third Battalion, Ninth Marines, Third Marine Division (Rein), FMF, in the Republic of Vietnam. During a search and destroy operation, Petty Officer Ashby's company came under intense fire from a large, North Vietnamese Army force deeply entrenched in a cleverly-concealed and heavily-defended bunker complex, and suffered heavy casualties during the first few minutes of the fierce battle. Responding immediately, Petty Officer Ashby dashed from his position of relative safety and, seemingly impervious to the murderous hostile, automatic-weapons fire sweeping the area, moved through the open terrain, treating and encouraging the wounded. Completely aware of the grave danger involved in remaining in a position exposed to the withering enemy fire, he staunchly refused to seek cover while there were wounded Marines in need of assistance, placing the welfare of his wounded comrades above his own personal safety. As he knelt over a seriously wounded Marine, shielding the Marine with his own body while administering lifesaving first aid, Petty Officer Ashby was mortally wounded by enemy sniper fire. By his inspiring courage in the face of great personal danger, his deep compassion for his conrades-in-arms, his outstanding professional ability, and his unfaltering devotion to duty, he succeeded in saving the lives of many Marines and upheld the highest traditions of the United States Naval Service.

*ASTON, JAMES M.

Citation: For extraordinary heroism while serving as a Mortar Ammunition Man with Company H, Second Battalion, Twenty-sixth Marines, Ninth Marine Amphibious Brigade in connection with combat operations against the enemy in the Republic of Vietnam on 19 March 1969. Private First Class Aston was participating in a company-sized operation through thick brush and chest high elephant grass in Quang Nam Province when he tripped a hidden enemy explosive device. Fully aware of the probable consequences of his daring action but thinking only of the welfare of several nearby companions, he unhesitatingly threw himself across the lethal object and was mortally wounded as he absorbed the concussion of the detonation. His heroic and timely actions inspired all who observed him and were instrumental in saving the lives of several Marines. By his courage, selfless concern for his fellowmen and unwavering devotion to duty, Private First Class Aston upheld the highest traditions of the Marine Corps and the United States Naval Service.

He gallantly gave his life for his country.

*AYERS, DARRELL E.

Citation: For extraordinary heroism while serving as a Platoon Sergeant with the First Force Reconnaissance Company, First Marine Division in connection with combat operations against the enemy in the Republic of Vietnam. On 19 March 1970, Sergeant Ayers was leading a seven-man patrol on a mission to locate primary enemy infiltration routes in the western section of Quang Nam Province. Two days previously, the aircraft by which the team had been helilifted into the territory had come under intense hostile fire as the Marines were disembarking and, in the intervening period, Sergeant Ayers had skillfully avoided any contact which would compromise his mission. As the Marines approached a small river which was spanned by a bamboo bridge, Sergeant Ayers, realizing the danger of encountering the enemy at this position, moved ahead of the point man and, accompanied by another Marine, reconnoitered the approach to the river. When the two men halted to analyze the surrounding terrain, they suddenly came under a heavy volume of automatic weapons fire from enemy soldiers concealed nearby. In an effort to shield his comrade, Sergeant Ayers placed himself between the fusillade of hostile fire and his companion. Mortally wounded moments thereafter, Sergeant Ayers, by his valiant and selfless efforts, was directly responsible for saving the life of a fellow Marine. His heroic actions were in keeping with the highest traditions of the Marine Corps and of the United States Naval Service.

BACK, JAMES B.

Citation: For extraordinary heroism on 28 February 1968 while serving as the Regimental Surgeon with the First Marines, First Marine Division, in connection with operations against enemy aggressor forces in the Republic of Vietnam. When a Marine was admitted to the regimental aid station suffering from serious wounds sustained when his tracked vehicle came under intense B-40 rocket fire, Lieutenant Back, upon treating the casualty, alertly observed a large, cylindrical, foreign object imbedded in the casualty's lower right side. Unable to identify the object, he requested assistance and was informed the projectile appeared to be an M-79 grenade. Fully aware of the dangers involved, Lieutenant Back operated and found a colored metal cylinder. He resolutely proceeded with the delicate operation without the aid of body armor and despite the danger of the device exploding upon the slightest movement. Displaying extraordinary courage and exceptional professional competence, Lieutenant Back continued his task until he had completely freed the object and carried it outside for disposal. Upon closer examination, it was revealed that the wound had been caused by the fuse of a B-40 rocket, an extremely sensitive and highly explosive device. By his bold initiative, outstanding professional skill, and selfless devotion to duty at great personal risk, Lieutenant Back upheld the highest traditions of the United States Naval Service.

BADNEK, SAMUEL J.

Citation: For extraordinary heroism while serving with Company "H", Second Battalion, Fourth Marines during Operation STARLITE near Chu Lai, Vietnam on 18 August 1965. Private Badnek's platoon was temporarily pinned down by intense automatic weapons, mortar and grenade fire delivered by an insurgent communist (Viet Cong) assault force. In the early moments of the engagement, two enemy grenadiers were silenced, causing the Viet Cong to fall back and regroup, all the while keeping the Marines under intense fire. Realizing the seriousness of the situation, and with total disregard for his own safety, Private Badnek stripped all combat equipment from his body and boldly dashed forty-five yards through heavy fire to reach the enemy. Hurling several grenades into the enemy position, he personally killed eight of the guerrillas. Stunned by his one man assault, the remaining enemy forces rapidly became disorganized and were unable to conduct a counterattack on the Marines now advancing on them. Although he sustained a head wound during his heroic act, Private Badnek remained undeterred as he continued to ferociously engage the enemy, directing accurate and effective rifle fire into the enemy position. Later, after withdrawing to a helicopter evacuation site, he assisted in loading his wounded comrades aboard the aircraft, refusing evacuation himself until all other casualties had embarked. Private Badnek's courageous actions, inspiring combative spirit and loyal devotion to duty reflected great credit upon traditions of the United States Naval Service.

*BAGGETT, CURTIS F.

Citation: For extraordinary heroism while serving as a Platoon Sergeant with Company K, Third Battalion, Fifth Marines, First Marine Division (Reinforced), in connection with operations against the enemy in the Republic of Vietnam. On the afternoon of 6 February 1968, Sergeant Baggett's platoon was attached to Company G, Second Battalion, Third Marines, Third Marine Division, which was heavily engaged with a numerically superior North Vietnamese Army force occupying fortified positions in the village of Phong Luc (1) in Quang Nam Province. As his unit assaulted the enemy, the Marines came under intense automatic weapons, mortar, and B-40 rocket fire. Although armed with only a .45-caliber pistol, Sergeant Baggett quickly rallied his men and led them in a determined assault against the hostile emplacements, overrunning one position and seizing a light machine gun after annihilating two enemy soldiers. Ignoring the hostile fire around him, he unhesitatingly led his men in assaulting the enemy, who were firing from positions in a nearby tree line, utilizing the confiscated machine gun to deliver effective fire as he advanced. Observing that the enemy was located in a well prepared trench line, he disregarded his own safety and courageously maneuvered to a position approximately five meters from the rear of the North Vietnamese emplacements. He exposed himself to enemy hand grenades and .50-caliber machine-gun fire in order to bring effective fire to bear on the entrenched enemy. Subsequently moving to a partially destroyed Vietnamese hut, he delivered a heavy volume of fire against the enemy and repeatedly maneuvered into the fire-swept area to pinpoint the source of enemy fire and direct the actions of his men. Disregarding his personal safety, he steadfastly maintained his vulnerable position until he was killed by a North Vietnamese B-40 rocket round. By his intrepid fighting spirit, superior leadership, and unwavering devotion to duty at the risk of his own life, Sergeant Baggett inspired all those who observed him, contributed significantly to the defeat of the enemy, and upheld the highest traditions of the Marine Corps and the United States Naval Service. He gallantly gave his life for his country.

BAILEY, WALTER F.

Citation: For extraordinary heroism while serving as Weapons Platoon Sergeant with Company E, Second Battalion, Fifth Marines, First Marine Division in connection with combat operations against the enemy in the Republic of Vietnam. On the night of 21 March 1970, Sergeant Bailey's unit was tasked with the security of Liberty Bridge in Quang Nam Province. While on watch, he observed a bamboo raft, laden with high explosives, floating downstream toward the bridge. Immediately alerting his fellow Marines, he directed them in delivering a heavy volume of fire at the floating object in an attempt to detonate the explosives before the raft reached the bridge. However, the Marines' fire failed to detonate the raft's cargo and it subsequently lodged among the bridge's pilings. Surveying the situation, Sergeant Bailey discovered that the raft contained a 250-pound bomb and numerous additional explosives, as well as a large number of connecting wires and cables which trailed off into the water. He then dived into the water and, with two other Marines, struggled for fifteen minutes to free it from the bridge's supports and push it back into the current. As it floated downstream, he observed the raft lodge on a sandbar approximately twenty-five meters away. Sergeant Bailey quickly swam to the sandbar, placed a small explosive charge around the bomb, shoved the raft back into the river current, and then detonated the charge. When the charge failed to detonate the bomb, he continued to follow the raft downstream until it again lodged on a sandbar, where he immediately secured it in place and subsequently directed an explosive ordnance team to the site to destroy the bomb. By his selfless courage, bold initiative, and steadfast devotion to duty in the face of great personal danger, Sergeant Bailey prevented probable serious damage to a vital bridge and upheld the highest traditions of the Marine Corps and of the United States Naval Service.

BAKER, HAROLD L.

Citation: For extraordinary heroism in action on the night of 20 December 1970 while serving as the rear security for a five-man SEAL patrol on an interdiction mission deep within enemy territory in the Republic of Vietnam. Immediately after inserting ashore, the patrol came under withering enemy fire from automatic weapons, grenades, and rockets, mortally wounding the patrol leader and the automatic weapons man, and critically wounding the patrol's radioman and Vietnamese guide. Although he was not wounded, Petty Officer Baker found himself in the river waters struggling to keep his head above the surface. Through sheer determination, he pulled himself and the body of a fallen comrade onto the bank and then returned a heavy volume of automatic weapons fire toward the enemy in an effort to stave off an assault on the squad's position. Subsequently, Petty Officer Baker administered lifesaving first aid to the two wounded members of the patrol and directed the recovery of the bodies of the patrol leader and the automatic weapons man. By his great personal valor and fighting spirit in the face of heavy enemy fire, he upheld the highest traditions of the United States Naval Service.

BARATKO, ROBERT E.

Citation: For extraordinary heroism on 15 September 1970 while serving as the aircraft commander of an attack helicopter, attached to Helicopter Attack (Light) Squadron THREE, during operations against enemy forces in the Republic of Vietnam. Lieutenant (jg) Baratko participated in a mission to provide cover for a medical evacuation helicopter which had previously attempted to evacuate several seriously wounded personnel in the face of intense enemy fire. As his plane and three others entered the evacuation area, the surrounding treelines erupted with intense fire which downed two aircraft and seriously damaged a third. Lieutenant (jg) Baratko's aircraft sustained several critical hits, including one through the fuel tank. With the only flyable attack helicopter on the scene, he provided gun-ship coverage while the medical evacuation helicopter eventually succeeded in rescuing the downed crews. As he was flying this coverage, Lieutenant (jg) Baratko's plane was again subjected to heavy fire and sustained several more hits. After the medical evacuation helicopter departed the area, Lieutenant (jg) Baratko flew to a nearby landing strip with his fuel supply practically exhausted. By his perseverance and great personal valor in the face of almost overwhelming odds, he was directly instrumental in saving the lives of several of his shipmates. His selfless and determined efforts were in keeping with the highest traditions of the United States Naval Service.

BARBER, WILLIAM B.

Citation: For extraordinary heroism on 25 November 1968 while serving as a corpsman with Company "I", Third Battalion, Fourth Marines, Third Marine Division in connection with combat operations against enemy aggressor forces in the Republic of Vietnam. During the afternoon hours, Petty Officer (then Hospitalman) Barber was accompanying a platoon engaged in patrol activities in Quang Tri Province. While crossing an abandoned landing zone, the unit was attacked by a well-entrenched North Vietnamese army force employing command-detonated mines, rocket-propelled grenades, and automatic weapons which wounded four Marines and forced the others to seek cover in a nearby wooded area. Observing that the four casualties were lying dangerously exposed to hostile fire, Petty Officer Barber disregarded his own safety to reach one of the fallen men. After administering first aid, Petty Officer Barber moved the man to a safer position and, undaunted by the extremely heavy volume of enemy fire, boldly maneuvered across the area on two more occasions to provide medical care and assist the second and third casualties to covered positions. He then braved the intense fire for a fourth time, placing himself between the last of the wounded Marines and the enemy fire during the fifteen minutes required to administer first aid. With the supporting fire of helicopters on station and the concentrated fire of his platoon, Petty Officer Barber was able to remove the wounded Marine to the relative safety of the wooded area. He then skillfully rendered medical aid and comforted all four casualties, directing their movement to a medical evacuation helicopter for embarkation and extraction. By his superb professional skill, outstanding valor, and unwavering devotion to duty in the face of great personal danger, Petty Officer Barber inspired all who observed him and was instrumental in saving four lives. His daring initiative was in keeping with the highest traditions of the United States Naval Service.

BARNES, ROBERT C.

Citation: For extraordinary heroism as a squad leader, with Company B, Third Reconnaissance Battalion, Third Marine Division (Reinforced) in Vietnam on 17 December 1966. Corporal (then Lance Corporal) Barnes was the assistant patrol leader of a nine man reconnaissance patrol penetrating deep into enemy controlled territory. Sighting two Viet Cong on a hill during the course of an ambush which the patrol was conducting, Corporal Barnes fired on them, mortally wounding one Viet Cong. Receiving instructions from the patrol leader to check out the area, Corporal Barnes and three men advanced toward the hill. Before they were half way to their objective the small team suddenly came under a hail of automatic weapons and machine gun fire. At the same time, the remainder of the patrol also came under fire from these same Viet Cong and an additional force of equal size. At this point, with the two teams separated and out of communications, the patrol was in imminent danger of destruction by the withering fire and advancing enemy. After surveying the situation, Corporal Barnes unhesitatingly led his small team into a fierce and direct assault on the enemy position. Shouting encouragement and directions, he bravely directed his men in an almost impossible advance across 200 meters of open terrain through heavy automatic weapons fire. Corporal Barnes personally accounted for two enemy killed and several wounded. In the face of this fiercely determined and unexpected assault, the enemy was forced to withdraw. By his courageous actions, inspiring leadership and loyal devotion to duty, Corporal Barnes reflected great credit upon himself and the Marine Corps and upheld the highest traditions of the United States Naval Service.

BARNETT, ROBERT L.

Citation: For extraordinary heroism while serving as a Machine Gun Squad Leader with Company A, First Battalion, Fifth Marines, First Marine Division, in connection with combat operations against the enemy in the Republic of Vietnam. On 9 May 1969, during a battalion-sized reconnaissance in force in Quang Nam Province, Corporal Barnett was moving with the point position across rice paddies bordered by tree lines when the Marines came under intense small-arms fire and were pinned down by a large North Vietnamese Army force. During the initial burst of enemy fire, four men in the lead platoon were wounded, including Corporal Barnett. Observing the wounded corpsman and another Marine lying in a dangerously exposed position, Corporal Barnett completely disregarded his own safety as he rushed across the fire-swept terrain to reach his fallen comrades and administer first aid. Locating another casualty, he ignored his own painful injuries as he braved the enemy fire to run 100 meters across the open terrain to reach the wounded Marine. Although injured a second time, he managed to assist in moving the casualty to a covered position. He refused evacuation for himself and boldly delivered effective fire which killed four North Vietnamese soldiers and suppressed the hostile fire sufficiently to enable the aircraft to land. Although wounded again by enemy fire, he remained oblivious to the intense pain and valiantly continued to deliver a heavy volume of accurate and effective covering fire while the casualties were embarked and the helicopter lifted out of the hazardous area. Despite his weakened condition, he continued to aggressively engage the enemy until wounded a fourth time and medically evacuated. His heroic actions inspired all who observed him and contributed materially to the defeat of the enemy. By his courage, bold initiative, and unwavering devotion to duty in the face of great personal danger, Corporal Barnett upheld the highest traditions of the Marine Corps and the United States Naval Service.

BARRETT, JAMES J.

Citation: For extraordinary heroism while serving as a Squad Leader with Company I, Third Battalion, Twenty-sixth Marines, Third Marine Division (Reinforced), in the Republic of Vietnam on 19 September 1967. While positioned in an area southwest of Con Thien, Corporal Barrett's company came under heavy mortar, rocket and artillery fire followed by a supported infantry assault by a numerically superior North Vietnamese Army force. In the initial attack, numerous casualties were taken and the company was forced to withdraw to a more advantageous position. Undaunted, Corporal Barrett courageously maintained his squad's position and directed accurate counter fire against the hordes of assaulting enemy. Assuming control of the platoon when his platoon commander became a casualty, he rallied his men, reorganized the platoon and led them in an effective counterattack against the enemy. With complete disregard for his own safety, he moved from position to position, encouraging his men and resupplying them with ammunition. Unhesitatingly, he aided the wounded and directed their evacuation. During the six hour ordeal, he repositioned his men five times to thwart the enemy advance and inflicted numerous casualties on the enemy force. By his bold initiative, gallant fighting spirit and loyal devotion to duty, Corporal Barrett reflected great credit upon himself and the Marine Corps and upheld the highest traditions of the United States Naval Service.

BARRETT, JOHN J.

Citation: For extraordinary heroism in aerial flight while serving as a Pilot with Marine Medium Helicopter Squadron 263 in connection with combat operations against the enemy in the Republic of Vietnam. After aborting two resupply missions to a Marine company on the night of 26 February 1969 due to mechanical difficulties and extremely adverse weather conditions, Captain Barrett launched at midnight as Section Leader in a flight of two CH-46 transport helicopters assigned the emergency resupply of ammunition to the beleaguered unit heavily engaged with a large hostile force two miles northwest of An Hoa. Realizing the seriousness of the situation when informed that the Marines had expended nearly all their small-arms ammunition, he resolutely elected to attempt the mission despite only a slight improvement in the weather. Acquiring his external load at An Hoa, he extinguished his aircraft's exterior lights and skillfully maneuvered his helicopter below the 800-foot ceiling in the designated area. Captain Barrett, guided only by a single strobe light and undaunted by the extremely heavy volume of hostile machine-gun fire directed against his CH-46, fearlessly maneuvered his aircraft in a tight spiral approach to a hover and boldly remained in his dangerously exposed position to stabilize his load before dropping the critically needed ammunition to the waiting Marines. Quickly lifting out of the fire-swept area, he maneuvered his helicopter up through the overcast and proceeded above the clouds to the Marble Mountain Air Facility. Captain Barrett's courage, superior airmanship, and unwavering devotion to duty in the face of great personal danger were instrumental in the accomplishment of the hazardous mission and were in keeping with the highest traditions of the Marine Corps and the United States Naval Service.

BASKIN, RICHARD W.

Citation: For extraordinary heroism as Squad Leader, First Squad while serving with Security Platoon, Sub Unit #1, Headquarters Company, 26th Marines, 9th Marine Amphibious Brigade near Khe Sanh, Republic of Vietnam on 6 June 1967. Sergeant Baskin with seventeen men was responsible for security of the vital radio relay position on Hill 950 near Khe Sanh, when in the early morning hours the position was suddenly attacked by a ninety man enemy company employing mortars, rocket launchers, machine guns and grenades. Six men were immediately killed and four others seriously wounded. Sergeant Baskin directed that artillery fire be called in and quickly organized his men, positioning them in the most advantageous positions to return a heavy volume of fire upon the enemy and effectively block enemy penetration. Throughout the night, although painfully wounded, Sergeant Baskin, with complete disregard for his personal safety exposed himself continously to enemy machine gun fire located only fifteen yards from his position. Shouting encouragement to his men, he led them on several occasions to positions that blocked enemy attempts to outflank and overrun the position. After over seven hours of close and continous combat, during which time he tended the wounded and assembled all available weapons, Sergeant Baskin led his remaining men in a fierce counterattack which overran an enemy machine gun emplacement, killing one enemy and capturing another. This last attack resulted in the enemy fleeing, carrying some of their dead and wounded. Sergeant Baskin, then consolidated the position and directed the evacuation of the dead and wounded before he himself was evacuated. As a result of his dauntless leadership, Sergeant Baskin and his men inflicted great damage on the enemy who left ten of their dead and one wounded. Sergeant Baskin's bold initiative, exceptional fortitude and valiant fighting spirit served to inspire all who observed him and upheld the highest traditions of the Marine Corps and the United States Naval Service.

BATCHELLER, GORDON D.

Citation: For extraordinary heroism while serving as Commanding Officer, Company A, First Battalion, First Marines, First Marine Division (Reinforced), in the Republic of Vietnam on 31 January 1986. Elements of Company A were assigned the mission of reinforcing a unit of the Army of the Republic of Vietnam in the city of Hue. Joining a small armored column north of Phu Bai in Thua Thien Province, the unit proceeded along National Route One toward Hue. On the southern edge of the city the column was ambushed by a numerically superior enemy force using automatic weapons, mortars, recoiless rifles and B-40 rockets. Quickly organizing his outnumbered forces into a defensive perimeter and unmindful of the danger, Captain Batcheller boldly began directing his unit's return fire. Exhibiting sound tactical judgement and calm presence of mind under enemy fire, he formulated a plan of attack and courageously exposed himself to the intense enemy barrage as he began shifting his men to more advantageous positions from which they delivered accurate suppressive fire against the hostile emplacements. Although injured by fragments of an exploding enemy rocket round, he aggressively led his men in a fierce assault against the enemy blocking positions, steadfastly advancing until he reached a besieged Popular Force compound. As the enemy increased the intensity of their attack, one of the Marine tanks was hit by hostile automatic weapons fire and B-40 rockets which wounded several of the crew members. Ignoring the danger from enemy rounds exploding all around him, Captain Batcheller unhesitatingly moved to the damaged vehicle to assist in removing the casualties. Simultaneously, he reorganized his force and succeeded in routing the enemy from its fortified positions. As the intensity of enemy fire to the front lessened, the column began receiving heavy automatic weapons fire from both flanks, seriously wounding Captain Batcheller in both legs. Exhibiting great courage and physical stamina, he supported himself with his elbows and resolutely continued to direct his men in repulsing the enemy until, weakened by the loss of blood from his serious injuries, his voice fell to a whisper. Even then, he bravely encouraged those near him as he lay receiving medical treatment. As a result of his determined efforts, National Route One was reopened, enabling the reaction force to reach the embattled city of Hue. By his exceptional heroism, outstanding tactical ability and steadfast devotion to duty at great personal risk, Captain Batcheller upheld the highest traditions of the Marine Corps and the United States Naval Service.

BATEMAN, KENT C.

Citation: For extraordinary heroism as a Pilot of an A6A Intruder Aircraft with Marine All Weather Attack Squadron 533 in the Republic of Vietnam on 25 October 1967. Assigned the mission of attacking a heavily defended airfield complex, Major Batemen launched his aircraft that night. Aware of the intense enemy surface-to-air missile fire, he formulated and executed a plan to penetrate the hostile defenses. Exposed to interception by enemy fighters at high level, he descended on instruments to minimum altitude. Maneuvering his aircraft over and around treacherous and uncertain terrain, he successfully pierced the enemy's outer missile ring and penetrated deep within his inner defenses. As he neared the initial attack point, Major Bateman was subjected to intense enemy tracking fire. Although losing radio contact with an electronic counter measure aircraft and realizing that it placed his aircraft and himself in serious danger, he nonetheless courageously continued his attack. Disregarding the intense enemy antiaircraft fire and surface-to-air missiles, he completed his daring attack. By his bold initiative, gallant fighting spirit and loyal devotion to duty, Major Bateman was instrumental in destroying an enemy airfield, thereby reflecting great credit upon himself and the Marine Corps and upholding the highest traditions of the United States Naval Service.

*BEAULIEU, LEO V.

Citation: For extraordinary heroism as a machine gunner serving with Company E, Second Battalion, Fifth Marines, First Marine Division, in action near Chu Lai, Republic of Vietnam, on 16 May 1966. Private Beaulieu's squad was engaged in search and destroy operations against Communist insurgent forces when it was ambushed by a Viet Cong force of sixty men. Heavy machine gun and automatic rifle fire from three sides pinned down the squad in an area offering little or no protection. Private Beaulieu was hit in the first volley of fire and knocked away from his machine gun. Although critically wounded in the chest, he crawled back to his gun and put it into action, delivering heavy, accurate fire on the enemy. He refused to take advantage of the limited cover available in order to bring punishing fire on the ambushing force, and as a result he was hit a second time as the machine gun malfunctioned. Still disregarding his own personal safety, he worked desperately to clear the weapon, and while doing so he received a third wound, which was fatal. Through his extraordinary initiative and inspiring valor in the face of almost certain death, he kept the enemy at a distance until reinforcements arrived, and enabled most of the members of his squad to be rescued. Private Beaulieu's calm and courageous actions under hostile fire upheld the highest traditions of the Marine Corps and the United States Naval Service. He gallantly gave his life in the cause of freedom.

BELL, VAN D., JR. (Gold Star in lieu of second award — first award during Korean Conflict, 1950-53)

Citation: For extraordinary heroism while serving as Commanding Officer, First Battalion, First Marines in Vietnam on 6 June 1966. Lieutenant Colonel Bell led a small complement consisting of himself, ten Marines and three Ontos deep into enemy controlled territory to personally take charge of one of his platoons that was heavily engaged in enemy fire. Arriving on the scene with the battle still in progress, he immediately employed the fire of the Ontos to suppress the enemy fire and called in artillery fire inflicting heavy casualties on the enemy and causing them to withdraw. He then proceeded through extremely hazardous terrain to visit Company B, which had recently established a patrol base well within the enemy stronghold. Enroute, one of the Ontos ran out of fuel, causing the small group to be stranded adjacent to the enemy-controlled village of Phong Ho (2). Realizing the seriousness of the situation, he immediately established a hasty defense and called for fuel resupply by helicopter. The helicopter arrived with the fuel and as it began to depart, the landing zone was attacked with heavy enemy small-arms fire. Lieutenant Colonel Bell directed the fire of his small unit to suppress the enemy fire and protect the helicopter. Almost simultaneously, the small unit was brought under a withering hail of small-arms and automatic weapons fire from three sides in an all out effort by the enemy to annihilate the small group. With complete disregard for his own personal safety, he moved from Ontos to Ontos pin-pointing targets and encouraging his men. With full knowledge of the risk involved, he elected to keep the enemy engaged rather than withdraw while he maneuvered a platoon from more than a mile away to trap the enemy. This valiant and daring action was a resounding success and resulted in over thirty enemy killed and the capture of sixteen weapons. With darkness drawing near, Lieutenant Colonel Bell elected to return to his Command Post. At a point located two miles from friendly units, the lead Ontos hit an enemy mine, totally destroying it and causing severe injuries to Lieutenant Colonel Bell and three other Marines. Again the enemy brought the group under fire and although in considerable pain, he gallantly rallied his small remaining force of seven, and once more repelled an enemy attack. Upon sighting the relief column and realizing that the safety of the remainder of his group was assured, he calmly called in a helicopter and directed the evacuation of himself and the other wounded Marines. Through his dynamic leadership, inspiring valor and loyal devotion to duty, Lieutenant Colonel Bell reflected great credit upon himself and the Marine Corps and upheld the highest traditions of the United States Naval Service.

*BENDORF, DAVID G.

Citation: For extraordinary heroism while serving as a Machine Gun Team Leader of the Second Platoon of Company L, Third Battalion, Ninth Marines, Third Marine Division (Reinforced), in the Republic of Vietnam on 20 May 1967. The company was moving to bring a relief force to an embattled sister company when it engaged a strong blocking force. Lance Corporal Bendorf and his gunner had volunteered to provide point for the platoon. When the enemy opened up in the darkness, he led his gunner to a foremost position and directed accurate fire into the enemy positions to support the assault. After a vicious exchange of fire and grenades, during which many

Marines were wounded, the platoon was forced to withdraw and regroup. Lance Corporal Bendorf knew that without the fire power of his gun the platoon would be unable to recover the casualties and carry them back to safety. Calmly accepting whatever consequences their bravery might cost, he and his gunner held their position under heavy automatic fire and a barrage of grenades, allowing the others to pull out of the trap. Both men were aware that death was inevitable and they chose to face the enemy alone in the infested area. As a direct result of their heroic sacrifice, a successful assault was launched which relieved the pressure on the other company and saved an untold number of lives, if not the entire unit. His outstanding courage, valiant fighting spirit and selfless devotion to duty were in keeping with the highest traditions of the Marine Corps and the United States Naval Service. He gallantly gave his life for his country.

*BENOIT, FRANCIS A.

Citation: For extraordinary heroism on 16 March 1967 while serving with Company "E", Second Battalion, Ninth Marines in the Republic of Vietnam. While returning to the Company Command Post from a night platoon patrol base, Petty Officer Benoit's platoon was suddenly attacked by an enemy force employing small arms, automatic weapons, and hand grenades. Observing several wounded men, Petty Officer Benoit rushed forward into the intense enemy fire to administer medical aid, but was wounded, himself, by a hand grenade before reaching the casualties. Stunned and temporarily unable to move, he waited for the wounded to be brought to him, and then quickly and competently rendered medical assistance while exposed to enemy fire. After the attack had subsided and the wounded had been put aboard an evacuation helicopter, he refused to be evacuated and thus leave the platoon without a corpsman. When the second helicopter came in, the landing zone was hit by enemy mortar fire, inflicting additional casualties. Petty Officer Benoit again stayed behind to treat the wounded. He was helping the last wounded man into the third helicopter, before boarding himself, when he was fatally wounded by an enemy mortar round. By his technical skill, courage and inspiring devotion to duty, Petty Officer Benoit undoubtedly saved the lives of many of his fallen comrades. His heroic actions were in keeping with the highest traditions of the United States Naval Service.

BENOIT, RONALD R.

Citation: For extraordinary heroism in action while serving as a Platoon Commander with Company "D", First Reconnaissance Battalion, First Marine Division in the Republic of Vietnam on 25 February 1967. Second Lieutenant Benoit and his platoon were inserted by helicopter deep into hostile territory on a reconnaissance mission. He and half of his platoon were in the first helicopter which landed in a heavily booby trapped and mined area, and immediately came under intense enemy small arms and .60 caliber machine gun fire. Quickly assessing the situation he exposed himself to the withering small arms fire to wave off the second helicopter. With extreme composure under fire, he immediately called for and directed artillery fire on the Viet Cong emplacements. Constantly exposed to enemy fire, he secured medical attention for his wounded, guided the second helicopter in and directed the evacuation of his wounded. While deploying the remainder of the platoon, a booby trap was detonated, killing one Marine, wounding others and rupturing Second Lieutenant Benoit's eardrums. At the same time his unit was hit again by intense enemy fire and although in extreme pain and almost totally deaf, he courageously and skillfully directed effective air strikes on the enemy. With the enemy fire suppressed, enabling the helicopters to land again, he expertly supervised the loading of the wounded and only after his entire platoon had been embarked aboard the aircraft did he allow his own retraction. By his extraordinary initiative, uncommon courage and complete disregard for his own safety, he undoubtedly saved numerous Marine lives, reflected great credit upon himslef, the Marine Corps and upheld the highest traditions of the United States Naval Service.

BERGER, DONALD J.

Citation: For extraordinary heroism while serving as an Aircraft Commander with Marine Medium Helicopter Squadron ONE HUNDRED SIXTY-THREE in operations in the Republic of Vietnam on 11 and 12 March 1966. Lieutenant Berger was assigned to participate in a mission to evacuate a large number of American and Vietnamese personnel from the besieged garrison at As Hau. Controlling his aircraft with exceptional skill, he hovered over the trees thirty to fifty feet tall while the stranded personnel were hoisted aboard. After discharging the passengers at Heu Phu Bai, Lieutenant

Berger returned to As Hau and was directed to another clearing where two Special Forces personnel and six Vietnamese soldiers awaited rescue. Since jungle growth prevented landing, he was attempting to hoist the defenders aboard when hostile automatic weapons fire damaged the tail pylon of his aircraft, causing complete loss of tail rotor control. Exhibiting great presence of mind, Lieutenant Berger effected a controlled crash landing and promptly instructed the copilot and one of the crewmembers to board another rescue helicopter. Due to the darkness and inclement weather precluding further rescue attempts, he calmly guided the outpost defenders through difficult terrain where they encountered and successfully fought off an enemy patrol. After putting a defensive plan into action and maintaining a watch throughout the night, he moved the group to another location at first light, then signaled for help and succeeded in getting a rescue aircraft to hoist the exhausted men aboard. His stalwart effort was directly responsible for saving his crewmen, as well as the group of outpost survivors, from capture or death at the hands of the Viet Cong. By his intrepid fighting spirit, brilliant initiative and fortitude in the face of grave danger, and unfaltering dedication to duty, Lieutenant Berger upheld the highest traditions of the Marine Corps and of the United States Naval Service.

BINNS, RICARDO, C.

Citation: For extraordinary heroism as a Scout Team Leader, Company C, First Reconnaissance Battalion, First Marine Division (Reinforced), in Vietnam on the night of 15-16 June 1966. Corporal Binns' platoon established an observation post deep within communist controlled territory to observe enemy movement. At 0100 a massive assault was launched against the Marine position by a determined and well trained North Vietnamese battalion. The murderous enemy fire was so intense that five of the eighteen-man platoon were killed and the remainder wounded. On two separate occasions, with complete disregard for his personal safety, Corporal Binns braved the withering enemy fire to forcibly pull to the ground severely wounded Marines who had unconsciously exposed themselves to almost certain death. Realizing that his Platoon Leader was wounded and unable to move, and preoccupied with the direction of close support aircraft, Corporal Binns took it upon himself to direct the fire of the remaining seven Marines, redistribute the ammunition of those who could not use it, and care for the wounded. Although painfully wounded in both legs,

Corporal Binns displayed magnificent courage throughout the night and long into the following morning. His selfless devotion to duty, superb professional skill, deep concern for his fellow Marines, and extraordinary heroism inspired all who observed him and were in keeping with the highest traditions of the Marine Corps and of the United States Naval Service.

BIRD, WILLIAM C.

Citation: For extraordinary heroism while serving as a Rifleman with Company E, Second Battalion, Fifth Marines, First Marine Division, in the Republic of Vietnam on 15 May 1969. The First Platoon of Company E was assigned the mission of relieving a friendly unit heavily engaged in combat with a North Vietnamese Army battalion near An Hoa in Quang Nam Province. As the point squad of Company E crossed an open field, it came under a heavy volume of rocket and automatic weapons fire from a large hostile unit occupying well-camouflaged bunkers. Alertly observing two wounded Marines lying dangerously exposed to the enemy fire, Private First Class Bird, despite the intense volume of hostile rounds impacting near him, pulled his comrades to a position of relative safety. Reacting instantly, he fearlessly stood up and, effectively firing his M-16 rifle, provided enough covering fire to enable a corpsman to reach the wounded Marines. Continuing to expose himself to the intense hostile fire, he delivered accurate covering fire for the corpsman as he moved throughout the hazardous area and administered emergency medical treatment to all the wounded. At dusk, another reaction force and two supporting tanks were deployed from the company command post. Alertly observing that the tank commanders were having difficulty discerning the enemy targets because of the approaching darkness, Private First Class Bird unhesitatingly climbed aboard the lead tank, despite the intense volume of enemy fire directed at him and, skillfully pointing out the hostile positions to the tank commander, was instrumental in bringing devastating fire to bear upon the enemy. As the platoon withdrew to a night defensive position, Private First Class Bird personally carried two wounded Marines to the friendly perimeter and subsequently assisted in loading the remainder of the casualties aboard the tanks for rapid evacuation. When an enemy rocket impacted on one of the tanks, seriously wounding the driver, Private First Class Bird positioned himself between the tank and the nearby hostile emplacement and, accurately firing his rifle, suppressed the enemy fire while the tank crew reorganized and continued firing. Private First Class Bird was directly responsible for saving the lives of six Marines. His courage, aggressive fighting spirit and unwavering devotion to duty upheld the highest traditions of the Marine Corps and the United States Naval Service.

*BLANN, STEPHEN

Citation: For extraordinary heroism as a squad leader with the Third Platoon, Company E, Second Battalion, Ninth Marines, Third Marine Division against North Vietnamese Army forces in Quang Tri Province, Republic of Vietnam. On 16 February 1969, Company E was attacking south along an enemy road with the Third Platoon providing rear security. Intermittent sniper fire had been received throughout the day. In the afternoon the company halted to conduct a reconnaissance of a large open area and to secure a stream-crossing site before continuing its movement. As the lead elements resumed the attack, Lance Corporal Blann observed a number of enemy troops flanking the company in an attempt to attack from the rear. Without hesitation he deployed his squad to counter the enemy's movement as the sporadic sniper fire increased to a heavy volume of small-arms and automatic-weapons fire. Lance Corporal Blann immediately evaluated the situation and maneuvered his squad with great professional skill into an assault position against the encircling enemy as one of his men was immediately wounded. Noticing the seriousness of the man's wounds and hearing his painful cry for help, Lance Corporal Blann, while under an intense volume of fire and disregarding his own personal safety, moved into the open area to the wounded man. Shouting encouragement to his squad and continuing to direct the attack upon the enemy, Lance Corporal Blann shielded the wounded man with his own body by kneeling in front of him in line with the enemy fire. While trying to administer first aid and move the man to a safer position, Lance Corporal Blann was mortally wounded. By his extraordinary heroism and selfless devotion to duty, Lance Corporal Blann saved the life of his fellow Marine and upheld the highest traditions of the Marine Corps and the United States Naval Service. He gallantly gave his life for his country.

*BLEVINS, THOMAS L., JR.

Citation: For extraordinary heroism while serving as a Squad

Leader with Company C, First Battalion, Twenty-Sixth Marines, Ninth Marine Amphibious Brigade in connection with combat operations against the enemy in the Republic of Vietnam. On 31 May 1969, while Corporal Blevins maneuvered his squad as the point element of a company-sized search and destroy operation in Quang Nam Province, the Marines came under a heavy volume of automatic weapons fire from a large enemy force occupying well-concealed, fortified emplacements. Observing that three of his men had been wounded and had fallen in an unprotected area close to the hostile positions, Corporal Blevins unhesitatingly left his relatively secure position and ran across the fire-swept terrain to the side of his companions. After kneeling in a dangerously exposed position to administer first aid to one of his comrades, he removed the man to waiting medical attention behind the friendly line. He then again braved the hostile fire raking the area and, after administering brief emergency treatment to the second wounded Marine, moved him back to the company's defensive perimeter. When he raced to the aid of the third man, they both became pinned down by concentrated enemy fire. Corporal Blevins, in full view of the enemy troops, hurled a hand grenade which diverted their attention sufficiently to allow him time to move the injured Marine to safety, but before he could attain a covered position himself, he was mortally wounded by small-arms fire. His heroic efforts and selfless concern for his fellowmen inspired all who observed him and were instrumental in saving the lives of three Marines. By his courage, aggressive fighting spirit and unwavering devotion to duty, Corporal Blevins upheld the highest traditions of the Marine Corps and of the United States Naval Service.

BLONSKI, THOMAS J.

Citation: For extraordinary heroism on 10 May 1972 as a naval flight officer of jet aircraft in Fighter Squadron NINETY-SIX, embarked in USS CONSTELLATION (CVA-64), during a major airwing strike against an enemy rail yard in North Vietnam. As the radar intercept officer in the lead aircraft of a section carrying out target combat air patrol, Lieutenant Blonski maintained visual contact with a formation of approximately sixteen enemy fighter aircraft and warned the retiring strike force of the oncoming threat. In the face of the overwhelming enemy odds, he aided his pilot in engaging the numerically superior aircraft and in pressing home several hard-fought attacks which resulted in the destruction of two enemy planes and the dispersion of the remaining aircraft out of range of the strike force. Lieutenant Blonski's professional skill, courage and dedication reflected great credit upon himself and the United States Naval Service.

BOGAN, RICHARD E.

Citation: For extraordinary heroism while serving as a Fire Team Leader with Company C, First Battalion, Fifth Marines, First Marine Division (Reinforced), in the Republic of Vietnam on 12 April 1968. While conducting a night ambush near the village of Thon Ha Vinh, Thua Thien Province, Lance Corporal (then Private First Class) Bogan alertly observed several North Vietnamese Army soldiers approaching his position. Reacting instantly, he directed a heavy volume of fire upon the hostile force, inflicting numerous casualties and forcing the enemy to disperse. Within a few moments, an enemy grenade landed among the Marines, and exploded harmlessly. Almost immediately, another grenade impacted extremely close to Corporal Bogan and a companion. Disregarding his own safety, he shouted a warning to his comrade and unhesitatingly jumped on top of the missile, absorbing the blast with his body. Although seriously wounded, he moved to his squad leader's position and informed him of the situation. By his dauntless courage, initiative and selfless efforts in behalf of another, Corporal Bogan saved his comrade from serious injury or possible death and upheld the highest traditions of the Marine Corps and the United States Naval Service.

BRADY, EUGENE R.

Citation: For extraordinary heroism and intrepidity in action while serving as Commanding Officer of Marine Medium Helicopter Squadron 364, Marine Aircraft Group Sixteen, First Marine Aircraft Wing in connection with combat operations against the enemy in the Republic of Vietnam. On 15 May 1969, Lieutenant Colonel Brady launched as Aircraft Commander of a transport helicopter assigned the mission of medically evacuating several seriously wounded Marines from an area northwest of An Hoa in Quang Nam Province. Arriving over the designated location, he was advised by the ground commander that the vastly outnumbered unit was surrounded by the enemy, some as close as thirty meters to the Marines' positions. Fully aware of the dangers involved, and despite rapidly approaching darkness and deteriorating weather conditions, Lieutenant Colonel Brady elected to complete his mission. As he commenced a high-speed, low-altitude approach to the confined zone, he came under a heavy volume of hostile automatic weapons fire which damaged his aircraft but did not deter him from landing. During the considerable period of time required to embark the casualties, the landing zone was subjected to intense enemy mortar fire, several rounds of which landed perilously close to the transport, rendering additional damage to the helicopter. However, Lieutenant Colonel Brady displayed exceptional composure as he calmly relayed hostile firing positions to fixed-wing aircraft overhead and steadfastly remained in his dangerously exposed position until all the wounded men were safely aboard. Demonstrating superb airmanship, he then executed a series of evasive maneuvers as he lifted from the fire-swept zone, and subsequently delivered the casualties to the nearest medical facility. His heroic and determined actions inspired all who observed him and were instrumental in saving the lives of eight fellow Marines. By his courage, superior aeronautical ability, and unfaltering devotion to duty in the face of grave personal danger, Lieutenant Colonel Brady upheld the highest traditions of the Marine Corps and of the United States Naval Service.

BRANDTNER, MARTIN L.

Citation: For extraordinary heroism while serving as Commanding Officer of Company D, First Battalion, Fifth Marines, First Marine Division, in connection with operations against the enemy in the Republic of Vietnam. On 3 September 1968, while conducting a reconnaissance in force near the village of Lan Phouc in Quang Nam Province, the lead platoon of Company D became pinned down by intense automatic weapons fire from a large North Vietnamese Army force. As he moved forward to assess the situation, Captain Brandtner was wounded by grenade launcher fire from an enemy soldier standing in a nearby trench. With complete disregard for his own safety, Captain Brandtner boldly exposed himself to the hostile fire and hurling a hand grenade, killed the North Vietnamese soldier. Suddenly, the Marines came under an intense North Vietnamese hand grenade attack, and when one of the lethal objects landed at Captain Brandtner's feet, he unhesitatingly seized the grenade and threw it back at the enemy. On two more occasions he completely disregarded his own safety to seize hand grenades which were thrown near his position and hurl them toward the hostile force. When another grenade landed in the midst of four nearby Marines, Captain Brandtner fearlessly rushed to their position, picked up the lethal object and hurled it away from his companions. Then, concerned only for the welfare of his fellow Marines, he knocked two of the men to the ground and quickly placed himself on top of them, thereby absorbing the fragments from the exploding grenade in his protective armor and preventing possible death or serious injury to his companions. Realizing the numerical superiority of the enemy, he consolidated his company's position and skillfully adjusted effective supporting arms fire which caused the hostile force to flee and enabled his Marines to overrun the objective. By his courage, intrepid fighting spirit, and selfless devotion to duty at the risk of his life, Captain Brandtner sustained and enhanced the highest traditions of the Marine Corps and of the United States Naval Service.

BRANDTNER, MARTIN L. (Gold Star in lieu of second award)

Citation: For extraordinary heroism in action while serving as the Commanding Officer, Company D, First Battalion, Fifth Marines, First Marine Division (Reinforced) in the Republic of Vietnam on 11 September 1968. Assigned a mission to conduct a search and destroy operation near the village of My Binh, Quang Dia Loc District, Quang Nam Province, Captain Brandtner selected his defensive position and began deploying his platoons for their assigned night activities. As the First Platoon departed, en route to their night ambush site, they began receiving intense small arms, automatic weapons and rocket fire from a numerically superior North Vietnamese Army force. Simultaneously, the enemy, approximately the size of the two North Vietnamese Army companies, began an attack on the Command Group with 82mm mortars, intense automatic weapons fire and P40 rockets. Quickly analyzing the situation and immediately realizing the seriousness and the danger involved, Captain Brandtner disregarded his own personal safety and moved forward to an extremely exposed position in order that he could personally control the battle at hand. When the enemy began the first of a series of "human wave" sapper attacks against the company's position, he calmly and with outstanding presence of mind moved from position to position reorganizing, encouraging and rallying his outnumbered and dazed company into an inspired fighting unit which completely stopped the momentum of the enemy attack and forced them to withdraw. Realizing the enemy were regrouping for subsequent attacks, he calmly adjusted his supporting artillery fire to within 200 meters of his lines, again raising havoc and confusion within the enemy's ranks. When the North Vietnamese Army units began their second attack, the devastating fires of a well organized Marine Corps rifle company caught them off balance and inflicted heavy enemy casualties. Twice more, the determined enemy launched massive "human wave" assaults on the perimeter of Company D, but the steadfast efforts of the men of the company proved to be too much for the now overwhelmed and demoralized enemy. After more than two hours of persistent attempts to overrun the company, the enemy broke contact. Daylight revealed 67 North Vietnamese dead as mute testimony to the ferocious encounter that had taken place. The number of enemy dead and wounded evacuated could not be estimated. Company D suffered only one Marine killed and fourteen wounds serious enough to require evacuation. By his outstanding courage, superb leadership and unswerving devotion to duty, Captain Brandtner served to inspire all who observed him and upheld the highest traditions of the Marine Corps and the United States Naval Service.

*BRANTLEY, LEROY

Citation: For extraordinary heroism while serving as a Squad Leader with Company G, Second Battalion, Fifth Marines, First Marine Division in the Republic of Vietnam on 28 March 1969. During a search and clear operation in Quang Nam Province, Company G's lead platoon was entering the village of Phu Nhuan (1) when it came under intense rocket and automatic weapons fire from a North Vietnamese Army company occupying well-fortified positions in the village and surrounding tree lines. Reacting instantly Corporal Brantley completely disregarded his own safety as he maneuvered his squad to defilade positions and skillfully directed the delivery of a heavy volume of return fire. Although seriously wounded while deploying his men, he ignored his own painful injury and repeatedly exposed himself to hostile fire as he rallied his men and boldly led them in an assault against the enemy. Wounded a second time by North Vietnamese fire, Corporal Brantley refused medical attention as he valiantly remained with his men to sustain the momentum of the attack. Fearlessly directing the actions of his squad and exhorting them to greater efforts, he continued to brave the intense enemy fire while aggressively leading the advance toward the hostile emplacements until he was struck for the third time by hostile fire. Undaunted by the North Vietnamese rounds impacting near him and weakened by his serious injuries, Corporal Brantley resolutely continued to move his men and direct their actions and, as he boldly pushed through the tree line toward a suspected hostile emplacement, he was mortally wounded. His intrepid fighting spirit and daring initiative inspired all who observed him and contributed significantly to the accomplishment of his unit's mission. By his courage, superb leadership and unwavering devotion to duty, Corporal Brantley upheld the highest traditions of the Marine Corps and of the United States Naval Service. He gallantly gave his life for his country.

*BRINDLEY, THOMAS D.

Citation: For extraordinary heroism while serving as a Platoon Commander with Company I, Third Battalion, Twenty-Sixth Marines, Third Marine Division (Reinforced) in the Republic of Vietnam on 20 January 1968. Lieutenant Brindley's unit was maneuvering toward Hill 881 near Khe Sanh when the lead elements suddenly came under intense small-arms and automatic weapons fire and sustained several casualties. Reacting instantly, he directed a heavy volume of fire against the enemy and moved his second squad to the point of heaviest contact. Despite the tall elephant grass which restricted movement, he effectively deployed and controlled his men, while suppressing the hostile fire sufficiently to enable the casualties to be taken from the area. Quickly shifting his unit to the base of the hill, under covering fire, Lieutenant Brindley led an aggressive assault against the opposing force which was entrenched in well-fortified positions supported by .50 caliber machine-gun emplacement. Ignoring the fire impacting around him, he continuously moved among his men, encouraging them, controlling the squads and directing his unit's return fire. As the Marines reached the crest of the hill and overran the North Vietnamese positions, they again came under intense fire and suffered additional casualties. In an attempt to pinpoint the source of enemy fire, Lieutenant Brindley, while freely moving throughout the fire-swept area, was struck by hostile fire and fell mortally wounded. By his inspiring leadership and unyielding devotion to duty in the face of overwhelming odds, he upheld the highest traditions of the Marine Corps and the United States Naval Service. He gallantly gave his life for his country.

BROWN, CHARLES E.

(Records indicate that a recommendation for award of the Navy Cross to Corporal Charles E. Brown, U.S. Marine Corps was approved 19 July 1968. At this printing a copy of Corporal Brown's citation cannot be located in service files. However, a statement of facts, as follows, is provided in Review Board memoranda.)

For extraordinary heroism while serving as a Squad leader with Combined Action Platoon H-8, Third Combined Action Group, Third Marine Amphibious Force in connection with operations against the enemy in the Republic of Vietnam in the early morning hours on 31 January 1968.

*BROWN, DAVID H.

Citation: For extraordinary heroism in action against the enemy while serving as a Platoon Sergeant with Company L, Third Battalion, Twenty-sixth Marines, Third Marine Division (Reinforced), in the Republic of Vietnam on 10 September 1967. While moving in support of a sister company, southwest of Con Thien on Hill 48, Sergeant Brown's platoon came under devastating enemy rocket, mortar, automatic weapons, small-arms, and grenade fire from a numerically superior enemy force. Quickly assessing the situation, he established a defensive position and brought fire to bear on the enemy. With complete disregard for his own safety, he charged the enemy positions, hurling grenades and temporarily disrupting an enemy assault. Upon depleting his grenade supply, he returned through the intense enemy fire and obtained an M-79 grenade launcher and again single-handedly assaulted the enemy positions, once again breaking up their assault and accounting for several enemy killed. Upon completion of this task, he moved among his men, directing their fire and encouraging them until he was mortally wounded. By his bold initiative, gallant fighting spirit and loyal devotion to duty, Sergeant Brown was instrumental in stopping an enemy attack, thereby saving numerous Marine casualties and upholding the highest traditions of the Marine Corps and the United States Naval Service. He gallantly gave his life for his country.

*BROWN, FRANCIS

Citation: For extraordinary heroism on 8 June 1967 in connection with an armed attack on USS LIBERTY (AGTR-5) in the Eastern Mediterranean. During the early afternoon hours, LIBERTY was attacked without warning by jet fighter aircraft and three motor torpedo boats. Subjected to intense incendiary, machine-gun, and rocket fire, and placed in extreme jeopardy by a torpedo hit below the waterline on the starboard side, LIBERTY sustained numerous personnel casualties and severe structural damage. Serving as Quartermaster, Petty Officer Brown was on the bridge during the initial phase of the air attack. When the helmsman became incapacitated, Petty Officer Brown fearlessly exposed himself to overwhelmingly accurate rocket and machine-gun fire while assuming the helmsman's duties. He steadfastly maintained the ordered course while many men in the immediate proximity received serious and fatal injuries, remaining on his post until felled by strafing fire from the torpedo boats at the moment the torpedo struck the ship. By his aggressiveness, composure under fire, and courageous actions, Petty Officer Brown upheld the highest traditions of the United States Naval Service.

BROWNING, RANDALL A.

Citation: For extraordinary heroism while serving as an Ontos Commander with Company A, Third Antitank Battalion, Third Marine Division (Reinforced) in support of the Third Battalion, Twenty-sixth Marines in the Republic of Vietnam on 10 September 1967. While engaged in a search and destroy operation in the northern sector of Quang Tri Province near the Demilitarized Zone, the battalion came under a heavy enemy bombardment of artillery and mortar fire. Although painfully wounded by fragments from an artillery round, Corporal (then Lance Corporal) Browning quickly had his injury treated and immediately returned to his Ontos where he learned that his was the only tracked vehicle in operation. Rapidly assessing the situation, he maneuvered his vehicle through the intense hostile fire to a forward position and began delivering highly effective machine-gun and recoilless rifle fire against the enemy. Successfully repulsing the first of several human wave assaults, he remained undaunted by the vicious enemy fire and steadfastly continued to deliver a heavy volume of fire during ensuing fanatical attacks. His aggressive actions repelled the hostile force on each occasion and inflicted heavy losses on the enemy. When his recoilless rifle ammunition was expended and his machine gun became inoperable, Corporal Browning unhesitatingly manned a sub-machine gun and continued to deliver devastating fire on the enemy. Due largely to his fearless initiative during the four hour battle, he was undoubtedly instrumental in thwarting the enemy's attempt to overrun the battalion's position and prevented the capture, injury or possible death of many Marines. By his resolute determination, dauntless courage and selfless devotion to duty at great personal risk, Corporal Browning inspired all who observed him and upheld the highest traditions of the Marine Corps and the United States Naval Service.

*BRYAN, CHARLES W.

Citation: For extraordinary heroism while serving as a Patrol Leader with Company B, Third Reconnaissance Battalion, Third Marine Division in connection with operations against insurgent communist (Viet Cong) forces in the Republic of Vietnam. On 20 January 1968, a seven man reconnaissance patrol led by Corporal Bryan was maneuvering with an infantry company toward Hill 881 North near the Khe Sanh Combat Base. The patrol was assigned to detach itself from the unit inconspicuously and reconnoiter the terrain surrounding Hill 881 North. In addition, Corporal Bryan was instructed to abort the mission and withdraw if the infantry unit became engaged with the enemy. As the unit approached the designated area, the Marines suddenly came under intense hostile small arms and automatic weapons fire, sustaining several casualties. Reacting instantly, Corporal Bryan deployed his men to establish an emergency helicopter landing zone to evacuate the wounded men. Subsequently, the infantry unit was directed to attack the hostile emplacements, and realizing the unit was greatly depleted by casualties, Corporal Bryan requested permission from his unit to reinforce the infantry company with his patrol. Quickly integrating his men with an infantry squad, he was assigned as Squad Leader and skillfully maneuvered his unit toward its assigned objective. Upon approaching the designated area, the Marines began receiving intense fire from an enemy machine gun position. Undaunted by the hostile fire, he maneuvered his men around the flank of the emplacement and launched an aggressive attack which silenced the position. Alertly observing one of his men fall wounded in an area dangerously exposed to enemy fire, he fearlessly ran across the fire-swept terrain to the side of his comrade. While skillfully administering first aid to the casualty, Corporal Bryan was mortally wounded. His heroic and timely actions inspired all who observed him and were instrumental in the subsequent defeat of the enemy force. By his courage, superb leadership and selfless devotion to duty, Corporal Bryan upheld the highest traditions of the Marine Corps and of the United States Naval Service. He gallantly gave his life in the service of his country.

BRYANT, JAROLD O.

Citation: For extraordinary heroism while serving as a Fire Team Leader of the Third Squad, Third Platoon, Company K, Third Battalion, First Marines, in action against communist insurgent forces in Quang Ngai Province, Republic of Vietnam, during Operation TEXAS on 21 March 1966. When the third platoon came under a vicious enemy cross fire, Corporal Bryant's squad was ordered to destroy an enemy stronghold on the right flank. While in the assault, his squad suffered numerous casualties including the squad leader. Unhesitatingly, Corporal Bryant moved from his position, coolly and courageously disregarding the intense fire, to assist four of the wounded to positions of safety. Displaying exceptional initiative and devotion to duty, he rallied to two remaining members and continued the assault by skillfully maneuvering through a barren rice paddy. Despite the predominant advantage of the enemy forces in numbers and prevailing positions, he single-handedly charged through the fury of hostile automatic weapons fire, overrunning the vital position by killing two of the enemy and causing the other to flee. Corporal Bryant's daring exploits were a determining factor in the rapid seizure of the company objective and the saving of many lives. By his courageous actions, initiative, and unswerving devotion to duty in the face of overwhelming odds, Corporal Bryant upheld the highest traditions of the Marine Corps and the United States Naval Service.

BUCHANAN, RICHARD W.

Citation: For extraordinary heroism while serving as an Automatic Rifleman with Company M, Third Battalion, Twenty-seventh Marines, First Marine Division (Reinforced) in the Republic of Vietnam on 24 May 1968. While participating in Operation ALLEN BROOK in Quang Nam Province, Corporal Buchanan's company was serving as battalion reserve, following in trace of Company K, as the unit moved against well-entrenched North Vietnamese Army forces in the village of Le Bac (1). Advancing into the objective area, Company K was ambushed by an enemy force in a tree line and two platoons were separated from the remainder of the company. As Corporal Buchanan's platoon quickly maneuvered toward the beleaguered Marines, it suddenly came under intense small-arms and automatic weapons fire from a North Vietnamese Army unit entrenched in a series of bunkers and spider holes. In the initial burst of fire, several Marines were killed or seriously wounded, including the platoon commander, platoon sergeant, all the squad leaders and the radio operator. Observing a well-hidden enemy bunker, he fearlessly assaulted the position and directed accurate rifle fire into the emplacement. Then, retrieving the platoon radio and shouting to his comrades to follow, he led the Marines to the relative safety of a nearby pagoda where he established a hasty defense. Unable to establish radio communication with his company and upon observing several medical evacuation helicopters in the vicinity, he relayed a request for armed helicopter support. As he directed numerous air strikes on the enemy positions, often within ten feet of his position, he courageously rushed into the fire-swept area to move the casualties to better protected positions. Upon discovering an adjacent bunker occupied by several North Vietnamese Army soldiers, Corporal Buchanan boldly assaulted it single-handedly, silencing the hostile fire. Throughout the intense three-hour battle, his superb command ability and calm presence of mind in hazardous situations undoubtedly saved numerous Marine lives and inspired all who observed him. By his outstanding leadership, intrepid fighting spirit and selfless devotion to duty Corporal Buchanan upheld the highest traditions of the Marine Corps and the United States Naval Service.

BULL, LYLE F.

Citation: For extraordinary heroism on 30 October 1967 as a bombardier/navigator in Attack Squadron ONE NINE SIX, embarked in USS CONSTELLATION (CVA-64). Exercising exceptional professional skill and sound judgment, Lieutenant Bull assisted in the planning and execution of an extremely dangerous, single-plane, night, radar bombing attack on the strategically located and heavily defended Hanoi railroad ferry slip in North Vietnam. Although the entire Hanoi defensive effort was concentrated upon his lone bomber, he flawlessly assisted his pilot in navigating the aircraft to the target area and commencing an attack. Seconds before bomb release, six enemy surface-to-air missiles were observed to be tracking on his plane. Undaunted by this threat to his personal safety, Lieutenant Bull assisted his pilot in taking swift and effective action to avoid the missiles and complete the attack, releasing all weapons in the target area with extreme accuracy. After release, four more missiles were fired at his aircraft in addition to the intense antiaircraft-artillery fire. In spite of this intense enemy opposition, Lieutenant Bull completed his mission and was directly responsible for dealing a significant blow to the North Vietnamese logistics efforts. His indomitable perseverance and conspicuous gallantry were in keeping with the highest traditions of the United States Naval Service.

*BURKE, JOHN R.

Citation: For extraordinary heroism while serving as a Sniper Team Leader with Headquarters and Service Company, First Battalion, Twenty-sixth Marines, Third Marine Division (Reinforced), in the Republic of Vietnam on 6 June 1967. Assigned the mission of defending an outpost on Hill 950 at Khe Sanh, Quang Tri Province, Corporal Burke's team was taken under attack by a numerically superior enemy force. During the initial assault, Corporal Burke was wounded by an enemy grenade. Ignoring his wound, he administered first aid to a severely wounded comrade and placed him in a relatively safe position, covering the wounded man with his own body to protect him from further injury. Heeding a call for help from outside the bunker, he unhesitatingly went to the aid of another Marine. While he and a companion were moving the man to the security of the bunker an enemy grenade exploded, knocking him and his comrade into the bunker. Although seriously wounded, he moved the wounded man to a tunnel to protect him from the devastating enemy fire. With all his team members' casualties, Corporal Burke unhesitatingly and with complete disregard for his own safety armed himself with grenades, and shouting words of encouragement to his men, stormed from the bunker in a valiant one-man assault against the enemy positions. While firing his weapon and throwing grenades at the enemy positions, Corporal Burke was mortally wounded. By his dauntless courage, bold initiative and devotion to duty, he was instrumental in stopping the enemy attack and saving his men from possible further injury or death, thereby reflecting great credit upon himself and the Marine

Corps and upholding the highest traditions of the United States Naval Service. He gallantly gave his life for his country.

BURNAND, ROBERT W., JR.

Citation: For extraordinary heroism in action from 12 through 16 October 1966 while serving in a detachment of Helicopter Anti-Submarine Squadron SIX, temporarily embarked in USS INTREPID (CVS-11), flying as plane commander of an armored search and rescue helicopter during a series of related rescue missions in support of combat operations in Southeast Asia. Lieutenant Burnand was vectored to an inland area of North Vietnam on three separate search and rescue flights in valiant attempts to rescue a downed Navy pilot. Although encountering severe enemy ground fire, he persisted in his attempts to locate and rescue the survivor. During the final search into the same area, he and his crew demonstrated fearless bravery while under fire. An accompanying helicopter was riddled by intense enemy automatic-weapons fire which completely disabled one of its engines, forcing it to retire toward the sea. Observing this action, and realizing that it was absolutely mandatory that the operation continue in the same location, Lieutenant Burnand and his crew decided to take a calculated risk and expose themselves to enemy fire in a valiant attempt to thwart the North Vietnamese and complete their mission. By executing skillful evasive maneuvers and effectively directing accurate counterfire at the enemy, he and his crew suppressed enemy resistance to such an extent that they successfully completed their assigned mission. By his outstanding courage, exceptional skill and fearless devotion to duty, Lieutenant Burnand upheld the highest traditions of the United States Naval Service.

BURNHAM, THOMAS R.

Citation: For extraordinary heroism while serving as a Fire Team Leader with Company F, Second Battalion, Fifth Marines, First Marine Division (Reinforced), at Nong Son, Quang Nam Province, Republic of Vietnam on 1 October 1967. While in a defensive position, Corporal (then Lance Corporal) Burnham observed a trip flare burning outside the perimeter of his unit. He was directed to lead his fire team to search and secure the area. Assessing the situation, he cautiously deployed his men to carry out the assignment. While slowly maneuvering toward the position, an enemy hand grenade landed in the midst of the fire team. Unhesitatingly and with complete disregard for his own safety, he shoved a comrade to the ground and dived on the grenade. While lying on the deadly missile, he yelled instructions to his men to take cover. As the moments passed, it became evident that the grenade had malfunctioned, however, the slightest jar could still activate the grenade. Courageously remaining in this precarious position for approximately ten minutes, Corporal Burnham, after considering the consequences, hurled himself into a ditch approximately four feet away. The grenade failed to detonate; however, had it exploded, his fearless action could well have saved the lives of his fellow Marines. By his bold initiative and grave concern for others, Corporal Burnham reflected great credit upon himself and the Marine Corps and upheld the highest traditions of the United States Naval Service.

*BURNS, DEWEY R., JR.

Citation: For extraordinary heroism on 13 September 1969 as a corpsman serving with Combined Action Platoon 1-3-9, III Marine Amphibious Force, during operations against the enemy in the Republic of Vietnam. During a concentrated enemy attack upon the village of An Phong in Quang Ngai Province, Petty Officer Burns, on several occasions, charged across the fire-swept terrain, rendered medical aid to wounded civilians and defending soldiers and Marines, and carried them to positions of safety. On one occasion, Petty Officer Burns was directly responsible for saving the lives of his patients when he defeated an enemy soldier in hand-to-hand combat. Observing that the platoon's interpreter was wounded and had fallen in the direct line of fire of enemy machine guns, Petty Officer Burns directed nearby Marines to provide covering fire and raced to the side of the casualty. Although he, himself, was seriously wounded while treating the fallen interpreter, he resolutely continued his lifesaving actions until he had stopped his patient's bleeding. He then commenced leading his charge toward a location of relative security, but was mortally wounded before he could attain his objective. Petty Officer Burns' valiant and determined actions served to inspire the other members of his platoon to heroic efforts, resulting in the complete routing of the enemy. By his intrepid fighting spirit, daring initiative, and unwavering devotion to duty, he succeeded in saving several lives, and upheld the highest traditions of the United States Naval Service.

BURNS, LEON R.

Citation: For extraordinary heroism in connection with operations against the enemy while serving as a Platoon Commander with Company B, First Battalion, Ninth Marines, Third Marine Division (Reinforced), in the Republic of Vietnam on 2 July 1967. Company B was engaged in a search and destroy operation when it was taken under intense small-arms, automatic weapons, mortar and rocket fire from an estimated two battalions of North Vietnamese troops. In the initial burst of enemy fire, the commanding officer and two platoon commanders became casualties. Immediately reacting to the situation, Staff Sergeant Burns moved his platoon forward only to be pinned down by a heavy volume of small-arms fire from both flanks and the front. He moved through the intense fire, with complete disregard for his own safety, to call in and adjust air strikes against the numerically superior enemy force. The air strikes erupted within fifty meters of his position, disrupting an enemy assault against his flanks. Exposing himself to the intense enemy fire, he organized the remnants of the company into a hasty defense and began treating and evacuating the wounded. Upon being joined by a relief column, he unhesitatingly volunteered to go forward to guide the column and assist in recovering the wounded and dead Marines. After the fulfillment of this mission, he led his men in a withdrawal along the highway. As the column moved along the highway, they were taken under devastating enemy mortar and artillery fire. Again exhibiting fearless leadership, he moved up and down the column encouraging his men and directing them into fighting holes to organize a defense position and personally carried two wounded Marines to the landing zone. By his bold initiative, dauntless courage and exceptional fortitude, Staff Sergeant Burns reflected great credit upon himself and the Marine Corps and upheld the highest traditions of the United States Naval Service.

BUSEY, JAMES B., IV

Citation: For extraordinary heroism on 21 August 1967 as a pilot in Attack Squadron ONE HUNDRED SIXTY-THREE, embarked in USS ORISKANY (CVA-34). During a combat mission over North Vietnam, Commander (then Lieutenant Commander) Busey was the leader of a section in a six-aircraft bombing element which attacked the Hanoi thermal power plant in the face of the enemy's most sophisticated and complex arsenal of air defense weapons. As he commenced his attack, Commander Busey sustained antiaircraft hits to his aircraft. He skillfully regained control of his aircraft and, although his plane was severely damaged, renewed his attack, placing his weapon precisely on target. Subsequent bomb damage assessment photography confirmed that he inflicted heavy damage to his assigned portion of the thermal power plant. Although still severely handicapped by his damaged aircraft, Commander Busey evaded four surface-to-air missiles during his egress from the target area. Then, through skillful airmanship, he returned his crippled aircraft to the aircraft carrier. By his tenacious aggressiveness, professionalism, and heroic actions in the face of the enemy's massed and determined defenses, Commander Busey upheld the highest traditions of the United States Naval Service.

CAINE, LAWRENCE B., III

Citation: For extraordinary heroism while serving as a Weapons Squad Leader with Company I, Third Battalion, Fifth Marines, First Marine Division (Reinforced) in the Republic of Vietnam on 13 May 1967. During Operation UNION, Corporal Caine's squad was providing covering fire during a recovery operation of Marine dead and wounded, when he observed a large force of well entrenched enemy forces to his front. From their positions, the enemy was able to cover an area of over 2,000 meters in width with grazing and interlocking fire. He quickly took the enemy under fire and killed 20 North Vietnamese Army soldiers in front of his position. Observing a series of caves adjacent to his position he, with complete disregard for his own personal safety, entered them and while searching them accounted for two more enemy killed. Returning to his position, he continued to employ machine-gun, rocket, and small-arms fire with devastating effect upon the enemy. Upon gaining fire superiority, helicopters were able to successfully evacuate the dead and wounded. As the battle ensued, he moved his squad into a tree line maintaining accurate and devastating fire on the enemy. Although painfully wounded during a mortar attack, he refused medical evacuation and continued to defend his company's front until all helicopter evacuation of dead and wounded was completed. As the numerically superior enemy force advanced on the company position, Company I was ordered to withdraw 200 meters and call air strikes and artillery fire on their former position. He directed the fire of his squad covering the successful withdrawal of the company with automatic weapons and a

3.5 inch rocket fire from his tree line position. Corporal Caine was wounded the second time when he was struck by a bomb fragment. As his squad withdrew, 62 enemy bodies were counted in the intermittent stream bed to his front. By his intrepid fighting spirit, exceptional fortitude and gallant initiative, Corporal Caine served to inspire all who observed him and contributed in large measure to the success of his unit. His great personal valor reflected the highest credit upon himself and enhanced the finest traditions of the Marine Corps and the United States Naval Service.

*CALHOUN, JOHN C.

Citation: For extraordinary heroism while serving as an Automatic Rifleman with Combined Action Platoon H-6, Third Combined Action Group, III Marine Amphibious Force, in the Republic of Vietnam on 7 January 1968. Corporal Calhoun's platoon, while defending an outpost in Nuoc Ngot Village, Thua Thien Province suddenly came under a heavy volume of mortar and rocket fire, followed by an aggressive assault by a numerically superior Viet Cong force. The enemy quickly seized the northern wall of the compound as the Marines and Popular Forces soldiers moved to the sandbagged southern wall. During the ensuing fire fight, the Marines became dangerously low of ammunition. Realizing the seriousness of the situation, Corporal Calhoun unhesitatingly ran across 30 meters of fire-swept terrain to obtain the ammunition and deliver it to his comrades. Ignoring the danger around him, he repeatedly crossed the hazardous area, resupplying the defenders, until he was mortally wounded. His heroic and timely actions inspired all who observed him and were instrumental in repelling the enemy force. By his conspicuous valor, strong initiative and complete dedication to duty, Corporal Calhoun upheld the highest traditions of the Marine Corps and of the United States Naval Service. He gallantly gave his life for his country.

*CAMERON, KENNETH R.

Citation: For extraordinary heroism as a Prisoner of War in North Vietnam from 18 May 1967 to 4 October 1970. Under constant pressure from the North Vietnamese in their attempt to gain military information and propaganda material, he experienced severe torture with ropes and by beatings and was kept in solitary confinement. As they persisted in their hostile treatment of him, he continued to resist by feigning sickness and refusing to eat anything but a bare minimum of food. Through those means he was successful in his attempt to keep himself unacceptable in appearance to the North Vietnamese, thus discouraging them from forcing him to meet visiting antiwar delegations for propaganda purposes. He gallantly evaded exploitation by the North Vietnamese throughout his lengthy confinement. By his exceptional courage, determination, and resourcefulness in a most difficult line of resistance, he reflected great credit upon himself and upheld the highest traditions of the Naval Service and the United States Armed Forces.

*CAMPBELL, JOSEPH T.

Citation: For extraordinary heroism while serving as Executive Officer of Company I, Third Battalion, Fifth Marines, First Marine Division, in connection with operations in the Republic of Vietnam. On 15 June 1968 during operation MAMELUKE THRUST in Quang Nam Province, Company I became heavily engaged with a large enemy force and sustained several casualties. As the company prepared to evacuate its wounded, an artillery round impacted nearby, killing the company commander, a platoon commander, and the company gunnery sergeant. Although seriously wounded by fragments, Lieutenant Campbell realized that he was his unit's only remaining officer and refused medical aid in order to assume command of the company. Despite his weakened condition due to the loss of blood, he ensured that a landing zone was secured and selflessly directed the evacuation of the other casualties. When the medical evacuation helicopter arrived and immediately came under intense enemy ground fire, Lieutenant Campbell fearlessly moved among his men to direct suppressive fire on the hostile positions, enabling the helicopter to extract the casualties. Ignoring his weakened condition, he directed a second helicopter into the zone to complete the emergency medical evacuation. He subsequently succumbed to his wounds before he could be evacuated. By his courage, inspiring leadership, and selfless devotion to duty despite the severity of his wounds, Lieutenant Campbell undoubtedly saved the lives of numerous Marines and upheld the highest traditions of the Marine Corps and of the United States Naval Service. He gallantly gave his life for his country.

CANLEY, "J" "L"

Citation: For extraordinary heroism while serving as Company Gunnery Sergeant of Company A, First Battalion, First Marines, First Marine Division during operations against the enemy in the Republic of Vietnam from 31 January to 6 February 1968. On 31 January, when his company came under a heavy volume of enemy fire near the city of Hue, Gunnery Sergeant Canley rushed across the fire-swept terrain and carried several wounded Marines to safety. Later, with the company commander seriously wounded, Gunnery Sergeant Canley assumed command and immediately reorganized his scattered Marines, moving from one group to another to advise and encourage his men. Although sustaining shrapnel wounds during this period, he nonetheless established a base of fire which subsequently allowed the company to break through the enemy strongpoint. Retaining command of the company for the following three days, Gunnery Sergeant Canley on 4 February led his men into an enemy-occupied building in Hue. Despite fierce enemy resistance, he succeeded in gaining a position immediately above the enemy strongpoint and dropped a large satchel charge into the position, personally accounting for numerous enemy killed, and forcing the others to vacate the building. On 6 February, when his unit sustained numerous casualties while attempting to capture a government building, Gunnery Sergeant Canley lent words of encouragement to his men and exhorted them to greater efforts as they drove the enemy from its fortified emplacement. Although wounded once again during this action, on two occasions he leaped a wall in full view of the enemy, picked up casualties, and carried them to covered positions. By his dynamic leadership, courage, and selfless dedication, Gunnery Sergeant Canley contributed greatly to the accomplishment of his company's mission and upheld the highest traditions of the Marine Corps and of the United States Naval Service.

*CARROLL, JAMES J.

Citation: For extraordinary heroism as Commanding Officer, Company K, Third Battalion, Fourth Marines, Third Marine Division in action against North Vietnamese Army forces during Operation PRAIRIE in the Republic of Vietnam from 27 September to 5 October 1966. On 27 September as Company K moved through a thick jungle canopy toward Hill 400, the point platoon was hit hard by enemy automatic weapons fire, electrically detonated mines and booby traps, and the other platoons of the company came under an intense mortar attack. Captain Carroll quickly seized a piece of high ground, and utilizing it for a temporary landing zone was able to evacuate his wounded quickly and establish a company defensive position from which he could attack the determined and well fortified enemy bunkers that defended Hill 400. On 28 September, he called in close air support to within fifty meters of his front lines in an attempt to destroy the enemy positions which had halted the Battalion for two days. Utilizing the shock action of bombs and napalm, Captain Carroll and seven of his Marines crawled to within hand-grenade range of the enemy. Aggressively and decisively launching the final assault and gaining a quick foothold on the hill, he employed the rest of his company to aid in securing the objective then under heavy counterattack from three sides. Despite a painful wound from an enemy mortar round, Captain Carroll continued to direct his men in the securing of the hill. On 5 October while directing supporting fire for Company M, he was mortally wounded by an exploding shell fragment. His courageous fighting spirit, great personal valor, and unswerving devotion to duty served to inspire all who observed him and were in keeping with the highest traditions of the Marine Corps and the United States Naval Service. He gallantly gave his life for his country.

CARTER, MARSHALL N.

Citation: For extraordinary heroism while serving as Commanding Officer, Company "C", First Battalion, First Marines during a heliborne raid against insurgent Viet Cong forces in Quang Nam Province, Republic of Vietnam on 14 January 1967. Upon debarking in the landing zone the company encountered determined resistance from a reinforced company of Viet Cong who delivered heavy small arms, automatic weapons, and mortar fire in defense of the objective area. In a highly professional manner, Captain Carter deployed his company, suppressed the enemy fire, and after inflicting heavy casualties on the enemy, overran the objective. During the withdrawal to the landing zone for reembarkation, one platoon was pinned down by rapidly increasing Viet Cong forces. Appreciating the significance of a delay on the success of the operation, Captain Carter moved immediately to the point of crisis. Efforts to evacuate the body of a fallen comrade under intense enemy fire prevented the platoon from being withdrawn. With complete disregard for his personal safety,

Captain Carter exposed himself to the heavy volume of enemy fire by crawling forward and bringing the fallen Marine to a point where he could be further evacuated. Captain Carter then covered the withdrawal of the platoon to the reembarkation site by single-handedly hurling grenades at the Viet Cong in close combat. Upon returning to the landing zone he supervised the loading of his entire company into helicopters before he himself would leave. Captain Carter's personal valor and professional excellence assured the success of the operation. By his conspicuous gallantry and heroic action in the face of great personal risk, Captain Carter reflected great credit upon himself and upheld the highest traditions of the Marine Corps and of the United States Naval Service.

*CASEBOLT, HENRY C.

Citation: For extraordinary heroism as Second Squad Leader, Third Rifle Platoon, Company F, Second Battalion, First Marines, in the Thua Thien Province, Republic of Vietnam, on 28 February 1966. While his company was engaged in a search and destroy operation it was taken under heavy machine gun and mortar fire by an entrenched Viet Cong battalion. Without hesitation, Corporal Casebolt maneuvered his squad through intense hostile fire in order to position them in a location where they could block the enemy's retreat. His skillful deployment of his squad enabled his men to kill approximately twenty-five Viet Cong and successfully stop the retreat of many others. When an enemy squad attempted to envelop his squad from the left, Corporal Casebolt and two other Marines assaulted the Viet Cong squad, killing them all. Without stopping to catch his breath, he gave orders to his squad to cover him with fire while he crossed a seventy-meter rice paddy in an attempt to destroy an enemy mortar position that he had detected. With complete disregard for his own safety he aggressively ran across the open rice paddy toward the enemy shouting instructions to his squad and directing their fire. When he was almost across the open area, the heavy enemy fire knocked him into the rice paddy. Although mortally wounded, he crawled to a mound of earth where he could observe the enemy. From this position, and still the object of intense enemy fire, Corporal Casebolt continued to direct his squad's fire by pinpointing the enemy positions for them and ordering them to deploy to positions where they could better block the Viet Cong retreat. By his tremendous devotion to duty, professional ability, and inspiring leadership, Corporal Casebolt upheld the highest traditions of the Marine Corps and the United States Naval Service. He gallantly gave his life in the cause of freedom.

*CASEY, MICHAEL J.

Citation: For extraordinary heroism while serving as a Platoon Commander with Company C, First Battalion, First Marines, First Marine Division (Reinforced), in connection with operations against the enemy in the Republic of Vietnam. On the afternoon of 18 March 1968, during Operation FORT, Lieutenant Casey's company was maneuvering across a large open area in Thau Thien Province. Suddenly, the Marines came under intense automatic weapons, mortar, recoilless rifle and antitank rocket fire from a well concealed North Vietnamese Army force. Reacting instantly, Lieutenant Casey rapidly deployed his men, ably directing their fire and shouting words of encouragement to them. Realizing that the forward elements of his platoon were dangerously low on ammunition and that several wounded Marines were lying in an area exposed to the hostile fire, he unhesitatingly ran across seventy meters of fire swept terrain, distributing weapons and ammunition. Picking up a wounded man, he ignored the enemy fire impacting around him and carried the casualty to the platoon's defensive perimeter. On two other occasions, he fearlessly exposed himself to distribute urgently needed ammunition and to move wounded Marines to covered positions. With complete disregard for his own safety, Lieutenant Casey stood in full view of the enemy, while skillfully directing supporting arms fire and air strikes against the enemy positions. When hostile snipers began firing from concealed emplacements to the rear of his platoon, he again rose to his feet, attracting the attention of the snipers and drawing their fire away from his men. While pinpointing the enemy's positions, he was mortally wounded by a burst of automatic weapons fire. His bold initiative and sincere concern for the welfare of his comrades were an inspiration to all who served with him, and contributed significantly to the accomplishment of his unit's mission. By his exceptional courage, aggressive fighting spirit and selfless devotion to duty, Lieutenant Casey upheld the highest traditions of the Marine Corps and of the United States Naval Service. He gallantly gave his life for his country.

*CASEY, ROBERT M.

Citation: For extraordinary heroism on 16 May 1968 while serving as a corpsman with Company "G", Second Battalion, Seventh Marines, First Marine Division in connection with operations against the enemy in the Republic of Vietnam. During Operation ALLEN BROOK, Company "G" was moving through a fortified village in Quang Nam Province to engage an estimated 200 North Vietnamese Army Regulars. Suddenly, the point elements came under heavy enemy fire, sustaining numerous casualties. Petty Officer Casey unhesitatingly moved forward under the intense hostile fire and administered medical aid to one of the wounded Marines. Although wounded himself, he disregarded his own injury as he proceeded to another casualty to render medical treatment. Wounded again while assisting his comrade, Petty Officer Casey steadfastly continued his efforts and moved to the aid of still another casualty, receiving two additional wounds while treating the Marine. When other Marines moved forward to evacuate Petty Officer Casey, he adamantly refused to leave the battle area, stating that he wanted to continue to treat the wounded. After being evacuated to the rear by his companions, he encouraged the casualties around him and provided instructions to others in applying battle dressings. Upon hearing a wounded Marine call for aid, Petty Officer Casey dauntlessly crawled to the man and, while treating his injuries, was mortally wounded. By his unflagging courage, selfless concern for the welfare of his comrades, and unfaltering devotion to duty, Petty Officer Casey upheld the highest traditions of the United States Naval Service.

*CASEY, THOMAS M., JR.

Citation: For extraordinary heroism while serving as a Fire Team Leader with Comapny D, First Battalion, Seventh Marines, First Marine Division, in connection with operations against the enemy in the Republic of Vietnam. On the afternoon of 16 February 1969, Company D was assaulting a large North Vietnamese Army force occupying a well-entrenched position in Quang Nam Province. Alertly observing an enemy fortification, Lance Corporal Casey launched a determined assault upon the hostile position, delivering accurate fire as he fearlessly maneuvered across fifty meters of fire-swept terrain. Upon reaching the hostile bunker, he boldly hurled grenades into it, destroying the North Vietnamese emplacements and killing an enemy soldier. Disregarding his own safety, he went to several casualties, and ignoring the hostile rounds impacting near him, skillfully administered first aid to his wounded comrades. Realizing the need for an M-79 grenade launcher, he again rushed across the hazardous area and, obtaining the weapon, returned to the point of heaviest contact. When two additional Marines were wounded, he unhesitatingly commenced maneuvering through a hail of fire to assist the injured men, but as he approached the casualties he was mortally wounded. His heroic actions and aggressive fighting spirit inspired all who observed him and were instrumental in saving the lives of several Marines. By his courage, sincere concern for the welfare of his comrades, and selfless devotion to duty, Lance Corporal Casey upheld the highest traditions of the Marine Corps and the United States Naval Service. He gallantly gave his life for his country.

CASTILLO, WILLIAM

Citation: For extraordinary heroism while serving as an Ammunition Man with Company E, Second Battalion, Fourth Marines, Third Marine Division, in connection with combat operations against the enemy in the Republic of Vietnam. On 25 February 1969, Company E was occupying a defensive position at Fire Support Base Russell, northwest of the Vandegrift Combat Base in Quang Tri Province. Suddenly, the Marines came under a vicious ground attack by a North Vietnamese Army sapper unit strongly supported by mortars and rocket-propelled grenades. During the initial moments of the attack, several men were trapped inside demolished bunkers and Private First Class Castillo worked feverishly to free the Marines. Then, diving into his gun pit, he commenced single-handedly firing his mortar at the invaders, and although blown from his emplacement on two occasions by the concussion of hostile rounds impacting nearby, resolutely continued his efforts until relieved by some of the men he had freed. Observing a bunker that was struck by enemy fire and was ejecting thick clouds of smoke, he investigated the interior, and discovering five men blinded by smoke and in a state of shock, led them all to safety. Maneuvering across the fire-swept terrain to the command post, he made repeated trips through the hazardous area to carry messages and directions from his commanding officer, then procured a machine gun and provided security for a landing zone until harassing hostile emplacements were destroyed. Steadfastly determined to be of assistance to his wounded comrades, he carried the casualties to waiting evacuation helicopters until he collapsed from exhaustion. By his courage, bold initiative, and unwavering devotion to duty in the face of grave personal danger,

Private First Class Castillo contributed significantly to the accomplishment of his unit's mission and upheld the highest traditions of the Marine Corps and the United States Naval Service.

*CAVANAUGH, THOMAS J.

Citation: For extraordinary heroism while serving as a Platoon Sergeant with Company F, Second Battalion, Seventh Marines, Ninth Marine Amphibious Brigade in the Republic of Vietnam on 19 September 1968. Company F was conducting a reconnaissance in force in Quang Nam Province when the Marines encountered a large enemy force employing heavy automatic weapons and accurate sniper fire which pinned down elements of the company and caused numerous casualties. Rapidly assessing the situation, Corporal Cavanaugh skillfully deployed elements of his platoon to establish a strong base of fire which would enable the beleagured Marines to extract injured personnel. Completely disregarding his own safety, he fearlessly exposed himself to the intense hostile fire, shouting words of encouragement to his men and directing their fire against the enemy emplacements while assisting the wounded to positions of relative safety. As the last of the casualties were withdrawn from the battle area, Corporal Cavanaugh rapidly redeployed his forces to provide covering fire for another hard pressed platoon. Alertly observing one of his men seriously wounded and lying in a dangerously exposed position, he unhesitatingly began maneuvering across the fire-swept terrain to his companion's side when he was seriously wounded. Ignoring his injury, he resolutely continued to crawl toward his wounded comrade until he was no longer able to advance. Steadfastly refusing medical attention, he calmly directed his men in assisting his injured companion to a covered position. Once assured that the last of the wounded Marines had been treated, Corporal Cavanaugh allowed himself to be evacuated to a protected area where he succumbed to his injuries. His bold initiative and heroic efforts inspired all who observed him and contributed immeasurably to the accomplishment of his unit's mission. By his courage, sincere concern for the welfare of his fellow Marines and unwavering devotion to duty, Corporal Cavanaugh upheld the highest traditions of the Marine Corps and of the United States Naval Service. He gallantly gave his life for his country.

CHEATHAM, ERNEST C., JR.

Citation: For extraordinary heroism while serving as Commanding Officer of the Second Battalion, Fifth Marines, First Marine Division (Reinforced), in the Republic of Vietnam from 3 February to 3 March 1968. During Operation HUE CITY, Colonel Cheatham led his battalion in extremely heavy house-to-house fighting against a numerically superior North Vietnamese Army force. Advancing through the city on 4 February to assault the well-fortified Treasury Building/Post Office complex, his unit came under intense fire from concealed enemy positions. The enemy resistance halted the Marines' advance during two days of bitter fighting. Nevertheless, Colonel Cheatham remained steadfast in his determination to secure the enemy stronghold. Skillfully deploying a 106mm recoilless rifle squad into advantageous firing positions, he personally pinpointed the targets with M-16 tracer rounds and directed accurate fire on the enemy, which significantly reduced the pressure on his assaulting force. Completely disregarding his own safety, he joined the assaulting unit and aggressively led his men in routing the North Vietnamese from their entrenched positions. While proceeding through the city on 6 February, he organized his battalion for an assault on the enemy-held Provincial Headquarters Building. Ignoring the hostile fire all around him, he directed his men to covered positions while he fearlessly advanced to an exposed position from which he could locate the sources of enemy fire. Calling an Ontos forward, he directed effective suppressive fire on the enemy and then courageously led his unit as it continued the assault. Colonel Cheatham's dynamic and heroic leadership and his unflagging example inspired all who observed him and contributed greatly to the defeat of the enemy and to their subsequent withdrawal from the city. His dauntless courage and unfaltering devotion to duty upheld the highest traditions of the Marine Corps and the United States Naval Service.

CHEATWOOD, PAUL R.

Citation: For extraordinary heroism while serving as a Mortarman with Company B, First Battalion, Fifth Marines, First Marine Division (Reinforced), in connection with operations against the enemy in the Republic of Vietnam. On the morning of 16 February 1968, Corporal Cheatwood's company was attacking North Vietnamese Army forces occupying the city of Hue. Crossing an open area toward a building, the Marines suddenly came under enemy sniper fire, killing one man, wounding four others and pinning down the platoon. Realizing the seriousness of the situation, Corporal Cheatwood unhesitatingly exposed himself to the hostile fire as he assumed a kneeling position and skillfully delivered suppressive fire at the enemy emplacement, enabling a corpsman to move to the assistance of the casualties. After assisting the corpsman in providing first aid for two casualties, his unit was again pinned down by automatic weapons fire. Reacting instantly, he rapidly directed a heavy volume of rifle fire at the hostile position and, crawling forward, assisted a wounded Marine. When the corpsman arrived, Corporal Cheatwood maneuvered toward the sniper's position and hurled several hand grenades into the building, killing two North Vietnamese soldiers. Subsequently volunteering to lead a search for an enemy machine gun that had been firing at his company, Corporal Cheatwood became separated from his men as he moved through a building. Electing to continue his mission, he alertly observed eight enemy soldiers in a nearby structure. Reacting instantly, he threw numerous hand grenades and fired his pistol into the building. Although painfully wounded, he inflicted numerous casualties on the enemy soldiers and forced the remainder to flee in panic and confusion. His bold initiative and outstanding professionalism were an inspiration to all who observed him and contributed significantly to the accomplishment of his unit's mission. By his exceptional courage, aggressive fighting spirit and selfless devotion to duty in the face of great personal danger, Corporal Cheatwood upheld the highest traditions of the Marine Corps and the United States Naval Service.

CHRISTENSEN, PAUL K.

Citation: For extraordinary heroism while serving as a Machine Gunner with the Third Combined Action Group, III Marine Amphibious Force in connection with operations against enemy forces in the Republic of Vietnam on 19 November 1967. Corporal (then Lance Corporal) Christensen was serving with a twelve-man combat patrol, along a known enemy route, when the patrol surprised and engaged a force of approximately fifty Viet Cong. He quickly placed his machine gun into action mortally wounding several Viet Cong and forced the remainder to withdraw. When the patrol leader and another Marine went forward to search the battle area to capture wounded enemy soldiers and weapons, they were taken under intense enemy automatic and rocket fire which wounded several Marines. With complete disregard for his own safety, Corporal Christensen moved through the hostile fire to deliver a heavy volume of fire on the enemy position. Rallying his men, he quickly established a base of fire and courageously advanced into the open area to assist the patrol leader to a covered position. Quickly assuming command of the patrol, he integrated a defensive perimeter and requested that a reactionary force be dispatched to reinforce his patrol. He called in illumination fire and a medical evacuation helicopter to evacuate the wounded. As the battle ensued he repeatedly exposed himself to the intense enemy fire to encourage his men and adjust their fire. When the relief force arrived, he directed them into position and led an assault into the enemy position, routing the enemy force. By his bold initiative, gallant fighting spirit and loyal devotion to duty, Corporal Christensen reflected great credit upon himself and the Marine Corps and upheld the highest traditions of the United States Naval Service.

*CHRISTMAN, WILLIAM J., III

Citation: For extraordinary heroism while serving as a Platoon Commander with Company A, First Battalion, Ninth Marines, Third Marine Division, in connection with operations against the enemy in the Republic of Vietnam. Early on the afternoon of 22 February 1969, Company A was patrolling north of Ashau Valley in Quang Tri Province when its lead element was pinned down by intense fire from a large North Vietnamese Army force well concealed in a heavily fortified bunker complex. Reacting instantly, Second Lieutenant Christman deployed his platoon to the right flank of the lead platoon and skillfully maneuvered his men forward in a coordinated attack until halted and pinned down by the extremely heavy volume of cross fire from the North Vietnamese emplacements and numerous sniper positions in trees. He directed the fire of his machine guns and light antitank weapons against the North Vietnamese emplacements and mounted such an aggressive assault that his platoon moved through the forward enemy positions. Undaunted by the enemy rounds impacting around him, he fired his light antitank assault weapon, and fearlessly charging across the fire-swept terrain, hurled hand grenades into a hostile emplacement, killing seven North Vietnamese soldiers and silencing their machine gun. Coming under fire from an adjacent bunker, he was mortally wounded while attempting to fire his light antitank assault weapon against the emplacement. With his remaining strength, he resolutely propped himself up on one arm to direct his men in outflanking and destroying the enemy bunker. His heroic actions inspired his men to such aggressive action in a coordinated company attack that 105 North Vietnamese soldiers were killed and a large bunker complex was destroyed. By his courage, bold initiative, and unwavering devotion to duty, Second Lieutenant Christman upheld the highest traditions of the Marine Corps and the United States Naval Service.

CHRISTMAS, GEORGE R.

Citation: For extraordinary heroism while serving as the Commanding Officer of Company H, Second Battalion, Fifth Marines, First Marine Division in connection with operations against the enemy in the Republic of Vietnam. On the afternoon of 5 February 1968 during Operation HUE CITY, Company H was attacking a complex of buildings known to be an enemy strong point consisting of mutually supporting bunkers, fighting holes, and trench lines. During the ensuing fire fight, two platoons seized the corner building of a city block, but intense hostile small-arms, automatic weapons, and B-40 rocket fire temporarily halted the advance. Realizing the seriousness of the situation and the urgent need to sustain the momentum of the attack, Captain Christmas, undaunted by the heavy volume of enemy fire, completely disregarded his own safety as he moved across thirty-five meters of open area to join the lead element and assess the situation. Returning across the fire-swept area, he rejoined the remaining platoon, issued an attack order, and then ran seventy meters across open terrain, ignoring automatic weapons fire, hand grenades, and satchel charges striking around him to reach a tank he had requested. Braving enemy fire and two B-40 rockets that hit the tank, he fearlessly stood atop the vehicle to direct accurate fire against the hostile positions until the intensity of enemy fire diminished. Immediately realizing the tactical advantage, he jumped from the tank, and directed his company in an aggressive assault on the hostile positions, personally leading his men in room-to-room fighting until the building complex was secured. In a large measure due to his bold initiative and courageous actions, he provided the impetus which inspired his men to aggressive action and enabled them to successfully accomplish the mission. By his dynamic leadership, unfaltering determination and selfless devotion to duty in the face of extreme personal danger, Captain Christmas upheld the highest traditions of the Marine Corps and the United States Naval Service.

*CISNEROS, ROY

Citation: For extraordinary heroism while serving as a Squad Leader with Company B, First Battalion, Third Marines, Third Marine Division in the Republic of Vietnam on 11 September 1968. While conducting a reconnaissance in force, Company B came under intense small arms and automatic weapons fire from a North Vietnamese Army company occupying fortified positions on Hill 461 in Quang Tri Province. During the ensuing fire fight, Corporal Cisneros skillfully maneuvered his squad across the hazardous terrain and, directing the fire of his men with devastating accuracy, was instrumental in the destruction of three enemy bunkers. When his men were pinned down by a heavy volume of fire from a fourth emplacement, he boldly advanced and singlehandedly attempted to destroy the enemy position. After firing a light antitank assault weapon into the bunker, he fearlessly hurled hand grenades at the defenders as he aggressively continued his assault. Disregarding his own safety, he commenced firing his rifle and was delivering effective fire upon the North Vietnamese emplacements, when he was mortally wounded by enemy fire. His resolute determination and intrepid fighting spirit inspired all who observed him and were instrumental in his unit accounting for 45 North Vietnamese soldiers confirmed killed. By his courage, aggressive leadership and selfless devotion to duty, Corporal Cisneros upheld the highest traditions of the Marine Corps and the United States Naval Service. He gallantly gave his life for his country.

CLAY, RAYMOND D.

Citation: For extraordinary heroism as a Platoon Corpsman, 1st Platoon, Company "G", 2d Battalion, 7th Marines in the Quang Tri Province, Republic of Vietnam on 24 September 1966. When a Marine from his platoon suffered a severe head wound shortly after the company encountered a North Vietnamese force estimated at regimental strength and employing intense mortar and small-arms fire, Hospitalman Clay, without hesitation, crawled approximately twenty meters through intense fire to aid the wounded Marine. As he began to treat the wounded man, an enemy grenade exploded about ten meters away. Although bleeding profusely from wounds caused by flying shrapnel, Hospitalman Clay continued treating the Marine until two more grenades landed near him, one falling so close to his legs that he immediately kicked it into the bushes, while the second grenade fell next to him and the wounded Marine. Hospitalman Clay quickly threw himself between the grenade and his patient and, in so doing, absorbed the shrapnel and shock with his own body, saving the wounded Marine from further injury and possible death. The force of this explosion hurled Hospitalman Clay into the bushes, where yet another grenade exploded, increasing the number of his wounds. He then laboriously and with great pain crawled to the rear. Hospitalman Clay's exceptional spirit and fortitude greatly increased the morale of the wounded Marines around him. His inspiring and courageous actions in jeopardizing his own life in order that his patient might live were in keeping with the highest traditions of the United States Naval Service.

CLAYBIN, EDWARD A.

Citation: For extraordinary heroism while serving as a cannoneer with Battery D, Second Battalion, Eleventh Marines, in Vietnam on 20 June 1966. When his battery came under a concentrated enemy mortar attack at 0010 on that date, Private First Class Claybin became a casualty almost immediately, receiving severe shrapnel wounds along the left side of his body. While he lay critically wounded, a hand grenade landed some distance from him in the gun pit. With complete disregard for his own personal safety he rolled and crawled until he covered the grenade with his own body in order to protect his fellow Marines from the expected blast. Although it failed to explode, Private First Class Claybin refused to move from the grenade until the other wounded were evacuated and the remaining members of his gun section were clear of danger. By his fearless action, he demonstrated his complete willingness to sacrifice his own life for his fellow Marines. Private First Class Claybin's outstanding courage, daring initiative and steadfast devotion to duty were in keeping with the highest traditions of the Marine Corps and the United States Naval Service.

*COBB, PAUL F.

Citation: For extraordinary heroism while serving as a Platoon Commander with Company A, First Battalion, Seventh Marines, First Marine Division in the Republic of Vietnam on 16 May 1968. During Operation ALLEN BROOK in Quang Nam Province, Lieutenant Cobb's platoon was assigned the mission of reinforcing an adjacent unit which was heavily engaged with a well-entrenched enemy force and had sustained numerous casualties. Under intense fire, he led his men to a position behind the most heavily engaged element of the besieged company where he prepared to continue the attack against the enemy. In order that the pinned-down Marines could evacuate their casualties from the fire-swept area, he established a base of fire utilizing small arms and M-79 grenade launcher fire and began maneuvering his unit across the hazardous terrain. Forced to crawl forward toward the hostile emplacements due to the heavy volume of the enemy's automatic weapons, machine gun, B-40 rocket and mortar fire, he ignored the fire striking around him, as he shouted directions and encouragement to his men. As he approached to within 20 meters of the enemy's positions, he was wounded by hostile fire, however, he aggressively led his men in hand-to-hand combat. While maneuvering forward with his men, he was mortally wounded by the enemy fire. His courageous leadership during the initial and ensuing assaults inspired his men to continue to advance and overwhelm the enemy to the point of defeat. By his bold determination and unwavering and selfless dedication to duty, Lieutenant Cobb upheld the highest traditions of the Marine Corps and the United States Naval Service. He gallantly gave his life for his country.

*COCHRAN, ROBERT F., JR.

Citation: For extraordinary heroism in Company A, First Amphibian Tractor Battalion, Third Marine Division (Reinforced), during Operation STARLITE near Chu Lai, Vietnam, on the morning of 18 August 1965. While leading an amphibian tractor supply column to the front lines, he had momentarily stopped the column in order to check his positions, when it came under intense enemy mortar, recoilless rifle and small-arms fire. Although he was exposed to enemy fire, he calmly and unhesitatingly directed his vehicles into defensive positions. The amphibian tractor on which Lieutenant Cochran was located was hit by recoilless rifle fire. Disregarding his own safety he ordered his crew to evacuate the vehicle and alertly pointed out a good position for them to occupy. Despite the imminent danger of the amphibian tractor exploding and the attempts of the enemy to enter the vehicle, he, in order to deprive the enemy of this source of supply, removed the machine gun ammunition before he left the tractor. With full knowledge of the situation and complete disregard for his own personal safety, Lieutenant Cochran moved through intense enemy cross fire to his disabled vehicle, directing the wounded and dazed personnel to the safety of two amphibian tractors which had gained hull defilade positions behind a rice paddy bank. When he was assured that all his men were safe, he determined which vehicle would afford the best observation of the battle area. As he moved toward this tractor he was severely wounded. Knowing that to ask his men to open the main ramp of the tractor would endanger their lives, he unselfishly chose to mount the vehicle through the top hatch. As a result of his heroic action he succumbed on the top of the amphibian tractor. His personal bravery, and fearless devotion to duty reflected great credit upon himself and the Marine Corps and were in keeping with the highest traditions of the United States Naval Service. He gallantly gave his life in the cause of freedom.

COFFMAN, CLOVIS C., JR.

Citation: For extraordinary heroism in action against Communist Forces while serving as a Platoon Leader with Company C, First Reconnaissance Battalion, First Marine Division in the Republic of Vietnam on 10 October 1966. Sergeant Coffman was leading a thirteen man patrol assigned the mission of observing a valley near Long Bihn, Quang Ngai Province for enemy activity. Early in the afternoon, while leading his unit from their observation post to a helicopter landing zone, the patrol came under a heavy small arms and grenade attack from an estimated thirty-five to fifty man enemy force. Reacting immediately, Sergeant Coffman skillfully organzied and directed the return fire of his out-numbered unit. Fearlessly disregarding his own safety, he repeatedly exposed himself in order to deploy his force and deliver maximum fire power against the attackers. On one occasion during the ensuing fierce action, he observed a wounded Marine lying helpless forward of his position. Courageously he went to his stricken comrade's aid. Although wounded himself, he killed three of the enemy at point blank range in order to reach the stricken Marine. Sergeant Coffman was successful in his effort to return his stricken comrade to friendly lines. When the patrol's medical corpsman was disabled by wounds, he skillfully administered first aid to four seriously wounded Marines. Sergeant Coffman directed fixed wing and armed helicopter attacks against the enemy with devastating accuracy, with the result that helicopters were able to land and extract the force. Although wounded, he remained until all of his men were safely embarked, resolutely defending the landing zone. As the last rescue helicopter was loading, he and another Marine held the landing zone alone, killing four of the enemy in close combat. Only after all of his patrol were embarked, did he board the aircraft and depart the embattled area. By his courageous devotion to duty, and extraordinary leadership, Sergeant Coffman reflected great credit upon himself and the Marine Corps and upheld the highest traditions of the United States Naval Service.

COKER, GEORGE T.

Citation: For extraordinary heroism during an extremely daring escape from a solitary confinement cell while a Prisoner of War in Hanoi, North Vietnam on 12 October 1967. During a period of particularly harsh treatment, he and another prisoner executed an escape as a two-man team despite the high risk of brutal reprisal or possible loss of life. That night, after opening the cell door by removing door bolt brackets from inside the room, he proceeded over the wall and through several blocks of housing to the Domer Bridge. Walking under the bridge to the Red River's edge, he swam downstream all night and at sunrise buried himself in a mudbank in an effort to remain concealed. He was later discovered, recaptured, severely beaten for many hours, and banished to solitary confinement for two and a half years. His extraordinary courage, aggressiveness in the face of the enemy, and dedication to his country reflected great credit upon himself and upheld the highest traditions of the Naval Service and the United States Armed Forces.

COLLINS, BRYANT C.

Citation: For extraordinary heroism as a scout team leader in Company A, Third Reconnaissance Battalion, Third Marine Division (Forward), Fleet Marine Force, on 12 July 1965. Deep in Viet Cong insurgent territory on a reconnaissance patrol, Corporal Collins, in the company of another Marine, was serving as point man when the patrol became heavily engaged with enemy forces firing machine guns and automatic weapons from concealed positions. In the opening moments he brought fire to bear and killed three enemy soldiers, then withdrew to the advance party, which consisted of the company commander and three men, two of whom were wounded. In an open field being swept by a hail of small arms fire, the company commander was struck and killed as he was attempting to aid one of the wounded men. Corporal Collins immediately took charge of the situation, and coolly exposing himself to extremely heavy fire, manned an M79 grenade launcher and silenced an enemy machine gun. He bandaged one wounded man and laid down covering fire to enable him to crawl out of range. After having recovered the commander's body, he again advanced to the fire-swept field and carried the remaining wounded man toward cover until met by assistance. He then organized the party and ordered their return to the main body located 100 yards to the rear. He personally carried his dead commander back to the main line through heavy fire received from the flanks. His heroic actions and brave demeanor served as an inspiration to all who observed him and contributed to the successful withdrawal of the other members of the patrol. By his superb leadership and valiant fighting spirit Corporal Collins reflected distinct credit upon himself and the Marine Corps and upheld the finest traditions of the United States Naval Service.

COMPTON, BRYAN W., JR.

Citation: For extraordinary heroism as a pilot and as Commanding Officer of Attack Squadron ONE HUNDRED SIXTY-THREE, embarked in USS ORISKANY (CVA-34), on 21 August 1967. As the strike leader of a major coordinated air attack against the Hanoi Thermal Power Plant, Hanoi, North Vietnam, Commander Compton, with precise navigation and timing, led the strike group to the target area through an extremely intense array of sophisticated enemy defenses, including at least twenty-eight surface-to-air missiles and heavy, accurate antiaircraft fire. Despite the continuing heavy enemy opposition in the target area, Commander Compton skillfully maneuvered his srike forces and led them in an attack which inflicted major damage upon the target. During the attack, strike aircraft incurred extensive battle damage from the heavy flak opposition. With complete disregard for his own safety, Commander Compton remained in the vicinity of the target until the damaged aircraft exited the area safely. In addition to assisting the egressing strike pilots by calling evasive maneuvers necessary for them to avoid surface-to-air missiles and heavy concentrations of antiaircraft artillery fire, he succeeded in taking seventeen pictures with a hand-held camera which provided immediate and invaluable damage assessment of this most significant target. By his superb leadership, outstanding courage and inspiring devotion to duty in the face of extremely heavy enemy opposition, Commander Compton contributed greatly to the success of a most hazardous mission and upheld the highest traditions of the United States Naval Service.

CONE, FRED "J"

Citation: For extraordinary heroism in action against the enemy while serving as a Pilot of an A6A Intruder Aircraft with Marine All Weather Attack Squadron 242 in the Republic of Vietnam on 25 October 1967. Assigned the mission of attacking an airfield deep in enemy controlled territory, Major Cone coordinated and led the second flight of four aircraft in a coordinated three flight strike attack. He led his flight across rugged terrain with no navigational aids. Skillfully navigating to the exact letdown point, he began his descent to evade enemy radar. Undaunted by the intense enemy antiaircraft fire, he skillfully maneuvered his aircraft towards the objective. Major Cone's surface-to-air missile warning device indicated that a missile had been launched. He banked his Intruder into a head-on collision course and with split second timing, snapped the aircraft down and away from the missile so that it exploded harmlessly in the air. Observing a second missile being launched, he skillfully avoided it 300 feet above the ground. While nearing the target and engulfed in intense enemy ground fire, he encountered a third and fourth missile. Utilizing the same tactics, he skillfully avoided the third missile, however, the fourth missile exploded above his aircraft tossing it into a violent maneuver. Although his plane was damaged, Major Cone continued on his course. Quickly putting his aircraft into a steep climb so that safe separation from the blast of his bombs could be achieved, he dropped four and one-half tons of ordnance, devastating the target. While turning outboard, he encountered a fifth missile. Quickly assessing the situation, he jettisoned his drop tanks to gain speed and maneuverability, thus avoiding the missile. By his bold initiative, devotion to duty and superb aeronautical skill, Major Cone was instrumental in destroying an enemy airfield, reflecting great credit upon himself and the Marine Corps and upholding the highest traditions of the United States Naval Service.

CONFER, MILTON W.

Citation: For extraordinary heroism on 13 February 1970 while serving in the Republic of Vietnam as an advisor to the patrol officer in charge of two Vietnamese river patrol boats which were escorting a resupply mission to advanced tactical support bases. The column included two heavy logistics craft loaded with seven tons of ammunition and a fuel barge with eight thousand gallons of fuel. Suddenly, both banks of the narrow river erupted in a storm of enemy rocket and heavy machine gun fire. With his patrol boat situated between the heaviest enemy firing positions and the transports, Petty Officer Confer attempted to man the after fifty-caliber machine gun but was knocked to the deck as the first of several rockets hit his boat. He then manned the midships gun and fired suppressive volleys into the enemy positions until his ammunition was exploded. Subsequently, he again attempted to man the after gun. This time he was wounded in the side by an enemy bullet, but succeeded in firing the gun until he was obliged to direct his boat alongside one of the logistics craft to rearm. While rearming, his boat received numerous heavy machine gun hits which damaged both engines and started a fire. Despite his painful wound, Petty Officer Confer began another firing run on the heaviest of the enemy positions as the boats finally neared the end of the kill zone. Only when he was relieved by units scrambled to aid his beleaguered convoy did he attend to his wound. By his great personal valor and dauntless perseverance, Petty Officer Confer contributed in large measure to the success of the mission and upheld the highest traditions of the United States Naval Service.

CONKLIN, RICHARD F.

Citation: For extraordinary heroism while serving as a Field Artillery Batteryman with Battery D, Second Battalion, Thirteenth Marines, First Marine Division (Reinforced), in connection with operations against the enemy in the Republic of Vietnam. On 10 May 1968, Corporal Conklin was a member of a detachment of two howitzers at the United States Army Special Forces camp at Ngok Tavak in Quang Tin Province. In the early morning hours, the camp was attacked by a reinforced North Vietnamese Army battalion which penetrated the camp's defensive wire in two places, and, utilizing grenades, mortars, B-40 rockets, and automatic weapons, attempted to overrun the hill-top position. Realizing the seriousness of the situation, Corporal Conklin manned a .30-caliber machine gun and delivered a heavy volume of accurate fire against the enemy reaching the crest of the hill. Sustaining heavy casualties from the machine-gun fire, the enemy concentrated its automatic weapons fire on his position and attacked it with grenades. Although seriously wounded by grenade fragments, Corporal Conklin resolutely remained at his position and continued to deliver effective fire on the assaulting North Vietnamese. Observing numerous grenades land in his position, he quickly retrieved them and threw them back at the enemy. Wounded a second time by grenade fragments, he temporarily lapsed into unconsciousness and slumped over the weapon, severely burning himself on the hot barrel. Regaining consciousness, he continued to deliver fire for another fifteen minutes until he collapsed from his multiple wounds. When he was subsequently evacuated, three unexploded grenades were found in his emplacement. By his exemplary courage, unfaltering determination, and steadfast devotion to duty at great personal risk, Corporal Conklin was instrumental in repulsing the enemy assault and upheld the highest traditions of the Marine Corps and the United States Naval Service.

*CONNELL, JAMES J.

Citation: For extraordinary heroism as a Prisoner of War in North Vietnam from April 1968 to June 1969. Under constant pressure from the North Vietnamese in their attempt to gain military information and propaganda material, he experienced severe torture with ropes and was kept in almost continuous solitary confinement. As they persisted in their hostile treatment of him, he continued to resist by feigning facial muscle spasms, incoherency of speech, and crippled arms with loss of feeling in his fingers. The Vietnamese, convinced of his plight, applied shock treatments in an attempt to improve his condition. However, he chose not to indicate improvement for fear of further cruelty. Isolated in a corner of the camp near a work area visited daily by other prisoners, he established and maintained covert communications with changing groups of POW's, thereby serving as a main point of exchange of intelligence information. By his exceptional courage, determination, and resourcefulness in this most difficult line of resistance, he reflected great credit upon himself and upheld the highest traditions of the Naval Service and the United States Armed Forces.

CONNELLY, MATTHEW J., III

Citation: For extraordinary heroism on May 10 1972 as pilot of a jet aircraft in Fighter Squadron NINETY-SIX, embarked in USS CONSTELLATION (CVA-64), during a major air-wing strike against an enemy rail yard in North Vietnam. As the flight leader of a section of aircraft on target combat air patrol, Lieutenant Connelly sighted a formation of approximately sixteen enemy fighter aircraft threatening the retiring strike force. Despite the overwhelming enemy odds, he engaged the numerically superior aircraft, pressing home hard-fought attacks which resulted in the destruction of two enemy planes and the dispersion of the remaining aircraft out of range of the strike force. Lieutenant Connelly's superb airmanship, courage and dedication reflected great credit upon himself and the United States Naval Service.

COOK, CLARENCE L.

Citation: For extraordinary heroism while serving as copilot of a Search and Rescue Helicopter, attached to Helicopter Support Squadron SEVEN, Detachment ONE HUNDRED FOUR, embarked in USS PREBLE (DLG-15) operating as a unit of the United States SEVENTH Fleet, in connection with the rescue of two downed aviators in North Vietnam on 19 June 1968. Providing exceptional support to the pilot of his aircraft throughout this daring, night rescue mission which was carried out despite extremely formidable enemy opposition, Lieutenant (jg) Cook rendered invaluable assistance in locating and maintaining references to the position of the survivors, and in utilizing his machine gun to suppress hostile small-arms and automatic-weapons fire which was directed at the rescue helicopter with growing intensity during four difficult descents which culminated in the successful rescue of the survivors. By his professional skill, prompt actions, and great personal valor in the face of intense enemy fire, Lieutenant (jg) Cook contributed in large measure to the success of this rescue mission and upheld the highest traditions of the United States Naval Service.

COOLICAN, JAMES J.

Citation: For extraordinary heroism in action in the city of Hue, Thua Thien Province, Republic of Vietnam on 31 January 1968. In the early morning hours, without warning, the enemy assaulted simultaneously all positions of the Hue Military Assistance Command, Vietnam Compound perimeter with 122mm and B-40 rockets, mortar and intense small-arms fire. Captain Coolican, with disregard for his own safety, dashed 150 meters through the hail of exploding enemy rounds to a guard post where he moved four wounded personnel to the dispensary. Within a short time, the enemy scored a direct hit on a 20-foot tower, mortally wounding the guard. Quickly, Captain Coolican ran to the tower under heavy enemy fire, recovered the wounded man and carried him down the ladder to an awaiting stretcher. After this, he returned to the tower guard post where he silenced the enemy with a fierce blanket of M-79 grenade fire. At daybreak, because of the critical condition of two wounded men, an emergency air medical rescue was planned from a landing zone approximately 400 meters from the MACV compound. Captain Coolican organized a small force and, after two futile attempts at evacuation of the wounded, he finally succeeded on the third trip and carried critically needed ammunition back to the compound. When a relief force coming to the aid of the compound was ambushed and sustained numerous casualties, Captain Coolican assembled his men and sped to the scene of intense fighting. Under unrelenting hostile fire, he skillfully directed the collection of the injured and evacuation to the Hue MACV dispensary. Throughout the battle of Hue, he skillfully effected medical evacuations under enemy observation and fire. He succeeded in saving many lives with no loss to his own force. Captain Coolican's conspicuous gallantry, professionalism and extraordinary devotion to duty were in keeping with the highest traditions of the Marine Corps and the United States Naval Service.

CORSETTI, HARRY J.

Citation: For extraordinary heroism in action while serving as a team leader with the Third Force Reconnaissance Company, Third Reconnaissance Battalion, Third Marine Division, in connection with operations against the enemy in the Republic of Vietnam. On 15 August 1968, while conducting a long-range reconnaissance patrol southeast of the Con Thien Combat Outpost, Corporal Corsetti alertly observed a numerically superior North Vietnamese Army force approaching his team's position. Rapidly deploying his men, he assigned them fields of fire, and upon learning that a wire on a command-detonated mine was defective, he fearlessly moved to within thirty meters of the advancing enemy soldiers to repair the faulty device. During the ensuing three-hour fight, he skillfully coordinated supporting arms fires with those of his men, successfully halting the advance of the enemy until a tank-infantry reaction force arrived. Mounting one of the armored vehicles to direct its fire, Corporal

Corsetti assumed command when the tank commander was wounded, and ignoring the intense hostile fire, he directed highly effective fire against the North Vietnamese until they were forced to flee in panic and confusion. When his team came under intense fire from a numerically superior hostile force on 17 August, Corporal Corsetti immediately deployed his men and coordinated accurate artillery fire and gunship attacks against the enemy. On one occasion, he completely disregarded his own safety as he fearlessly exposed himself to draw hostile fire, enabling the supporting armed helicopter pilots to locate the North Vietnamese positions. Undaunted by the enemy rounds impacting near him, he moved across the fire-swept terrain to establish a landing zone and subsequently directed the embarkation of his men aboard an extraction aircraft. By his courage, bold initiative, and selfless devotion to duty in the face of great personal danger, Corporal Corsetti inspired all who served with him and upheld the highest traditions of the Marine Corps and the United States Naval Service.

*COUSINS, MERRITT T.

Citation: For extraordinary heroism while serving as a Radio Operator with Battery B, First Battalion, Twelfth Marines, Third Marine Division attached to Company F, Second Battalion, Third Marines, Third Marine Division in the Republic of Vietnam on 8 July 1967. Lance Corporal Cousins, serving with a Forward Observer Team, was engaged in a search and clear operation in Cam Lo District, southwest of Con Thien. En route to their objective, the second squad was taken under heavy small-arms and automatic weapons fire by a numerically superior enemy force. The third squad, to which Lance Corporal Cousins was attached, immediately proceeded to assist them. Before contact was made with the second squad, the third squad was taken under heavy automatic weapons fire and a devastating mortar attack by an estimated reinforced North Vietnamese Army unit. In the initial moments of the battle he was wounded by shrapnel, and he and four comrades were cut off forward of their unit and completely surrounded by the enemy. Despite his painful wounds, he called in artillery and advised the command post of their situation. He called artillery in so close that shrapnel was hitting their position. As the artillery fire rocked the enemy position, they made an assault toward the Marine perimeter. Hand-to-hand combat ensued and Lance Corporal Cousins was wounded a second time. Disregarding his painful wounds, and aware of the desperate need for artillery fire and the needs of his fellow Marines, he refused to leave his radio and continued to adjust artillery fire upon the enemy and relay their situation until he succumbed to his wounds with his radio handset in his hands. By his bold initiative, gallant fighting spirit and selfless devotion to duty, he was instrumental in repulsing a large scale attack and saving the lives of the beleaguered Marines, reflecting great credit upon himself and the Marine Corps and upholding the highest traditions of the United States Naval Service. He gallantly gave his life for his country.

*COVELLA, JOSEPH F.

Citation: For extraordinary heroism as Light Weapons Infantry Advisor, Third Battalion, First Regiment, First Infantry Division, Army of the Republic of Vietnam, on 3 January 1966. Sergeant Covella was accompanying the First Company of his battalion when that unit came under scorching fire from their front, pinning them in a ditch while the numerically superior enemy force continued to rain murderous fire upon them. When the order to withdraw was given, one platoon was instructed to remain in position to provide covering fire, and Sergeant Covella, with no regard for his personal safety, volunteered to remain with the platoon. The remainder of the company made an orderly withdrawal and the platoon was told to evacuate. As soon as the order was implemented, three Vietnamese soldiers and one American advisor were wounded. Realizing that without covering fire his platoon would be destroyed, Sergeant Covella stayed with the wounded to aid them and cover the retreat in the face of a merciless enemy advance. He was able to halt the enemy long enough for his platoon to escape from the trap. His battalion found him later with the men he had tried to protect. By his personal bravery, consummate courage and willing self-sacrifice for his comrades, Sergeant Covella reflected great credit upon himself and the Marine Corps and upheld the highest traditions of the United States Naval Service. He gallantly gave his life in the cause of freedom.

COVER, ROBERT L.

Citation: For extraordinary heroism while serving with Marine Light Helicopter Observation Squadron Two, Marine Aircraft Group Sixteen, First Marine Aircraft Wing in connection with combat operations against the enemy in the Republic of Vietnam. On 17 March 1969, Master Sergeant Cover, then a Gunnery Sergeant, launched as Aerial Gunner aboard an armed helicopter assigned the mission of supporting a Marine company which was heavily engaged in combat with a large North Vietnamese Army force near An Hoa in Quang Nam Province. Arriving over the designated location, he was informed that the unit on the ground had sustained several casualties and had been pinned down in an open rice paddy by a heavy volume of automatic weapons fire. Throughout the ensuing four-hour period, while his pilot maneuvered the helicopter close to hostile emplacements, Master Sergeant Cover delivered intense machine gun fire at the enemy. Despite his vigorous efforts, the withering fire of the hostile troops still prevented the Marines from recovering their casualties from exposed locations. The pilot of the helicopter subsequently elected to land his craft in the contested area to evacuate the wounded men. During the landing, the aircraft became a vulnerable target for intensified hostile fire. Although Master Sergeant Cover attempted to suppress the enemy fire and to destroy the nearby enemy positions with his machine gun, he observed that the hostile fusillade raking the friendly lines prevented the Marines from reaching the casualties. Quickly dismounting his machine gun and providing his own covering fire, he ran thirty meters across the hazardous terrain to the side of one of the wounded and, assisted by a companion, carried the critically wounded Marine back toward the helicopter. Before he could reach the aircraft, he was seriously wounded by enemy small-arms fire, but steadfastly continued his mission and embarked the casualty. On three additional occasions, the pilot landed to embark casualties and each time, concealing his painful wound from his comrades, Master Sergeant Cover braved the hostile fire to set up his machine gun and provide covering fire for the Marines carrying wounded to the aircraft. His heroic and selfless actions inspired all who observed him and were instrumental in saving the lives of four fellow Marines. By his courage, initiative, and devotion to duty, Master Sergeant Cover upheld the highest traditions of the Marine Corps and of the United States Naval Service.

COX, CHARLES J.

Citation: For extraordinary heroism on the morning of 15 September 1968 while serving with United States forces engaged in riverine assault operations against communist aggressor forces in the

Republic of Vietnam. As Commander of River Assault Division 11-1, Lieutenant Cox was leading a column of assault craft down the Ben Tre River in Kien Hoa Province when the column was ambushed by a Viet Cong unit. After ordering return fire from all weapons, Lieutenant Cox exposed himself to fierce enemy fire while evaluating the tactical situation and marking beach sites for his boats. Although painfully wounded at the outset by exploding rocket fragments, he continued to issue orders and maintain tight control over his division, landing embarked troops on both enemy flanks. In order to insure the safe arrival of the medical aid boat to attend to his numerous casualties, he ordered a monitor at the aid boat's location to provide fire support, and then directed his boat and another monitor back through the ambush. As the front and rear units met in a hail of enemy fire, Lieutenant Cox ordered his two monitors to reverse course and, while running the ambush for the third time, led all four boats to a position of relative safety. He then supervised the treatment or evacuation of his wounded before submitting to much-needed attention for his own injuries. Because of his rare tactical brilliance, the infantry units were landed at optimal positions to assault the enemy from both flanks and inflict serious damage while sustaining little themselves. During two subsequent, intense engagements on 15 and 16 September 1968, Lieutenant Cox led his men with the same high degree of courage and competence. His exemplary performance of duty with consistent disregard for his own safety or his painful wounds throughout two days was instrumental in the success of an operation which inflicted numerous enemy casualties. By his inspiring leadership, great personal valor, and selfless devotion to duty, Lieutenant Cox upheld the highest traditions of the United States Naval Service.

*CRAWFORD, CHARLES H.

Citation: For extraordinary heroism on 29 May 1967 while serving as a corpsman with Company "M", Third Battalion, Fourth Marines, Third Marine Division, during Operation PRAIRIE VI against elements of the North Vietnamese Army in Quang Tri Province, Republic of Vietnam. While attacking the heavily fortified enemy bunker complex on Hill 174, the lead elements of Company "M" were pinned down by a heavy volume of automatic-weapons fire delivered from well-prepared enemy positions, and sustained numerous Marine casualties in the initial stage of the battle. Despite the concentrated fire which made it virtually impossible to reach the wounded who were trapped only a few feet from the main enemy bunker, Petty Officer Crawford immediately ran through the deadly hail of enemy fire to reach his injured comrades. After administering first aid to the most seriously wounded Marine, and while moving the casualty to a relatively safe area, Petty Officer Crawford himself was fatally wounded. Through his fearless courage and uncommon concern for his comrades, he inspired the other Marines, and undoubtedly saved the life of the wounded Marine he treated. Petty Officer Crawford's daring actions and unswerving devotion to duty were in keeping with the highest traditions of the United States Naval Service.

CROCKETT, JOSEPH R., JR.

Citation: For extraordinary heroism while serving as a team leader with First Force Reconnaissance Company, First Reconnaissance Battalion, First Marine Division, in connection with operations against the enemy in the Republic of Vietnam. On 23 April 1969, Sergeant Crockett's team was clandestinely observing a major North Vietnamese Army supply route west of An Hoa in Quang Nam Province when the Marines came under a ground assault by an estimated hostile platoon supported by a heavy volume of automatic weapons fire, and in the initial moments of the attack sustained several casualties. Sergeant Crockett seized a grenade launcher from one of his wounded men and moved across 50 meters of exposed terrain to deliver fire upon the enemy. As a group of North Vietnamese soldiers approached his team's defensive perimeter, he quickly killed one and wounded four others; then, having exhausted his ammunition, utilized a radio to adjust supporting artillery fire to within 50 meters of his men. He then ran from one Marine position to another gathering grenades, which he hurled at the hostile soldiers, forcing them to regroup and withdraw. As the enemy soldiers retreated they lighted several brush fires that rapidly spread toward the team's emplacement. Unable to extinguish the flames with his jacket, Sergeant Crockett repeatedly assisted in moving his injured Marines to safety, stopping only to render first aid and deliver suppressive fire upon the North Vietnamese force. In order to expedite evacuation of his critically injured men, he tied an air panel to his back and boldly moved into an open clearing where he stood in full view of the enemy to mark the landing zone for the helicopters and gunships as they arrived on station. Although nearly exhausted, Sergeant Crockett refused to be extracted, and assisted in a search of the vicinity. By his courage, aggressive fighting spirit, and selfless devotion to duty in the face of grave personal danger, Sergeant Crockett upheld the highest traditions of the Marine Corps and the United States Naval Service.

*CRUSE, JAMES D.

Citation: For extraordinary heroism in action on 15 June 1968 while serving as a corpsman with Company "M", Third Battalion, Fourth Marines, Third Marine Division, in connection with operations against enemy aggressor forces in the Republic of Vietnam, Hospitalman Cruse's platoon was conducting a search and destroy operation near the Khe Sanh Combat Base when the platoon suddenly came under intense automatic-weapons fire from a large North Vietnamese Army force. During the initial moments of the fire fight, lead elements of the platoon were pinned down in an open area, and the two point men were seriously wounded. Disregarding his own safety, Hospitalman Cruse unhesitatingly advanced from his position of relative safety and maneuvered across the fire-swept terrain to assist his injured comrades. Upon reaching the first casualty, he efficiently rendered medical aid and spoke words of comfort and encouragement before moving forward to the other Marine casualty who lay exposed to enemy fire. While treating and comforting the second wounded Marine, Hospitalman Cruse was himself mortally wounded. By his courage, bold initiative, and selfless devotion to duty, he served to inspire all who observed him and upheld the highest traditions of the United States Naval Service.

*CUMMINGS, ROGER W.

Citation: For extraordinary heroism while serving as a Rifleman with Company K, Third Battalion, Seventh Marines, First Marine Division in the Republic of Vietnam on 20 April 1969. Private First Class Cummings' platoon was directed to assault heavily fortified North Vietnamese Army emplacements located in the mountainous Thoung Duc area of Quang Nam Province. As the platoon commenced the attack, the Marines came under vicious automatic weapons fire from concealed machine gun positions, pinning down the unit and inflicting several casualties. Realizing the need for immediate action to prevent further Marine injuries, Private First Class Cummings unhesitatingly left his relatively secure rear position and charged across the fire-swept terrain to assault the hostile bunker complex. With enemy rounds impacting about him, he raced from one emplacement to another, firing his rifle and throwing hand grenades in a splendid display of valor which enabled his companions to resume the attack. Demoralized by the impetus of the attack, the North Vietnamese soldiers began a retreat from the area and, as they withdrew, one of the men hurled an explosive device at Private First Class Cummings which injured him extensively and rendered him unable to walk. Although suffering great pain, he resolutely determined to prevent the escape of the hostile unit, and struggling desperately, he dragged himself on his elbows and hands to a vantage point from which he continued to fire upon the enemy soldiers until he succumbed to his wounds. His heroic efforts and selfless concern for his fellowmen were instrumental in his unit's securing the objective. By his courage, aggressive fighting spirit and unwavering devotion to duty, Private First Class Cummings upheld the highest traditions of the Marine Corps and the United States Naval Service. He gallantly gave his life for his country.

CUNNINGHAM, RANDALL H.

Citation: For extraordinary heroism on 10 May 1972 while serving as a pilot with Fighter Squadron NINETY-SIX, embarked in USS CONSTELLATION (CVA-64), during a major air-wing coordinated strike against the strategic and heavily defended Hai Duong marshalling rail yard joining the port of Haiphong to the industrial center of Hanoi in North Vietnam. As leader of a section of F-4J flak-suppressor aircraft assigned to protect the less maneuverable and heavily loaded attack group, Lieutenant Cunningham positioned his unit between the retiring strike force and a large formation of approximately sixteen enemy aircraft attempting to intercept the bombers. Displaying extraordinary courage and brilliant aerial skill, he inspired and motivated his outnumbered shipmates in resisting several enemy assaults, and personally accounted for three of the six enemy aircraft destroyed in the fierce battle. Although his aircraft was struck by a surface-to-air missile and later burst into flame, Lieutenant Cunningham managed to barrel-roll his crippled fighter to the Tonkin Gulf where he ejected and was picked up shortly by a rescue helicopter. His great personal courage and invaluable contribution to the success of an extremely important mission were in keeping with the highest traditions of the United States Naval Service.

CURLEY, RONALD T.

Citation: For extraordinary heroism as Squad Leader of the First Squad, First Platoon, Company F, Second Battalion, Twenty-sixth Marines in the Quang Tri Province, Republic of Vietnam on 16 May 1967. During Operation PRAIRIE IV, the platoon in front of Sergeant Curley's platoon came under heavy small-arms and automatic weapons fire from a North Vietnamese Army battalion entrenched in fortified bunkers. As the platoon moved to envelop the enemy, the platoon commander and numerous other Marines were wounded, and the platoon was pinned down by a heavy volume of enemy fire coming from all sides. Sergeant Curley immediately took charge of the platoon and moved to an exposed position from which he could better direct the fire fight. Fully aware of the personal risk involved, he repeatedly exposed himself to enemy fire during the three hour battle while directing his platoon. On two occasions he single-handedly assaulted enemy bunkers, silencing the automatic weapons inside. Moving from place to place on the battlefield, he distributed ammunition to men in exposed positions and personally visited each of the wounded men. When the major battle had subsided, he continued to set an example of courage by making three trips to the landing zone with wounded men, a distance of 400 meters, under enemy sniper fire. By his daring initiative, gallant fighting spirit and selfless devotion to duty in the face of insurmountable odds, Sergeant Curley saved the lives of many of his comrades and contributed materially to the success of his company's mission. His outstanding courage and valiant leadership were in keeping with the highest traditions of the Marine Corps and the United States Naval Service.

CURTIS, RUSSELL W.

Citation: For extraordinary heroism while serving with Supply Battalion, First Force Service Regiment in the Republic of Vietnam on 21 August 1967. Upon discovery of a large mine, Gunnery Sergeant Curtis was called upon to aid in its removal since it was located on a vital trail network. After assessing the situation, it was determined that the only feasible method to remove the mine was by hand. When the small force at the scene came under vicious sniper fire from a nearby tree line, he immediately dispersed his men to give covering fire and proceeded to remove the mine. Estimating that it was a twenty-five pound tetronal, he and a comrade proceeded to remove the fuse and check the mine for additional booby traps. While the mine was being removed Gunnery Sergeant Curtis noticed an M-26A1 hand grenade fixed to the mine. With complete disregard for his own safety, he shoved his comrade aside and shouted a warning. Unable to throw the grenade because of the close proximity of the friendly troops, Gunnery Sergeant Curtis elected to absorb the impact of the explosion with his own body thereby saving his comrades from death or injury. By his bold initiative, dauntless courage, and unselfish concern for his fellow Marines, Gunnery Sergeant Curtis reflected great credit upon himself and the Marine Corps and upheld the highest traditions of the United States Naval Service.

DALTON, ROBERT G.

Citation: For extraordinary heroism while serving as a Squad Leader with Company K, Third Battalion, Third Marines, Third Marine Division in the Republic of Vietnam on 25 May 1969. While Company K was participating in Operation VIRGINIA RIDGE near the Demilitarized Zone, the lead platoon came under a heavy volume of machine gun and automatic weapons fire supported by rocket-propelled grenades, directional mines and mortars. In the initial burst of fire, the platoon commander and point squad leader were seriously wounded. Realizing the need for immediate action, Corporal Dalton rallied his companions, then, seizing the machine gun of an injured Marine, dauntlessly moved forward to a vantage point on the crest of a hill and, although this made him a vulnerable target for hostile gunners, resolutely maintained his dangerously exposed position as he relentlessly delivered rapid fire at enemy emplacements, thus enabling other Marines to treat the casualties behind him. Aware that the hilltop had to be taken before medical evacuation helicopters could land and embark the wounded, Corporal Dalton picked up the machine gun and two cans of ammunition and, wrapping his shirt around the red-hot barrel of the weapon, initiated an aggressive assault up the slope. As he led his comrades in the attack, the North Vietnamese Army soldiers retreated from their entrenched positions. Having expended his ammunition and armed only with a pistol and a hand grenade, Corporal Dalton observed an enemy bunker 30 meters to his front and, boldly charging the remaining emplacement, routed the enemy. His heroic actions and determined efforts were instrumental in the defeat of the North Vietnamese Army force. By his aggressive fighting spirit and unwavering devotion to duty, Corporal

Dalton upheld the highest traditions of the Marine Corps and the United States Naval Service.

DANNER, DAVID J.

Citation: For extraordinary heroism as a Tank Maintenance Man and Crewman with Company A, Third Tank Battalion, Third Marine Division, in connection with operations against the enemy in the Republic of Vietnam on 8 May 1967. While operating in support of the First Battalion, Fourth Marines, Sergeant Danner's tank was hit and heavily damaged by enemy fire during a savage mortar and infantry attack on the battalion's positions at Gio Linh by a 400-man North Vietnamese Army force. Although wounded himself, Sergeant Danner helped his dazed and wounded fellow crewmen from the wreckage to the medical aid station. Realizing that enemy soldiers were in the Command Post area, having penetrated the defensive perimeter during their initial assault, he refused first aid and resolutely returned to his disabled tank to retrieve a .30-caliber machine gun. Mounting the weapon on the ground, he commenced delivering a heavy volume of fire on the attackers. With complete disregard for his own safety, he repeatedly left his position to deliver badly needed ammunition to the infantrymen in the fighting holes and to assist in moving casualties to safer positions. On one occasion, observing a seriously wounded Marine in need of immediate medical treatment, Sergeant Danner carried the man through intense enemy fire to the corpsman's bunker where he could receive life-saving first aid, which prevented him from bleeding to death. Demonstrating uncommon courage and tenacity, he then returned to his machine gun where he continued to provide covering fire for his comrades, moving his weapon to alternate positions in order to deliver maximum fire on the enemy. Although in extreme pain from fragment wounds in his arms and back and suffering severe burns and a loss of hearing as a result of an explosion, he selflessly disregarded his own welfare throughout the vicious fire fight in order to assist his comrades in repulsing the North Vietnamese attack. By his exceptional professional skill and bold initiative, he personally killed fifteen enemy soldiers and undoubtedly wounded many more. Sergeant Danner's daring and heroic actions at great personal risk, inspiring leadership, and unwavering devotion to duty reflected great credit upon himself and were in keeping with the highest traditions of the Marine Corps and of the United States Naval Service.

DANNHEIM, WILLIAM T.

Citation: For extraordinary heroism on 20 October 1970 during an attack by enemy forces on the Advance Tactical Support Base at Song Ong Doc, Republic of Vietnam. As Senior Advisor to River Patrol Division SIX TWO, and as the senior officer present on the base at the time of the coordinated enemy rocket, mortar, and automatic weapons attack, Lieutenant Commander (then Lieutenant) Dannheim immediately proceeded to Naval Operations Center to organize and direct the defense of the base. With mortar fire intensifying and fires springing up in several places on the base, he gave orders for the boats moored alongside to get underway and defend the base from the adjacent river. This decision was responsible for saving the lives of many United States Navy and Vietnamese personnel by moving them from their static and suddenly lethal position to a maneuverable protected position on the River Assault Craft (monitors). In the face of the mounting enemy fire attack, Lieutenant Commander Dannheim remained in the Naval Operations Center in order to direct air strikes by attack helicopters. Finally, after a secondary fire caused a loss of power to the Naval Operations Center, Lieutenant Commander Dannheim left the burning building to search for any remaining personnel on the base. After completing this search and helping to carry some wounded men aboard a waiting boat, he then moved to a monitor moments before the Naval Operations Center he had just vacated received a direct hit. From the monitor, Lieutenant Commander Dannheim continued to direct gunfire and air support until early morning at which time he moved his operations to the USS GARRETT COUNTY. By his outstanding professionalism, leadership and courage, he was directly instrumental in saving many lives and in inflicting heavy casualties upon the enemy, thereby upholding the highest traditions of the United States Naval Service.

*DARNELL, DANA C.

Citation: For extraordinary heroism as a 60mm Mortar Ammunition Carrier attached to Company B, First Battalion, Ninth Marines, Third Marine Division in the Republic of Vietnam on 24 April 1967. Company B was engaged in a search and destroy operation against the Viet Cong and North Vietnamese Forces in Quang Tri Province. Lance Corporal Darnell's platoon was entering a clearing, when it was ambushed by North Vietnamese Army Forces, using heavy small arms and automatic weapons fire. As the ambush was sprung, the mortar gunner was knocked unconscious while seeking cover. Exhibiting sound judgment and extraordinary calmness in the face of the intense enemy fire, Lance Corporal Darnell retrieved the mortar. Due to the urgency of the situation, he was unable to set the mortar up properly. Holding it between his legs and steadying it with his hands, he began firing the mortar from a position exposed to the enemy fire and delivered accurate fire into the enemy positions. When he had exhausted all of his ammunition, he moved from man to man, collecting mortar ammunition to keep his mortar in action. He repeated this selfless performance many times, until the enemy fire was silenced. At this time, the platoon was ordered to withdraw from the clearing. Lance Corporal Darnell was dragging two wounded Marines from the clearing when he was temporarily blinded by enemy fire, which knocked dirt and rock fragments into his eyes. He refused to be evacuated and within an hour was again assisting in the care of the wounded. By his outstanding courage, exceptional fortitude and valiant fighting spirit he served to inspire all who observed him and upheld the highest traditions of the Marine Corps and the United States Naval Service.

*DAVIS, DENNIS D.

Citation: For extraordinary heroism while serving as a Rifleman with Company K, Third Battalion, Seventh Marines, First Division in connection with combat operations against the enemy in the Republic of Vietnam. On 28 August 1969, while Company K was conducting a search and destroy operation in Quang Nam Province, the lead platoon was pinned down by enemy small arms, automatic weapons, and antiaircraft fire. Crawling toward a vantage point from which to better observe enemy activities when he saw a hostile soldier moving into a bunker, Private First Class Davis raced across ten meters of open terrain and, leaping to the top of the fortification, hurled a grenade into the rear aperture. When a hostile grenade landed beside him, he quickly retrieved it and heaved it toward the opening of the bunker. However, the grenade detonated prematurely and the resultant explosion knocked Private First Class Davis to the ground, seriously wounded him and rendered his weapon useless. Undaunted, he crawled under the enemy fire, to the front of the fortification and pushed another grenade through the firing aperture, fatally wounding the hostile occupant. Quickly entering the smoking bunker, he captured an enemy machine gun and utilized it to deliver devastating fire at other nearby hostile positions until the weapon malfunctioned. When he saw a companion fall in a position dangerously exposed to the enemy fire, he dashed through the hostile fusillade to the side of the casualty, picked him up, and moved across twenty meters of fire-swept terrain to a relatively covered location. Despite the pain of his own wounds, he then armed himself with the casualty's rifle and charged forward to attack another enemy fortification, but was mortally wounded before he could reach it. By his courage, aggressive fighting spirit and unwavering devotion to duty in the face of grave personal danger, Private First Class Davis contributed significantly to the accomplishment of his unit's mission and upheld the highest traditions of the Marine Corps and of the United States Naval Service.

*DAWSON, JOHN R.

Citation: For extraordinary heroism while serving as a Forward Observer with Battery G, Third Battalion, Twelfth Marines, Third Marine Division (Reinforced), in action against the enemy in the Republic of Vietnam on 27 October 1967. During Operation GRANITE, Lieutenant Dawson was attached to Company B, First Battalion, Fourth Marines during a search and destroy operation in Thua Thien Province. As the company was moving down a narrow jungle trail, it suddenly came under intense enemy fire from well concealed North Vietnamese Army and Viet Cong forces on three sides, sustaining immediate casualties, and was temporarily pinned down by the heavy volume of automatic weapons and small-arms fire and grenade attack. Although the enemy ambush continued with relentless intensity, Lieutenant Dawson completely disregarded his own safety as he dauntlessly moved from his position at the rear of the platoon to the side of the company commander in the foreground of the attack. After the two officers conferred to determine how artillery could best be employed against the enemy, Lieutenant Dawson quickly called for and accurately adjusted supporting arms fire on the enemy positions. While he continued to direct artillery fire, the commanding officer was struck by an enemy round and fell to the ground, exposed to further injury or possible death on the open trail. Quickly obtaining a rifle, Lieutenant Dawson unhesitatingly positioned himself by the side of his wounded comrade, using his own body as a shield in an effort to protect him from the hostile fire. Exhibiting a sincere concern for the welfare of his companion and a determined fighting spirit, he courageously returned fire upon the enemy until he was mortally wounded. His heroic action at the risk of his own life was instrumental in saving the life of his fellow Marine and contributed significantly in repulsing the enemy force. By his intrepid fighting spirit, daring initiative and selfless devotion to duty, Lieutenant Dawson upheld the highest traditions of the Marine Corps and the United States Naval Service. He gallantly gave his life for his country.

*DAY, EDWARD

Citation: For extraordinary heroism as a rifleman with Company L, Third Battalion, Third Marines, Third Marine Division in the Republic of Vietnam on 26 August 1968. Company L was occupying a defensive position near the Rockpile in Quang Tri Province when the Marines came under intense mortar fire. Following the attack, a listening post alertly observed a reinforced North Vietnamese Army platoon advancing toward the company's position. Realizing the importance of denying the enemy access to the avenue of approach to the Marine perimeter, which was blocked by his position forward of the company lines, Lance Corporal Day fearlessly moved to a dangerously exposed location and began delivering an accurate volume of fire upon the North Vietnamese soldiers. Disregarding his own safety, he steadfastly remained in the hazardous area as he effectively employed his weapon, successfully destroying an enemy machine gun and killing all members of its crew. Alertly observing an injured Marine who was pinned down by the intense enemy fire he unhesitatingly moved from his firing position, and as he was maneuvering to the aid of his comrade, Lance Corporal Day was mortally wounded. His daring initiative and heroic efforts were inspiring to all who observed him and contributed significantly to the accomplishment of his unit's mission. By his courage, sincere concern for the welfare of his comrades and steadfast devotion to duty, Lance Corporal Day upheld the highest traditions of the Marine Corps and the United States Naval Service. He gallantly gave his life for his country.

DE BONA, ANDREW D.

Citation: For extraordinary heroism while serving as Commanding Officer Company M, Third Battalion, Twenty-sixth Marines, Third

Marine Division (Reinforced), in the Republic of Vietnam on 10 September 1967. During a search and destroy operation in the vicinity of Con Thien, Company M was providing flank security for the battalion, when the enemy commenced a heavy and accurate artillery, rocket, and mortar barrage, followed by an assault by an estimated North Vietnamese Army Regiment. The second and third platoons absorbed the brunt of the preliminary attack with their commanders and platoon sergeants becoming casualties during the action. Quickly grasping the situation, Captain DeBona unhesitatingly, and with full knowledge of the risks involved, moved in among his men, rallying them to drive off the enemy assault. After supervising the evacuation of his wounded to a secure area to await medevac helicopters, he conducted an orderly withdrawal of his troops and casualties toward prepared positions on the ridge line. Constantly exposing himself to the enemy while repulsing another enemy assault and concurrently organizing a defensive perimeter, he displayed a tremendous degree of composure and calm, inspiring his Marines by his presence of mind and outstanding courage. Shortly after dusk approximately 20 Marines became pinned down in a bomb crater 25 meters in front of the lines. Moving swiftly, Captain DeBona gathered a small reaction force and led it, under intense fire, to the bomb crater. Upon reaching the crater, he effectively organized his men into casualty bearers and a covering party. The volume of fire laid down by the covering party allowed the removal of all of the casualties. Captain DeBona ordered his men to withdraw, remaining behind to cover the withdrawal. His bravery and determination throughout the bitter action were instrumental in driving back three waves of enemy assault and inspired all who observed him. By his intrepid fighting spirit, daring initiative and unwavering devotion to duty, Captain DeBona reflected great credit upon himself and the Marine Corps and upheld the highest traditions of the United States Naval Service.

DENGLER, DIETER

Citation: For extraordinary heroism during an extremely daring escape from a prisoner-of-war stockade on 30 June 1966. Playing a key role in planning, preparing for, and developing an escape and evasion operation involving several fellow prisoners and himself, Lieutenant (jg) Dengler, keenly aware of the hazardous nature of the escape attempt, boldly initiated the operation and contributed in large measure to its success. When an unplanned situation developed while the escape operation was being executed, he reacted with the highest degree of valor and gallantry. Through his courageous and inspiring fighting spirit, Lieutenant (jg) Dengler upheld the highest traditions of the United States Naval Service.

DENTON, JEREMIAH A., JR.

Citation: For extraordinary heroism while serving as a Prisoner of War in North Vietnam from February 1966 to May 1966. Under constant pressure from North Vietnamese interrogators and guards, he experienced harassment, intimidation and ruthless treatment in their attempt to gain military information and cooperative participation for propaganda purposes. During this prolonged period of physical and mental agony, he heroically resisted cruelties and continued to promulgate resistance policy and detailed instructions. Forced to attend a press conference with a Japanese correspondent, he blinked out a distress message in Morse Code at the television camera and was understood by United States Naval Intelligence. When this courageous act was reported to the North Vietnamese, he was again subjected to severe brutalities. Displaying extraordinary skill, fearless dedication to duty, and resourcefulness, he reflected great credit upon himself, and upheld the highest traditions of the Naval Service and the United States Armed Forces.

DE PLANCHE, MARK B.

Citation: For extraordinary heroism as a fire team leader while serving with Company G, Second Battalion, Ninth Marines, Third Marine Division (Reinforced), Fleet Marine Force in Quang Nam Province, Republic of Vietnam on the night of 13-14 January 1966. Assigned to lead a patrol set up to help defend his platoon's position, Corporal DePlance established an ambush in one position, and when ordered to move to a second site, he detected a Viet Cong moving on the ground to his left front. Seconds later he saw 30 to 40 Viet Cong moving into a skirmish line in the same area. Shouting for his fire team to launch the attack, he opened fire, and as they followed his command the four Marines, undaunted by numerical odds, assaulted the Viet Cong force and drove them in retreat to high ground. As the foe fell back they began to deliver heavy automatic weapons fire and a shower of grenades at the patrol, and although Corporal DePlanche was wounded he continued in pursuit and secured the area. Calling by radio, he notified his platoon commander of the situation and requested a reserve squad to be sent. After having repulsed three Viet Cong counter-attacks, he then took part in the assault which drove the insurgents from the hill. His exceptional initiative and aggressive action in assailing a force much larger than his own resulted in the capture of four 60mm mortars, 81 rounds of 60mm mortar ammunition, 15 rifles, and the death of four Viet Cong. His courageous and daring actions reflected distinct credit upon himself and the Marine Corps and upheld the finest traditions of the United States Naval Service.

DEVRIES, MARVIN H.

Citation: For extraordinary heroism while serving as a Platoon Commander with Company E, Second Battalion, Third Marines, Third Marine Division in connection with combat operations against the enemy in the Republic of Vietnam. During the early morning hours of 10 August 1969, while occupying a night defensive position near the Demilitarized Zone in Quang Tri Province, First Lieutenant Devries' platoon came under a ground attack by a North Vietnamese Army company reinforced by sappers utilizing automatic weapons fire, rocket-propelled grenades, and satchel charges. During the initial moments of the assault, the momentum of the enemy movement enabled the hostile soldiers to penetrate a portion of the Marines' defensive perimeter. Reacting instantly to this threat, First Lieutenant Devries ran across the fire-swept terrain to the point of heaviest contact and, shouting directions to the Marines there, skillfully realigned the defensive perimeter in such a way that the North Vietnamese Army soldiers were again outside the friendly lines. Completely disregarding his own safety, First Lieutenant Devries then moved from one Marine position to another to encourage his men and to insure that every possible avenue of enemy approach was adequately covered with firepower. While rushing across the hazardous area to counter a new threat, First Lieutenant Devries was severely wounded by fragments from a rocket-propelled grenade which impacted hear him. Refusing medical attention, he directed a vigorous defense of the perimeter, personally accounting for five enemy casualties. He then moved to a dangerously exposed vantage point and, heedless of the rounds impacting around him, skillfully adjusted supporting Marine artillery fire with such accuracy that the North Vietnamese Army force lost the advantage of its numerical superiority and retreated. His heroic and determined actions over a prolonged period of time were instrumental in minimizing Marine casualties and turning a potential disaster into a resounding victory. By his courage, dynamic leadership, and unwavering devotion to duty in the face of grave personal danger, First Lieutenant Devries upheld the highest traditions of the Marine Corps and of the United States Naval Service.

*DICKSON, EDWARD A.

Citation: For extraordinary heroism on 7 February 1965 while serving as a jet attack pilot with Attack Squadron ONE HUNDRED FIFTY-FIVE, aboard the USS CORAL SEA (CVA-43), during a retaliatory air strike against the Dong Hoi Army Barracks and staging area in North Vietnam. When his aircraft was struck by intense enemy antiaircraft fire on the low-level run-in to the target area and burst into flame, Lieutenant Dickson elected to remain with his burning plane until he had released his bombs on the target area. Following his attack, he headed toward the sea where he ejected from his flaming aircraft. By his inspiring and courageous devotion to duty, Lieutenant Dickson upheld the finest traditions of the United States Naval Service.

*DICKSON, GROVER L.

Citation: For extraordinary heroism as squad leader of the Second Platoon, Company K, Third Battalion, Third Marines in Vietnam during Operation PRAIRIE on 11 November 1966. When the Second Platoon came under heavy enemy automatic weapons fire during a search and destroy mission which seriously wounded his platoon commander and two other Marines, Corporal Dickson quickly formed his squad into an effective fighting force. Seeing a wounded Marine in front of his position, he charged forward, with complete disregard for himself, and succeeded in carrying his wounded comrade to safety. Then, realizing that his platoon commander lay seriously wounded beneath the aperture of an enemy bunker, Corporal Dickson seized a grenade launcher and tried to quell the automatic rifle fire coming from the enemy emplacement. Aware that this action was not successful, he returned to his squad's position, picked up a fragmentation hand grenade and, without regard to the unrelenting fury of automatic weapons fire, charged the bunker. He threw the grenade through the aperture and momentarily neutralized the position, enabling the removal of his platoon commander to a safe location and subsequent evacuation. Automatic weapons fire again erupted from the same bunker. Ignoring the personal dangers involved, Corporal Dickson seized two hand grenades and charged the bunker again, but before he could reach his objective, he was mortally wounded. His daring initiative, valor and selfless efforts in behalf of his comrades were in keeping with the highest traditions of the Marine Corps and the United States Naval Service. He gallantly gave his life for his country.

DILLARD, HENRY C.

Citation: For extraordinary heroism while serving as a 3.5 inch Rocket Gunner with Company M, Third Battalion, Fourth Marines, Third Marine Division (Reinforced) in the Republic of Vietnam on 29 May 1967. During Operation PRAIRIE IV, in Quang Tri Province, Company M was assigned the mission of attacking a well camouflaged and heavily fortified enemy bunker complex defending Hill 174. The unseen enemy opened devastating automatic weapons fire on the advancing Marines, inflicting numerous casualties. As rifle fire was virtually ineffective against the enemy fortification, Corporal (then Private First Class) Dillard, with complete disregard for his own safety, moved his rocket launcher, through the devastating enemy fire, to the main point of the ensuing battle and although completely exposed to the intense fire, he single-handedly assaulted the enemy stronghold. Stopping momentarily, only ten meters in front of the enemy stronghold, he fired his rockets with deadly accuracy at the position. As the exploding rockets threw him to the ground, he quickly rallied and regained his position. Expending all his rocket rounds, he continued his daring one-man assault with hand grenades and rifle fire, silencing the enemy position and killing six enemy soldiers. By his aggressive fighting spirit and initiative, Corporal Dillard served to inspire all who observed him and contributed directly to the security of his company. His great personal valor reflected the highest credit upon himself and enhanced the finest traditions of the Marine Corps and the United States Naval Service.

DINSMORE, HARRY H.

Citation: For extraordinary heroism on 1 October 1966 while serving as Chief of Surgery at U. S. Naval Support Activity, Danang, Republic of Vietnam. With full knowledge of the serious hazards involved and with complete disregard for his own personal safety, Captain Dinsmore volunteered to perform a surgical operation to remove a live 60mm mortar shell from the chest wall of Private First Class Nguyen Luong, Army of the Republic of Vietnam. The impact fuse of the mortar shell was partially activated and could easily have detonated at any time during the operation, resulting in certain death to Captain Dinsmore and his patient. Exhibiting outstanding professional skill and calmness, Captain Dinsmore took command of the situation and successfully removed the shell. By his heroic conduct and fearless devotion to duty, Captain Dinsmore saved the life of the patient and upheld the highest traditions of the United States Naval Service.

DITTMAN, CARL R.

Citation: For extraordinary heroism while serving as a scout with the Intelligence Section of the Third Marines, Third Marine Division in connection with operations against the enemy in the Republic of Vietnam. On 14 November 1968, Corporal Dittman was accompanying Company A during a reconnaissance in force in the vicinity of Hill 461 in Quang Tri Province when the lead elements came under intense fire and were pinned down. In a forward position, Corporal Dittman alertly observed a North Vietnamese soldier throw a hand grenade toward him and, shouting a warning to his companions, reached cover as the grenade exploded. Then circling around the hill to where Marines were pinned down so close to the hostile bunker that the enemy could be heard talking, he gathered all the grenades he could carry and, advancing under fire, launched a single-handed assault against the entrenched North Vietnamese solders. Forced back by intense mortar and automatic weapons fire, Corporal Dittman waited until the attack subsided and advanced again in full view of the enemy and threw the remainder of his grenades against the stronghold in a fierce attempt to rout the hostile soldiers. Rejoining his companions, he aided the wounded until the unit was directed to withdraw to more advantageous positions. Although painfully wounded in the face and right arm, Corporal Dittman was attempting to carry a seriously injured Marine down the hill when the enemy concentrated a heavy volume of fire on him. Disregarding his own safety, he quickly placed his fallen comrade in a fighting hole and shielded him with his own body as mortar fire began impacting all around him. Refusing to seek cover and ignoring his own weakened condition, Corporal Dittman aided and comforted the injured man throughout the night. At daybreak, he skillfully attracted the attention of an aerial observer who directed a medical evacuation helicopter to the isolated hillside position to evacuate the two men. His heroic action and resolute determination in saving the life of a fellow Marine were an inspiration to all who served with him. By his courage, bold initiative, and selfless devotion to duty at great personal risk, Corporal Dittman upheld the highest traditions of the Marine Corps and the United States Naval Service.

DONALDSON, BILLY M.

Citation: For extraordinary heroism as a Team Leader with the First Force Reconnaissance Company, Third Reconnaissance Battalion, Third Marine Division, during operations against the enemy sixteen miles west of Dong Ha, Vietnam, on 8 August 1966. Deep in enemy controlled territory, Staff Sergeant Donaldson was leading a four-man reconnaissance team when he observed fifteen Viet Cong. Realizing the valuable opportunity to capture a prisoner, he suggested that a platoon reaction force be landed in the area. The platoon landed, made a fruitless search and commenced helilifting the force and the reconnaissance team out of the area. Staff Sergeant Donaldson declined to be withdrawn with the initial helilift, as he felt he could assist the Platoon Commander in the evacuation of the remainder of the force. All but twenty-four of the Marines had been flown out when an estimated two companies of North Vietnamese and Viet Cong launched a vicious rocket, machine gun fire and grenade attack. The attacks continued late into the night, killing four Marines and wounding numerous others. The casualties were moved to foxholes within the defensive perimeter. Subsequently, while under heavy grenade attack from thirty or forty North Vietnamese and Viet Cong, Staff Sergeant Donaldson saw a grenade land in a foxhole containing a wounded man. With complete disregard for his own safety, he leaped into the foxhole, picked up the grenade, and threw it back toward the Viet Cong. As the grenade left his hand, it exploded, wounding him severely in the arm and head. By his heroic actions, initiative, and loyal devotion to duty at great personal risk, Staff Sergeant Donaldson undoubtedly saved the wounded Marine's life, reflected great credit upon himself and the Marine Corps and upheld the highest traditions of the United States Naval Service.

DONOVAN, JOSEPH P.

Citation: For extraordinary heroism while serving as a Pilot with Marine Medium Helicopter Squadron 364 in the Republic of Vietnam on 22 February 1969. First Lieutenant Donovan launched as Wingman in a flight of two CH-46 transport helicopters assigned the emergency medical evacuation of a seriously wounded Marine from an area north of the Nam O Bridge in Quang Nam Province. When the section leader's aircraft experienced mechanical difficulties and returned to its base, First Lieutenant Donovan resolutely elected to continue the mission. Approaching the designated area, he observed a hostile rocket launching site and dispatched his gunships to destroy the emplacement. When informed that the injured Marine was in a critical condition, First Lieutenant Donovan, undaunted by the extremely heavy volume of enemy fire and lacking gunship support, fearlessly maneuvered to a landing on the fire-swept area and embarked the casualty. Wounded by fragments from hostile grenades and mortar rounds which also severely damaged his helicopter and caused it to vibrate violently as it lifted out of the zone, he ignored his painful injuries as he fought to regain control of the CH-46 and then skillfully maneuvered it to the nearest medical facility. After receiving medical attention and ascertaining that his aircraft was operable, he boldly launched on a second emergency medical evacuation mission and again entered an extremely hazardous area, without gunship support, to take the wounded to a medical facility. Informed that eight seriously injured Marines in another area required immediate evacuation, First Lieutenant Donovan unhesitatingly proceeded to the site, coordinated his approach with gunship fire, and landed in the perilous zone. He resolutely remained in his dangerously exposed position until all the casualties were embarked, and then lifted out of the area. As he began to depart, he learned that additional casualties had been brought to the landing zone, two of whom were in critical condition. With complete disregard for his own safety, he again braved the heavy volume of enemy fire and landed in the fire-swept area, embarked the wounded Marines, and departed to the nearest medical facility. By his courage, superior airmanship and unwavering devotion to duty in the face of great personal danger, First Lieutenant Donovan was instrumental in the accomplishment of the hazardous mission and upheld the highest traditions of the Marine Corps and the United States Naval Service.

DONOVAN, JOSEPH P.   (Gold Star in lieu of second award)

Citation: For extraordinary heroism while serving with Marine Medium Helicopter Squadron 364, Marine Aircraft Group Sixteen, First Marine Aircraft Wing during combat operations against the enemy in the Republic of Vietnam. On 21 April 1969, First Lieutenant Donovan, launched as pilot of a transport helicopter assigned the mission of medically evacuating seriously wounded Marines from an open rice paddy northwest of Liberty Bridge in Quang Nam Province. Arriving over the designated area, he commenced a high-speed, low-altitude approach toward a tree line north of the site, and immediately came under machine-gun fire which damaged the forward section of his transport. Undaunted by the hostile fire, he maneuvered the helicopter to the area where the casualties lay, maintaining his helicopter in a hover while the wounded men were embarked. Still taking a heavy volume of enemy fire, First Lieutenant Donovan departed the area and delivered his patients to the hospital at Danang. After an inspection of the battle damage revealed that the helicopter was no longer airworthy, he took command of a second aircraft and immediately received a request for another medical evacuation mission from the same area. Proceeding at once to the site, he commenced his second approach into the hazardous zone, again flying through intense enemy fire. As he awaited the embarkation of the casualties, additional enemy fire erupted which prevented the Marines on the ground from embarking the remainder of the casualties. When informed that his starboard gunner had been wounded, First Lieutenant Donovan lifted from the zone to evaluate the man's wound and to appraise the damage to his aircraft. Determining that the aircraft was still capable of accomplishing the evacuation and that his gunner was not seriously wounded, he advised the ground unit that he was again ready to enter the hazardous zone, but was informed that another helicopter had been designated to complete the mission. By his courage, superior aeronautical ability, and unwavering devotion to duty in the face of grave personal danger, First Lieutenant Donovan was directly instrumental in saving the lives of several fellow Marines and upheld the highest traditions of the Marine Corps and of the United States Naval Service.

*DORRIS, CLAUDE H.

Citation: For extraordinary heroism while serving as the Marine

Squad Leader/Advisor of Combined Action Platoon H-6, Third Combined Action Group, III Marine Amphibious Force, in the Republic of Vietnam. During the early morning hours of 7 January 1968, Sergeant Dorris' platoon was defending an outpost in Nuoc Ngot Village, Thua Thien Province. Suddenly, the compound came under a heavy volume of mortar and rocket fire, followed by an aggressive assault by a numerically superior Viet Cong force. The enemy quickly seized the northern wall of the compound as the Marines and Popular Forces soldiers moved to the sandbagged southern wall. Realizing that several Marines had been in their living quarters when the attack commenced, Sergeant Dorris unhesitatingly exposed himself to the hostile fire to ensure that the Marines were manning their fighting positions. Although painfully wounded in both legs soon after the attack commenced, he resolutely crawled from one burning hut to another, ensuring that none of his men had been trapped in the structures. Observing a wounded Vietnamese boy run into the compound, Sergeant Dorris skillfully administered first aid to the child. Despite the enemy fire impacting around him, he fearlessly remained in his dangerously exposed position in an attempt to halt the advancing enemy force until he was mortally wounded by an enemy rocket round. His heroic and timely actions inspired his men and prevented the enemy from overrunning the compound. By his courage, bold initiative, and selfless devotion to duty, Sergeant Dorris upheld the highest traditions of the Marine Corps and the United States Naval Service. He gallantly gave his life for his country.

*DOWD, JOHN A.

Citation: For extraordinary heroism while serving as Commanding Officer of the First Battalion, Seventh Marines, First Marine Division in connection with combat operations against the enemy in the Republic of Vietnam on 12 August and 13 August 1969. During this two day period, Lieutenant Colonel Dowd aggressively led his battalion against North Vietnamese Army forces attempting to infiltrate the vital An Hoa and DaNang areas. In the early morning hours of 12 August, Company B was preparing to depart its defensive position when the Marines came under coordinated mortar, rocket-propelled grenade, and small arms fire. Unhesitatingly leaving his relatively secure position, Lieutenant Colonel Dowd fearlessly traveled over 400 meters of enemy territory to the beleaguered unit's position and, after a rapid assessment of the tactical situation, boldly moved to a forward position from which he directed preparations for an aggressive attack against the enemy. Personally leading the subsequent assault, he simultaneously coordinated the movement of adjacent units along three fronts, causing the hostile force to attempt to withdraw. Aware of the enemy plan, Lieutenant Colonel Dowd deployed his men along all possible routes of egress, thereby denying the North Vietnamese Army force the opportunity to escape. As the battalion continued its search and destroy efforts, Company D was heavily engaged in combat by a large North Vietnamese Army force. When Company B was similarly engaged while en route to assist the beleaguered Marines, Lieutenant Colonel Dowd, completely disregarding his own safety, boldly moved to the point of heaviest contact and, calling for reinforcements, effected the encirclement of the hostile soldiers. Displaying outstanding tactical ability, he then adeptly maneuvered his units in an aggressive assault against the trapped enemy, the impetus of which completely demoralized the hostile unit and caused its defeat. On the following day, the battalion was advancing along a four company front when the Marines came under a heavy volume of small arms, automatic weapons, and machine gun fire from North Vietnamese Army soldiers occupying well-fortified emplacements in a tree line. After adjusting fixed wing air strikes and artillery fire on the enemy positions, Lieutenant Colonel Dowd, seeming to be completely without fear, was moving to an advantageous location from which to control the movement of his forces when he was mortally wounded by hostile machine gun fire. His resolute determination and bold initiative inspired all who observed him and were instrumental in his battalion accounting for 140 hostile soldiers killed, the apprehension of six prisoners, and the seizure of vast quantities of enemy weaponry. By his courage, dynamic leadership and unwavering devotion to duty, Lieutenant Colonel Dowd upheld the highest traditions of the Marine Corps and of the United States Naval Service. He gallantly gave his life in the service of his country.

DOWNING, TALMADGE R.

Citation: For extraordinary heroism while serving as Weapons Platoon Sergeant with Company M, Third Battalion, First Marines in the Republic of Vietnam on 5 March 1966. During Operation UTAH in Quang Ngai Province, Sergeant Downing was serving with an assault element which was engaged in seizing the battalion objective held by units of a North Vietnamese regiment. As the battle progressed, one of the Marine machine gun squads and a rifle squad were pinned down by intense automatic weapons fire and hand grenades originating from concealed, fortified positions. When fire from maneuvering friendly forces endangered a group of Marine casualties, Sergeant Downing exhibited exceptional presence of mind, gallantly exposing himself, shouting and giving hand signals until the errant fire was corrected. In his daring effort, he sustained a painful shoulder wound from an enemy grenade. Undaunted, he directed and helped the wounded men to a relatively safe position. With forceful leadership, he organized an assault unit which attacked and destroyed a position which was manned by a numerically superior enemy force. He single-handedly destroyed another enemy position with his pistol and a hand grenade. Running low on ammunition, he calmly picked up an automatic weapon from a destroyed enemy position and courageously directed the final assault on the Viet Cong strongpoint, personally hurling the grenade which completely silenced the position. His gallant effort contributed in large measure to the success of Operation UTAH. By his extraordinary leadership, resolute fighting spirit and selfless dedication to duty throughout, Sergeant Downing upheld the highest traditions of the Marine Corps and the United States Naval Service.

DRISCOLL, THOMAS B.

Citation: For extraordinary heroism while serving as a Forward Air Controller for Company D, First Battalion, Fifth Marines, First Marine Division (Reinforced), in the Republic of Vietnam on 4 and 6 September 1967. On 4 September, Company D came under devastating enemy automatic weapons, mortar and grenade fire from an estimated regiment of North Vietnamese Regulars, wounding several Marines and the forward observer. Corporal (then Lance Corporal) Driscoll immediately assumed the duties of the forward observer, calling in and adjusting artillery with uncanny accuracy and breaking up the enemy attack. During darkness, it was necessary to mark the landing zone for the emergency medical evacuation of casualties. Undaunted by the heavy sniper fire, he unhesitatingly procured a strobe light and held it over his head to guide in the helicopters. On 6 September, the company was again taken under heavy enemy fire. Observing two Marines wounded and lying in an open area approximately 100 meters from his position, he courageously and with complete disregard for his own safety, moved forward and retrieved one man. Being assured the man was in a safe position, he returned to the second wounded Marine and carried him back to safety. When fifteen to twenty Viet Cong attempted to penetrate the perimeter, he boldly exposed himself to the withering small-arms fire and gallantly led a one-man assault on the enemy, hurling grenades and breaking up the enemy attack. Upon returning to his position, he supervised the establishment of a defensive perimeter. By his bold initiative, gallant fighting spirit and loyal devotion to duty, Corporal Driscoll reflected great credit upon himself and the Marine Corps and upheld the highest traditions of the United States Naval Service.

DRISCOLL, WILLIAM P.

Citation: For extraordinary heroism on 10 May 1972 while serving as a radar intercept officer with Fighter Squadron NINETY-SIX, embarked in USS CONSTELLATION (CVA-64), during a major air-wing coordinated strike against the strategic and heavily defended Hai Duong marshalling rail yard joining the port of Haiphong to the industrial center of Hanoi in North Vietnam. Flying with the leader of a section of F-4J flak-suppressor aircraft assigned to protect the less maneuverable and heavily loaded attack group, Lieutenant (jg) Driscoll rendered invaluable assistance when a large formation of approximately sixteen enemy aircraft attempted to intercept the retiring strike group. Visually acquiring the enemy fighters, and skillfully directing defensive maneuvers, Lieutenant (jg) Driscoll aided his pilot in shooting down three of the six enemy aircraft destroyed in the fierce battle. Although his aircraft was struck by a surface-to-air missile and later burst into flame, Lieutenant (jg) Driscoll remained with the crippled aircraft and assisted the pilot in reaching the Tonkin Gulf where both men ejected and were picked up shortly by a rescue helicopter. Lieutenant (jg) Driscoll's great personal courage and invaluable contribution to the success of an extremely important mission were in keeping with the highest traditions of the United States Naval Service.

*DUFF, BARRY W.

Citation: For extraordinary heroism while serving as a Fire Team Leader with Company C, First Battalion, Ninth Marines, Third

Marine Division (Reinforced), in the Republic of Vietnam on 21 May 1966. While on a patrol, Corporal Duff's squad came under intense rifle, machine-gun, mortar, and recoilless rifle fire from a reinforced Viet Cong company. The initial burst of enemy fire caused several casualties. Realizing that the casualties were lying fully exposed to the enemy fire, Corporal Duff immediately moved to a small knoll overlooking the enemy and his wounded comrades. During the next half hour the enemy launched three assaults in an effort to annihilate the wounded Marines and capture their weapons. With complete disregard for his own safety, he repeatedly exposed himself to turn back the enemy's attacks with accurate rifle fire. Although wounded during the second attack when he was shot in the leg and knocked from the knoll, he gathered more ammunition and hand grenades and gallantly regained his position to protect his wounded comrades. He courageously held his position until mortally wounded while exposing himself to throw a hand grenade. By his bold initiative, indomitable fighting spirit and loyal devotion to duty, Corporal Duff was instrumental in saving his comrades from further injury or possible death, thereby upholding the highest traditions of the Marine Corps and the United States Naval Service. He gallantly gave his life for his country.

*DUNCAN, RICHARD W.

Citation: For extraordinary heroism while serving as a Machine Gun Squad Leader with Company M, Third Battalion, Fifth Marines, First Marine Division (Reinforced), in the Republic of Vietnam on the afternoon of 8 November 1967. During Operation ESSEX, Corporal Duncan's company was attempting to seize a small but heavily fortified village in Quang Nam Province when it suddenly came under intense mortar and automatic weapons fire which killed the acting platoon commander and seven other Marines, and temporarily pinned down the lead platoon in a rice paddy. Quickly assessing the situation, Corporal Duncan displayed unusual courage, leadership and composure under fire, as he maneuvered his machine gun team across the open area to a position behind a dike. He directed a heavy volume of fire against the North Vietnamese Army force, suppressing its fire sufficiently to enable the Marines lying in the open field to move to relatively safe positions. As he was moving his team back to rejoin the platoon, he was painfully wounded. When a defensive perimeter was established and his squad was assigned to provide cover for the left flank, he ignored his own injury as he deployed his men and moved along the perimeter to insure their firing positions provided maximum security for their sector against hostile attacks. As darkness fell, the enemy force launched an assault but was repulsed by the extremely heavy volume of fire from Corporal Duncan's team. The enemy then commenced a grenade attack to destroy the Marines' firing positions. Observing one of his men completely exposed to the incoming grenades, Corporal Duncan, completely disregarding his own safety and the intense pain of his wound, moved to aid his fellow Marine. When a grenade landed nearby, he fearlessly used his own body to shield the man. He repeatedly exposed himself to the enemy's fire, as he moved into the open to deliver covering fire while the squad reached more secure positions. After all members of his team had reached safety, Corporal Duncan was mortally wounded as he advanced to join his men at the new position. His bravery and daring actions throughout the engagement inspired his men to steadfastly maintain their position and repulse the fanatical enemy assault. By his courageous fighting spirit, bold initiative and unswerving devotion to duty at great personal risk, he upheld the highest traditions of the Marine Corps and the United States Naval Service. He gallantly gave his life for his country.

DUTTERER, CARROLL E., JR.

Citation: For extraordinary heroism on 15 September 1967 during action against communist insurgent (Viet Cong) forces in the Mekong Delta region of the Republic of Vietnam. As Boat Captain of Armored Troop Carrier 111-6, a unit of River Assault Flotilla ONE, operating in support of the Second Brigade, Ninth United States Army Infantry Division, Petty Officer Dutterer participated in a combat mobile riverine assault operation against a Viet Cong stronghold in the Cam Son Secret Zone. While proceeding in formation with embarked Army troops, the riverine assault units came under intense automatic-weapons, recoilless-rifle, and rocket fire from enemy positions on both banks of the narrow stream. Petty Officer Dutterer's boat, one of the lead units in the formation, was returning maximum fire when it was hit simultaneously by two enemy rockets, wounding Petty Officer Dutterer and four other crewmen, and destroying all communications equipment. Unable to receive instructions by radio, or to observe movements of the other craft through the dense pall of smoke, he was unaware that other units had been ordered to reverse course and retire to a safe area for casualty evacuation. Determined to carry out his assigned mission, Petty Officer Dutterer fought his craft, alone and with no fire support, through the entire 1800-meter enemy barrage, and landed his troops. When the troops were pinned down by enemy fire, he directed fire from his exposed position topside and rebeached his boat to pick up the troops. During the reembarkation, Petty Officer Dutterer was seriously wounded when his boat was again hit by an enemy rocket. Despite his wounds, he maintained control of his craft until reembarkation was completed. His courage and inspiring devotion to duty were in keeping with the highest traditions of the United States Naval Service.

EADES, LAWRENCE M.

Citation: For extraordinary heroism while serving with Combined Action Company P, Third Combined Action Group, III Marine Amphibious Force, in connection with operations against the enemy in the Republic of Vietnam. During the early morning hours of 2 February 1968, Corporal Eades' unit came under intense enemy small-arms, automatic weapons, mortar and rocket fire supporting an aggressive ground assault by a North Vietnamese Army battalion. Reacting instantly, Corporal Eades ran across the fire swept terrain to his defensive position and commenced delivering a heavy volume of accurate machine-gun fire upon the attacking force. Observing an enemy platoon attempting to penetrate the perimeter to his right, he quickly directed a deadly volume of fire at the onrushing enemy hordes, and although the enemy concentrated their fire at him, he steadfastly remained in his precarious position firing belt after belt of ammunition as the enemy rounds erupted around him. As the enemy closed within hand grenade range of his position, Corporal Eades stood up in the intense enemy fire to better observe them and fire his weapon. Although wounded by an enemy rocket round, he resolutely stood his ground and singlehandedly drove off the advancing enemy force. By his bold initiative, intrepid fighting ability and loyal devotion to duty, Corporal Eades was instrumental in repulsing a numerically superior enemy force, thereby reflecting great credit upon himself and the Marine Corps and upholding the highest traditions of the United States Naval Service.

EBBERT, TERRY J.

Citation: For extraordinary heroism while serving as Commanding Officer of Company E, Second Battalion, Fifth Marines, First Marine Division in the Republic of Vietnam on 24 December 1966. When Company G was encircled by a Viet Cong force near the village of Phu Tay (1), First Lieutenant Ebbert's company was assigned the mission of conducting a relief operation to assist the beleaguered unit. After landing on the beach by assault boats, his company was entering the village when the point platoon came under heavy enemy machine gun, mortar, recoilless rifle and small arms fire. The platoon sustained several casualties and was unable to advance due to the intense enemy fire. With complete disregard for his own safety, First Lieutenant Ebbert courageously moved forward, under the observation and fire of the enemy, to evaluate the situation and lead the attack. Under his inspiring leadership, his unit quickly gained fire superiority and forced the enemy to withdraw from the area. He directed his company to resume its advance, but almost immediately, the point platoon was halted by intense automatic weapons fire and mortars from elements of a Viet Cong battalion. Once more, First Lieutenant Ebbert daringly moved to the front of his unit, directing return fire, rallying and encouraging his men, and supervising the evacuation of the wounded to a position of safety. Observing an opportunity to envelop the well entrenched enemy force, he aggressively led a squad of Marines across fifty meters of fire-swept, open terrain and flanked the enemy positions, forcing them to halt their firing and retreat. As he directed artillery fire on the Viet Cong force, First Lieutenant Ebbert was seriously wounded in the chest by enemy fire. But he steadfastly remained at his exposed vantage point, continuing to direct his company's efforts in inflicting heavy losses on the enemy, until he fell unconscious from his wounds. First Lieutenant Ebbert's daring initiative, indomitable fighting spirit, and loyal devotion to duty at great personal risk reflected great credit upon himself and were in keeping with the highest traditions of the Marine Corps and the United States Naval Service.

EDWARDS, CRAIG A.

Citation: For extraordinary heroism on 20 August 1970 while serving as Commanding Officer of Company H, Second Battalion, Seventh Marines, First Marine Division, in connection with combat operations against enemy forces in the Republic of Vietnam. After leading a relief force to the site of a beleaguered combat patrol unit which had sustained three casualties, including the platoon commander, First Lieutenant Edwards braved the intense, hostile, automatic-weapons fire to move to a forward position. Here he observed four of his own men lying wounded in an area dangerously close to one of the enemy's machine-gun emplacements. Although enemy soldiers concentrated their fire on him as he raced toward the emplacement, he managed to hurl three grenades into the enemy position, destroying the emplacement along with its occupants. Pinned down by fire from another hostile position before he could administer first aid to his four wounded comrades, First Lieutenant Edwards, upon observing a grenade land in proximity to the casualties, succeeded in kicking it to one side and jumped in front of his companions to protect them from the blast. Despite a painful leg wound caused by fragments from the exploding grenade, he proceeded to hack a path to the river, returned to his position and, assisted by a corpsman, carried the most seriously wounded man one hundred meters upstream in the face of enemy fire to a designated landing zone. He then returned with the corpsman and carried a second casualty up the river to safety, following which he directed the evacuation of all remaining casualties before weakness from loss of blood forced his own removal to a medical facility. By his indomitable courage, determined fighting spirit, and selfless devotion to duty, First Lieutenant Edwards was directly instrumental in saving the lives of several of his fellow Marines, thereby upholding the highest traditions of the Marine Corps and the United States Naval Service.

EGGERT, LOWELL F.

Citation: For extraordinary heroism on 10 May 1972 as pilot of a jet aircraft, while serving as Commander, Attack Carrier Air Wing NINE, embarked on board USS CONSTELLATION (CVA-64), in connection with a coordinated strike against a heavily defended enemy railway yard in North Vietnam. In the face of intense opposition, Commander Eggert, as planner of the mission, led his strike force in dive-bombing runs which placed all ordnance directly on target and destroyed a major enemy railway center. Exiting the target area, Commander Eggert's strike group was attacked by approximately sixteen enemy fighter aircraft. In the resultant dogfight, five enemy planes were shot down. By his brilliant planning and foresight, along with his flawless professional leadership, Commander Eggert contributed immeasurably to the success of this mission and upheld the highest traditions of the United States Naval Service.

ENNIS, JOSEPH J.

Citation: For extraordinary heroism on 4 April 1968 while serving with friendly forces engaged in armed conflict against communist insurgent (Viet Cong) forces in the Republic of Vietnam. As Boat Engineer and 30-caliber gunner, Petty Officer Ennis was aboard Armored Troop Carrier (ATC) 92-2 during strike operations in support of United States Army units along the Song Ba Lai River in the Mekong Delta region. When the Viet Cong launched an attack on the entire column of boats with rockets, recoilless rifles, automatic weapons, and small arms, Petty Officer Ennis immediately returned fire with his machine gun which was mounted in the well-deck forward. Seconds later, a rocket exploded on the canopy directly over Petty Officer Ennis, knocking him down and severely wounding him. Although stunned and in great pain, he returned to his weapon, only to find it inoperable. After making his way aft to the boat's magazine to obtain another machine gun, he returned to the forward well deck and immediately fired the weapon from a hand-held position against the enemy until his ammunition was exhausted. Petty Officer Ennis then began administering first aid to other wounded personnel in the well deck. As the boat neared the bank, he quickly reloaded his weapon, stood on the ramp fully exposed to the enemy fire, and put down a withering base of cover fire for the assault troops, maintaining his position until every able-bodied soldier had gotten ashore and had reached a relatively safe position in the tree line. After an hour of fierce combat, ATC 92-2 cleared the area. Petty Officer Ennis continued to assist in treating and moving other wounded until all had been removed to a medical aid boat. Only then, when he was nearing collapse from loss of blood, did he proceed to the medical aid boat for treatment of his severe wounds. By his outstanding professionalism, concern for his fellow men, sense of responsibility, and courage under fire, Petty Officer Ennis upheld the highest traditions of the United States Naval Service.

ENOCH, BARRY W.

Citation: For extraordinary heroism on 9 April 1970 in connection with operations against enemy forces in the Republic of Vietnam. While serving with a detachment of SEAL Team ONE, Chief Petty Officer Enoch was the senior advisor and radioman/grenadier to a combined United States Vietnamese SEAL combat patrol against the Viet Cong infrastructure leaders in Long Phu District, Ba Xuyen Province. After insertion and patrolling to the target area, Chief Petty Officer Enoch observed six armed Viet Cong attempting to evade. Rushing forward and exposing himself to hostile fire, he succeeded in accounting for three enemy casualties. The SEALs then came under intense B-40 rocket and automatic weapon fire. Realizing that his small force was surrounded, Chief Petty Officer Enoch deployed his men in a defensive perimeter, and although under intense fire, continually shifted position to more effectively employ his weapon, relocate his men, and survey the enemy's locations and tactics. Although his radio was damaged by enemy fire, Chief Petty Officer Enoch directed fixed-wing and helicopter air strikes on the enemy's positions, some strikes as close as twenty meters to his position. With his men running low on ammunition and still encircled, Chief Petty Officer Enoch directed air strikes on the shortest route between his position and the river, and then led the patrol through the enemy encirclement before the latter could close the gap caused by the air strikes. By his heroic and decisive efforts in the face of almost overwhelming odds, Chief Petty Officer Enoch was directly responsible for the safe extraction of the patrol members and upheld the highest traditions of the United States Naval Service.

ENSCH, JOHN C.

Citation: For extraordinary heroism in action against the enemy as a naval flight officer of jet aircraft while serving with Fighter Squadron ONE HUNDRED SIXTY-ONE embarked in USS MIDWAY (CVA-41). On 23 May 1972, in support of an air strike against the Haiphong petroleum products storage in North Vietnam, the Combat Air Patrol element, in which Lieutenant Ensch participated as a Radar Intercept Officer, was taken under attack by six enemy fighter aircraft. Lieutenant Ensch was instrumental in providing critical tactical information to his pilot and in covering the stern of the patrol element. In the ensuing low-altitude aerial combat, he materially contributed to the success of the mission in which he and his pilot were credited with the confirmed downing of two enemy fighter aircraft. Lieutenant Ensch's superb airmanship and courage reflected great credit upon himself and were in keeping with the highest traditions of the United States Naval Service.

ESTRADA, MANUEL A.

Citation: For extraordinary heroism while serving as a Squad Leader with Company A, Third Reconnaissance Battalion, Third Marine Division in the Republic of Vietnam, on 24 and 25 August 1968. Lance Corporal Estrada and his eight-man reconnaissance team were helilifted into enemy controlled territory near Con Thien and were proceeding across an open rice paddy when the point man encountered twelve North Vietnamese Army soldiers followed by a force estimated to be battalion size. Reacting instantly, the point man fired his weapon and killed three of the enemy. While the surprised North Vietnamese unit recovered from its momentary confusion, Lance Corporal Estrada rapidly deployed his men and adjusted supporting arms fire which, in coordination with the fire of his team, successfully held the determined North Vietnamese unit at bay. As a reaction force, sent to the relief of the beleaguered team, disembarked in a nearby landing zone, it was pinned down by a heavy volume of enemy mortar and automatic weapons fire and suffered several casualties. Skillfully shifting supporting artillery fire and the direction of his team's firepower, he enabled the relief force to join his team, and when the officer leading the infantrymen was severely wounded, Lance Corporal Estrada unhesitatingly assumed command of the combined forces, although he had been seriously injured during the early moments of the engagement. With the arrival of helicopters containing further reinforcements, he boldly stood in the hazardous area and utilized a strobe light to guide the aircraft to a landing. Relieved by an officer accompanying the new unit, Lance Corporal Estrada, twice, steadfastly refused medical evacuation and, ignoring his painful injury, crawled from one position to another, distributing ammunition and water and encouraging the men in their efforts to contain the enemy assault. Resolutely remaining with his team, he assisted in repulsing repeated attacks until the reconnaissance team was extracted the following day. By his courage, resolute determination and unfaltering devotion to duty he upheld the highest traditions of the Marine Corps and the United States Naval Service.

*EVANS, RICHARD A., JR.

Citation: For extraordinary heroism while serving as a Fire Team Leader with Company D, First Battalion, Fifth Marines, First Marine Division, in connection with operations against the enemy in the Republic of Vietnam. On 29 August 1968, Private Evans was maneuvering his fire team toward known enemy positions when the Marines suddenly came under antitank rocket and automatic weapons fire from a well entrenched North Vietnamese Army company. Although seriously wounded during the initial burst of fire, he resolutely refused medical attention for himself in order to continue leading his men against the enemy. Observing five North Vietnamese soldiers maneuvering to a position on his unit's flank, Private Evans quickly moved across the fire-swept terrain to a vantage point where he delivered highly accurate fire that killed all five enemy soldiers. Wounded a second time by fire from another hostile emplacement, he realized that his team was in an untenable position. Concerned only for the welfare of his comrades, Private Evans directed his men to withdraw to a more defensible position and, ignoring his own painful injuries, selflessly remained behind providing covering fire for their movement. Continuing his gallant efforts in an attempt to ensure that his fellow Marines would reach a position of relative safety, he fearlessly rushed forward in a determined assault, firing his rifle into the hostile emplacement until he was mortally wounded by enemy machine-gun fire. His bold initiative and uncommon valor undoubtedly saved the lives of three of his fellow Marines. By his courage, intrepid fighting spirit, and selfless devotion to duty, Private Evans inspired all who observed him and sustained and enhanced the highest traditions of the Marine Corps and the United States Naval Service. He gallantly gave his life for his country.

FAIRFIELD, RUPERT E., JR.

Citation: For extraordinary heroism as a Copilot of a UH-1E Helicopter attached to Marine Observation Squadron SIX near Quang Ngai, Republic of Vietnam on 19 August 1967. While conducting a regularly assigned mission, Captain Fairfield's aircraft monitored a transmission giving the approximate location of four soldiers from a downed helicopter. The UH-1E diverted from its mission to this site and found the soldiers in the midst of an estimated thirty to fory Viet Cong, who were bayoneting and beating them with rifle butts. They began a series of low level attacks, and the Viet Cong scattered and withdrew to a tree line. Upon making a second low level pass, they observed one man raise his arm in a gesture for help. Immediately the helicopter landed on the beach between the men and the enemy, who were now firing furiously at the aircraft. Seeing that two men were unable to move a wounded man to the aircraft, Captain Fairfield exited the aircraft to go to their aid. As he stepped onto the ground, three Viet Cong appeared on top of a small sand dune, only ten feet from the aircraft. He quickly removed one of the machine guns from its mount and killed the enemy with a short burst of fire. Replacing the weapon, he drew his pistol and ran into the hail of fire to aid in carrying the wounded man to the aircraft. With all but one of the wounded men aboard, Captain Fairfield once again braved the enemy fire to race to the aid of the remaining soldier, only to find he had succumbed to his wounds. Returning to the aircraft, he leaped into the cockpit. The helicopter, being subjected to intense enemy fire and overloaded, was barely able to fly, as they made their way to a field hospital. By Captain Fairfield's bold initiative, indomitable fighting spirit and selfless devotion to duty, he was instrumental in saving the men's lives and thereby upheld the highest traditions of the Marine Corps and the United States Naval Service.

*FANTE, ROBERT G.

Citation: For extraordinary heroism while serving as a squad leader with Company F, Second Battalion, Fifth Marines, First Marine Division, in connection with operations against the enemy in the Republic of Vietnam. On 6 August 1968, while participating in a search and clear operation south of the Thu Ben River during Operation MAMELUKE THRUST II, Corporal Fante's platoon came under a heavy volume of small-arms fire from an estimated North Vietnamese Army company entrenched in a tree line. In the initial moments of the attack, Corporal Fante disregarded his own safety to pinpoint enemy positions and maneuver his men forward. When his squad became pinned down, he directed his grenadier to fire into the tree line, effectively suppressing the hostile fire and enabling his men to advance. Subsequently pinpointing an enemy 75mm recoilless rifle position, Corporal Fante skillfully suppressed the fire with supporting arms, and then single-handed, he assaulted the hostile position, capturing the weapon and forcing the enemy soldiers to flee. Repeatedly exposing himself to hostile fire, he continued maneuvering his Marines through the fortified positions, destroying bunkers with hand grenades and boldly pursuing the fleeing enemy. When one of his men was seriously wounded, Corporal Fante unhesitatingly moved to his side and provided security while the corpsman treated the Marine's wounds and evacuated him to a covered position. Alertly observing a camouflaged enemy bunker, he quickly attacked it with hand grenades, killing two North Vietnamese soldiers. As he was advancing across open terrain to attack another hostile fortification, Corporal Fante was mortally wounded by enemy automatic weapons fire. His heroic actions inspired all who observed him and saved numerous fellow Marines from possible death or serious injury. By his courage, superb leadership, and selfless devotion to duty, Corporal Fante upheld the highest traditions of the Marine Corps and the United States Naval Service. He gallantly gave his life for his country.

*FEDEROWSKI, ROBERT A.

Citation: For extraordinary heroism while serving as a Squad Leader with Company D, First Battalion, Fifth Marines, First Marine Division, in connection with operations against the enemy in the Republic of Vietnam. On the evening of 24 May 1968, Corporal Federowski's unit had established an ambush on a suspected enemy infiltration route in Thua Thien Province and became heavily engaged with a numerically superior North Vietnamese Army force. Ignoring the hostile small-arms fire and B-40 rockets impacting around him, Corporal Federowski boldly moved about the hazardous terrain, shouting words of encouragement to his men and skillfully directing their fire. Suddenly, an enemy hand grenade landed near him and several other Marines. With complete disregard for his own safety, Corporal Federowski fearlessly placed himself between the grenade and his comrades. As he attempted to hurl it away from his position, the grenade detonated, and he was mortally wounded. His bold initiative and sincere concern for the welfare of his comrades inspired all who observed him and saved the lives of several fellow Marines. By his courage, aggressive fighting spirit, and selfless devotion to duty, Corporal Federowski upheld the highest traditions of the Marine Corps and the United States Naval Service. He gallantly gave his life for his country.

FEERRAR, DONALD L.

Citation: For extraordinary heroism as a rocket ammunition man with Company "G", Second Battalion, First Marines, in the Republic of Vietnam on 20 March 1967. A squad of the first platoon was positioned in a night ambush against the communist insurgent forces in Quang Nam Province in the early morning hours. Lance Corporal (then Private First Class) Feerrar was with two other Marines in a camouflaged position. During the night, an enemy grenade was hurled into his position, hitting one of his comrades on the arm. Instantly, Lance Corporal Feerrar gave the alarm and knocked the other Marine to the ground. He then grasped the deadly bomb, threw it out of the position and at the same instant threw himself on the Marine he had knocked out of the way, covering the Marine's body with his own. The enemy grenade exploded harmlessly several meters away. Through his extraordinary initiative and inspiring valor in the face of almost certain death, Lance Corporal Feerrar saved his comrades from injury and possible loss of life, thereby reflecting great credit upon himself and upholding the highest traditions of the Marine Corps and the United States Naval Service.

FELTON, SAMUEL L., JR.

Citation: For extraordinary heroism while serving as a Fire Team Leader with Company C, First Battalion, Fifth Marines, First Marine Division, in connection with combat operations against the enemy in the Republic of Vietnam. Early on the morning of 11 June 1969, Company C was established in a battalion night defensive perimeter two miles west of An Hoa Combat Base when its sector came under a heavy volume of rocket, mortar, recoilless rifle, and automatic-weapons fire followed by a determined assault by an estimated 100 North Vietnamese Army soldiers. When communications with a three-man listening post seventy-five meters forward of the perimeter were lost, Private First Class Felton established voice contact and learned that all three Marines were wounded and unable to return to the perimeter unassisted. With resolute determination, he left his fighting hole and although wounded by enemy fire, continued across the open terrain until he reached the beleaguered Marines. After administering first aid and ensuring that no equipment or ordnance was left behind, he provided covering fire as he directed the two least seriously wounded men across the hazardous area to the company lines. Despite his weakened condition from loss of blood, Private First Class Felton began to carry the most seriously injured Marine through the knee-deep mud and water of the rice paddy. Suddenly two hostile soldiers jumped in front of him, blocking his chance to return to friendly lines. Reacting instantly, he fired his M-16 rifle with one hand while supporting the wounded Marine with his injured arm, killing both of the enemy, and fearlessly continued his herculean efforts until he delivered his wounded comrade to the battalion aid station. He then returned to the perimeter and continued fighting the attacking force until the enemy was repulsed. His heroic actions and bold fighting spirit inspired all who observed him and were instrumental in saving the lives of several fellow Marines. By his courage, daring initiative, and unwavering devotion to duty in the face of great personal danger, Private First Class Felton upheld the highest traditions of the Marine Corps and the United States Naval Service.

*FINLEY, MICHAEL P.

Citation: For extraordinary heroism while serving as a Grenadier with First Platoon, Company A, First Battalion, Fourth Marines, Third Marine Division (Reinforced) at Con Thien, Quang Tri Province, Republic of Vietnam on 8 May 1967. Two squads from the First Platoon were maneuvering across an open strip to stop the enemy penetration of the perimeter at Con Thien when they were pinned down by intense fire from a numerically superior North Vietnamese Army force in a revetment behind two burning amphibious tractors. Realizing that the squad was taking heavy casualties Lance Corporal Finley, with complete disregard for his own personal safety, leaped from his covered position and accurately fired two M-79 grenades at the enemy position. Although he was wounded, he scored two direct hits on an enemy machine gun, destroying it and killing its crew. Once again with complete disregard for his own safety, he lunged forward through a hail of enemy fire to give aid to a wounded Marine lying in the open. After giving first aid to the wounded Marine, he noticed that his squad leader was also seriously wounded. Again he fearlessly exposed himself to give assistance to his squad leader, but was mortally wounded. By his daring initiative, valiant fighting spirit and selfless devotion to duty in the face of insurmountable odds, Lance Corporal Finley was responsible in a great measure for saving many of his comrades and thereby upheld the highest traditions of the Marine Corps and the United States Naval Service. He gallantly gave his live for his country.

*FISHER, THOMAS W.

Citation: For extraordinary heroism while serving as a Fire Team Leader with Company M, Third Battalion, Fifth Marines, First Marine Division (Reinforced), in the Republic of Vietnam on 4 September 1967. While advancing toward Hill 63 in Quang Tin Province during Operation SWIFT, Lance Corporal Fisher's platoon came under heavy mortar, machine-gun and small-arms fire from well-entrenched elements of the North Vietnamese Army and was temporarily pinned down. In the initial moments of the vicious attack, he fearlessly exposed himself to enemy fire to encourage and direct his fire team and observe enemy positions. Pinpointing an enemy automatic weapon, he directed accurate rifle fire into the position, silencing the weapon. When another automatic weapon immediately opened fire on his team's position he boldly stood up in full view of the enemy and quieted the weapon with a rapid burst of rifle fire before an enemy round damaged his rifle and wounded him in the arm. Then, despite the painful wound and lack of a weapon, Lance Corporal Fisher daringly ran through a barrage of enemy fire to assist a companion fire team, pinned down in an extremely hazardous position. Upon learning that a seriously wounded Marine was lying in an exposed area approximately forty meters from the left flank, he courageously braved concentrated fire in an attempt to rescue the disabled man. Undaunted by painful wounds, Lance Corporal Fisher crawled forward, bravely continuing to advance until he was wounded again. Even then, when a Marine reached his side to assist him, he refused aid, urging the man to aid the wounded man whom he so courageously had tried to save. Although he ultimately succumbed to his multiple wounds, he inspired all who observed him to heroic endeavor in repulsing the enemy attack. By his extraordinary courage, bold initiative and selfless devotion to duty, Lance Corporal Fisher upheld the highest traditions of the Marine Corps and the United States Naval Service. He gallantly gave his life for his country.

*FITZGERALD, WILLIAM C.

Citation: For extraordinary heroism on 7 August 1967 while serving as senior advisor to Vietnamese Navy Coastal Group SIXTEEN in connection with combat operations against the communist insurgents (Viet Cong) in the Republic of Vietnam. When Coastal Group SIXTEEN was taken under a coordinated attack by numerically superior Viet Cong forces, Lieutenant Fitzgerald immediately established communications with the Vietnamese Navy commanding officer, and attempted to coordinate assistance with free-world forces in the area. The enemy fire soon became too intense for the outnumbered base defense force to resist successfully and the Viet Cong completely overran the base. Aware that his bunker was the only remaining source of resistance, Lieutenant Fitzgerald requested an artillery barrage to be laid down on his own position and ordered his men to evacuate the base toward the river. He gallantly remained in the command bunker in order to provide cover fire for the evacuating personnel. Before Lieutenant Fitzgerald could carry out his own escape, he was fatally shot by the Viet Cong aggressors. By his fearless dedication to duty, courage under fire, and heroic actions in defense of the base, despite overwhelming odds, Lieutenant Fitzgerald served as an inspiration to all persons engaged in the counterinsurgency effort in Vietnam and upheld the highest traditions of the United States Naval Service.

*FLOREN, JIMMY E.

Citation: For extraordinary heroism while serving as a Fire Team Leader with Company H, Second Battalion, Fifth Marines, First Marine Division (Reinforced), in operations against the enemy in the Republic of Vietnam on 6 November 1967. During Operation ESSEX, near Quang Duc, Quang Nam Province, Corporal Floren's company was taken under devastating small-arms, automatic weapons and mortar fire from a well entrenched and numerically superior enemy force. During the initial burst of enemy fire, a Marine was wounded and fell in an open rice paddy, fifteen meters from an enemy machine-gun emplacement. Quickly deploying his men, and with complete disregard for his own safety, Corporal Floren crawled across the fire-swept terrain to the side of the injured man and moved him to a position of relative safety behind a rice paddy dike. Observing that all the members of a machine-gun team were wounded and unable to operate the weapon, he moved forward, seized the weapon and began delivering intense fire in the enemy positions. Although in an exposed position, he continued to fire the weapon until it was rendered useless by enemy machine-gun fire which wounded him. Ignoring his wound, he seized an M-79 Grenade Launcher from a wounded Marine and fearlessly moved to a vantage point on top of a paddy dike from which he delivered accurate fire upon the enemy emplacements, until he was mortally wounded. By his bold initiative, gallant fighting spirit and loyal devotion to duty, Corporal Floren reflected great credit upon himself and the Marine Corps and upheld the highest traditions of the United States Naval Service. He gallantly gave his life for his country.

*FORD, PATRICK O.

Citation: For extraordinary heroism on 21 June 1968 while serving with friendly forces engaged in armed conflict against the communist insurgent (Viet Cong) forces in the Republic of Vietnam. Petty Officer Ford was serving as after machine gunner on a River Patrol Boat (PBR) which was ambushed during a combat patrol by a Viet Cong force using rockets and heavy machine guns. The enemy rocket fire disabled his craft and started a fire on board, causing the PBR to go out of control and head for the shore line directly in front of enemy firing positions. Although seriously wounded, Petty Officer Ford returned a continuous volume of fire into the Viet Cong positions. Realizing that his boat was out of control, and in the face of point-blank hostile fire, he assisted three of his more seriously wounded shipmates from the PBR into the water. Only after insuring that all the surviving crew members had left the boat did Petty Officer Ford give any thought to his own safety. He was the last man to leave the boat. As a result of his heroic actions and fearless devotion to duty, Petty Officer Ford saved the lives of two of his shipmates, gallantly sacrificing his own in doing so. His extraordinary heroism under fire was in keeping with the highest traditions of the United States Naval Service.

FOWLER, EARL W.

Citation: For extraordinary heroism while serving as a Squad Leader with Company C, First Battalion, Seventh Marines in action against insurgent communist forces (Viet Cong) in the Republic of Vietnam on 28 March 1966. During Operation INDIANA, Corporal Fowler's platoon was engaged in an assault on a hostile village in Quang Ngai Province. The intense volume of enemy machine-gun and automatic weapons fire soon inflicted heavy Marine casualties and halted the advance of the two attacking squads. Quickly appraising the situation, Corporal Fowler skillfully deployed his squad to provide covering fire and, with complete disregard for his own safety, courageously moved across an open field where three wounded

Marines lay helpless only about ten yards from a Viet Cong machine gun bunker. As he reached the position of his stricken comrades, he was knocked to the ground by a barrage of enemy concussion grenades. Undaunted, he picked himself up and took the Viet Cong under fire with his M-79, killing and wounding several and forcing the remainder to withdraw temporarily. As he was administering medical aid to the casualties, the Viet Cong returned. Again Corporal Fowler drove them back, killing two with his pistol at a distance of five feet. After helping to carry the wounded men to a covered position, he replenished his supply of ammunition and recrossed the fire-torn field, directing covering fire while other casualties were withdrawn. Although he was wounded in his valiant effort, he stalwartly refused evacuation and remained with his squad through the night, helping to defend the perimeter. By his indomitable fighting spirit and determination to aid his comrades at the risk of his own life, Corporal Fowler upheld the highest traditions of the Marine Corps and the United States Naval Service.

*FREDERICK, JOHN W., JR.

Citation: For extraordinary heroism while interned as a Prisoner of War in Southeast Asia from June 1967 to August 1968. During this period, Chief Warrant Officer Frederick distinguished himself by his relentless rejection of any attempts to gain his cooperation or assistance. His steadfast resistance in the face of grave personal danger was an inspiration to other POW's who observed him. As a result of his dogged resistance, in spite of the fury and relentless cruelty of his captors, fellow prisoners were able to emulate his highly professional example and to find additional personal strength by which to resist interrogation and indoctrination. As a hard-core resister, and with full knowledge of the serious personal hazards to his life, Chief Warrant Officer Frederick personified leadership, bravery, and resistance far beyond that which could reasonably be expected. By his loyalty, perseverance, and courageous actions, Chief Warrant Officer Frederick upheld the highest traditions of the Marine Corps and the United States Naval Service.

*FREUND, TERRENCE J.

Citation: For extraordinary heroism in action on 26 October 1966 while serving with the United States River Patrol Force, near An Lac

119

Thon Village, Republic of Vietnam. As forward machine gunner on board River Patrol Boat Forty during a combat patrol on the Bassac River, Petty Officer Freund was instrumental in preventing an enemy battalion from crossing the river, and assisted in the dispersal of that force. By determined and accurate gunfire, he repeatedly suppressed enemy fire from the river banks during the hotly-contested action. When an attempt to capture an enemy craft resulted in the recovery party being forced into the river by hostile fire, Petty Officer Freund's covering fire was instrumental in their rescue. Although mortally wounded, he continued to fire into enemy positions so that his craft and other friendly forces could be extricated from their perilous positions close to the enemy. By his heroic conduct, he enabled his unit to retire from the action without further loss of life or damage. Petty Officer Freund's performance distinguished him among his gallant comrades, contributed to a victory over the enemy, and was in keeping with the highest traditions of the United States Naval Service.

FRYMAN, ROY A.

Citation: For extraordinary heroism on 29 April 1968 as a Platoon Commander, First Force Reconnaissance Battalion, First Marine Division during operations against enemy aggressor forces in Vietnam. While leading a long-range reconnaissance patrol through the southeastern portion of Phu Loc Valley, Thua Thien Province, Sergeant Fryman, hearing enemy troops approaching along the trail leading to the patrol's position, immediately organized and triggered an ambush, firing bursts from his automatic rifle which killed one of the hostile soldiers, while the patrol killed another. During this brief fire fight, an enemy grenade landed in the position occupied by Sergeant Fryman and three companions. He quickly picked up the deadly missile and hurled it back at the enemy, killing another hostile soldier. Although suffering a slight concussion from the explosion, Sergeant Fryman steadfastly refused medical aid and moved his patrol 100 meters south of the trail where he deployed three-man ambush teams. Subsequently, he and his men succeeded in killing three more enemy troops and wounding two. Following this action, Sergeant Fryman prepared a landing zone for a medical helicopter in order to evacuate the wounded prisoners. He then established a defense perimeter and remained at the scene with the point man to halt the advance of a numerically superior enemy force while the rest of the unit withdrew from the area. As a result of Sergeant Fryman's exceptional knowledge of patrol techniques and tactics, his patrol accomplished its hazardous mission without a single Marine casualty. His great personal valor, aggressive leadership, and unfaltering devotion to duty throughout these actions reflect the highest credit upon himself, the Marine Corps, and the United States Naval Service.

*FULLER, JOHN L., JR.

Citation: For extraordinary heroism in action against insurgent communist (Viet Cong) forces while serving as Platoon Leader, Third Platoon, Company E, Second Battalion, Fifth Marines on 23 March 1967. During Operation NEW CASTLE, Second Lieutenant Fuller's platoon was maneuvering toward the fortified village of Dai Khuong (1), Quang Nam Province, when they were undertaken by intense small arms, mortar and recoilless rifle fire from a well entrenched enemy force. Moving with the lead squad, Second Lieutenant Fuller was wounded by the initial burst of fire. Unmindful of his wound, he stationed himself to direct fire on the advancing enemy and while positioning and encouraging his men, he was struck again by enemy fire. Although suffering from a severe loss of blood he courageously began maneuvering toward the radio position of the platoon, with the intention of directing artillery fire on the enemy knowing it would save the lives of the other Marines. In his advance toward the radio, he received his fatal wound; however, his profound sense of duty and determination enabled him to reach the radio, but he lost consciousness and subsequently died of his wounds while attempting to call in the artillery fire. Inspired by his apparent calm, valiant fighting spirit and dynamic leadership, his Marines went on to defeat the Viet Cong in this fierce battle. Second Lieutenant Fuller's daring initiative and his undying devotion to duty reflected great credit upon himself and upheld the highest traditions of the Marine Corps and the United States Naval Service. He gallantly gave his life for his country.

FULLER, ROBERT B.

Citation: For extraordinary heroism as a Prisoner of War (POW) in North Vietnam during the month of October 1967. During this period, as a prisoner at Hoa Lo POW Prison, he was subjected to severe treatment at the hands of his North Vietnamese captors. As they persisted in their harsh treatment of him, he continued in his refusal to give out biographical data demanded by the North Vietnamese. He heroically resisted all attempts by his captors to break his resistance indicating his willingness to suffer any deprivation and torture to uphold the Code of Conduct. Through those means, he inspired other POW's to resist the enemy's efforts to demoralize and exploit them. By his gallantry and loyal devotion to duty, he reflected great credit upon himself and upheld the highest traditions of the Naval Service and the United States Armed Forces.

*GALBREATH, BOBBY F.

Citation: For extraordinary heroism while serving as a Pilot with Marine Observation Squadron SIX, in the Republic of Vietnam on 16 February 1968. Captain Galbreath launched as Wingman in a flight of two armed UH-1E helicopters diverted to support the emergency extraction of an eight man reconnaissance team which was heavily engaged with a numerically superior North Vietnamese Army force six miles northwest of Dong Ha. Arriving over the designated area, he immediately initiated his attack and made repeated strafing runs on the enemy positions. Although five Marines had been recovered, subsequent attempts to rescue the remaining men failed due to a heavy volume of ground fire which had seriously damaged three helicopters. Realizing the seriousness of the situation, Captain Galbreath volunteered to evacuate the surrounded men. Fully aware of the extreme danger to himself and his crew, he unhesitatingly commenced his approach, but was forced to abandon the landing when his aircraft sustained several hits. Completely disregarding his own safety, he initiated his second approach and skillfully maneuvered his aircraft through the hostile fire into the landing zone. Ignoring the intense fire which was striking his aircraft, he remained in the fire swept area while the men embarked. Lifting from the hazardous zone, his helicopter was struck by a burst of enemy fire and crashed, mortally wounding Captain Galbreath. By his courage, bold initiative and selfless devotion to duty, he inspired all who served with him and upheld the highest traditions of the Marine Corps and the United States Naval Service. He gallantly gave his life for his country.

*GALE, ALVIN R.

Citation: For extraordinary heroism while serving as a Radio Operator with Company G, Second Battalion, Twenty-sixth Marines, Ninth Marine Amphibious Brigade in the Republic of Vietnam on 28

January 1969. During Operation LINN RIVER, the Second Platoon of Company G was patrolling along a stream in Quang Nam Province when the Marines came under a heavy volume of fire from hostile soldiers occupying well-concealed emplacements and, after sustaining several casualties, deployed to the marginal shelter of a bomb crater. Observing that the platoon leader was among the casualties, Private First Class Gale volunteered to accompany his platoon commander and a fire team and fearlessly went to the aid of the beleaguered unit. Noting that the casualties were lying in an unprotected area near the hostile emplacements and would have to be evacuated prior to the utilization of supporting artillery fire, he unhesitatingly accompanied his companions across the fire-swept terrain and effected the rescue of three of the injured men. As he, with his platoon commander, again boldly entered the enemy kill zone and approached to within five meters of the hostile soldiers to evacuate the remaining helpless Marine, the two men came under intense fire which fatally wounded the platoon commander. Determined to save his injured comrade and, if possible, retrieve the officer, Private First Class Gale immediately delivered suppressive fire on the North Vietnamese position and was attempting to gain fire superiority, when he was mortally wounded. By his courage, selfless concern for his fellowmen and unwavering devotion to duty, Private First Class Gale upheld the highest traditions of the Marine Corps and the United States Naval Service. He gallantly gave his life for his country.

GALLAGHER, GARY G.

Citation: For extraordinary heroism on 10 and 11 October 1968 while serving with friendly foreign forces engaged in armed conflict in the Mekong Delta region of the Republic of Vietnam. Distinguishing himself by his exemplary leadership and selfless courage, Petty Officer Gallagher, serving in the capacity of reconnaissance Unit Adviser, led his unit in a capture mission deep into an enemy-controlled area. As the operation progressed and the unit began picking up prisoners, the unit split and advanced on both sides of a small canal in an effort to capture additional members of the Viet Cong infrastructure. At this time, an earlier-acquired captive made a warning sound to his comrades in the vicinity. Immediately, heavy fire from a numerically-superior enemy force was encountered by the separated half of Petty Officer Gallagher's patrol unit. In order to prevent his prisoners from escaping, he forced them to lead the way while crossing the canal to assist his stricken troops. Rallying his reconnaissance unit, Petty Officer Gallagher boldly exposed himself to the hostile fire while directing return fire on the enemy. His driving determination to succeed in his mission served to inspire his men and resulted in the temporary neutralization of the enemy attack. Petty Officer Gallagher then led a hasty, yet professionally executed, withdrawal — with his entire unit and all prisoners-of-war intact. Before concluding the extraction phase, he administered lifesaving first aid to a seriously wounded companion and carried the man over eight kilometers to safety. Petty Officer Gallagher's heroic response while leading this Vietnamese force, his demonstrated initiative and valor, and his selfless dedication under concentrated enemy fire were in keeping with the highest traditions of the United States Naval Service.

GALLAGHER, PATRICK

Citation: For extraordinary heroism as an ammunition carrier in a machine-gun team with Company H, Second Battalion, Fourth Marines near Cam Lo, Republic of Vietnam, in the early morning of 18 July 1966. The company was set in defensive positions at 0145, when enemy soldiers who had infiltrated the area threw a grenade into the position which Lance Corporal Gallagher and three other Marines were manning. Lance Corporal Gallagher, awake and displaying keen presence of mind, immediately kicked the grenade out of the position where it exploded at a safe distance. Another enemy grenade followed and landed in the position between two of his comrades. Without hesitation, in a valiant act of self-sacrifice, Lance Corporal Gallagher threw himself upon the deadly grenade in order to absorb the explosion and save the lives of his comrades. The other three Marines moved to safety while two other grenades landed in the position and exploded, miraculously injuring no one. Lance Corporal Gallagher's Squad Leader then ordered him to throw the grenade into the nearby river where it exploded upon hitting the water. Through his extraordinary heroism and inspiring valor in the face of almost certain death, he saved his comrades from probable injury and possible loss of life. His daring actions were in keeping with the highest traditions of the Marine Corps and the United States Naval Service.

GALLAGHER, ROBERT T.

Citation: For extraordinary heroism on 13 March 1968 while serving with SEAL Team Detachment ALFA engaged in armed conflict against the communist insurgent forces (Viet Cong) in the Republic of Vietnam. Senior Chief Petty Officer Gallagher served as assistant patrol leader for a SEAL night combat operation deep in an enemy battalion base area. His patrol penetrated 5,000 yards into the Viet Cong base camp, locating a large barracks area occupied by approximately 30 well-armed insurgents. Senior Petty Officer Gallagher led three men into the barracks. When discovered by a Viet Cong sentry, the patrol came under heavy enemy fire. Although wounded in both legs, Senior Chief Petty Officer Gallagher accounted for five enemy Viet Cong killed. Discovering that his patrol leader was seriously wounded, Senior Chief Petty Officer Gallagher took command and led his patrol 1,000 yards through heavily occupied enemy territory to an open area where he radioed for helicopter support. He continually exposed himself to heavy enemy automatic-weapons fire to direct friendly helicopter gunships and extraction ships. While assisting his patrol to the evacuation point, Senior Chief Petty Officer Gallagher was again wounded, but, despite his multiple wounds, succeeded in leading his men to a safe extraction. By his courage, professional skill, and devotion to duty, he was directly responsible for the safe withdrawal of his patrol and for killing a large number of the enemy in their own base area. His heroic achievements were in keeping with the highest traditions of the United States Naval Service.

GATES, MICHAEL L.

Citation: For extraordinary heroism on 10 July 1969 while serving with friendly foreign forces engaged in armed conflict against the North Vietnamese and Viet Cong communist aggressor forces in the Republic of Vietnam. As Boat Engineer of a River Patrol Boat, Petty Officer Gates served with River Division 533 which was patrolling the upper reaches of the Vam Co Dong River in a special holding operation to protect Tay Ninh City from expected heavy enemy attack. While settling into waterborne guard-post positions, the units came under heavy automatic-weapons fire. During the first volley, Petty Officer Gates fell to the deck with a serious bullet wound which temporarily paralyzed the lower half of his body. When the units cleared the ambush only to come under a second enemy attack, Petty Officer Gates, despite his severe wound, grabbed a grenade launcher and, from his prone position on the deck of the boat, returned the enemy's fire until the boats again cleared the ambush. After he was transported to the flight deck of a troop carrier to await medical evacuation by helicopter, the enemy once more ambushed the boats. Lying on his back completely exposed to the enemy fire, Petty Officer Gates manned an M-16 rifle which he had requested, and proceeded to assist his shipmates in suppressing the enemy fire. His great personal valor, dauntless initiative, and inspiring devotion to duty in the face of grave personal danger were in keeping with the highest traditions of the United States Naval Service.

*GAUTHIER, BRIAN J.

Citation: For extraordinary heroism while serving as a Marine Rifle Squad Leader with Company "A", First Battalion, Third Marines, Third Marine Division (Reinforced), in the Republic of Vietnam during the early morning of 11 July 1965. While moving to an ambush position eight miles southwest of Danang, Corporal Gauthier's squad suffered heavy casualties from the detonation of an enemy mine and subsequent secondary explosions. Shortly thereafter his unit came under Viet Cong fire from several directions. Although mortally wounded by the initial blast, he persistently refused medical aid until all of the casualties had been treated, meanwhile reorganizing his squad, establishing a defensive perimeter around the wounded, and directing fire against the enemy. During this time a helicopter attempted to evacuate the casualties but was driven off by intensive enemy machine gun fire. For a period of over two hours he continued to shout encouragement and direction to his men until he succumbed to his wounds. Corporal Gauthier's gallant leadership, indomitable fighting spirit, and inspiring devotion to duty reflected great credit upon himself and the Marine Corps and upheld the highest traditions of the United States Naval Service. He gallantly gave his life in the cause of freedom.

*GERRISH, ALAN R.

Citation: For extraordinary heroism on 23 August 1968 while serving as a hospital corpsman with the Third Military Police Battalion, Force Logistic Command, Fleet Marine Force, Pacific, in connection with operations against communist aggressor forces (Viet Cong) in the Republic of Vietnam. During a combined United States Marine Corps and Army of the Republic of Vietnam combat sweep near Danang Airfield, Hospitalman Gerrish's unit came under intense machine-gun fire and grenade attack. Without hesitation, he responded to the pleas for aid from wounded Marines. Braving an open fire-swept field to reach his fallen comrades Hospitalman Gerrish was struck by shrapnel from an exploding grenade and fell to the ground near an open foxhole where he could have attained cover and tended to his wounds. Instead, in the face of the heavy enemy opposition, he chose to advance to the position of the wounded Marines in order to render medical aid. Crawling forward, he inserted himself between the enemy fire and a wounded Marine, using his body as a shield to protect the casualty from the hail of bullets. Critically wounded by enemy fire while engaged in administering first aid to the wounded Marine, Hospitalman Gerrish, by his heroic actions and selfless concern for his fallen comrades, served to inspire all who observed him, and upheld the highest traditions of the United States Naval Service.

*GETLIN, MICHAEL P.

Citation: For extraordinary heroism as Commanding Officer, Company "I", Third Battalion, Ninth Marines in the Republic of Vietnam on 30 March 1967. The company was engaged in establishing platoon night ambush sites against communist insurgent forces in Quang Tri Province when all elements became engaged simultaneously, and the company's command group and a small security element were attacked by a North Vietnamese reinforced company utilizing heavy automatic weapons fire and mortar barrages. Captain Getlin, despite multiple shrapnel and gunshot wounds, while under constant mortar and small-arms fire, remained on the exposed forward slope of the hill where he calmly called in artillery fire and directed helicopter strikes on the advancing enemy. When the attack built to the point of overrunning the Marine position, Captain Getlin moved to the most critical position and delivered devastating shotgun fire into the assaulting enemy. The barrel of his weapon split due to the rate of fire. With complete disregard for the danger involved, he reloaded and continued to fire, personally killing at least six enemy soldiers. Realizing that the position was not tenable, Captain Getlin directed his men to move to a better position while he covered their move. At this time three grenades fell within his immediate position. He threw one grenade back at the enemy and was mortally wounded attempting to retrieve the others. As a result of his professional ability, extraordinary courage, and stirring example, the Marines gained the new position and repulsed the enemy attack of over sixty North Vietnamese. Captain Getlin's great personal valor reflected the highest credit upon himself and the Marine Corps and upheld the highest traditions of the United States Naval Service. He gallantly gave his life for his country.

GIBSON, GEORGE R.

Citation: For extraordinary heroism as an Automatic Rifleman while serving with the Second Platoon, Company B, Second Battalion, Fourth Marines during Operation PRAIRIE in Vietnam on 8 August 1966. His platoon was being evacuated by helicopter from an area northwest of Cam Lo, Quang Tri Province, when it was attacked by North Vietnamese Army units utilizing automatic weapons fire and barrages of hand grenades. The half of the platoon that had not been successfully evacuated was quickly surrounded. Casualties mounted as enemy forces in reinforced company strength threatened to overrun the friendly positions. Corporal Gibson observed a Marine, wounded and helpless, almost within the grasp of the advancing enemy. He immediately, with complete disregard for his own safety, left his covered position and exposed himself to murderous enemy fire to provide fire support for the evacuation of the wounded man. The Platoon Commander rallied the platoon for a counter-attack and Corporal Gibson leaped from protective cover and charged into the enemy fire. Although painfully wounded by a grenade, he continued to press the attack until the original positions had been retaken. Knowing their only chance to hold was to obtain more ammunition, he unhesitatingly crossed twenty-five meters of fire-swept terrain and returned with the badly needed ammunition. Observing a machine gun that was not manned, Corporal Gibson immediately put it into action and, disregarding barrages of enemy grenades and accurate small-arms fire directed at him, courageously stood his ground until the North Vietnamese withdrew to reorganize for another attack. The second attack was accompanied by vicious automatic-weapons fire and grenades, and despite being painfully wounded again by machine gun fire, he continued to fight, killing six additional enemy. The North Vietnamese set up a machine gun that threatened to enfilade the Marine position. Corporal Gibson moved out on the fire-swept slope in full view of the enemy, flanked the weapon, and single-handedly knocked it out, killing its crew. His courageous initiative, indomitable fighting spirit and unselfish devotion to duty were contributing factors in the successful removal of the wounded and in saving the lives of many of his comrades. His great personal valor reflected the highest credit upon himself, the Marine Corps and the United States Naval Service.

GILLELAND, RICHARD M.

Citation: For extraordinary heroism while serving as a Platoon Sergeant with Company M, Third Battalion, Seventh Marines, First Marine Division, in connection with combat operations against the enemy in the Republic of Vietnam. On 23 February 1969, the Second Platoon of Company M was dispatched to the Bo Ban area of Hieu Duc District in Quang Nam Province to assist a squad from another platoon, which had become heavily engaged with a well-entrenched North Vietnamese Army battalion. Having reached their objective, the Marines commenced a reconnaissance in force across a rice paddy covered with heavy grass. Unhesitatingly leading the nearest squad, Sergeant Gilleland was immediately engaged in fierce hand-to-hand combat with hostile soldiers who had been concealed in the tall grass. He inspired his men by his example, and during the initial moments of the fierce engagement, the Marines killed twelve hostile soldiers in fierce close combat. After pausing momentarily to allow fixed-wing strikes on the enemy, Sergeant Gilleland initiated another aggressive assault enabling his men to force the North Vietnamese soldiers back into concealed areas. When the Marines approached within a few meters of the hostile emplacements they sustained a number of casualties, and Sergeant Gilleland valiantly crossed the fire-swept area on six separate occasions to lead the wounded men to places of relative security, thereby saving their lives. His heroic and determined efforts inspired all who observed him and were instrumental in his platoon's accounting for thirty-six hostile soldiers killed and vast quantities of enemy weapons and equipment captured. By his courage, bold initiative, and unwavering devotion to duty in the face of grave personal danger, Sergeant Gilleland upheld the highest traditions of the Marine Corps and the United States Naval Service.

*GILLESPIE, MARTIN L., JR.

Citation: For extraordinary heroism as platoon corpsman, 2nd Platoon, Company D, First Battalion, Fourth Marines during

Operation TEXAS in the Republic of Vietnam against communist insurgent guerrilla forces on 21 March 1966. While engaged in a search and destroy mission, the Second Platoon came under a devastating volume of accurate small arms semi-automatic weapons fire and heavy caliber machine gun fire from concealed, fortified enemy positions about 75 meters to their front. Observing a Marine wounded as he attempted to knock out the enemy emplacements with a rocket launcher, Petty Officer Gillespie fearlessly dashed across 30 meters of exposed ground, completely disregarding the intense volume of fire. Upon reaching the critically wounded Marine, he quickly began administering life saving aid with calm professionalism. Although the surrounding area was raked continually with increasingly accurate enemy fire, Petty Officer Gillespie continued to work, remaining in the exposed position for several minutes until he had stopped the bleeding, and then, as he began to move the wounded Marine to cover, he was mortally struck by enemy fire. As a result of his expert professional skill and his selfless daring actions, the life of a Marine was spared. Petty Officer Gillespie gallantly gave his life in the service of his country.

*GILLINGHAM, RICHARD K.

Citation: For extraordinary heroism in connection with operations against enemy forces while serving as a Squad Leader with Company H, Second Battalion, Ninth Marines, Third Marine Division (Reinforced) in the Republic of Vietnam on 19 May 1967. While on a search and destroy operation in Quang Tri Province, Corporal Gillingham's squad was taken under heavy small arms and automatic weapons fire. In the initial burst of fire, one of his men was seriously wounded and unable to move from his exposed position. With complete disregard for his own safety, Corporal Gillingham rushed into the open terrain to administer aid to the fallen Marine, who was twenty meters away. Although wounded three times, he courageously persisted in his efforts until he had moved his wounded fellow Marine to a secure position. While heroically attempting to return to his squad, he succumbed to his grievous wounds. By his outstanding courage, exceptional fortitude and valiant fighting spirit, Corporal Gillingham served to inspire all who observed him and upheld the highest traditions of the Marine Corps and the United States Naval Service. He gallantly gave his life for his country.

GILLOTTE, KEVIN

Citation: For extraordinary heroism on 11 January 1969 while serving with United States forces engaged in riverine assault operations against enemy aggressor forces in the Republic of Vietnam. With Petty Officer Gillotte embarked as engineer, Assault Support Patrol Boat (ASPB) 92-8 was assigned as a participating unit of Operation GIANT SLINGSHOT. The craft had moored in a night defensive position alongside an Army LCM-8 Mobile Fire Support Base on a shallow, narrow canal when ASPB 92-8 came under sudden mortar attack, finding itself in the center of the impact area. Although wounded in the leg, Petty Officer Gillotte responded immediately to the seriousness of the situation by assisting the boat captain in rousing the crew to man their stations, and then made his way forward to throw off the entangled mooring line. Standing exposed to incoming mortar rounds on the forecastle of the boat, Petty Officer Gillotte was again wounded by shrapnel, but eventually succeeded in freeing the fouled line. Upon hearing the cries of the machine gunner, he climbed on top of the gun mount, removed his seriously wounded shipmate, rendered immediate medical aid, and threw his own body over the incapacitated victim to shield him from further injury. After ASPB 92-8 cleared the kill zone, Petty Officer Gillotte risked harmful burns when he entered the engine compartment to work on an engine damaged by shrapnel that caused extreme overheating. He remained at his station tending the damaged engine until the boat secured alongside a landing ship on the main river; only then allowing himself to be relieved in order to seek medical attention. His inspiring courage and selfless dedication were in keeping with the highest traditions of the United States Naval Service.

GOMEZ, ERNESTO

Citation: For extraordinary heroism while serving with Marine Medium Helicopter Squadron 262, in connection with operations against the enemy in the Republic of Vietnam. On 25 January 1968, Corporal Gomez was the Crew Chief aboard a CH-46 transport helicopter assigned an emergency medical evacuation mission on Hill 881 near the Khe Sanh Combat Base. The pilot proceeded to the designated area and landed in the zone as two Marines began leading a casualty, whose head and eyes were covered with bandages, toward the helicopter. When the entire landing zone was subjected to intense enemy fire, the two men were forced to drop to the ground. Observing the blindfolded casualty attempting to reach the aircraft unassisted, Corporal Gomez unhesitatingly left the helicopter and rushed across 25 meters of fire-swept terrain to the side of the injured man. Quickly pulling the Marine to the ground, he selflessly used his own body to shield his comrade from the hostile fire impacting around them, and as the enemy fire continued, he took cover with the casualty in a nearby rocket crater. Corporal Gomez remained in this exposed area until another crew member rushed to his assistance. Then the two Marines, protecting their wounded comrade from further injury, carried him to the helicopter. The Pilot was quickly informed that the injured Marine was aboard, and the aircraft lifted from the hazardous area for the medical facility at Khe Sanh. Corporal Gomez's heroic actions were instrumental in saving his companion's life and inspired all who observed him. By his courage, selfless concern for the safety of his fellow Marine, and unswerving devotion to duty at great personal risk, he upheld the highest traditions of the Marine Corps and the United States Naval Service.

GONZALES, DANIEL G.

Citation: For extraordinary heroism while serving as a 60mm mortar section leader with Company B, First Battalion, Seventh Marines, First Marine Division, in connection with combat operations against the enemy in the Republic of Vietnam. In the early morning hours of 7 June 1969, Corporal Gonzales was stationed in Quang Nam Province at a company patrol base which was being defended by one platoon and his mortar section. Suddenly, the position was attacked by a determined North Vietnamese Army force utilizing automatic weapons and rocket propelled grenades, which either killed or wounded all of the Marines in the western defensive sector except Corporal Gonzales. Realizing the need for drastic action to prevent the overrunning of the command group, he fearlessly left his covered emplacement, and armed only with a pistol, utilized the scant natural cover available as he assaulted the enemy. Repeatedly exposing himself to the intense hostile fire to accurately fire his pistol, he boldly ran forward alone, killing three enemy soldiers and forcing the remainder to retreat. He then continued to pursue the hostile soldiers by fire until other Marines came to his assistance. His heroic actions and determined efforts prevented the death of his injured companions and the capture of a 60mm mortar. By his courage, bold initiative, and unwavering devotion to duty in the face of grave personal danger, Corporal Gonzales upheld the highest traditions of the Marine Corps and the United States Naval Service.

*GOODSELL, WILLIAM J.

Citation: For extraordinary heroism while serving with Marine Observation Squadron SIX in the Republic of Vietnam on 16 June 1966. Serving as Tactical Air Coordinator (Airborne) in an armed UH-1F helicopter, Major Goodsell made repeated rocket and machine gun attacks against an enemy battalion that had encircled and trapped a Marine reconnaissance unit. When a relieving force was airlifted into the battle, he guided the transport helicopters to the landing zone and delivered such devastating attacks on the enemy positions that only one aircraft in the assault force was struck by hostile fire. He then proceeded to fly dangerously low to seek out enemy positions and aid the assault force in their rescue of the beleaguered reconnaissance unit. When a juncture of the units was accomplished, he guided the medical evacuation helicopters to the friendly positions where eighteen wounded Marines lay waiting. Realizing the necessity to accurately mark the Marine positions because of the close proximity of the enemy, he courageously elected to fly very low and slow over the position to mark it with a smoke grenade. As his mark landed directly on target, he was taken under fire by several automatic weapons positions and although mortally wounded he maintained control of his aircraft until relieved by his copilot. By his bravery and fearless devotion to duty, Major Goodsell reflected great credit upon himself and the Marine Corps and upheld the highest traditions of the United States Naval Service. He gallantly gave his life in the cause of freedom.

*GRANT, GOLLIE L.

Citation: For extraordinary heroism on 19 September 1966 as a corpsman with Company B, First Battalion, Twenty-Sixth Marines, Third Marine Division in connection with operations against insurgent communist (Viet Cong) forces in the Republic of Vietnam. When the lead squad came under intense automatic-weapons and sniper fire from well-concealed enemy positions during the approach to Gia Binh Village in Quang Tri Province during Operation PRAIRIE, Hospitalman Grant unhesitatingly ran forward and moved approximately twenty-five yards through deadly enemy fire to aid the wounded. While moving toward the nearest wounded Marine, he himself was struck by small-arms fire. Ignoring his painful wound, he courageously continued his advance by crawling toward his wounded comrade. As he was applying a battle dressing to the man, Hospitalman Grant was wounded a second time by enemy fire. Continuing to administer first aid, he selflessly completed the treatment and directed the casualty to friendly lines. As he proceeded toward another injured Marine, Hospitalman Grant was mortally wounded by a third enemy round. His professional skill, great personal courage and inspiring devotion to duty at the risk of his own life undoubtedly saved the life of one Marine and were in keeping with the highest traditions of the United States Naval Service.

GRAY, GEORGE E.

Citation: For extraordinary heroism while serving as an Antitank Assaultman with Company E, Second Battalion, Ninth Marines, Third Marine Division (Reinforced), in connection with operations against the enemy in the Republic of Vietnam. On 2 February 1968, Company E was advancing to seize a hill in Quang Tri Province overlooking National Route Nine to prevent the enemy from interdicting the road. Suddenly, Lance Corporal (then Private First Class) Gray's platoon came under heavy fire from mutually supporting fortified North Vietnamese Army positions on the hill, pinning down the platoon and inflicting several casualties. Observing an enemy mortar emplacement, he disregarded his own safety as he repeatedly exposed himself to hostile fire in order to bring effective fire to bear against the North Vietnamese position. On three separate occasions, he was wounded as he fired his antitank rocket weapon, however he ignored his painful wounds and refused medical attention for himself. Having expended his rocket ammunition, Corporal Gray obtained an M-16 rifle and began delivering a heavy volume of accurate fire against the enemy. When he observed a wounded Marine lying in an area exposed to hostile fire, he ran across the fire-swept area to the side of his fallen comrade, carried him to safety and began administering first aid. After he was joined by two other Marines who assisted in providing medical treatment to the wounded man, he heard the sound of an incoming enemy mortar round and, reacting instantly, pushed his two companions to the ground and covered the injured man with his own body. Although severely wounded by fragments from the exploding round, Corporal Gray successfully protected his fellow

Marine from sustaining further injury. Still refusing medical attention for himself even though he was again wounded by enemy fire, he continued to aggressively engage the enemy until the critical phase of the battle was over. By his steadfast courage, intrepid fighting spirit and selfless devotion to duty at great personal risk, Corporal Gray inspired all those who observed him and upheld the highest traditions of the Marine Corps and the United States Naval Service.

GREEN, JOHN S.

Citation: For extraordinary heroism in action against enemy forces while serving as Company Gunnery Sergeant, Company F, Second Battalion, Fifth Marines, First Marine Division (Reinforced) in the Republic of Vietnam on 2 June 1967. During Operation UNION II, Company F came under intense enemy small arms, automatic weapons and mortar fire from a well entrenched enemy force and was temporarily halted. Gunnery Sergeant Green, with complete disregard for his own safety, led a frontal assault against the enemy positions. Leading his men across 800 meters of open, fire-swept rice paddy, he quickly overran the Viet Cong machine gun position and personally accounted for ten enemy killed. After seizing the objective, he immediately established a hasty defense and began redistributing ammunition to his men. He fearlessly braved the intense enemy fire by exposing himself in carrying wounded to positions of relative safety. By his daring initiative, valiant fighting spirit and selfless devotion to duty in the face of insurmountable odds, Gunnery Sergeant Green was responsible in great measure for saving many of his comrades and thereby upheld the highest traditions of the Marine Corps and the United States Naval Service.

GREEN, MAURICE O. V.

Citation: For extraordinary heroism while serving as the Intelligence Officer of the First Battalion, Fifth Marines, First Marine Division, in the Republic of Vietnam on 27 October 1968. First Lieutenant Green traveled to the Company D Command Post in Quang Nam Province to interrogate two North Vietnamese Army prisoners. During the night, the Marine perimeter was breached by an enemy engineer unit hurling satchel charges throughout the position. Simultaneously, a large North Vietnamese force initiated a savage attack employing mortars, small arms, automatic weapons and antitank rockets. Alertly observing the commanding officer among the seriously wounded, First Lieutenant Green unhesitatingly assumed command of the company and repeatedly exposed himself to the continuous hail of enemy fire as he began rallying the Marine defenders. Completely disregarding his own safety, he fearlessly moved about the fire-swept terrain to each Marine position, shouting words of encouragment to the men and directing their fire at the hostile soldiers. Ignoring the enemy rounds impacting near him, he swiftly retrieved a radio from a seriously injured radio operator and boldly adjusted supporting arms fire on the attackers with pinpoint accuracy, forcing them to withdraw in panic and confusion. Rapidly assessing the turn of events, First Lieutenant Green courageously mounted and skillfully directed a determined counterattack in pursuit of the fleeing enemy soldiers while continuing to direct effective supporting arms fire on them. After contact had been broken with the enemy, he ensured that the wounded were medically treated and made arrangements for their evacuation. His daring initiative and heroic efforts inspired all who served with him and were instrumental in his company's accounting for eight hostile soldiers confirmed killed. By his courage, bold leadership and unwavering devotion to duty in the face of great personal danger, First Lieutenant Green upheld the highest traditions of the Marine Corps and the United States Naval Service.

GREGORY, ROBERT B., JR.

Citation: For extraordinary heroism while serving as a Rifleman with Combined Action Platoon 2-1-2, III Marine Amphibious Force, in the Republic of Vietnam on 23 and 25 February 1969. Lance Corporal Gregory's platoon was participating in a search and destroy operation near the village of Hoa Huong in Quang Nam Province when the Marines sustained several casualties as they came under a heavy volume of hostile automatic weapons fire from a numerically superior force occupying well-fortified emplacements. Realizing the necessity for immediate action, Lance Corporal Gregory rushed across the fire-swept terrain to a machine gun which had been dropped by a wounded Marine and, with complete disregard for his own safety, provided covering fire which enabled his companions to remove the injured men to positions of relative safety. Having exhausted his ammunition and heedless of the enemy rounds impacting about him, he again ran forward and assisted a casualty to safety, after which he repeatedly crossed the dangerous terrain to retrieve weapons and equipment left behind by wounded men. When a medical evacuation helicopter arrived, he fearlessly exposed himself to the intense hostile fire raking the landing zone as he assisted the casualties to embark. On 25 February, during the same operation, Lance Corporal Gregory's platoon was directed to assist another unit which was heavily engaged with the enemy. Arriving at the designated location, he observed a wounded Marine fall in a position dangerously exposed to the hostile fire. After crawling to the man's side, he was treating the casualty when he detected an enemy soldier preparing to fire at his injured companion. Although realizing the explosion would reveal his presence to the hostile force, Lance Corporal Gregory immediately threw a hand grenade and killed the enemy soldier. Ignoring the hostile rounds that were being concentrated on his now revealed position, he began carrying the casualty from the area. Although struck by enemy fire three times, he refused to abandon his wounded comrade and successfully reached a position of relative safety. He refused medical evacuation to ensure that his comrade and other wounded were cared for. Although weak from his wounds and loss of blood, he continued to aid his fellow Marines until he received a fourth wound and was forced to abandon his selfless tasks. By his courage, bold initiative and unfaltering devotion to duty, Lance Corporal Gregory upheld the highest traditions of the Marine Corps and the United States Naval Service.

GRESHAM, MICHAEL E.

Citation: For extraordinary heroism while serving as a Squad Leader with Company D, First Battalion, Fifth Marines, First Marine Division, in connection with operations against the enemy in the Republic of Vietnam. On the night of 11 September 1968, while occupying a defensive position in Quang Nam Province, Company D came under intense rocket and mortar fire, immediately followed by a heavy volume of grenades and satchel charges supporting a human wave assault by a North Vietnamese Army company. When the hostile attack was initiated, Sergeant (then Lance Corporal) Gresham was at the platoon command post, and when the building was struck by several rocket rounds, the platoon commander, platoon sergeant, and both other squad leaders were wounded seriously. Momentarily stunned, Sergeant Gresham recovered quickly and, realizing that he was the senior Marine remaining uninjured, unhesitatingly assumed command of the platoon. With complete disregard for his own safety, he raced through the intense enemy fire, and moving from one position to another, shouted words of encouragement to his men and directed their fire, inflicting numerous losses on the advancing hostile soldiers. Ignoring the enemy rounds impacting nearby, he moved throughout the fire-swept area redistributing ammunition and assisting injured men to covered positions. Assessing the situation, he concluded that the rapid expenditure of ammunition and number of casualties his platoon had sustained made his position untenable. Quickly repairing an inoperable radio, Sergeant Gresham appraised the company commander of the situation and, at his direction, skillfully redeployed his men to an alternate location. Obtaining ammunition and hand grenades from adjacent units, Sergeant Gresham rapidly distributed them to his men and, when the enemy force again attacked, he directed his platoon's devastating fire and successfully repelled the hostile onslaught. His heroic and decisive action prevented the platoon from being overrun and saved the lives of several Marines. By his courage, bold initiative, and selfless devotion to duty, Sergeant Gresham inspired all who observed him and upheld the highest traditions of the Marine Corps and the United States Naval Service.

GRESKO, RICHARD W.

Citation: For extraordinary heroism while serving with Headquarters and Service Company, Third Battalion, Fifth Marine Regiment, First Marine Division in the Republic of Vietnam. On the night of 11 March 1970, Sergeant (then Lance Corporal) Gresko was in one element of an ambush set up to protect a village from enemy attack. Around midnight, his element ambushed a Viet Cong unit which was attempting to enter the village. During the ensuing fight, Sergeant Gresko observed an enemy hand grenade land near his position. With complete disregard for his own personal safety and fully aware of the dangers involved, he unhesitatingly threw himself on top of the grenade, absorbing most of the blast fragments with his own body in order to protect his men from certain injury and possible death. Although painfully wounded, he continued to direct his men's actions until the squad made their sweep. By his bold and heroic action on behalf of his fellow Marines, Sergeant Gresko reflected great credit upon himself and upheld the highest traditions of the Marine Corps and the United States Naval Service.

*GRIFFITH, JOHN G.

Citation: For extraordinary heroism in aerial flight on 24 February 1968 as a naval flight officer in Attack Squadron THIRTY-FIVE, embarked in USS ENTERPRISE (CVA(N)-65). As leading bombardier/navigator, Lieutenant Commander (then Lieutenant) Griffith flew on a night air strike against a vital and heavily defended port facility in the heart of North Vietnam. Navigating his aircraft at perilously low altitudes in the monsoon weather, he successfully penetrated intense and accurate enemy defenses en route to the target. Disregarding the threatening surface-to-air missiles and antiaircraft artillery defending the target area, Lieutenant Commander Griffith maintained a steady radar tracking of the target until bomb release, thereby ensuring an optimum bombing solution. Because of his daring and highly professional navigation and radar-bombing skill, his bombs found their mark, inflicting heavy damage upon the port facilities. By his technical competence, courage, and loyal devotion to duty in the face of intense enemy opposition, Lieutenant Commander Griffith contributed materially to United States efforts in Southeast Asia and upheld the highest traditions of the United States Naval Service.

GRIMES, PAUL E., JR.

Citation: For extraordinary heroism as a Rifleman with Company F, Second Battalion, Seventh Marines in the Republic of Vietnam on 4 March 1967. During Operation DE SOTO, Company F was conducting a search and destroy mission in the vicinity of Thanh Hieu (1), Quang Ngai Province, when the second squad, third platoon was taken under intense enemy automatic weapons fire from a heavily fortified bunker. The initial enemy fire wounded one Marine and pinned down the remaining members of the second squad behind a rice paddy dike which lay approximately 100 meters from the enemy emplacement. The Company Commander joined the second squad and asked for a volunteer to advance on the bunker and attempt to destroy it by firing LAW's into the aperture. Lance Corporal grimes immediately volunteered and after obtaining two LAW's moved from his covered position and advanced thirty meters toward the bunker through the devastating enemy fire. After firing the two LAW's and striking the bunker both times, he returned to his previous position. Seconds later the clattering of the enemy automatic weapons was again heard from the bunker. Realizing that the LAW's had not penetrated the heavily fortified bunker and that the enemy must be silenced in order to evacuate the Marine who had been previously wounded, Lance Corporal Grimes took two grenades in hand and assaulted the bunker. As he advanced through the devastating enemy fire, bullets ripped at his flack jacket and two grenades were thrown at him. Upon reaching the enemy bunker, he fearlessly climbed up to the aperture, pulled the pins on his grenades, and thrust them through the opening. The destruction of the enemy bunker was the turning point in a violent action taken against the enemy. By his outstanding courage, exceptional fortitude and valiant fighting spirit, Lance Corporal Grimes served to inspire all who observed him and upheld the highest traditions of the Marine Corps and the United States Naval Service.

GROCE, DONALD B.

Citation: For extraordinary heroism while serving as the Advisor to Vietnamese Navy ZIPPO Boat (HG-6533) when that vessel was ambushed by enemy forces in the Republic of Vietnam on 4 September 1970. During the initial moments of the ambush, enemy rockets, recoilless rifle and automatic weapons fire inflicted heavy casualties upon crew members of the ZIPPO boat. The first rocket round wounded Chief Petty Officer Groce in the arms and legs and knocked him out of the coxswain'a flat and into the main deck gunwhale. Despite his serious wounds, he made his way back to his battle station and had resumed his duty of advising and assisting the Vietnamese Boat Captain in the counterattack when shrapnel from another enemy rocket again wounded him, causing a deep hip wound and a compound fracture of his right thumb. Disregarding his grievous injuries, Chief Petty Officer Groce managed to crawl forward on the open deck to the flame mounts which were not firing. While exposed to the full force of the enemy fire, he calmly aligned the flame system and shouted encouragement to the other crew members. Subsequently, he personally operated one flame mount and supervised the employment of the flame throwers against the enemy's positions until the enemy fire was effectively suppressed. Chief Petty Officer Groce's exemplary professionalism, bravery under fire, and courageous devotion to duty were in keeping with the highest traditions of the United States Naval Service.

GROSZ, NICHOLAS H., JR.

Citation: For extraordinary heroism as Commanding Officer of Headquarters and Service Company, Second Battalion, Seventh Marines, in the Republic of Vietnam on 18 December 1965, during Operation HARVEST MOON in Quang Tin Province near the hamlet of Ky Phy. When savage small arms, automatic weapons and mortar fire pinned his company down in a muddy and exposed rice paddy area, Lieutenant Grosz immediately informed his battalion of the seriousness of the situation and summoned help. Completely ignoring his own personal safety, he repeatedly ran the gauntlet of intense enemy fire to personally evacuate four wounded Marines. He returned to his men and gave them encouragement as he rallied them and directed their fire toward Viet Cong positions. In order to permit a few of the lesser wounded to make their way to relative safety while a rifle company was coming to the rescue, he personally engaged automatic weapons with a grenade launcher while enemy rounds were striking his pack and equipment. After returning to retrieve weapons and sundry abandoned gear, and to make certain that none of his men were left behind, he finally made his way to the main battle position and organized his company to support the battalion in its subsequent attack and mopping up operations. By his daring actions, indomitable fighting spirit, and loyal devotion to duty in the face of great personal danger, Lieutenant Grosz reflected distinct credit upon himself and the Marine Corps and upheld the highest traditions of the United States Naval Service.

GUARINO, TIMOTHY S.

Citation: For extraordinary heroism while serving as a Machine Gun Ammunition Man with Company G, Second Battalion, Ninth Marines, Third Marine Division in the Republic of Vietnam on 1 June 1969. Company G came under a vicious ground attack by a determined hostile force utilizing satchel charges, automatic weapons fire and rocket-propelled grenades. While resolutely defending his position in a sector of the perimeter which had been penetrated by the enemy, Private First Class Guarino observed a wounded companion fall in a position dangerously exposed to the enemy advance. Completely disregarding his own safety, he fearlessly crossed the fire-swept area and carried his injured comrade to a place where medical aid was available. As he was assisting in treating the casualty, an enemy hand grenade landed beside the corpsman and the wounded Marine. Fully aware of the possible consequences of his actions and thinking only of the safety of his companions, Private First Class Guarino unhesitatingly knocked the corpsman to the ground beside the wounded Marine and valiantly threw himself over their bodies, thus absorbing the full force of the grenade's detonation and sustaining extensive wounds. His heroic and bold efforts inspired all who observed him and saved the lives of two comrades. By his courage, selfless concern for his fellowman and unwavering devotion to duty in the face of grave personal danger, Private First Class Guarino upheld the highest traditions of the Marine Corps and the United States Naval Service.

GUAY, ROBERT P.

Citation: For extraordinary heroism while serving with Marine Medium Helicopter Squadron TWO HUNDRED SIXTY-ONE in Vietnam on 19 March 1966. As Flight Leader of ten UH-34D aircraft on a mission to transport reinforcement troops into the outpost at An Hoa, which was rumored to have been overrun by the enemy during the previous night, Major Guay, upon approaching the outpost, held the flight at altitude while a visual reconnaissance was made. Advised that all appeared quiet and that Vietnamese civilians and military personnel had waved to the aircraft in a friendly manner, Major Guay proceeded with landing operations. As the first two aircraft were about to land, Viet Cong in ambush positions around the landing zone opened intense antiaircraft, small-arms and automatic weapons fire. Courageously braving the barrage, Major Guay completed the landing and disembarked the troops. Realizing that the Viet Cong completely controlled the area and had forced their prisoners to lure the aircraft into the trap, he made several additional attempts to land, then returned to the staging area at Quang Ngai. Volunteering to attempt the rescue of the Vietnamese soldiers just landed in the zone, Major Guay, as Flight Leader, directed the helicopter back to the beleaguered outpost and executed a single plane approach to the nearby landing zone. Although his aircraft sustained a damaging hit from enemy fire, he fearlessly continued his approach and successfully embarked a load of Vietnamese. Despite the continuing danger and battle damage to his aircraft, he remained in the vicinity to direct the efforts of other aircraft in the flight. His courageous actions, inspiring leadership and extraordinary airmanship undoubtedly prevented the friendly troops from being killed or captured by the enemy, reflected great credit upon himself and were in keeping with the highest traditions of the Marine Corps and the United States Naval Service.

GUERRA, VICTOR J.

Citation: For extraordinary heroism while serving as a Platoon Sergeant with Company L, Third Battalion, First Marines, First Marine Division in connection with combat operations against the enemy in the Republic of Vietnam. On the night of 27 October 1969, while Staff Sergeant Guerra was returning to the Company Patrol Base with his men, he saw an enemy grenade land before him on the road in proximity to three of his companions. Fully aware of the possible consequences of his actions, he shouted a warning and then unhesitatingly threw himself over the grenade. Although realizing that every second's delay increased his chances of being mortally wounded, he remained in a prone position over the grenade until he was satisfied that the other Marines had attained covered positions. Then, rising to his knees, he hurled the grenade away from the Marines where it detonated harmlessly. His heroic and determined actions inspired all who observed him and undoubtedly saved three comrades from serious injury or possible death. By his courage, bold initiative, and selfless devotion to duty in the face of great personal risk, Staff Sergeant Guerra upheld the highest traditions of the Marine Corps and of the United States Naval Service.

HALL, MICHAEL R.

Citation: For extraordinary heroism on 24 February 1968 as a bombardier/navigator in Attack Squadron SEVENTY-FIVE, embarked in USS KITTY HAWK (CVA-63), and launched from USS ENTERPRISE (CVA(N)-65) in a joint attack with Attack Squadron THIRTY-FIVE. Lieutenant Commander Hall participated in a coordinated, night, low-level strike against the heavily defended port facilities within the city of Hanoi, North Vietnam. Soon after launching, serious systems difficulties developed in his aircraft. Through the professionalism and determination of Lieutenant Commander Hall and his pilot, this discrepancy was overcome and they rejoined the flight to continue the attack. En route to, and in the target area, extremely heavy and accurate antiaircraft fire was encountered and the aircraft received a hit in the left wing.

Notwithstanding this battle damage, Lieutenant Commander Hall aggressively navigated his aircraft to the target through multiple surface-to-air missile attacks which were successfully evaded through extremely low-altitude maneuvering. He then delivered his ordnance directly on the target. During egress from the target area, he again came under an intense attack from surface-to-air missiles and was forced to maneuver violently at very low altitude. One missile was seen to explode aft and below his aircraft, buffeting it violently. By his daring action, exceptional skill, and loyal devotion to duty in the face of intense enemy opposition, Lieutenant Commander Hall upheld the highest traditions of the United States Naval Service.

*HALSTEAD, LEE M.

Citation: For extraordinary heroism while serving as a Pilot with Marine Light Helicopter Squadron 167 in connection with operations against insurgent communist (Viet Cong) forces in the Republic of Vietnam. On 29 August 1968, Lieutenant Halstead was Aircraft Commander aboard an armed UH-1E helicopter providing support for a UH-34 helicopter assigned to evacuate three wounded Marines from an area southwest of Danang in Quang Nam Province. Seeking to determine the source of enemy fire, he boldly commenced a low-level pass over the friendly position and immediately came under intense hostile fire, which struck a box of ammunition in the crew's compartment. As the evacuation helicopter prepared to land, Lieutenant Halstead skillfully delivered covering fire on the hostile positions. Suddenly, the transport aircraft was damaged by enemy fire and crash-landed in hostile territory 500 meters from the friendly unit. With complete disregard for his own safety, Lieutenant Halstead commenced an approach to the disabled aircraft while simultaneously expending all remaining rockets and delivering a heavy volume of machine-gun fire around the damaged helicopter. Although the evacuation aircraft was receiving intense enemy antitank rocket and small-arms fire, he fearlessly continued his gallant efforts and executed a landing beside the downed crew members. Despite the hostile fire impacting nearby, he steadfastly remained on the ground until all the survivors had boarded his aircraft and, skillfully maneuvering his dangerously overloaded helicopter through the accurate fire, sustained additional damage as he departed the hazardous area. His heroic actions and extraordinary aeronautical skill inspired all who observed him and undoubtedly saved the lives of five Marines. By his courage, intrepid fighting spirit, and selfless devotion to duty in the face of grave personal danger, Lieutenant Halstead sustained and enhanced the highest traditions of the Marine Corps and the United States Naval Service.

HAMMOND, ROBERT J.

Citation: For extraordinary heroism as a crewmember of the USS PUEBLO (AGER-2) during their period of captivity in North Korea from 24 January to 23 December 1968. Following his capture, Sergeant Hammond, through his unyielding resistance and fierce loyalty to his shipmates and his country, became a symbol of resistance, courage, and dedication to the United States. This infuriated the North Koreans, who singled him out for more frequent and far more severe brutalities than were administered to the other prisoners. When the North Koreans learned that the PUEBLO crew had duped them in their international propaganda efforts, they intensified their efforts to break the will and spirit of the crew through the administration of indiscriminate beatings. Realizing that many of his shipmates were in danger of being permanently injured or killed, Sergeant Hammond willingly attempted to sacrifice his own life in order that his shipmates might be spared further torture. The following day the North Koreans ceased their beatings and tortures. Sergeant Hammond's devotion to duty and heroic actions against seemingly impossible odds reflected great credit upon himself and upheld the highest traditions of the Marine Corps and the United States Naval Service.

HAMPTON, GREGORY O.

Citation: For extraordinary heroism on 20 August 1969 while serving with friendly foreign forces engaged in armed conflict against enemy aggressor forces in the Republic of Vietnam. As an M-60 machine-gun operator, Seaman Hampton took part in a two-boat night patrol on the Vam Co Dong River. When sounds of approaching personnel on the beach were detected, his unit held its fire, due to lack of visibility, until a better target could be obtained. Suddenly, a hand grenade was tossed aboard his patrol boat and landed in the darkness. Quick to act, Seaman Hampton called to all personnel to take cover, dived across the wet slippery deck, succeeded in locating the lethal weapon, and hurled it over the side of the patrol boat. As the grenade hit the water, it exploded and showered the craft with water and shrapnel. Seaman Hampton then manned the M-60 machine gun and began to deliver suppressive fire on the suspected enemy position until his boat could clear the kill zone. His craft received one rocket round close aboard as it cleared the zone. Discovering that no damage had been inflicted, the patrol boat returned to make a second firing run on the enemy position. By his daring initiative, unfaltering courage, and heroic spirit of self-sacrifice in the face of almost certain death, Seaman Hampton was directly instrumental in saving many lives, along with his patrol boat. His unswerving devotion to duty was in keeping with the highest traditions of the United States Naval Service.

*HANCOCK, EUGENE S.

Citation: For extraordinary heroism on 24 February 1969 while serving as a Corpsman with Company "I", Third Battalion, Seventh Marines, First Marine Division, in connection with operations against enemy aggressor forces in the Republic of Vietnam. With a squad from Company "I" conducting a search and destroy operation east of Highway 5 near La Chau (2) in Quang Nam Province, when the unit came under a heavy volume of small-arms, automatic-weapons, and rocket-propelled grenade fire from a concealed and well-entrenched North Vietnamese Army company and sustained several casualties, Petty Officer Hancock immediately proceeded to the assistance of three casualties, treated their wounds and, aided by his comrades, removed all three men to a position of relative safety. Upon observing a critically-wounded Marine who was lying in an area dangerously exposed to the intense enemy fire, Petty Officer Hancock maneuvered across the fire-swept terrain and methodically applied tourniquets to the Marine's legs to stop the profuse bleeding. Assured of the casualty's immediate evacuation to friendly lines, Petty Office Hancock then valiantly ran through the intense hostile fire to yet another seriously injured comrade, but was himself mortally wounded by automatic-weapons fire before he could reach the Marine. By his heroic and inspiring efforts, Petty Officer Hancock was directly instrumental in saving the lives of four Marines. His courage, bold initiative, and selfless devotion to duty in the face of heavy enemy fire were in keeping with the highest traditions of the United States Naval Service.

HANSON, ANTHONY C.

Citation: For extraordinary heroism on 2 July 1967 while serving as combat aircrewman aboard a search and rescue helicopter embarked in USS REEVES (DLG-24). When the helicopter rescue of a wounded U. S. Air Force pilot, downed by hostile fire, was rendered impossible due to extensive jungle growth, Petty Officer Hanson, with full knowledge that enemy ground forces were closing the rescue scene, descended 150 feet from his helicopter to the wounded pilot, disengaged the latter from his parachute and, after carrying the downed airman one hundred yards through the dense undergrowth, fastened him to the hoisting equipment and guided him into the hovering helicoptr. By his heroic action and fearless devotion to duty, Petty Officer Hanson was directly instrumental in saving a life. His inspiring efforts were in keeping with the highest traditions of the United States Naval Service.

HARRINGTON, MYRON C.

Citation: For extraordinary heroism while serving as Commanding Officer for Company D, First Battalion, Fifth Marines, First Marine Division (Reinforced), in connection with operations against the enemy in the Republic of Vietnam. On the afternoon of 23 February 1968, Company D was attacking a well entrenched North Vietnamese Army force that was occupying a fortified section of the wall surrounding the Hue Citadel. As the Marines maneuvered forward, they began receiving a heavy volume of small arms, automatic weapons, mortar and antitank rocket fire. Realizing the seriousness of the situation, Captain Harrington skillfully deployed his 3.5 rocket teams into advantageous firing positions. Continuously moving from one position to another, he pinpointed enemy emplacements and skillfully directed the fire of his men. After silencing four hostile positions, he requested supporting arms fire and skillfully adjusted 60mm mortar fire to within twenty-five meters of the forward elements of his company, while simultaneously adjusting artillery fire. Disregarding his own safety, Captain Harrington then fearlessly maneuvered to the point of heaviest contact and, rallying his men, boldly led a determined assault against the enemy soldiers. Shouting words of encouragement to his men, he skillfully maneuvered his unit forward and directed the Marines' fire upon the hostile emplacements. Largely due to his resolute determination and intrepid fighting spirit, his men overran the hostile positions and routed the North Vietnamese soldiers, accounting for twenty-five enemy soldiers confirmed killed. By his courage, superb leadership and unfaltering devotion to duty in the face of extreme personal danger, Captain Harrington upheld the highest traditions of the Marine Corps and the United States Naval Service.

*HARTSOE, DAVID E.

Citation: For extraordinary heroism while serving as a Machine Gunner with Company L, Third Battalion, Ninth Marines, Third Marine Division (Reinforced) in the Republic of Vietnam on the evening of 20 May 1967. Company L was moving to bring a relief force to an embattled sister company when it engaged a strong enemy blocking force. Private First Class Hartsoe volunteered as point man to lead the company through the darkness to Company K. The enemy opened up on the relief force, and he positioned his gun in the foremost position. After a vicious fire fight the platoon was forced to withdraw to regroup. Private First Class Hartsoe knew that without the fire power of his gun, the platoon would be unable to recover the casualties and carry them to safety. Calmly accepting the consequences of their action, he and his team leader held their position under heavy automatic fire and a barrage of grenades, delivering covering fire while the others pulled out of the entrapped area. With complete disregard for his own safety, he held his own position until mortally wounded. By his dauntless courage, indomitable fighting spirit and loyal devotion to duty, Private First Class Hartsoe was instrumental in saving several Marine lives and thereby upheld the highest traditions of the Marine Corps and the United States Naval Service. He gallantly gave his life for his country.

HAYENGA, WILLIAM E., JR.

Citation: For extraordinary heroism on 4 February 1968 while engaged in armed conflict in the Republic of Vietnam. During Operation BOLD DRAGON I, Fireman Hayenga, as engineman on board River Patrol Boat (PBR) 731, participated in a four-PBR combat patrol on the Rach Hong Nhu River to assist a Vietnamese unit pinned down by a Viet Cong company. When PBR 728 was hit by three rockets and forced to beach in the middle of the ambush site, PBR 731, having also taken a direct rocket hit, returned to the stricken boat to attempt rescue of its crew. One crew member was rescued shortly after beaching. Realizing the gravity of the situation, Fireman Hayenga volunteered to search for the four missing crew members. Unarmed, he jumped ashore and made his way upstream toward the partially-sunken boat in search of his comrades. Finding no one on board the boat, he continued his search among the numerous thatched hutches along the river bank, and succeeded in locating two of the crewmen hidden in a drainage ditch. Both men were in a state of shock and one had sustained a serious leg wound. Assisting the wounded man and urging the other onward, Fireman Hayenga started to lead them back to PBR 731. Enemy fire was so effective at one point that the men were forced to crawl approximately thirty yards across an open space. On the other side of the clearing, Fireman Hayenga found a third crew member who was disoriented and in a state of shock. Upon reaching the embankment leading down to PBR 731, he sent the two ambulatory sailors to the boat and, once they were aboard, assisted the wounded man down the embankment and onto the boat. The Boat Commander of PBR 728 made his way to the rescue PBR approximately two minutes later, thus completing the rescue operation. Fireman Hayenga's heroic actions in the face of intense enemy fire were directly responsible for saving the lives of three of his comrades and were in keeping with the highest traditions of the United States Naval Service.

HAYES, DANIEL J.

Citation: For extraordinary heroism while serving as a Squad Leader with Company L, Third Battalion, Fifth Marines, First Marine Division, in connection with operations against the enemy in the Republic of Vietnam. On 28 November 1968, Lance Corporal Hayes was directed to escort a sniper to a tree line some distance forward of the company's defensive perimeter and to provide security for the man while he was in position. Utilizing what little natural cover was available, Lance Corporal Hayes skillfully maneuvered his eight-man squad across an open rice paddy and was into the tree line when the Marines came under a heavy volume of small arms and automatic weapons fire from a numerically superior hostile force occupying well-concealed emplacements. In the initial burst of fire, five Marines were seriously wounded, including Lance Corporal Hayes. Ignoring his painful injuries, he refused medical attention and provided covering fire while his wounded companions were treated. Quickly deploying his men into covered fighting positions, he directed their suppressive fire upon the enemy soldiers. Observing a casualty being further subjected to hostile fire, he unhesitatingly threw himself across the man's body to protect him from additional injury. With exceptional tactical skill, he then regrouped his men for an orderly withdrawal across the open terrain to the company lines and, disregarding his own safety, provided covering fire for his squad. His heroic and timely actions inspired all who observed him and undoubtedly saved the lives of his Marines. By his courage, bold initiative, and selfless devotion to duty in the face of grave personal danger, Lance Corporal Hayes upheld the highest traditions of the Marine Corps and the United States Naval Service.

HAZELBAKER, VINCIL W.

Citation: For extraordinary heroism while serving with Marine Observation Squadron TWO, Marine Aircraft Group SIXTEEN, First Marine Aircraft Wing during operations against enemy forces in Vietnam on 8 August 1966. While flying in support of ground operations in the vicinity of Ban Hieu, Major Hazelbaker observed two unsuccessful attempts to deliver ammunition to a Marine reaction force which had become surrounded by North Vietnamese forces. Realizing that the supplies were needed desperately by the besieged ground force, Major Hazelbaker daringly maneuvered his UH-1E helicopter through the darkness and intense hostile fire and skillfully landed near the Marines' position. Without regard for his own precarious situation, he resupplied the ground unit with three thousand rounds of his own supply of ammunition, and thereby provided the defenders with temporary means of continuing their battle against overwhelming enemy force. Returning to Dong Ha Airfield, Major Hazelbaker courageously volunteered to return to the hazardous area with an additional load of ammunition for the same troops. With keen airmanship and fortitude, he again braved withering fire from North Vietnamese forces on all sides as close as fifteen yards to the position. Shortly after he landed with eight hundred pounds of direly needed ammunition, his aircraft was disabled by enemy fire, and two of his crewmen were wounded. With exceptional presence of mind and composure, Major Hazelbaker contacted the infantry unit and was advised that their officers had been wounded or killed. Displaying superior professionalism and firm leadership, he immediately assumed command of ground operations, reorganizing the defense, supervising distribution of ammunition, ensuring that the casualties were cared for and controlling supporting air strikes. Largely as a result of his determined and gallant effort, the Marine unit was able to break the impetus of the vicious enemy attack and maintain the position until daylight, when retraction could be effected. By his extraordinary courage in the face of extreme danger, bold aeronautical skill, and unfaltering dedication to duty throughout, Major Hazelbaker upheld the highest traditions of the Marine Corps and the United States Naval Service.

HELLE, RONALD B.

Citation: For extraordinary heroism while participating in a pacification operation in the vicinity of Combat Base Baldy with his unit which was located in a popular force compound in the Moo Bai District, Republic of Vietnam. On the night of 28 January 1971, Sergeant Helle, an artillery scout and observer with Company G, Second Battalion, Fifth Marines was sitting in the command post and talking with other members of his unit and a newspaper correspondent. Stepping outside to make a routine check of the area, Sergeant Helle was struck on the back by an object which he quickly recognized to be a grenade. He then threw himself upon the missile and alerted everyone to take cover, following which he stood up and hurled the grenade out of the compound. By his prompt and courageous action in the face of almost certain death or serious injury to himself and other men in the vicinity, Sergeant Helle upheld the highest traditions of the Marine Corps and the United States Naval Service.

HENDERSON, BILLY K.

Citation: For extraordinary heroism while serving as a squad leader with Company H, Second Battalion, First Marines, First Marine Division, during operations against enemy forces in the Republic of Vietnam on the night of 17 July 1969. Occupying an ambush site when he spotted approximately twenty-five enemy soldiers heading toward his squad's position, Lance Corporal Henderson ordered his men to withhold their fire, surmising that the hostile group was the lead element of a much larger force. He then arranged for an on-call artillery fire mission. Later, when an approximately sixty additional hostile soldiers emerged from the tree line and prepared to attack the command post, Lance Corporal Henderson initiated the ambush and simultaneously called for supporting artillery fire. While directing his squad's fire, an enemy grenade landed among three of his companions. Reacting instantly, he threw himself on the grenade to prevent injury to the other Marines. Fortunately, the grenade failed to explode. Lance Corporal Henderson then stood upright and hurled the missile into the enemy's ranks, following which he resumed his fire-directing activities and called for fixed-wing air strikes until the enemy broke contact, having suffered heavy casualties. By his outstanding personal valor, aggressive leadership, and inspiring devotion to duty, Lance Corporal Henderson was directly responsible for saving the other members of his squad from probable serious injury or death. His courageous and heroic efforts reflect great credit upon himself, and were in keeping with the highest traditions of the Marine Corps and of the United States Naval Service.

HENDRICKS, ROBERT L.

Citation: For extraordinary heroism while serving as the 60mm Mortar Section Leader with Company H, Second Battalion, Seventh Marines, First Marine Division, in connection with operations against insurgent (Viet Cong) forces in the Republic of Vietnam. On the night of 19 February 1968, Corporal Hendricks was directing the 60mm mortar section as it conducted routine fire missions around the company perimeter when he observed an object about the size of a hand grenade land approximately fifteen feet from the mortar position. Locating the object, he found that it was a rock and, reporting the incident to the command post, alerted personnel along the defensive perimeter. A few minutes later, another rock landed on top of the ammunition storage area to the front of the mortar position. Again, Corporal Hendricks alerted those manning defensive positions and continued to direct the fire missions. Fifteen minutes later, a fragmentation grenade landed near the mortar position and only a few feet from two men sleeping on the ground. Reacting instantly and with complete disregard for his own safety, Corporal Hendricks jumped over the sandbag wall around the position, threw himself on the armed grenade and shouted to his companions to take cover. When all the men had reached safety and it appeared that the grenade would not detonate, he removed the explosive device to a safe area where it was destroyed. By his courage, bold initiative, and selfless devotion to duty at great personal risk, Corporal Hendricks upheld the highest traditions of the Marine Corps and the United States Naval Service.

HERBERT, ROBERT S.

Citation: For extraordinary heroism on 11 August 1970 while serving as Weapons Officer in USS CANON (PG-90) engaged in armed conflict against enemy forces in the Republic of Vietnam. Lieutenant (jg) Herbert was directing the harassment and interdiction fire of his gun crews while proceeding up the narrow Bo De river when his vessel suddenly came under intense enemy rocket, automatic-weapons, and small-arms attack from an estimated forty-man force in concealed positions on both banks of the river. During the initial hail of enemy fire, he and the commanding officer were both seriously wounded. Despite his own serious wounds, Lieutenant (jg) Herbert immediately removed the commanding officer to a position of relative safety and then, further exposing himself to enemy fire, continued to direct and coordinate the ship's gun crews. Although weak from loss of blood, he managed to communicate with the bridge, relaying the commanding officer's orders and keeping the latter informed of the status of the ship's armament, propulsion, and known damage. Due to Lieutenant (jg) Herbert's excellent training of and communication with the gun crews, a deadly and effective suppressive barrage was continued even after he was unable to personally direct the fire. When crew members found him lying on the deck, Lieutenant (jg) Herbert directed them to aid the commanding officer first. By his outstanding courage and valiant efforts in the face of heavy enemy fire, Lieutenant (jg) Herbert was directly instrumental in preventing the enemy from inflicting additional personnel casualties and material damage to the ship. His heroic actions were in keeping with the highest traditions of the United States Naval Service.

*HERRERA, FELIPE

Citation: For extraordinary heroism while serving with Company A, First Reconnaissance Battalion, First Marine Division, in connection with operations against the enemy in the Republic of Vietnam. On the afternoon of 20 September 1968, Corporal Herrera was the machine gunner of a reconnaissance team operating near Thoung Duc in Quang Nam Province when he alertly observed a large hostile force maneuvering to attack the Marines. Reacting instantly, he warned his comrades of the approaching enemy, and almost immediately the patrol came under a heavy volume of hostile automatic weapons fire. With complete disregard for his own safety, Corporal Herrera boldly moved from his position and fearlessly assaulted the enemy soldiers to within ten meters of their location, killing six of the attackers and halting their advance. Continuing his determined efforts, he resolutely remained in his dangerously exposed position and delivered intense machine-gun fire against the enemy until he was mortally wounded. His heroic and timely actions inspired all who observed him and were instrumental in enabling his comrades to gain fire superiority and deploy into advantageous defensive positions. By his courage, aggressive fighting spirit, and steadfast devotion to duty, Corporal Herrera upheld the highest traditions of the Marine Corps and the United States Naval Service. He gallantly gave his life for his country.

*HERRON, LEE R.

Citation: For extraordinary heroism while serving as Executive Officer, Company A, First Battalion, Ninth Marines, Third Marine Division in the Republic of Vietnam on 22 February 1969. While patrolling north of Ashau Valley in Quang Tri Province, the lead elements of Company A came under intense fire and were pinned down by a large North Vietnamese Army force. First Lieutenant Herron maneuvered one of his platoons forward to reinforce the lead elements. When the second platoon commander was seriously wounded, he immediately assumed command and quickly organized the men into an assault force. Skillfully deploying his men, he led them in an aggressive attack until halted and pinned down by an extremely heavy volume of cross-fire from several enemy machine guns augmented by mortar, rocket-propelled grenade, small arms, and automatic weapons fire from the North Vietnamese emplacements, as well as numerous sniper positions in trees in the dense jungle canopy. Undaunted by the hostile rounds impacting around him, First Lieutenant Herron repeatedly exposed himself to enemy fire as he moved among his men to encourage them and urged them to inch forward to positions from which they could deliver more effective return fire. Aware that the fire from two mutually supporting hostile machine guns was holding his Marines in place and preventing the removal of the casualties, he completely disregarded his own safety as he exposed himself to North Vietnamese fire to direct a light antitank assault round which scored a direct hit on one of the machine gun bunkers. Boldly leaping to his feet, he fearlessly charged across the fire-swept terrain to hurl hand grenades and fire his weapon against the enemy emplacement, killing nine North Vietnamese soldiers who were in the bunker. While directing his men in the assault on the remaining bunker, First Lieutenant Herron was mortally wounded by enemy sniper fire. His heroic actions inspired his men to such aggressive action in coordinated company attack that 105 North Vietnamese soldiers were killed and the large bunker complex destroyed. By his courage, bold initiative and unwavering devotion to duty, First Lieutenant Herron upheld the highest traditions of the Marine Corps and the United States Naval Service. He gallantly gave his life for his country.

HICKEY, WILLIAM L.

Citation: For extraordinary heroism on 4 July 1966 as Senior Corpsman with Company K, Third Battalion, Ninth Marines, during a search and destroy operation in the Republic of Vietnam. When his company came under intense small-arms, automatic-weapons, and 57mm recoilless rifle fire from a numerically superior enemy force, Petty Officer Hickey braved the blistering enemy fire to move across an open field to aid a Marine trapped in an amphibian vehicle. Although he, himself, was wounded during this action, he succeeded in carrying the victim to a protected area. Realizing that two other corpsmen needed assistance in treating several casualties, he again exposed himself to the withering fire to reach their position and was wounded a second time. Disregarding the agonizing discomfort of his multiple injuries, he fearlessly moved about helping the other wounded and, upon reaching the company casualty collection point, was wounded a third time by an enemy rifle grenade. Displaying an uncommon devotion to his fellow comrades, Petty Officer Hickey refused evacuation for several hours so that he could render assistance and advice to the other corpsmen, remaining until all casualties could be treated and until evacuation of the seriously wounded was completed. His outstanding professional skill, and inspiring and unconquerable courage were in keeping with the highest traditions of the United States Naval Service.

HILGERS, JOHN J. W.

Citation: For extraordinary heroism as Battalion Operations Officer of the Second Battalion, Fourth Marines, Third Marine Division, in connection with operations against the enemy in Vietnam on 23 and 24 August 1966. During Operation PRAIRIE, when a company from

Captain Hilgers' battalion was attacked and surrounded by a numerically superior North Vietnamese force in the Thon Son Lam area, he immediately realized the seriousness of the situation and unhesitatingly volunteered to lead a reaction force to the company's aid. The battalion's disposition and the nature of its mission prevented dispatching one company as a unit, so a composite company was quickly formed and helilifted into the area just after dark. After analyzing the enemy's weaknesses, he fearlessly led his unit through 400 meters of enemy infested, dense, and unfamiliar jungle, dispatching one unit to halt the enemy's attack and neutralize deadly automatic weapons fire on the left flank. After joining the besieged unit, which was located in a bowl-shaped depression, Captain Hilgers selflessly exposed himself to heavy automatic weapons fire and grenades in order to move to the forward slope of the position to direct his forces better and insure that the beleaguered unit was obtaining the maximum support available. During the early morning hours of 24 August, the North Vietnamese launched three vicious assaults on the position, threatening to annihilate the trapped company. The combined force, under Captain Hilgers' inspiring and aggressive leadership, successfully repulsed each attack, inflicting heavy casualties on the enemy. Throughout the seemingly endless fourteen-hour battle, he repeatedly exposed himself to the devastating enemy fire to direct and control fire support and encourage his gallant fighting men. As a result of his heroic actions, the combined force successfully defeated the enemy attacks and relieved the pressure on the besieged company. By his outstanding leadership, fearless determination, great professional skill, and unfaltering dedication to duty in the face of extreme danger, Captain Hilgers reflected great credit upon himself and the Marine Corps and upheld the highest traditions of the United States Naval Service.

*HILL, LAMONT D.

Citation: For extraordinary heroism as a Machine Gunner serving with the Weapons Platoon, Company "I", Third Battalion, Fourth Marines, Third Marine Division in Vietnam on 6 March 1967. While conducting a company sweep near the village of Tan Lich in Quang Tri Province, Private First Class Hill was attached to the Third Platoon when it was subjected to heavy automatic weapons fire from a well entrenched enemy. In the initial burst of enemy fire, he was fatally wounded. However, realizing the gravity of the situation, Private First

Class Hill, disregarding his own serious and painful wound, manned his machine gun and brought deadly, well aimed fire to bear on the enemy. Refusing medical treatment except when he stopped to reload his weapon, he provided covering fire so that his wounded comrades could be moved to defiladed positions of relative safety. Then he immediately shifted his weapon and began to provide a base of fire on the entrenched enemy which enabled two squads of the platoon to make a successful assault, killing twenty of the enemy. Private First Class Hill, succumbing to his wound, fell unconscious upon his machine gun. His heroic actions were responsible for saving the life of at least one Marine and were instrumental in the defeat of the enemy with no further friendly casualties. Private First Class Hill's courageous actions, aggressive fighting spirit and loyal devotion to duty reflected great credit upon himself and the Marine Corps and upheld the highest traditions of the United States Naval Service. He gallantly gave his life for his country.

HOAPILI, JOHN

Citation: For extraordinary heroism while serving as a Platoon Commander with Company K, Third Battalion, Twenty-sixth Marines, Third Marine Division, in connection with operations against the enemy in the Republic of Vietnam. On 9 May 1968, Gunnery Sergeant (then Staff Sergeant) Hoapili led a patrol composed of two five-man teams into an ambush position in Quang Tri Province. Arriving at the designated site, he skillfully deployed his two teams into mutually supporting positions. Alertly observing numerous North Vietnamese soldiers approaching his position, he immediately delivered a heavy volume of fire against the enemy, killing two hostile soldiers and initiating the ambush. After his men killed the remaining North Vietnamese, the Marines were conducting a thorough search of the area when they suddenly came under intense hostile fire. Reacting instantly, Sergeant Hoapili led his men to a predesignated rendezvous and established a perimeter defense. Pinpointing an enemy machine-gun emplacement, he moved about the hazardous area, shouting words of encouragement to his men and gathering numerous hand grenades. Disregarding his own safety, he fearlessly rushed across the fire-swept terrain hurling hand grenades at the hostile position. As he maneuvered forward, he was knocked to the ground and seriously wounded when an enemy grenade detonated near him. Ignoring his painful injuries, he regained his feet and aggressively continued forward, delivering automatic rifle fire which killed the North Vietnamese soldiers and silenced their machine gun. His heroic and timely actions inspired all who observed him and forced the enemy to break contact and flee. By his daring initiative, intrepid fighting spirit, and unwavering devotion to duty in the face of extreme personal danger, Sergeant Hoapili contributed significantly to the accomplishment of his unit's mission and upheld the highest traditions of the Marine Corps and the United States Naval Service.

*HODGKINS, GUY M.

Citation: For extraordinary heroism while serving as a Platoon Sergeant with Company I, Third Battalion, Ninth Marines, Third Marine Division, near An Hoa, Republic of Vietnam on 3 September 1966. While moving with the First Squad of his platoon, Sergeant Hodgkins came upon fifteen Viet Cong retreating along a trail and an adjoining trench line, and received heavy enemy automatic weapons fire. Reacting immediately, his men returned fire, forcing the Viet Cong to break contact and flee. To prevent the enemy's escape, he directed the squad in an aggressive pursuit of the Viet Cong for two hundred meters. Desperately setting up a hasty ambush in and around a concrete building, the enemy took cover and awaited their pursuers. Sergeant Hodgkins was cautiously leading his men forward when they suddenly received intense enemy fire, immediately sustaining three casualties. With complete disregard for his own safety, he courageously advanced, under heavy enemy fire, returning fire with a fallen Marines's weapon. Having expended all his rifle ammunition, he boldly continued to advance and, with only a grenade in each hand, assaulted the building from which the Viet Cong were delivering their most effective fire. He fearlessly moved to within point-blank range before throwing his grenades. His brave action resulted in three enemy deaths and the neutralization of Viet Cong fire from the building. Having accomplished his mission, he became the target of intense enemy fire and grenades and was finally struck and mortally wounded. Sergeant Hodgkins' heroic leadership, courage, and dedication to duty inspired his squad to assault and rout the entire enemy force. This resolute fighting spirit and great personal valor in the face of heavy odds reflected the highest credit upon himself and were in keeping with the highest traditions of the Marine Corps and the United States Naval Service. He gallantly gave his life in the cause of freedom.

HOFF, JOHN R., JR.

Citation: For extraordinary heroism while serving as a Platoon Commander with Company E, First Reconnaissance Battalion, First Marine Division in connection with combat operations against the enemy in the Republic of Vietnam. On 7 April 1970, while leading a seven-man patrol through a heavily jungled area southwest of Danang, Second Lieutenant Hoff detected signs of enemy soldiers in a hut and launched an aggressive assault, resulting in the destruction of the hut and four enemy dead. Continuing his mission, he led his men deeper into the confines of the camp where the Marines came under a heavy volume of grenade launcher fire from enemy soldiers occupying well-concealed emplacements. Although outnumbered, Second Lieutenant Hoff seized the initiative and led a counterattack against the enemy, boldly moving to a dangerously exposed vantage point from which he hurled hand grenades at the hostile soldiers. As a result of his valiant efforts and the accurate fire of his men, the enemy abandoned their positions and retreated. Shortly thereafter, Second Lieutenant Hoff located a large cache of arms and ammunition and was passing the supplies to his men when the patrol was subjected to intense grenade launcher fire from enemy soldiers who had maneuvered to a nearby position. Despite the rounds impacting around him, Second Lieutenant Hoff tenaciously held his ground, hurling hand grenades and delivering rifle fire with such accuracy that he accounted for several enemy casualties and forced the remainder of the enemy to retreat. The reconnaissance efforts of the patrol having now been seriously compromised, Second Lieutenant Hoff led his men to a nearby suitable landing zone and skillfully adjusted supporting Marine artillery fire around the site until they were safely extracted the following morning. His heroic and determined actions inspired all who observed him and contributed to the success of the mission without sustaining a single Marine casualty. By his courage, aggressive leadership, and unwavering devotion to duty, he upheld the highest traditions of the Marine Corps and of the United States Naval Service.

HOLMES, BILLIE D.

Citation: For extraordinary heroism on the night of 15-16 June 1966 as a Medical Corpsman, Company C, First Reconnaissance Battalion in the Republic of Vietnam. Serving with a platoon which was attacked by a determined and well-trained North Vietnamese battalion after the platoon had established an observation post deep within Viet Cong-controlled territory, Petty Officer Holmes, in the face of the intense enemy fire, left the meager cover of his position on the perimeter to render aid to the wounded. Oblivious to the shouted warnings of his Platoon Leader to take cover, he repeatedly exposed himself to the hostile fire by moving from one wounded man to the next, administering emergency treatment. On two separate occasions when there were enemy grenades exploding, he covered the body of his wounded companion with his own to prevent further injury. Although twice painfully wounded, he continued giving aid and comfort to the wounded throughout the night and morning. Petty Officer Holmes' outstanding professional skill, extraordinary heroism, and deep concern for his comrades were in keeping with the highest traditions of the United States Naval Service.

HOLMES, WALTER C.

Citation: For outstanding heroism as a 60mm Mortar Section Leader serving with Company B, First Battalion, Ninth Marines, in Vietnam on 27 December 1965. Sergeant Holmes was providing support for a combat patrol in the vicinity of Danang when a force of sixty to eighty well-armed Viet Cong opened fire from concealed positions about fifteen meters away. Situated thirty meters to the rear from where the intense fire immediately felled several Marines, he fearlessly advanced toward the guerrillas, who were positioned along high sand dunes. When the Viet Cong attempted to overrun the patrol, Sergeant Holmes, with relentless fighting spirit, stood his ground and fired with an accuracy that drove back the enemy and provided cover for Marines who were maneuvering forward. Taking a mortar and all the rounds he could carry from a casualty, he aggressively moved to higher ground, directing twelve rounds, in a matter of seconds, at the fleeing Viet Cong. With continued presence of mind, he organized a hasty defense and prepared for medical evacuation and relief forces. By his exceptional courage in the face of extreme peril, Sergeant Holmes saved the patrol from further casualties and upheld the highest traditions of the Marine Corps and the United States Naval Service.

*HONEYCUTT, JAMES E.

Citation: For extraordinary heroism while serving with the Third

Force Reconnaissance Company, Third Reconnaissance Battalion, Third Marine Division (Reinforced), in connection with operations against the enemy in the Republic of Vietnam on 16 February 1968. While on patrol southeast of Con Thien, Private Honeycutt's team established an ambush when seven enemy soldiers were observed moving toward their position. During the initial exchange of fire, one Marine was seriously wounded. Disregarding his own safety, Private Honeycutt moved to an exposed area where he provided covering fire for the corpsman who was treating the injured man. After annihilating the enemy force, the team moved toward a landing zone to evacuate the casualty. As the team moved forward, they were taken under devastating enemy small-arms, automatic-weapons and mortar fire from an estimated two companies of North Vietnamese soldiers. In the initial burst of enemy fire, three Marines were wounded. With complete disregard for his own safety, Private Honeycutt moved across the fire-swept terrain to the side of an injured comrade and administered first aid. He then provided covering fire and assisted in moving the casualties across forty meters of fire-swept terrain to a waiting evacuation helicopter. Displaying exceptional courage, he remained behind to deliver a heavy volume of fire that suppressed hostile fire sufficiently to allow the team to embark. Only after all were aboard did he then embark. Realizing that a wounded man remained in the zone and that the injured team leader had debarked to search the hazardous area, he unhesitatingly jumped from the helicopter to aid his fellow Marines. Upon the arrival of the second extraction aircraft, he then assisted his wounded comrades aboard. By his bold initiative, intrepid fighting spirit and loyal devotion to duty, Private Honeycutt reflected great credit upon himself and the Marine Corps and upheld the highest traditions of the United States Naval Service.

*HOPKINS, MICHAEL E.

Citation: For extraordinary heroism while serving as an Automatic Rifleman with Company K, Third Battalion, Ninth Marines, in the Republic of Vietnam on 4 July 1966. During a search and destroy operation, the company was taken under heavy small-arms, automatic-weapons, and 57mm recoilless rifle fire from a numerically superior Viet Cong force. When an LVT was hit by a 57mm recoilless rifle round, Private First Class Hopkins immediately ran through the hail of small-arms fire to aid the injured crew. After he had helped remove the injured men from the LVT, he and three other Marines were sent to a forward position in order to give covering fire. As the ammunition ran low, Private First Class Hopkins repeatedly exposed himself to heavy enemy fire as he ran across open ground to the supply point. After his sixth trip, he saw his squad leader fall from wounds. Although exhausted from the heat and carrying ammunition, he courageously exposed himself again to heavy incoming fire in order to administer immediate first aid to his squad leader. As he was treating the wounded Marine, he noticed a corpsman attempting to maneuver to his position. Seizing his rifle once again, he began giving covering fire to enable the corpsman to attain his objective. Seconds after the corpsman reached the location an enemy rifle grenade exploded nearby killing the squad leader and wounding the corpsman. Realizing that the enemy fire was too intense for anyone to come to their aid, Private First Class Hopkins, in a final valiant act of complete self-sacrifice, deliberately exposed himself in an effort to direct attention away from the wounded, absorbing with his own body the full force of the deadly enemy fire. Through his extraordinary loyalty and initiative in the face of almost certain death, he saved his comrades from further injury and possible loss of life, thereby upholding the highest traditions of the Marine Corps and the United States Naval Service. He gallantly gave his life for his country.

HOUGHTON, KENNETH J.

Citation: For extraordinary heroism as Commanding Officer, Fifth Marines, First Marine Division (Reinforced) in the Republic of Vietnam from 26 May to 5 June 1967. The Fifth Marine Regiment was launched on Operation UNION II to track down the remnants of the 21st North Vietnamese Regiment, which had been thoroughly decimated by them nine days previous. Responding to intelligence reports that the enemy was attempting to withdraw to the western mountains, Colonel Houghton committed two battalions in pursuit. The First Battalion swept overland while the Third Battalion was enveloped by helicopter near Cam La. The Third Battalion met with heavy resistance, but completely overran the enemy positions, causing many casualties. He was constantly in the operational area, bravely exposing himself to all the hazards of the battlefield. Colonel Houghton revised his tactics when intelligence reports indicated a much larger enemy force in the area, which was identified as the 3d North Vietnamese Regiment and pointed to a buildup along the Suio Cau Doi River, in the vicinity of Vinh Huy (2). Instantly reacting, he launched his attack from the east, with the First and Third Battalions abreast and the Second in reserve. On 2 June, the First Battalion came under intense enemy mortar, recoilless rifle and automatic weapons fire, indicating contact with the main force of the 3d North Vietnamese Army force. While the First and Third Battalions maintained heavy pressure on the enemy, he committed the Second Battalion to assault the enemy's flank. Although wounded at this time, he continued to aggressively advance on the enemy with renewed determination. Colonel Houghton launched a bold night attack which smashed through the enemy defenses, and annihilated the large enemy force. By his outstanding leadership, gallant fighting spirit and bold initiative, he contributed materially to the success of the First Marine Division, thereby upholding the highest traditions of the Marine Corps and the United States Naval Service.

HOUSE, CHARLES A.

Citation: For extraordinary heroism as Commanding Officer, Marine Medium Helicopter Squadron ONE HUNDRED SIXTY-THREE, in action in the Republic of Vietnam on 9 and 10 March 1966. Colonel House's helicopter was disabled by intense enemy fire in the landing zone at As Hau, where the garrison had been under siege for several days. After ensuring that all personnel had abandoned the aircraft, Colonel House immediately rallied his crew members and joined a group of seventy exhausted survivors of the garrison. With inspiring leadership and dogged determination, he skillfully led the group into the jungle to escape capture. Chopping a trail through the dense underbrush, he moved into the hills which surrounded the outpost, cleverly maneuvering between hostile positions and successfully evading enemy search patrols. Although the group was subjected to harassing fire throughout the march, Colonel House managed to overcome the language barrier and instill in the Vietnamese a sense of confidence and encouragement which sustained them through the ordeal. With constant concern for the welfare of the survivors, many of whom were wounded, he halted the march several times to allow them to rest, stalwartly standing watch while others slept. When helicopters were sighted and signaled on the following afternoon, Colonel House's brilliant leadership motivated all who were able to help clear a position from which the rescue was subsequently effected. His valiant effort and determination throughout contributed in large measure to saving the members of his crew and many Special Forces and Vietnamese defenders from capture or death at the hands of the Viet Cong. By his intrepid fighting spirit, extraordinary ability as a leader, and unswerving dedication to duty, Colonel House upheld the highest traditions of the Marine Corps and the United States Naval Service.

*HOWARD, BILLY

Citation: For extraordinary heroism as Company Gunnery Sergeant, Company E, Second Battalion, Fourth Marines, during Operation TEXAS in Quang Ngai Province, Republic of Vietnam on 21 March 1966. Upon arrival in its assigned helicopter landing zone, Company E came under withering enemy small-arms and automatic weapons fire from three directions. The volume and effectiveness of this fire forced the battalion to modify its tactical plan and move Company E to a newly designated line of departure. Braving heavy enemy fire, Gunnery Sergeant Howard moved from heli-team to heli-team as they arrived in the landing zone providing instructions for this redisposition of forces. Once deployed on their assigned line of departure, and upon completion of preparatory air and artillery fires, Company E commenced an assault against the hamlet of Phuong Dinh (2). After crossing an open rice paddy, and when within twenty-five meters of the objective, Company E was struck with a vicious fusillade of small arms, automatic weapons, recoilless rifle, and mortar fire. The volume and intensity of the enemy fire immediately inflicted numerous friendly casualties and had the majority of the company pinned down, unable to move in any direction. Seeing his Company Commander trapped in heavy cross fire and incapable of movement, Gunnery Sergeant Howard immediately seized the initiative and dashed forward from a relatively secure position to the point of furthest contact. With full knowledge that his life was in jeopardy, he moved among the dead and wounded and supervised their evacuation to the rear. In complete defiance of the enemy and braving certain death, he rallied his fellow Marines to leave their covered positions and continue the assault. His indomitable fighting spirit, fearless leadership, and outstanding courage inspired his men to charge aggressively forward and destroy the enemy fortifications. Mortally wounded during this assault, Gunnery Sergeant Howard, by his great personal valor and unswerving devotion to duty, reflected great credit upon himself, the Marine Corps and the United States Naval Service. He gallantly gave his life for his country.

*HOWELL, GATLIN J.

Citation: For extraordinary heroism while serving as Intelligence Officer, First Battalion, Ninth Marines, Third Marine Division (Reinforced), in the Republic of Vietnam from 2 to 7 July 1967. While manning the command bunker at Con Thien on 2 July, First Lieutenant Howell was closely monitoring the progress of Company B, First Battalion, as it became heavily engaged with an estimated two battalions of North Vietnamese Army Regulars near the Demilitarized Zone. When the unit suffered heavy casualties and was in danger of being overrun, he volunteered to lead a relief force to rescue the beleaguered Marines. Displaying exceptional leadership and tactical skill during his advance, he fearlessly exposed himself to enemy mortar and small-arms fire as he kept the relief column intact, pointing out directions of fire for the tanks and providing effective flank security as he moved rapidly to Company B's position. Immediately evaluating the situation when he arrived in the battle area, he established a defensive perimeter and moved to rescue the forward elements of the besieged company. As he searched for the wounded, he observed two men in a hole fifteen meters beyond the friendly lines. With complete disregard for his own safety, First Lieutenant Howell ran through heavy small-arms fire to treat the men and carry them to the safety of the perimeter. When his right flank was threatened by a North Vietnamese squad, he directed heavy fire against the assaulting force, undoubtedly saving the lives of at least three injured Marines caught between the enemy and the friendly lines. Subject to intense enemy mortar and artillery fire and road mines that disabled two tanks, he moved the casualties to a landing zone. After ensuring that the casualty evacuation process was well under way, he refused medical treatment for himself and returned to the forward area to determine that all the wounded had been moved. During a rocket attack on 7 July at Con Thien, First Lieutenant Howell was killed in action. By his intrepid fighting spirit, daring initiative, and selfless devotion to duty at great personal risk, First Lieutenant Howell was instrumental in saving many of his fellow Marines from capture, injury or possible death, and upheld the highest traditions of the Marine Corps and the United States Naval Service. He gallantly gave his life for his country.

*HUBBARD, ROBERT W.

Citation: For extraordinary heroism while serving as an Advisor to the Revolutionary Development Cadre, Thua Thien Province, in the city of Hue, Republic of Vietnam, from 31 January to 4 February 1968. On 31 January, while carrying out his advisory duties within the city of Hue, the quarters in which Captain Hubbard was temporarily residing, together with two military and two civilian personnel, came under intense enemy ground attack. Quickly assuming command, he organized a defense against the repeated assaults from the enemy forces and covered the front door along with two of his companions. Every attempt by the enemy to overrun their strongpoint was thwarted, until finally, after two of his group were seriously wounded, withdrawal was necessary. Quickly assessing the situation, he braved the intense enemy fire while searching for a covered route through which his group could withdraw. Despite the ever increasing enemy fire, he elected to cover the withdrawal of his unit and inflicted numerous casualties upon the enemy. During the ensuing days, the enemy maintained almost complete control of the city of Hue, and Captain Hubbard's group of men found it necessary to move from shelter to shelter to escape death or possible capture. Although acting in the capacity as a civilian advisor at the time of the Tet Offensive, Captain Hubbard's skill as a Marine infantry officer instantly surfaced during this crisis. He was constantly moving, administering to the wounded, foraging for food and water for his companions, searching for assistance from friendly forces, and returning deadly accurate fire on the enemy. On 4 February, with all food, water and ammunition depleted, he led the group, armed only with a single hand grenade, in an attempt to reach friendly forces south of the city. During this time he was hit and mortally wounded by small-arms fire. By his brilliant leadership, intrepid fighting spirit and exceptional fortitude, Captain Hubbard was largely responsible for the escape of his fellow Americans. His outstanding courage and valiant devotion to duty reflected the highest credit upon himself, the Marine Corps and the United States Naval Service. He gallantly gave his life for his country.

HUFFCUT, WILLIAM H., II

Citation: For extraordinary heroism while serving as a Pilot with Marine Observation Squadron Six, Marine Aircraft Group Thirty-Six, First Marine Aircraft Wing in connection with combat operations against the enemy in the Republic of Vietnam. On the morning of 28 September 1969, Major Huffcut launched a Tactical Air Controller (Airborne) aboard an aircraft assigned the mission of conducting an aerial reconnaissance south of the Demilitarized Zone. Receiving urgent request to support an infantry unit which was heavily engaged in combat with a hostile force, he immediately proceeded to the designated area and was informed by the commander of the ground unit that his men were pinned down by machine-gun fire. Undaunted by the extremely heavy volume of enemy fire directed at his aircraft, Major Huffcut executed repeated attacks and delivered his ordnance with such devastating effectiveness that the hostile fire was suppressed sufficiently to enable the Marines to move to a more tenable position. When a flight of F-4 Phantom aircraft arrived, Major Huffcut skillfully coordinated and directed accurate air strikes upon the enemy emplacement, and carried out a series of strafing runs at right angles to the attack aircraft, a tactic which effectively distracted the enemy from firing on the Phantoms. As a result, the hostile machine gun emplacement was destroyed. Shortly thereafter, he skillfully executed the same flight and attack patterns on repeated passes which succeeded in destroying a second enemy position. Subsequently responding to an emergency request to assist a Marine reconnaissance team which was pinned down by a large enemy force, Major Huffcut expertly maneuvered his aircraft on both simulated and live rocket and strafing runs, and skillfully directed the air strikes of A-4 Skyhawk aircraft which routed the enemy. By his dauntless courage, superb airmanship, and unwavering devotion to duty in the face of great personal danger, Major Huffcut inspired all who observed him and upheld the highest traditions of the Marine Corps and the United States Naval Service.

HUGGINS, MICHAEL A.

Citation: For conspicuous gallantry and intrepidity in action while serving as a Rifleman with Company G, Second Battalion, Fourth Marines, Third Marine Division in connection with combat operations against the enemy in the Republic of Vietnam. On the morning of 27 June 1969, Private First Class Huggins' fire team, having secured a landing zone northwest of Fire Support Base Sierra in Quang Tri Province, was maneuvering up a hill when he observed a North Vietnamese Army squad in an ambush position. Reacting instantly, he skillfully deployed his men and initiated contact with the enemy. Although painfully wounded by the initial burst of hostile fire, Private First Class Huggins led his comrades in an assault against the enemy positions. Courageously moving throughout the fire-swept terrain, he shouted instructions and encouraged his men as he directed their fire at the enemy. When a hostile hand grenade landed between him and another Marine, Private First Class Huggins immediately picked up the grenade and threw it back at the enemy where it subsequently exploded. Relentlessly pursuing his objective, he continued his assault against the hostile bunkers, forcing the enemy to break contact. His heroic and timely actions inspired all who observed him and contributed significantly to the defeat of the North Vietnamese Army force. By his courage, superb leadership and unwavering devotion to duty in the face of extreme personal danger, Private First Class Huggins upheld the highest traditions of the Marine Corps and of the United States Naval Service.

HUGHES, STANLEY S. (Gold Star in lieu of second award — first award during the Korean Conflict, 1950-53)

Citation: For extraordinary heroism while serving as Commanding Officer of the First Marines, First Marine Division (Reinforced), in connection with operations against the enemy in the Republic of Vietnam on 3 February 1968. During Operation HUE CITY, Colonel Hughes displaced his command post from Phu Bai to Hue along National Route One through enemy controlled territory. Undaunted by the heavy volume of hostile fire around him as he entered the besieged city, he rapidly moved his men along the fire-swept streets to reach the Military Assistance Command, Vietnam Compound. Moving to a vantage point on a roof top, he directed accurate countermortar and sniper fire, effectively suppressing the hostile fire in the area. He then maneuvered two battalions in an aggressive assault against the enemy, repeatedly disregarding his own safety to move to the areas of heaviest fighting to advise his commanders, encourage his men and personally request and direct support arms fire. When the First Battalion, Fifth Marines was attached to his regiment during heavy fighting, he fearlessly crossed the footbridge over the Perfume River under heavy fire, joining the command group at the Citadel to brief the unit commanders of the tactical situation and remain abreast of the battalion's progress. He repeatedly traveled across dangerously exposed areas to ensure the availability and uninterrupted distribution of vital supply items and equipment to his units. By his bold initiative, intrepid fighting spirit and superior tactical skill, Colonel Hughes was instrumental in the defeat and annihilation of a numerically superior enemy force, thereby reflecting great credit upon himself and the Marine Corps and upholding the highest traditions of the United States Naval Service.

HUNNICUTT, HUBERT H., III

Citation: For extraordinary heroism on 16-18 April 1968 as a squad leader in Company C, First Battalion, Ninth Marines, Third Marine Division in connection with operations against enemy forces in the Republic of Vietnam. Participating in the attack against an enemy bunker complex on a hilltop near the Khe Sanh Combat Base when the battalion came under heavy fire, seriously wounding his platoon commander, Sergeant (then Corporal) Hunnicutt treated the officer's wounds and then directed squad members into a bomb crater to await a lull in the enemy activity. When Sergeant Hunnicutt attempted to emerge from the crater, he sustained serious wounds along with other members of his unit, and was unable to leave his position because of the continuing enemy fire raking the area. At dusk he left the position and crawled across the fire-swept terrain to secure medical aid for himself and the other casualties trapped in the bomb crater. En route, Sergeant Hunnicutt discovered his company commander lying in an open area, severly wounded. While attempting to render aid and assistance to the officer, Sergeant Hunnicutt was again wounded. Nonetheless, he was able to fire at the enemy positions and to hurl hand grenades, eventually silencing their fire. At the first rays of dawn, he managed to move the company commander to a covered position and then proceeded to seek medical assistance but, overcome by weakness from loss of blood, fell into a gulley where he lay for several hours. Alerted by the sound of an aircraft, he gathered his last remaining strength and attracted the attention of the pilot who thereupon landed, placed Sergeant Hunnicutt aboard the observation craft, and then relayed a message to pinpoint the location of the company commander. By his indomitable courage, his selfless concern for the safety and welfare of his fellow Marines, and his inspiring devotion to duty in the face of overwhelming adversity, Sergeant Hunnicutt upheld the highest traditions of the Marine Corps and the United States Naval Service.

HUNTER, CHARLES B.

Citation: For extraordinary heroism on 30 October 1967 as a pilot in Attack Squadron ONE NINE SIX, embarked in USS CONSTELLATION (CVA-64). Exercising exceptional professional skill and sound judgment, Commander (then Lieutenant Commander) Hunter, planned and executed an extremely dangerous, single-plane, night, radar bombing attack on the strategically located and heavily defended Hanoi railroad ferry slip in North Vietnam. Although the entire Hanoi defensive effort was concentrated upon his lone bomber, he flawlessly piloted his aircraft to the target area and commenced his attack. Seconds before bomb release, six enemy surface-to-air missiles were observed to be tracking on his plane. Undaunted by this threat to his personal safety, Commander Hunter took swift and effective action to avoid the missiles and then proceeded to complete his attack, releasing all weapons in the target area with extreme accuracy. After release, he guided his plane through the intense antiaircraft-artillery fire and four additional missiles which were fired at his aircraft. In spite of this intense enemy opposition, Commander Hunter completed his mission and was directly responsible for dealing a significant blow to the North Vietnamese logistics efforts. His indomitable perseverance and conspicuous gallantry were in keeping with the highest traditions of the United States Naval Service.

JAEHNE, RICHARD L.

Citation: For extraordinary heroism while serving as a Platoon Leader with Company K, Third Battalion, Seventh Marines, First Marine Division in connection with combat operations against the enemy in the Republic of Vietnam. On 28 August 1969, while moving through an open rice paddy during a company-sized search and clear operation in the Que Son-Hiep Duc Valley in Quang Nam Province, Second Lieutenant Jaehne's platoon came under intense mortar, automatic-weapons, and small-arms fire from a well-entrenched North Vietnamese Army force. Quickly assessing the situation, he deployed his platoon into firing positions and launched an aggressive counterattack. During the ensuing fire fight, he repeatedly disregarded his own safety to gain vantage points from which to direct the fire of his men against one hostile position after another. When one of his squads was temporarily pinned down by fire from a heavy machine gun, he inched his way through the deep rice paddy and, in full view of the enemy gunners, destroyed the machine gun with a hand grenade, using his pistol to dispose of the last of the enemy gunners in the emplacement. Although he had sustained a painful fragmentation wound in the shoulder and a bullet wound in the hand, Second Lieutenant Jaehne rallied his Marines, retrieved the radio from his fallen radio operator, restored communications, and continued the attack until the enemy broke contact and withdrew, leaving behind thirteen casualties, several crew-served weapons, and numerous rifles and items of equipment. By his courage, aggressive leadership, and unflagging devotion to duty in an extremely hazardous situation, Second Lieutenant Jaehne upheld the highest traditions of the Marine Corps and of the United States Naval Service.

JAMES, ALAN C.

Citation: For extraordinary heroism on 9 September 1968 while serving as senior corpsman with Company "B", First Battalion, Third Marines, Third Marine Division, in connection with operations against enemy aggressor forces in the Republic of Vietnam. Company "B" commenced an aggressive assault against a North Vietnamese Army battalion occupying well-fortified emplacements in the Mutter's Ridge area of Quang Tri Province. During the ensuing three-day engagement which culminated in a decisive rout of the numerically-superior enemy force, Petty Officer James personally organized the company aid stations and casualty clearing points, and attended each of the numerous casualties sustained by the company, continually exposing himself to intense artillery and mortar fire in order to maneuver across the hazardous terrain and treat his injured companions. On several occasions, Petty Officer James protected wounded Marines from further injury by shielding them with his own body. During one intense artillery attack, he rushed outside the defensive perimeter to aid a seriously-wounded Marine, and calmly rendered first aid before carrying the man to a medical evacuation helicopter. Petty Officer James demonstrated a sincere concern for the welfare of his comrades throughout this fierce battle, repeatedly refusing rest or protective cover in order to ensure the proper treatment and expeditious evacuation of his patients. His heroic actions and extraordinary professional skill undoubtedly saved the lives of several Marines and inspired all who observed him. By his courage, resolute determination, and selfless devotion to duty, Petty Officer James upheld the highest traditions of the United States Naval Service.

*JMAEFF, GEORGE V.

Citation: For extraordinary heroism while serving as a Platoon Sergeant with Company C, First Battalion, Fourth Marines, Third Marine Division in the Republic of Vietnam on 1 March 1969. While

Company C was attempting to seize Hill 484 north of the Rockpile, the lead platoon was pinned down by sniper fire and grenades from North Vietnamese Army soldiers who were acting as mortar forward observers and occupying well-fortified bunkers. Corporal Jmaeff, realizing that a frontal attack would produce excessive Marine casualties, directed three men to provide covering fire and, fully aware of the possible consequences of his daring action, initiated a lone assault on the hostile emplacements. Although seriously wounded by fragments of a hand grenade, he ignored his painful injuries and, resolutely obtaining his objective, destroyed the first enemy position. With the arrival of a reaction platoon, Corporal Jmaeff steadfastly refused medical treatment and continued to direct his men until ordered to receive medical aid. While his wounds were being tended, he observed several Marines injured during a new barrage of mortar fire and, tearing the intravenous fluid tube from his arm, unhesitatingly left his relatively secure location to aid his companions. As he dauntlessly struggled forward in a splendid display of valor, he was mortally wounded by the detonation of a mortar round. His heroic efforts and selfless concern for his fellowmen inspired all who observed him and were instrumental in his unit's securing the objective. By his courage, aggressive fighting spirit and unwavering devotion to duty, Corporal Jmaeff upheld the highest traditions of the Marine Corps and the United States Naval Service. He gallantly gave his life for his country.

JOHNSON, JAMES L., JR.

Citation: For extraordinary heroism while serving as a Squad Leader with Company E, Second Battalion, Ninth Marines, Third Marine Division, in connection with operations against the enemy in the Republic of Vietnam. On 17 February 1969, Corporal Johnson was directed to seize a hostile bunker complex which had pinned down elements of Company H in Ashau Valley. As the squad advanced through the hazardous area, the Marines came under a heavy volume of fire from an enemy machine gun 20 meters to their front. Not wishing to incur excessive casualties, Corporal Johnson called for supporting arms fire from gunships overhead and marked the hostile position with air bursts from his grenade launcher. When the pilots failed to locate the emplacements, he fearlessly stood in full view of the North Vietnamese Army force and waived air panels to indicate his position to the gunships. As the air strikes began, he brought his squad on line and directed the Marines toward the bunker complex, simultaneously adjusting the air strikes on his own position because of his proximity to the hostile soldiers. After the air strikes had ceased, the pilots informed him that his actions had driven 15 enemy soldiers into an open area behind the complex and that these North Vietnamese had been killed by the successive air strikes. Continuing his mission, Corporal Johnson led an aggressive assault against the bunkers during which he received a grenade fragment wound in his hand. Disregarding his injury, he resolutely proceeded across the fire-swept terrain, shouting words of encouragement to his men and directing their fire. Having sustained a second grenade fragment wound, this time in his leg, he steadfastly ignored his painful injuries, fearlessly made his way to the enemy bunker, and threw a hand grenade through the aperture of the bunker, razing the position and killing its three occupants. Deploying his men around the bunker, he directed a search of the area which revealed a complex of three more bunkers and two dead North Vietnamese soldiers. As he was preparing to rejoin the rest of his platoon, he heard moaning sounds from outside the squad's defensive perimeter. Suspecting an enemy trap, he alerted his men, then went alone to investigate the source of the noise and found one mortally wounded and one seriously wounded Marine from Company H, who had been injured in the previous engagement. Working rapidly and knowledgeably, Corporal Johnson rendered first aid to the casualty, thereby saving the man's life. Rejoining his platoon, he steadfastly refused medical attention until all other casualties had been treated and medically evacuated. His heroic and timely actions inspired all who observed him and were instrumental in minimizing Marine casualties. By his courage, intrepid fighting spirit, and unwavering devotion to duty in the face of grave personal danger, Corporal Johnson contributed significantly to the accomplishment of his unit's mission and upheld the highest traditions of the Marine Corps and the United States Naval Service.

*JOHNSTON, CLEMENT B., JR.

Citation: For extraordinary heroism as a member of a reconnaissance platoon, Company D, First Reconnaissance Battalion, First Marine Division (Reinforced), Fleet Marine Force, in action against enemy Viet Cong forces in the vicinity of Xuan Ngoc Village in Quang Ngai Province, Republic of Vietnam, on 28 April 1966. Corporal Johnston, a fellow Marine, and a Navy Corpsman were occupying a position when an undetermined number of insurgents (Viet Cong) quietly approached their location and threw two hand grenades into their midst. Corporal Johnston saw one of the grenades and leaped at his companions, knocking them to the ground and shielding them from the blast of the grenade. In so doing he absorbed the terrific force of the explosion and saved his friends from major injuries and possible loss of life. Corporal Johnston's courageous action and selfless devotion to duty upheld the highest traditions of the Marine Corps and the United States Naval Service. He gallantly gave his life in the cause of freedom.

*JONES, PHILLIP B.

Citation: For extraordinary heroism while serving as a Platoon Commander with Company G, Second Battalion, Twenty-sixth Marines, Ninth Marine Amphibious Brigade in the Republic of Vietnam on 28 January 1969. During Operation LINN RIVER, the Second Platoon of Company G was patrolling along a stream in Quang Nam Province when the Marines came under a heavy volume of fire from hostile soldiers occupying well-concealed emplacements and, after sustaining several casualties, deployed to the marginal shelter of a bomb crater. Observing that the platoon leader was among the casualties, Second Lieutenant Jones mustered his radio operator and a fire team and fearlessly went to the aid of the beleaguered unit. After rapidly assessing the situation and realizing the advantage held by the numerically superior enemy force, he elected to utilize supporting artillery fire upon the North Vietnamese Army positions, but was faced with the necessity to evacuate the casualties who were lying in an unprotected area near the hostile emplacements. Unhesitatingly leading his companion across the fire-swept terrain, he effected the rescue of three of the injured men. As he, with his radio operator, again boldly entered the enemy kill zone and approached to within five meters of the hostile soldiers to evacuate the remaining helpless Marine, Second Lieutenant Jones was seriously wounded, but, determined to save his comrade, ignored his painful injury and was delivering suppressive fire on the North Vietnamese positions when he was mortally wounded. By his courage, selfless concern for his fellowmen and unwavering devotion to duty, Second Lieutenant Jones upheld the highest traditions of the Marine Corps and the United States Naval Service. He gallantly gave his life for his country.

*JOYS, JOHN W.

Citation: For extraordinary heroism while serving with Company A, First Battalion, Fourth Marines, Third Marine Division, Fleet Marine Force, in the defense of a forward tank and artillery position at Cam Lo in Vietnam on 26 August 1966. Employing satchel charges, hand grenades and a heavy concentration of automatic weapons, the enemy launched a fanatic assault against the Marine perimeter, penetrating the First Platoon's lines. Staff Sergeant Joys, the platoon sergeant, was wounded by mortar fire during the initial phase of the attack. In spite of his painful wound, he proceeded to organize and coordinate the defenses in his sector, spotting targets, directing fires, and constantly exposing himself while moving up and down the lines through the area where enemy fire was the heaviest. He made repeated trips carrying desperately needed ammunition to the men on the line, stopping briefly to spot and shift targets while encouraging adamant determination of his men to stop the penetration. At one time, while moving across the open area between holes, a Viet Cong satchel charge exploded beside Staff Sergeant Joys, lifting him completely off the ground and slamming him down again. Bruised and battered, but undaunted, he picked himself up, retrieved his load and continued without hesitation. Constantly alert to the action within his perimeter, he saw a corpsman hit while in an open area. Without thought of his personal safety, Staff Sergeant Joys raced through a rain of intensive enemy fire to bring the wounded man to shelter. Noting that the momentum of the enemy's assault was endangering the safety of tanks in his area, he immediately organized part of his platoon to counterattack the enemy from the flank. While leading the assault, Staff Sergeant Joys was wounded for the second time. Although seriously injured and in intense pain, he courageously pressed the attack, and continued to move from man to man, uttering encouragement, helping the wounded, and directing fire until he himself fell mortally wounded by an enemy hand grenade. As a result of his dynamic leadership and stirring personal example, the enemy was contained, and the perimeter restored. Staff Sergeant Joys' professional ability and unfaltering courage reflected great credit upon himself and upheld the highest traditions of the United States Naval Service. He gallantly gave his life for his country.

*JUDGE, MARK W.

Citation: For extraordinary heroism as a Rifleman with Company E, Second Battalion, Fourth Marines, Third Marine Division in connection with operations against enemy forces in the Republic of Vietnam on 21 September 1967. Private First Class Judge was point man of the lead fire team on a search and destroy mission when the team came under attack from a well entrenched and concealed enemy force of an undetermined number. Wounded several times in the initial burst of enemy fire, Private First Class Judge instinctively returned their fire. During the following heavy exchange of fire he was again hit and, although seriously wounded, realized that the enemy was moving toward him from the flank, attempting to cut his team members off from their platoon. Private First Class Judge directed the other members to move back while he provided covering fire. As a result of his heroic action and fearless devotion to duty he eventually succumbed to his numerous wounds even while still unleashing a deadly hail of fire on the enemy. Through his extraordinary initiative and inspiring valor in the face of almost certain death, he saved his fellow Marines from injury and possible loss of life. Private First Class Judge's outstanding courage and devotion to duty reflected great credit upon himself and the Marine Corps, and upheld the highest traditions of the United States Naval Service. He gallantly gave his life for his country.

*KALER, RICHARD D.

Citation: For extraordinary heroism as a machine gunner with Company H, Second Battalion, Fourth Marines near Cam Lo, Republic of Vietnam, on 21 July 1966. The company was engaged in a search and destroy mission during Operation HASTINGS when the point man of Corporal Kaler's platoon was fired upon and killed by an enemy machine gun. Disregarding his own personal safety, he immediately moved forward through the heavy fire and carried the body back. The following day, the platoon attacked the same position. When several machine guns opened fire cutting down several of his comrades and pinning the rest of the platoon, Corporal Kaler, knowing the hazards involved, without hesitation and in complete disregard for his own safety, exposed himself to the intense fire and charged the enemy positions. Receiving a bullet in the thigh, he nevertheless closed with the North Vietnamese, silencing one position before he was struck and mortally wounded by enemy fire. By his daring initiative, valiant fighting spirit and selfless devotion to duty in the face of insurmountable odds, Corporal Kaler was responsible in a great measure for saving many of his comrades and thereby upheld the highest traditions of the Marine Corps and the United States Naval Service. He gallantly gave his life in the cause of freedom.

*KAUFMAN, DAVID M.

Citation: For extraordinary heroism while serving as First Sergeant of Company E, Second Battalion, Third Marines, Third Marine Division in the Republic of Vietnam on 15 June 1969. While Company E was participating in a search and destroy operation in Cam Lo Valley, the Marines came under a heavy volume of North Vietnamese Army mortar, small arms, and rocket-propelled grenade fire and sustained numerous casualties. Completely disregarding his own safety, First Sergeant Kaufman unhesitatingly left his position of relative security to assist the corpsman in treating the wounded men and, on several occasions, fearlessly crossed the fire-swept terrain to aid casualties to covered places. During the ensuing fierce engagement, First Sergeant Kaufman, seemingly oblivious to the hostile rounds impacting about him, boldly moved to vantage points and, in full view of enemy soldiers, encouraged his men and ensured that every possible avenue of approach was effectively covered with fire power. Then, as he dauntlessly moved from one fighting position to another along the company's defensive perimeter, exhorting his Marines to greater combat efforts, he was mortally wounded by North Vietnamese Army fire. By his courage, selfless concern for his fellowmen and unwavering devotion to duty, First Sergeant Kaufman upheld the highest traditions of the Marine Corps and the United States Naval Service. He gallantly gave his life for his country.

*KECK, RUSSELL F.

Citation: For extraordinary heroism while serving as a Machine Gun Squad Leader with Company A, Battalion Landing Team 1/3, Ninth Marine Amphibious Brigade, in the Republic of Vietnam on 18 May 1967. During Operation BEAU CHARGER, in Quang Tin Province, Corporal Keck's squad was landed by helicopter into a heavily defended enemy position. Due to the large volume of intense enemy ground fire, the helicopters were forced to disperse over a wide area, causing the isolation of many small units. Finding himself and his gun team separated from the main body of his company, Corporal Keck quickly placed his guns into action. Observing one machine gun within hand grenade range of the teeming enemy trench lines, he rushed to the aid of his men under vicious enemy fire, finding one lone survivor. He quickly evaluated the situation and decided to move the gun to a safer position to keep it in action. While breaking the gun down into two groups, he was wounded by an enemy grenade. Disregarding his painful wounds, he quickly killed the enemy soldier who had thrown the grenade with an accurate burst of machine gun fire. Realizing that only one man could possibly make it back across the deadly fire-swept terrain, Corporal Keck ordered his gunner to return, while he gave covering fire. During this unselfish action, he was mortally wounded. By his courageous actions, bold initiative, intrepid fighting spirit and sincere concern for others, Corporal Keck reflected great credit upon himself and the Marine Corps, and upheld the highest traditions of the United States Naval Service. He gallantly gave his life for his country.

KELLEY, EDWIN C., JR.

Citation: For extraordinary heroism while serving as Commanding Officer, Company M, Third Battalion, Fourth Marines, Third Marine Division, in connection with combat operations against the enemy in the Republic of Vietnam. On 13 March 1969, First Lieutenant Kelley was directed to retake Landing Zone Sierra near the demilitarized zone which had been previously abandoned by friendly forces and was subsequently occupied by a North Vietnamese Army force entrenched in well-fortified bunker complexes. After personally leading a reconnaissance patrol to within 100 meters of the hostile emplacements without detection, First Lieutenant Kelley formulated his plan of attack and initiated an aggressive assault on the enemy positions. During the ensuing protracted engagement, First Lieutenant Kelley directed his company in the destruction of a series of four bunker complexes without the aid of air support and with only limited artillery fire. When monsoon weather precluded helicopter resupply, he instructed his Marines in the employment of captured North Vietnamese Army weapons and grenades for a final assault against the remaining hostile fortification, thereby enabling his company to seize the objective and establish defensive positions. During the night, the Marines were subjected to a series of probing assaults, which increased in intensity until the early morning hours when the enemy penetrated a sector of the perimeter. First Lieutenant Kelley fearlessly led a bold counterattack resulting in the defeat of the North Vietnamese Army force. His heroic actions and aggressive leadership inspired all who observed him and were instrumental in defeating the tenacious hostile unit. By his courage, superb tactical skill, and unwavering devotion to duty in the face of grave personal danger, First Lieutenant Kelley contributed significantly to the accomplishment of his unit's mission and upheld the highest traditions of the Marine Corps and the United States Naval Service.

*KELLY, JAMES R., III

Citation: For extraordinary heroism while serving as a grenadier with Company I, Third Battalion, Third Marines, Third Marine Division in Vietnam on 24 March 1967. During a search and destroy mission, Corporal Kelly's platoon was engaged in a heavily contested conflict against enemy forces. As his platoon entered the village of An Hoa, it became subjected to intense enemy mortar and automatic weapons fire, which inflicted numerous casualties upon the Marines. With complete disregard for his own safety and with full knowledge of the hazards involved, Corporal Kelly assaulted an enemy bunker single-handedly and destroyed it. The enemy then attempted to flank the Marine platoon with six men armed with automatic weapons. Utilizing a well camouflaged trenchline, the enemy was close to accomplishing their objective when Corporal Kelly suddenly observed their movement. He rushed forward in the face of certain death, killed three of the enemy and caused the remainder to flee. Mortally wounded during this action, Corporal Kelly by his bold initiative and selfless concern for others undoubtedly saved the lives of many of his comrades. His daring display of courage was responsible for the eventual successful accomplishment of the platoon's mission and an inspiration to all who observed him. Corporal Kelly's indomitable fighting spirit, professional skill and loyal devotion to duty reflected great credit upon himself and the Marine Corps and upheld the highest traditions of the United States Naval Service. He gallantly gave his life for his country.

KELLY, ROBERT A.

Citation: For extraordinary heroism while serving as Executive Officer of Company I, Third Battalion, Ninth Marines, Third Marine Division, in the Republic of Vietnam on 3 and 5 September 1966. On 3 September, while commanding two Marine reaction forces, First Lieutenant Kelly directed an assault against a Viet Cong trench position; a number of the enemy were killed and some enemy weapons and equipment were captured. When a member of his squad was wounded by hostile fire, First Lieutenant Kelly requested helicopter evacuation. While the approaching rescue aircraft was subjected to heavy automatic weapons fire, he repeatedly exposed himself to direct the fire of his men, thereby diverting the enemy's attention and enabling the evacuation to be completed safely. On 5 September, he was serving as a Platoon Commander assigned to escort an Ontos to afford security on the left flank of a company sweep. Suddenly the left flank was engulfed in a barrage of mortar explosions, machine gun fire and hand grenades from a Viet Cong force later estimated at battalion strength. A mortar round exploded about five feet behind First Lieutenant Kelly, sending shrapnel through his hand and also wounding six other Marines. After quickly bandaging his own wounds he quickly gathered medical supplies and raced across the fire-torn field to one of his reaction forces which was pinned down by fire and taking casualties. After assisting the squad he returned to his original position and learning that an air strike was to be launched, he responded to a need for a machine gunner on the Ontos. While firing the weapon, First Lieutenant Kelly was hit by a ricocheting round in the shoulder and knocked from his post into the hatch. With grim determination, he regained his position and resumed his covering fire. During this gallant effort, he was hit twice more in the neck. Firmly aware of his responsibilities despite his intense suffering, he calmly radioed to the Company Command Post and forwarded a sound appraisal of the situation in his area before lapsing into unconsciousness. First Lieutenant Kelly's inspiring leadership, aggressive determination and valiant devotion to duty in the face of overwhelming odds were contributing factors in containing the hostile attack and thereby reflected the highest credit upon himself, the Marine Corps and the United States Naval Service.

KEMP, MARWICK L. — KIA on next tour 2/18/69

Citation: For extraordinary heroism as a 3.5" Rocket Squad Leader attached to Third Platoon, Company E, Second Battalion, Fourth Marines, in the Republic of Vietnam on 21 March 1966. As the company was engaged in search and destroy operations against the communist insurgent forces in Quang Ngai Province, it moved across an open rice paddy area and approached to within thirty-five meters of a small village and was taken under fire from a large Viet Cong force emplaced in heavy fortifications and trench lines completely surrounding the village. The Third Platoon came under particularly devastating fire as it was completely exposed to the enemy's automatic weapons fire, mortar fire, and grenade attacks. Within seconds the platoon commander, the platoon sergeant, the platoon guide, and two rifle squad leaders had been wounded and were out of action. Sergeant Kemp moved to the commander's side and offered aid, but was instructed to take over the platoon and continue the attack. Exposing himself to intense enemy fire from several fortified positions, he quickly reorganized the squads. He then directed the continuation of the attack, exposing himself to urge his men forward until word came down from the company commander to withdraw from the village. Simultaneously directing fire on the enemy, conducting the evacuation of the wounded, and personally carrying other wounded back to safety, he unselfishly risked his life time after time to insure that the withdrawal was performed in an orderly manner and that each wounded man was brought back to safety. During this entire period, Sergeant Kemp performed his duties in a fashion that would be considered extremely exceptional for men of higher grade and experience. His tireless devotion to duty, his unswerving courage in the face of great danger, and his brilliant display of professional skill were responsible for the saving of many lives and were directly responsible for over sixty Viet Cong killed by his platoon. His actions upheld the finest traditions of the Marine Corp and the United States Naval Service.

*KENISON, BENJAMIN A.

Citation: For extraordinary heroism in connection with operations against enemy forces while serving as a squad leader with Company D, First Battalion, Fourth Marines in Vietnam on 16 September 1966. During Operation PRAIRIE, the Second Platoon was caught in an ambush. In the initial burst of fire a member of Lance Corporal Kenison's squad was seriously wounded. Realizing that the wounded Marine could not be left unattended, Lance Corporal Kenison quickly maneuvered his squad into a position from which they could best provide covering fire. Then, with full knowledge of the hazards involved and with complete disregard for his own personal safety, he bravely advanced alone by crawling up a steep slope and going forward in the face of withering enemy fire in order to bring his wounded comrade back to safety. Upon reaching the Marine who was receiving fire in an exposed area, Lance Corporal Kenison gallantly attempted to carry him back to safety. At this time both men were hit by an enemy hand grenade and mortally wounded. Lance Corporal Kenison's fearless courage, inspiring leadership and loyal devotion to duty reflected great credit upon himself and the Marine Corps and upheld the highest traditions of the United States Naval Service. He gallantly gave his life for his country.

KENNEDY, JOHNNIE M.

Citation: For extraordinary heroism while serving as a Light Weapons Infantry Advisor with the 39th Ranger Battalion, Army of the Republic of Vietnam, on 19 April 1965. While conducting a search and destroy mission four kilometers west of Thang Binh in Quang Tin Province, a composite battalion-size force of armored personnel carriers, Vietnamese Infantry and Marines located on the battalion's flank was routed by two Viet Cong battalions and began to withdraw through the Ranger Battalion area. Sergeant Kennedy left his protected position and attempted to stop the retreating friendly forces and establish them in defensive positions. Although the heavy enemy fire forced the regrouping of his position on three occasions, he unceasingly rallied the men around him and by his personal example inspired several of the Vietnamese officers to try to hold the withdrawing troops. During the action he personally inflicted 25 casualties among the enemy and saved 75 friendly troops from imminent capture. His cool and skillful leadership, indomitable fighting spirit and fearless devotion to duty reflected great credit upon himself and the Marine Corps and upheld the highest traditions of the United States Naval Service.

KEYS, WILLIAM M.

Citation: For extraordinary heroism as Commanding Officer, Company D, First Battalion, Ninth Marines, while engaged in action against elements of the North Vietnamese Army and insurgent communist (Viet Cong) forces during Operation PRAIRIE II in the Cam Lo district of the Republic of Vietnam on 2 March 1967. While on a search and destroy mission, Captain Keys' company made contact with a large enemy force estimated to be two companies in strength. During this contact, the company command post group received heavy automatic-weapons and mortar fire from the rear. Realizing that his rifle platoons were heavily engaged, Captain Keys organized his command group into an assault element and led them against the enemy, who were firing into his position. Personally leading his small group against a numerically superior force, he succeeded in completely overrunning the North Vietnamese, personally killing six and destroying a machine gun position. Immediately following this fire fight he rushed to the rear of his center platoon where he could best direct the deployment of his company. During the next four hours his company repelled attack after attack by a determined enemy. This period found Captain Keys along the entire line of his company, shouting encouragement, shifting forces to meet each new attack, and successfully directing all aspects of his company's firepower and supporting arms. Following the enemy's last attack, Captain Keys immediately reorganized his company and attacked the enemy before they could withdraw to a safe area. While completely overrunning the enemy camp, his company succeeded in killing 183 North Vietnamese soldiers and capturing eight prisoners and nearly 200 weapons. Realizing that the surviving enemy would attempt to circumvent his company during the oncoming darkness and escape to the north, Captain Keys placed his company in a blocking position, thereby forcing the enemy to withdraw into a prearranged zone where they were pounded by air and artillery resulting in 44 more enemy killed. As a result of his professional skill and stirring example, the enemy forces in his area of operations were completely routed. By his daring performance and loyal devotion to duty in the face of great personal risk, Captain Keys reflected great credit upon himself and the Marine Corps and upheld the highest traditions of the United States Naval Service.

KINNARD, DONEL C.

Citation: For extraordinary heroism while engaged in armed conflict against enemy forces in the Republic of Vietnam on 20-21 January 1970. During this period, Chief Petty Officer Kinnard was serving with Underwater Demolition Team Twelve, Detachment Golf, and operating with the Second Battalion, Fifth Mobile Forces Command during a sweep and clear mission in the Ca Mau peninsula. On one occasion, Chief Petty Officer Kinnard was singled out as a target by an enemy force while he was attempting to beach a damaged sampan from which three of the enemy had leaped into the water and escaped. His courageous action resulted in the capture of the sampan and enemy weapons. On another occasion, when his unit was subjected to intense enemy rocket, machine-gun and automatic-weapons fire, Chief Petty Officer Kinnard was wounded in the arms and legs by shrapnel from an enemy hand grenade. He immediately hurled several hand grenades aross a canal into enemy positions. During the ensuing battle, he was suddenly attacked by one of the enemy who had crept up behind him. After several minutes of a fierce hand-to-hand struggle, Chief Petty Officer Kinnard succeeded in overcoming his attacker who was later identified as a North Vietnamese Army Lieutenant. By his personal courage and inspiring devotion to duty, Chief Petty Officer Kinnard contributed materially to the success of a vital mission and upheld the highest traditions of the United States Naval Service.

*KOELPER, DONALD E.

Citation: For extraordinary heroism in connection with the bombing of the Capital Kinh-Do Theater in Saigon, Republic of Vietnam, on the evening of 18 February 1964. Upon becoming aware of a bomb being placed in the lobby of the theater, Major Koelper, who was standing nearby with a companion, unhesitatingly entered the main area of the theater and shouted to the occupants, United States servicemen and their dependents, to take cover. This warning provided the time for numerous unsuspecting individuals to obtain cover by lying between the rows of seats. Seconds later the bomb exploded, fatally wounding Major Koelper and another person, and injuring approximately fifty others. Through his prompt and courageous actions in warning the theater patrons of the imminent explosion, Major Koelper undoubtedly saved many from serious injury or possible death. His self-sacrificing efforts were in keeping with the highest traditions of the United States Naval Service.

*KOLLMANN, GLENN E.

Citation: For extraordinary heroism in aerial flight on 24 February 1968 as the Commanding Officer of Attack Squadron THIRTY-FIVE, embarked in USS ENTERPRISE (CVA(N)-65). Commander Kollmann planned and led a night air strike against a vital and heavily defended port facility in the heart of North Vietnam. Piloting his aircraft at perilously low altitudes in the monsoon weather, he successfully penetrated intense and accurate enemy defenses. Disregarding the threatening surface-to-air missiles and the antiaircraft artillery defending the target area, Commander Kollmann maintained a smooth, level flight path until bomb release, thereby ensuring an optimum bombing solution. Because of his daring and highly professional flying skill, his bombs found their mark, inflicting heavy damage upon the port facilities. By his airmanship, courage, and loyal devotion to duty in the face of intense hostile fire, Commander Kollmann contributed materially to United States efforts in Southeast Asia and upheld the highest traditions of the United States Naval Service.

KOONTZ, LENOARD

Citation: For extraordinary heroism while serving as a radio operator with Company M, Third Battalion, Fourth Marines, Third Marine Division in the Republic of Vietnam on 27 May 1968. While Company M was on a patrol near the Khe Sanh Combat Base, Corporal (then Lance Corporal) Koontz' platoon became pinned down by intense automatic weapons fire from a large North Vietnamese Army force occupying fortified positions on the crest of Hill 542. Alertly locating the hostile defenses, Corporal Koontz gave his radio to another Marine and crawled across the fire-swept terrain toward the closest enemy fortification. Fearlessly moving on top of the North Vietnamese emplacement, he destroyed the bunker with a hand grenade, killing one enemy soldier. Immediately entering the remains of the position, Corporal Koontz killed a second North Vietnamese defender with his pistol. Pinpointing another hostile bunker from which enemy soldiers were throwing grenades at the Marines, he unhesitatingly assaulted the emplacement and, hurling hand grenades into the structure, killed its occupants. Realizing that the intense hostile fire was disrupting casualty evacuation efforts, he delivered suppressive fire against the enemy positions, enabling the Marines to assist their wounded comrades to positions of relative safety. Although partially dazed by an impacting North Vietnamese mortar round, he resolutely moved to aid two injured Marines and assisted them to a covered area. Returning to his dangerously exposed firing position, Corporal Koontz steadfastly continued to deliver effective fire upon the enemy until the last of his wounded companions had been evacuated. By his courage, aggressive fighting spirit and unwavering devotion to duty, Corporal Koontz was instrumental in saving several Marines from possible death or serious injury and by so doing he upheld the highest traditions of the Marine Corps and the United States Naval Service.

KORKOW, KENNETH A.

Citation: For extraordinary heroism while serving as Mortar Section Leader of Company B, First Battalion, Twenty-Sixth Marines, Third Marine Division, in the Republic of Vietnam on 30 March 1968. During a search and destroy operation in the vicinity of the Khe Sanh Combat Base, Company B suddenly came under intense small-arms and mortar fire from a well-entrenched North Vietnamese Army battalion. Fearlessly exposing himself to the hostile fire, Corporal Korkow quickly deployed his mortar section into firing positions and, moving about the fire-swept terrain from one squad to another, directed heavy barrages of accurate fire against the enemy, destroying four fortified bunkers. Alertly detecting a hidden mortar site which was pinning down elements of his company, he advanced to a position dangerously open to enemy fire and, employing his own mortar, single-handedly destroyed the hostile emplacement. As the battle intensified, Corporal Korkow repeatedly disregarded his own safety as he moved from one position to another, encouraging his men and directing their fire. Observing a Marine fall wounded by an enemy explosive device, he selflessly rushed into the hazardous area and assisted his injured comrade to an aid station established to the rear of his company. Although seriously wounded while returning to the forward area after assisting more casualties to the aid station, Corporal Korkow resolutely continued to encourage and assist his men and comfort the wounded until he was medically evacuated. His intrepid fighting spirit inspired all who observed him and contributed immeasurably to the final defeat of the numerically superior enemy force. By his uncommon valor and selfless devotion to duty in the face of extreme personal danger, Corporal Korkow reflected great credit upon himself and upheld the highest traditions of the Marine Corps and the United States Naval Service.

KOWALYK, WILLIAM

Citation: For extraordinary heroism while serving with Battery G, Third Battalion, Twelfth Marines during operations against the enemy near Cam Lo, Vietnam, on 26 August 1966. During the early morning Lance Corporal Kowalyk and two other Marines were manning a foxhole on the battalion perimeter when it was breached by a company of North Vietnamese Regulars. In the initial onslaught, all three men were wounded by a hand grenade. Although painfully wounded in the chest, arms, and face, Lance Corporal Kowalyk assured the others that he was not seriously hurt and continued to fire his weapon. The others noticed that he could barely lift his rifle and attempted to evacuate him, but he refused to be moved and selflessly resumed firing. Now surrounded, the two less seriously wounded Marines again took up their positions. At this time, unknown to the two, a North Vietnamese soldier leapt into the foxhole and attempted to strangle the nearly helpless Lance Corporal Kowalyk with a rope. Summoning all his strength, he threw off the attacker and, with a heroic effort, killed him with his rifle. Again his companions rushed to him and, realizing how badly he was hurt, evacuated him still protesting to the aid station. Through his daring and resolute determination he was instrumental in thwarting the enemy attack. By his courage, selfless actions, and inspiring devotion to duty, Lance Corporal Kowalyk reflected great credit upon himself and the Marine Corps and upheld the highest traditions of the United States Naval Service.

KRUEGER, ROGER W.

Citation: For extraordinary heroism on 24 March 1968 as a naval flight officer in Attack Squadron ONE HUNDRED SIXTY-FIVE, embarked in USS RANGER (CVA-61). Lieutenant Krueger served as the bombardier/navigator for the first U. S. Navy A-6A night, all-weather attack against the heavily defended and strategic Kinh No railroad yard, located on the vital northeast railroad of North Vietnam. Although encountering extremely intense enemy antiaircraft defenses, a barrage of four surface-to-air missiles, and a near miss that forced the aircraft into momentarily uncontrolled flight and degraded his weapon system, Lieutenant Krueger continued to operate the attack system and to provide the necessary navigational and attack parameters to accomplish a successful weapons release on this vital target. During egress, the flight encountered a line of thunderstorms and heavy enemy defenses necessitating an aerial refueling in order to safely outmaneuver these obstacles and complete the return to ship. Lieutenant Krueger's heroic actions, professionalism, and fearless devotion to duty in the face of grave personal danger were in keeping with the highest traditions of the United States Naval Service.

*KUZMA, MARC J.

Citation: For extraordinary heroism while serving as a Rifleman with Company A, First Battalion, Fourth Marines, Third Marine Division in connection with operations against the enemy in the Republic of Vietnam. On 26 April 1968, Private Kuzma's squad was assigned to reconnoiter a suspected enemy bunker complex located west of Con Thien. As the Marines approached the designated area, they suddenly came under a heavy volume of hostile fire, and during the ensuing engagement, the squad's radio was severely damaged and rendered inoperable. Realizing the seriousness of the situation, Private Kuzma unhesitatingly exposed himself to the hostile fire in order to return to the platoon patrol base and guide reinforcements to the location of his besieged squad. Quickly leading the Marines to a location near the ambush site, he accurately pointed out friendly and enemy positions to his platoon commander. Disregarding his own safety, he then commenced moving toward his squad's position and, as he ran across a dangerously exposed area, came under fire from a hostile bunker. Reacting instantly, he threw a grenade into the emplacement, killing the enemy soldier defending the position. Continuing his movement, he simultaneously delivered a heavy volume of rifle fire which killed two additional North Vietnamese soldiers. Arriving at his unit's location, he was informed that several wounded Marines were lying forward of the squad's perimeter. Unhesitatingly moving toward his wounded comrades, he came under fire from another well fortified bunker. Maneuvering close to the emplacement, he threw a grenade into the position, killing another enemy soldier. Continuing toward his fallen comrades, he was again fired upon and rapidly returned accurate fire which killed the hostile soldier. Almost immediately, he received fire from his flank, and as he turned to direct fire upon the enemy he was mortally wounded. His heroic and timely actions inspired all who observed him and were instrumental in saving the lives of numerous Marines. By his courage, intrepid fighting spirit and selfless devotion to duty, Private Kuzma upheld the highest traditions of the Marine Corps and of the United States Naval Service. He gallantly gave his life for his country.

LAIN, BOBBY D.

Citation: For extraordinary heroism as Commanding Officer, Company B, First Battalion, First Marines, First Marine Division in Vietnam on 19 February 1967. During Operation STONE, the battalion encountered a main force Viet Cong battalion. Company B was assigned the key mission of closing the last route of escape available to the enemy. Although suffering from a wound in the foot from a punji stick, Captain Lain refused evacuation and gallantly led his company through 5,000 meters of heavily mined and booby-trapped terrain to completely surround and entrap the enemy battalion which suffered more than 250 casualties. While aggressively advancing against the enemy to establish final contact with a friendly company, Captain Lain was critically wounded by an enemy mine, causing the ultimate loss of both lower limbs. Although stunned by the severity of his wounds, he thoroughly briefed his executive officer as to the situation and only after insuring that the company's tactical integrity was maintained and the entrapment of the enemy force complete, did he relinquish command of his unit. By his indomitable courage, superb leadership and valiant fighting spirit, Captain Lain served to inspire his men to heroic endeavor in their successful elimination of the enemy battalion as a fighting force. His great personal valor reflected the highest credit upon himself and was in keeping with the highest traditions of the Marine Corps and the United States Naval Service.

LANKFORD, ALBERT J., III

Citation: For extraordinary heroism while serving as a Platoon Commander with Company G, Second Battalion, Ninth Marines, Third Marine Division in connection with combat operations against the enemy in the Republic of Vietnam. During the early morning hours of 21 April 1969, while occupying a night observation position,

Company G came under a ground attack by a large North Vietnamese Army force. During the initial moments of the assault, enemy sappers succeeded in penetrating the defensive perimeter and attempting to destroy the command post with satchel charges. By shouting to attract the attention of the enemy soldiers and thereby determine the area of their heaviest concentration, First Lieutenant (then Second Lieutenant) Lankford became an excellent target for intense hostile fire. Heedless of the rounds impacting near him, he directed the suppressive fire of nearby Marines at the soldiers, then maneuvered across the hazardous terrain to the command post, where he mustered a group of men and launched an attack against the approaching sappers. As the North Vietnamese Army force swarmed against the defensive perimeter seeking a means of penetration, First Lieutenant Lankford saw an opportunity to seize the initiative and, rallying his exhausted men, led them in a counterattack. When the Marine beside him fell to the ground seriously wounded, First Lieutenant Lankford picked him up and, seemingly oblivious to the fire raking the area, carried him to a covered position. His heroic and determined actions inspired all who observed him and were instrumental in the defeat of a determined and numerically superior enemy force. By his courage, dynamic leadership, and unwavering devotion to duty in the face of grave personal danger, First Lieutenant Lankford upheld the highest traditions of the Marine Corps and of the United States Naval Service.

LA POINTE, ALVIN S.

Citation: For extraordinary heroism as a rifleman in Company C, First Battalion, Seventh Marines in Quang Ngai Province, Republic of Vietnam, on 28 March 1966. While engaged in a search and destroy operation against communist insurgent forces, Private LaPointe's platoon came under an intense volume of well aimed automatic weapons fire. While engaged in vicious hand-to-hand combat, Private LaPointe observed an enemy antiaircraft weapon raking his squad with a murderous volume of accurate fire. Facing almost certain death, he heroically crawled across the fire swept slope toward the enemy bunker armed only with his bayonet and hand grenades. Within ten feet of the emplacement, he fearlessly and aggressively leaped into the position and, landing astride the gun, stabbed and killed the gunner. Seeing his comrade killed, the second Viet Cong fled into a tunnel within the position. Courageous and oblivious to the imminent danger, Private LaPointe unhesitatingly followed and killed him.

Through his extraordinary initiative and inspiring valor in the face of almost certain death, he saved his comrades from injury and possible loss of life and enabled the platoon to seize and hold the vital enemy position. By his personal bravery, indomitable fighting spirit and devotion to duty, Private LaPointe reflected great credit upon himself and the Marine Corps and upheld the highest traditions of the United States Naval Service.

LA PORTE, ALFRED P., JR.

Citation: For extraordinary heroism while serving as Weapons Platoon Sergeant with Company H, Second Battalion, Fourth Marines, Third Marine Division, in connection with combat operations against the enemy in the Republic of Vietnam. During the early morning hours of 25 February 1969, while elements of the Second Battalion were occupying a defensive position at Fire Support Base Neville in Quang Tri Province, the Marines came under a vicious ground attack by a North Vietnamese Army sapper company supported by mortars, grenades, and satchel charges. Reacting instantly, Sergeant LaPorte commenced directing devastating countermortar fire and illumination on the assaulting force as it neared the battalion's perimeter wire, and as the Marines' supply of mortar rounds became depleted, he fearlessly moved about the fire-swept terrain to ensure the rapid resupply of mortar ammunition. When an enemy round detonated in an 81mm mortar emplacement and ignited an uncontrollable fire, Sergeant LaPorte quickly directed the men of his mortar crew to evacuate the position and led them to a covered location, then returned and organized a firefighting crew to extinguish the blaze. Observing two wounded Marines lying in positions dangerously exposed to the North Vietnamese fire, he boldly maneuvered through the hazardous area and assisted his injured companions to a location of relative security. As he reached the command post, an 81mm mortar round impacted in the vicinity. He unhesitatingly seized the extremely hot projectile and, despite severely burning his hands, threw it over an embankment, thereby preventing injury or destruction to nearby personnel and equipment. His heroic actions and calm presence of mind during a prolonged critical situation inspired all who observed him and saved the lives of numerous Marines. By his courage, selfless concern for his fellowmen, and unwavering devotion to duty in the face of grave personal danger, Sergeant LaPorte upheld the highest traditions of the Marine Corps and the United States Naval Service.

*LARAWAY, WILLIAM D.

Citation: For extraordinary heroism as a rifleman while serving with Combined Action Company "H", Sub Unit Number 4 of Headquarters Battalion, Third Marine Division in the Republic of Vietnam on the night of 11 April 1967. Lance Corporal Laraway was participating on a combined U. S. Marine and Republic of Vietnam Popular Forces patrol in Cau Hai Hamlet, Phu Loc District, when the main body of the patrol became separated from the point which included the patrol leader. As the point came under intense enemy fire, Lance Corporal Laraway quickly moved the main body to assist them. When they were taken under heavy fire at close range by an unknown number of Viet Cong from an ambush position, he quickly placed his M-60 machine gun in action and took the enemy under fire to cover the deployment of the other members of the patrol. The Medical Corpsman fell severely wounded in the initial burst of enemy fire. Disregarding the intense enemy fire, Lance Corporal Laraway unhesitatingly ran from his relatively sheltered position and carried the wounded corpsman to a less exposed position. He returned to his machine gun and again delivered heavy fire on the enemy, only to have a deadly barrage of hand grenades hurled at his position by the Viet Cong. He again raced to the aid of the wounded corpsman and shielded him from the grenades with his own body. He seized two of the incoming grenades and hurled them back at the enemy and kicked others from their position before they detonated. Oblivious of the continuing enemy fire and grenades, he again moved to his machine gun in a position between the wounded and the enemy. While attempting to place his machine gun in action he fell fatally wounded from an exploding enemy grenade. By his outstanding courage, valiant devotion to duty and selfless efforts in behalf of his wounded comrade, Lance Corporal Laraway upheld the highest traditions of the Marine Corps and the United States Naval Service. He gallantly gave his life for his country.

LARSEN, DAVID R.

Citation: For extraordinary heroism on 2 August 1969 while serving with friendly foreign forces engaged in armed conflict against North Vietnamese and Viet Cong communist aggressor forces in the

Republic of Vietnam. Petty Officer Larsen was serving as a gunner's mate aboard River Patrol Boat (PBR) 775 which was part of a two-boat night waterborne guard post stationed on the upper Saigon River. Operating in conjunction with the patrol, a six-man ambush team, which was providing bank security for the guard post, engaged four enemy soldiers who were part of an estimated 35 to 50-man force that returned the contact with accurate rocket fire, killing or critically wounding all but one member of the six-man ambush team. One man from the team managed to call for the PBR crewmen's help. Armed with a machine gun and several ammunition belts, Petty Officer Larsen hastened to the assistance of the ambush team. As he led his small force ashore, he saw three enemy soldiers about to overrun the friendly position. He immediately rushed toward them, firing his machine gun, and single-handedly turned back the enemy assault, killing at least one of the enemy. Petty Officer Larsen then maintained a one-man perimeter defensive position and, although under continuous enemy fire, succeeded in discouraging further enemy attacks until additional help arrived. Later, armed with three different weapons, Petty Officer Larsen was the first man to take his post on the perimeter established to provide security for the medical evacuation helicopter. By his extremely courageous one-man assault in the face of direct enemy fire, Petty Officer Larsen was responsible for saving the lives of three fellow servicemen, and for protecting his shipmates as they administered aid to the wounded. His valiant and inspiring efforts reflect the highest credit upon himself and the United States Naval Service.

*LAUER, CHARLES R.

Citation: For extraordinary heroism as a Crew Chief with Company A, Third Amphibian Tractor Battalion, First Marine Division (Reinforced) in the Republic of Vietnam on 18 June 1967. Following an assault by three amphibian tractors, Hill 11 continued to receive heavy, accurate, automatic fire from tree lines to the right and left and tunnels and bunkers on the hill itself. As a platoon of infantry endeavored to reach the hill, vicious enemy fire cut down the Platoon Commander, his radio operator and another Marine. Corporal Lauer was at this time manning a machine gun mounted atop his amphibian tractor. With complete disregard for his own safety, he nonetheless ordered his tractor forward and dropped its ramp to pull in the wounded. At this time the enemy concentrated its already intense fire on the medical evacuation in progress by his vehicle. Unhesitatingly and knowing the intimate danger involved, he elected to stay by the gun to deliver accurate counter fire into the surrounding tree lines. When the incoming fire became so intense that it began ripping into the interior of the tractor and endangering the wounded, he ordered his tractor to be turned stern to the fire, so that the engine could shield the casualties. At this time Corporal Lauer elected to remain atop the tractor to cover for another group of wounded, fully mindful of the intense danger. With enemy fire ripping across his tractor from two sides, he began to shift his position, and was mortally wounded. By his daring initiative, valiant fighting spirit and selfless devotion to duty in the face of imminent danger, Corporal Lauer was responsible for saving many of his comrades and thereby upheld the highest traditions of the Marine Corps and the United States Naval Service. He gallantly gave his life for his country.

LAZARO, LAWRENCE J.

Citation: For extraordinary heroism while serving as a Fire Team Leader with Company E, Second Battalion, Seventh Marines in Vietnam on 19 September 1966. While the second platoon of Company E was on a patrol in jungle terrain of Quang Tri Province, it came under heavy small-arms and automatic weapons fire from a large Viet Cong force. The squad leader was wounded during the initial exchange of fire and Corporal Lazaro immediately assumed command. Continually exposing himself to enemy fire, he moved from position to position inspiring the other men with his dynamic leadership and courageous fighting spirit. He redistributed ammunition and directed fire where it would be most effective against the enemy. Upon hearing that there were wounded comrades pinned down on the point, Corporal Lazaro and three volunteers fought their way under fire to the wounded. With complete disregard for his own safety, Corporal Lazaro calmly supervised the evacuation of the dead and wounded and then brought up rear security for the safe withdrawal of the patrol. By his daring initiative, inspiring leadership and outstanding courage, Corporal Lazaro served to inspire all who observed him and upheld the highest traditions of the Marine Corps and of the United States Naval Service.

*LEAL, ARMANDO G., JR.

Citation: For extraordinary heroism on 4 September 1967 while serving as a corpsman with the Second Platoon, Company "M", Third Battalion, Fifth Marines, First Marine Division (Reinforced), FMF, in connection with operations against enemy aggressor forces in the Republic of Vietnam. During Operation SWIFT, the Second Platoon was providing security for the Battalion Command Group when the platoon came under heavy enemy fire. Petty Officer (then Hospitalman) Leal ran through the fire-swept area, and began administering first aid to several casualties who were directly exposed to grazing fire. Although constantly exposed to heavy fire, and painfully wounded himself, he rendered aid for two hours to wounded Marines who were located between friendly and enemy lines. He refused to be evacuated in order that he might continue his mission of mercy. While treating his comrades and moving them to protected areas, Petty Officer Leal was severely wounded for a second time and, despite being immobilized, calmly continued to aid his wounded comrades. A Marine tried to drag him to a covered position, but was shot in the hand and, at that time, Petty Officer Leal received a third wound. Petty Officer Leal pushed the Marine and told him to take cover from the assaulting enemy whom they both could see. Suddenly a North Vietnamese soldier fired a machine gun from close range, mortally wounding Petty Officer Leal. Through his swift actions and professional skill in aiding and protecting the wounded, he significantly eased the suffering and undoubtedly saved the lives of several of his comrades. His exceptional courage and unfaltering dedication to duty in the face of great personal risk were in keeping with the highest traditions of the United States Naval Service.

LEBAS, CLAUDE G.

Citation: For extraordinary heroism as a rifleman with Company B, First Battalion, Third Marines, Third Marine Division (Reinforced), Fleet Marine Force at Quang Nam Province, Vietnam, on 2 April 1966. When his platoon came under heavy automatic-weapons and mortar fire, Corporal Lebas, sighting the enemy mortar position, withdrew to the rear and retrieved three assault weapons. Returning alone through an open area covered by heavy fire from two directions, he single-handedly destroyed the enemy mortar position just as it was adjusting fire on the company command group. Upon returning to his platoon, it was discovered that a machine gunner had been killed and that he and his weapon were one hundred meters forward of the secured position. Even though his platoon was assuming a reserve position, Corporal Lebas turned and, while shouting for covering fire, rushed out to retrieve the weapon. The enemy fire was so intense that his covering force was driven back to a more secure area. With complete disregard for his own safety, Corporal Lebas grabbed the gun and returned to safety amid a hail of bullets. It was later learned that two enemy rounds were imbedded in his haversack, stopped only by the rations he was carrying. Corporal Lebas' actions were in keeping with the highest traditions of the Marine Corps and the United States Naval Service.

LEDBETTER, WALTER R., JR.

Citation: For extraordinary heroism as Commanding Officer of Marine Medium Helicopter Squadron 263, Marine Aircraft Group 16, First Marine Aircraft Wing, during operations against the enemy in the Republic of Vietnam. On the morning of 31 January 1970, Lieutenant Colonel Ledbetter launched as flight leader of three helicopters assigned to transport assault teams during a Marine heliborne assault mission in Quang Nam Province. While carrying out his mission, he received an urgent request to assist elements of a platoon which had inadvertently entered a minefield while attacking enemy positions, and had sustained several casualties. Realizing that the Marines stood little chance of survival in their helpless position, Lieutenant Colonel Ledbetter, ignoring sporadic sniper fire from a tree line, cautiously maneuvered his helicopter to a landing in a small crater created by the explosion of one of the mines and remained in his perilous position until the casualties in that area were embarked. He then air taxied fifty meters to the second group of Marines and, undaunted by the extreme danger of landing in a mined area with only his main mount touching the area cleared by the detonated mine, carefully executed a landing. As the injured were being placed aboard, another mine exploded close to his aircraft, damaging the rotor system and aft pylon area. With complete disregard for his own safety, Lieutenant Colonel Ledbetter remained in his precarious position until all of the remaining Marines were aboard his aircraft, then lifted out of the hazardous area and departed for the hospital at Danang. By his courage, superb airmanship, and inspiring devotion to duty in the face of great personal danger, Lieutenant Colonel Ledbetter was instrumental in saving the lives of several of his fellow Marines, and upheld the highest traditions of the Marine Corps and the United States Naval Service.

LEDFORD, KENNETH, JR.

Citation: For extraordinary heroism on 15 September 1970 while serving with the 58th Medical Battalion, United States Army, engaged in armed conflict against enemy forces in the Republic of Vietnam. While flying as a medical evacuation pilot and aircraft commander of a rescue helicopter, First Lieutenant Ledford was attempting to extract six seriously wounded personnel from a landing zone when he came under heavy enemy small-arms and automatic-weapons fire. Forced to depart the area, he subsequently enlisted the aid of four Navy helicopters and returned to the scene for another rescue attempt. As the aircraft were making their descent into the zone, they came under intense small-arms, automatic-weapons, and .51 caliber fire. Two of First Lieutenant Ledford's cover ships were shot down, a third gunship was disabled, and a fourth was seriously damaged. Instantly, First Lieutenant Ledford went to the rescue of the crew of one of these aircraft which had autorotated into a lake. Despite intense enemy fire from several positions as he neared the stricken aircraft, he succeeded in rescuing the downed crew. Once airborne he enlisted the aid of the remaining attack helicopter to cover him while he attempted to extract the dead and wounded from the second downed aircraft. As he approached the wreckage, again coming under a hail of small-arms and automatic-weapons fire, he landed and at great personal risk held his position while his crew made two time-consuming extractions of the wounded men. As the extraction was completed, he took off through the continuing barrage of enemy bullets and impacting mortar rounds. First Lieutenant Ledford's professionalism, courage under fire, and inspiring dedication to duty were in keeping with the highest traditions of the United States Armed Forces.

LEFLER, ALAN C.

Citation: For extraordinary heroism while serving with Marine Light Helicopter Observation Squadron Two, Marine Aircraft Group Sixteen, First Marine Aircraft Wing in connection with combat operations against the enemy in the Republic of Vietnam. On 17 March 1969, Lance Corporal Lefler launched as Crew Chief aboard an armed helicopter assigned the mission of supporting a Marine company which was heavily engaged in combat with a large North Vietnamese Army force near An Hoa in Quang Nam Province. Arriving over the designated location, he was informed that the unit on the ground had sustained several casualties and had been pinned down in an open rice paddy by a heavy volume of automatic weapons fire. Throughout the ensuing four-hour period, while his pilot maneuvered the helicopter close to hostile emplacements, Lance Corporal Lefler delivered intense machine gun fire at the enemy. Despite his vigorous efforts, the withering fire of the hostile troops still prevented the Marines from recovering their casualties from exposed locations. The pilot of the helicopter subsequently elected to land his craft in the contested area to evacuate the wounded men. During the landing, the aircraft became a vulnerable target for intensified hostile fire. Although Lance Corporal Lefler attempted to suppress the enemy fire and to destroy the nearby enemy positions with his machine gun, he observed that the hostile fusillade raking the friendly lines prevented the Marines from reaching the casualties. Quickly dismounting his machine gun and providing his own covering fire, he ran thirty meters across the hazardous terrain to the side of one of the wounded and, assisted by a companion, carried the critically wounded Marine back toward the helicopter. On three additional occasions, the pilot landed to embark casualties and, each time, Lance Corporal Lefler braved the hostile fire to ensure the evacuation of the casualties. His heroic and selfless actions inspired all who observed him and were instrumental in saving the lives of four fellow Marines. By his courage, initiative, and selfless devotion to duty, Lance Corporal Lefler upheld the highest traditions of the Marine Corps and of the United States Naval Service.

LEFTWICH, WILLIAM G., JR.

Citation: For extraordinary heroism as the Senior Task Force Advisor to Task Force Alfa, Vietnamese Marine Brigade, in the vicinity of Hoai An Village, Binh Dinh Province, Republic of Vietnam, on 9 March 1965. Major Leftwich played a major part in all phases of the successful relief of the village of Hoai An, which was under heavy enemy attack by two Viet Cong battalions. Prior to the actual operation, he worked out a plan with the 22nd Division Air Liaison Officer for supporting aircraft to deliver their ordnance in extra-close proximity to the front lines, and then to continue simulated attacks while the Vietnamese Marines assaulted the enemy positions.

He participated in the planning of the approach march which, by using last-minute intelligence, avoided a massive ambush planned by the Viet Cong. As lead elements of the Task Force contacted the Viet Cong from an unexpected direction, he sensed the ideal opportunity to use the prearranged air support plan, and taking the radio, he moved under heavy fire to the forward-most elements of the Task Force. By his own personal example of shooting point-blank and shouting, he led the attack which overran the immediate Viet Cong positions and carried the assault to within forty meters of the crest of a hill overlooking Hoai An. Despite injuries by enemy machine-gun bullets in the back, cheek, and nose, he went to the aid of a mortally wounded comrade, and although bleeding profusely, he refused assistance and delayed his own evacuation until he could call for additional air strikes and brief the Task Force Commander of the situation. Through his heroic conduct and fearless devotion to duty in the face of personal risk, Major Leftwich upheld the highest traditions of the Marine Corps and the United States Naval Service.

LEWIS, DAVID H.

Citation: For extraordinary heroism while serving as a surgeon with the First Medical Battalion, First Marine Division in connection with combat operations against the enemy in the Republic of Vietnam. On 24 September 1969, a Marine was admitted to the battalion's emergency receiving area with a serious wound in his thigh. Subsequent x-rays revealed that an armed grenade launcher round was imbedded in the tissue adjacent to the bone. After directing all personnel not positively necessary to assist him as he operated to immediately leave the area, Lieutenant Commander Lewis supervised the careful removal of the wounded man to an operating room and then directed that sand bags be placed around the patient, leaving only room for himself to move while he worked with the casualty. Fully aware that the round could detonate at any moment, but concerned only for the welfare of the wounded man, Lieutenant Commander Lewis then skillfully operated on his patient and successfully extracted the projectile. His resolute determination and bold initiative inspired all who observed him and were instrumental in saving the life of the Marine. By his courage, fearless action, and selfless devotion to duty under extremely perilous conditions, Lieutenant Commander Lewis averted a potential disaster and upheld the highest traditions of the United States Naval Service.

LINDER, JAMES B.

Citation: For extraordinary heroism in aerial flight on 28 September 1967 as Commander, Attack Carrier Air Wing FIFTEEN, embarked in USS CORAL SEA CVA-43). Commander Linder planned, led, and directed an air-wing striking force consisting of thirty-one aircraft against the heavily defended and strategically important Haiphong railway/highway bridge in North Vietnam. Although subjected to intense and accurate barrages of multi-caliber antiaircraft-artillery fire, surface-to-air missiles, and enemy interceptor aircraft, he fearlessly and skillfully directed and controlled the striking forces assigned, resolutely pressing home a devastating attack which resulted in total destruction of the bridge and marked the culmination of the comprehensive attack plan to isolate the city. As the leader of four of the previous assaults on the strategic Haiphong bridge complex, Commander Linder, by his courageous leadership, comprehensive planning, and outstanding airmanship, contributed greatly to the total success of this daring and expansive attack strategy. Tactics which were planned and executed by Commander Linder encompassed over one hundred and fifty attack sorties and were consummated in the face of scores of accurate surface-to-air missile firings and fusillades of antiaircraft fire concentrated at the targets. Despite the enemy's determined and formidable opposition, the logistic lifeline of Haiphong was effectively severed by the destruction of these key bridges without the loss of a single strike aircraft. Commander Linder's brilliant planning, consummate flight leadership, and fearless devotion to duty in the face of grave personal danger were in keeping with the highest traditions of the United States Naval Service.

*LINEBERRY, JERRY E.

Citation: For extraordinary heroism while serving as a Platoon Sergeant with Company B, First Battalion, Seventh Marines, First Marine Division in connection with combat operations against the enemy in the Republic of Vietnam. On 12 February 1970, during a platoon-sized patrol in the Que Son Mountains of Quang Nam Province, the Marines came under a heavy volume of small-arms and automatic-weapons fire from North Vietnamese Army soldiers occupying well-concealed emplacements in a hedgerow to the front of the friendly unit. During the initial moments of the assault, the platoon sustained several casualties. Realizing the need for decisive action,

Staff Sergeant Lineberry directed one of his fire teams to execute a movement to the enemy's flank and initiate a counterattack. As the men moved across the open rice paddy, they were pinned down by a grenade launcher and automatic-weapons fire delivered from two different directions and sustained additional casualties. In a valiant effort to assist the beleaguered unit, Staff Sergeant Lineberry led a machine gun team across the fire-swept terrain. Although seriously wounded during this action, he shouted encouragement to the pinned-down men and directed other Marines as they evacuated the casualties. Despite his extreme pain, he refused to leave the hazardous area and, even after becoming a target for concentrated hostile fire, continued to direct his men and adjust supporting Marine artillery fire on enemy targets until he was mortally wounded. His heroic and determined efforts inspired all who observed him and contributed significantly to the defeat of the North Vietnamese Army force. By his courage, selfless actions, and unwavering devotion to duty, Staff Sergeant Lineberry upheld the highest traditions of the Marine Corps and of the United States Naval Service.

LIVINGSTON, LAWRENCE H.

Citation: For extraordinary heroism on 11 July 1972 while serving as Senior Advisor to the 1st Vietnamese Marine Corps Infantry Battalion during a heliborne assault into enemy-held territory northeast of Quang Tri City, Republic of Vietnam. When the battalion encountered unexpectedly heavy enemy fire while disembarking into the landing zone, and sustained numerous casualties, Captain Livingston moved throughout the hasty positions taken by the scattered and hesitant element and formed the Marines into an assault force. Despite the continuing heavy concentration of hostile fire, he began the assault on the initial objective — a treeline approximately 50 yards distant. Although blown from his feet by explosions and periodically delayed to reform and redirect his casualty-riddled force, he forged ahead, leading the Vietnamese Marines into the enemy-infested trench lines of the objective and a subsequent hand-to-hand battle. Upon seizure of the initial portion of the trench line, Captain Livingston shed his combat equipment, emerged from the trench line, and exposed himself to a hail of enemy fire to reach and carry his wounded naval gunfire spotter to a position of relative safety. Captain Livingston's repeated acts of heroism in the face of heavy enemy fire reflected great credit upon himself and the Marine Corps and were in keeping with the highest traditions of the United States Naval Service.

LONG, MELVIN M.

Citation: For extraordinary heroism while serving as Second Squad Leader, Third Platoon, Company F, Second Battalion, Fifth Marines, First Marine Division (Reinforced) Quang Tin Province, Republic of Vietnam, during Operation UNION II, on 2 June 1967. While advancing toward a designated objective, Company F came under an intense volume of enemy mortar, recoilless rifle, automatic weapons and small arms fire. Due to its exposed position, the Third Platoon was temporarily pinned down. Sergeant (then Corporal) Long was ordered to seize a critical piece of high ground in the tree line on the left flank. He moved his squad under intense enemy fire, across 200 meters of open, fire swept terrain into the tree line. With complete disregard for his own safety, he maneuvered his squad in an enveloping movement and assaulted the well-entrenched enemy position from the rear resulting in six enemy killed. Though painfully wounded, he led his men in overrunning the position and organized a hasty defense. From his newly won position, he observed another enemy machine gun position which was delivering accurate fire on the platoon. With complete disregard for his wounds and the intense enemy fire, he led another assault which resulted in two more enemy killed. He then organized a defensive position and defended their key terrain feature for three hours until the enemy finally withdrew. Upon learning of the enemy's withdrawal, Sergeant Long led his men to a landing zone some 600 meters to the rear and supervised the evacuation of his wounded. By his outstanding courage, exceptional fortitude and valiant fighting spirit, Sergeant Long served to inspire all who observed him and upheld the highest traditions of the Marine Corps and the United States Naval Service.

LOPEZ, JOSE G.

Citation: For extraordinary heroism while serving as a Patrol Leader with Company B, Third Reconnaissance Battalion, Third Marine Division (Reinforced), in the Republic of Vietnam on 2 September 1967. Sergeant Lopez's patrol was inserted near Khe Sanh into enemy infested and controlled territory. After moving from the landing zone, he spotted several enemy attempting to encircle his position. The patrol was taken under devastating enemy automatic and semiautomatic rifle fire from a numerically superior enemy force. Quickly assessing the situation, he deployed his men and returned accurate fire upon the enemy positions and directed close air support on the enemy, destroying their position. He quickly moved his men from an exposed position and established a hasty defense. Spotting six enemy soldiers approaching his position, Sergeant Lopez and another Marine assaulted them with tear gas grenades and annihilated them with rifle fire. Shortly thereafter, two more enemy attempted to maneuver to his position, but once again, with complete disregard for his own safety, he and a comrade assaulted the enemy with hand grenades and killed them. He then called fixed wing and armed helicopter strikes, sealing off further enemy reinforcements and destroying numerous enemy positions. He then skillfully led his patrol out of the area as gunships and fixed wing aircraft bombarded the enemy positions. By his bold initiative, gallant fighting spirit and loyal devotion to duty, Sergeant Lopez was instrumental in defeating a numerically superior enemy force, reflecting great credit upon himself and the Marine Corps and upholding the highest traditions of the United States Naval Service.

LOPEZ, STEVEN D.

Citation: For extraordinary heroism while serving as a Radio Operator with the First Platoon, Company A, Third Reconnaissance Battalion, Third Marine Division (Reinforced) near Khe Sanh, Republic of Vietnam, on 9 and 10 May 1967. Corporal (then Private First Class) Lopez was a member of a seven man reconnaissance patrol deep in enemy controlled territory. The patrol discovered numerous enemy bunkers and equipment and radioed the valuable intelligence information back. Towards evening they withdrew to high ground and established a night defense. Shortly after midnight, a North Vietnamese unit of approximately 50 men was heard moving toward their position. Several enemy troops walked into their position and started to unsling their weapons and Corporal Lopez quickly killed them with an accurate burst of automatic weapons fire. The enemy immediately began delivering a heavy volume of small arms fire into their perimeter. As the fire fight continued, numerous casualties were inflicted until only Corporal Lopez, who was wounded in the side, and another Marine were able to deliver fire on the enemy. Although wounded, he assumed the task of directing artillery on enemy positions around the patrol. Armed helicopters and flare ships arrived to add support to the besieged patrol. Wounded a second time, he still courageously directed supporting arms in dangerously close to his position as, on several occasions, the enemy was within 15 feet of his position. Two attempts to extract the patrol by helicopter failed, due to the intense enemy fire. Running low on ammunition, he moved among the bodies of his fallen comrades to retrieve ammunition and discovered one Marine seriously wounded. He moved him to a covered position and distributed the ammunition between himself and the other survivor. He once again called in air support so close that dirt from the exploding rockets and bombs showered them and was once again wounded when an enemy round grazed his head. A last desperate attempt was made for extraction by helicopter. Napalm, bombs, and rockets rocked the enemy's position as the three remaining members of the patrol were extracted. His steadfast determination and indomitable fighting spirit throughout the twelve hour ordeal were instrumental in inflicting numerous casualties on the enemy and saving the lives of several Marines. By his outstanding courage, bold initiative and selfless devotion to duty in the face of grave personal danger, Corporal Lopez upheld the highest traditions of the Marine Corps and the United States Naval Service.

*LOWERANITIS, JOHN L.

Citation: For extraordinary heroism while serving as Company Messenger of Company "I", Third Battalion, Ninth Marines in the Republic of Vietnam on 30 March 1967. The company was engaged in establishing platoon night ambush sites against communist insurgent forces in the Quang Tri Province when the company command group and a small security element were attacked by a North Vietnamese reinforced company utilizing heavy automatic weapons and mortar fire. At the initiation of the action Corporal Loweranitis moved through intense fire to the 60mm mortar position, reorganized the crew and delivered effective fire on the machine gun positions that were raking the Marine positions. When the mortar ammunition was expended he again exposed himself to small-arms fire and grenades as he moved from position to position evacuating wounded to the reverse slope of the hill. When the North Vietnamese Army attempted to overrun the Marine positions, he moved to the most threatened point and personally accounted for five enemy kills. Although wounded by small-arms fire and grenade fragments on two separate occasions, he refused to leave his position and resolutely covered the withdrawal of the command group to a more tenable position until he fell, mortally wounded. His heroic action, with complete disregard for his own life, allowed the Marines to gain the new position and account for numerous enemy casualties. By his outstanding courage, exceptional fortitude and valiant fighting spirit, Corporal Loweranitis served to inspire all who observed him and upheld the highest traditions of the Marine Corps and the United States Naval Service. He gallantly gave his life for his country.

LOWERY, STEVEN M.

Citation: For extraordinary heroism while serving as a patrol leader with Company C, Third Reconnaissance Battalion, Third Marine Division, in connection with combat operations against the enemy in the Republic of Vietnam. Early on the morning of 5 March 1969, Corporal Lowery's twelve-man reconnaissance patrol was occupying a defensive position at Fire Support Base Argonne south of the Demilitarized Zone. Suddenly, the Marines were assaulted by a North Vietnamese Army platoon employing mortars, hand grenades, and automatic weapons. In the initial moments of the fire fight, Corporal Lowery was seriously wounded in both legs by the intense enemy fire. Steadfastly remaining in his hazardous position, he boldly delivered accurate return fire and hurled grenades at the advancing enemy. When two hostile soldiers approached his position in an attempt to penetrate the Marine perimeter, Corporal Lowery calmly lobbed three hand grenades outside of his emplacement, killing several of the enemy and causing the others to retreat. Although suffering extensive pain and weakness from his wounds, he then commenced directing artillery fire upon the hostile force to within twenty meters of friendly lines and skillfully readjusted his defenses. When helicopters arrived to extract his team, he skillfully directed supporting gunships against the North Vietnamese unit and ensured that all other wounded Marines were aboard the extraction aircraft before allowing himself to be carried to the helicopter. His bold initiative and resolute determination inspired all who observed him and were instrumental in his unit's accounting for twenty North Vietnamese soldiers killed. By his courage, aggressive fighting spirit, and unwavering devotion to duty in the face of great personal danger, Corporal Lowery upheld the highest traditions of the Marine Corps and the United States Naval Service.

LOWNDS, DAVID E.

Citation: For extraordinary heroism while serving as Commanding Officer of the Khe Sanh Combat Base in connection with operations against the enemy in the Republic of Vietnam from August 1967 through March 1968. Upon assuming command of the vital combat base located in western Quang Tri Province and tasked with the responsibility of interdicting major North Vietnamese resupply routes and blocking any enemy invasion attempt from the west into the northern provinces of South Vietnam, Colonel Lownds immediately established combat outposts on Hills 881 South, 861, and 950, and launched extensive and highly effective patrol activities throughout his area of responsibility. Despite the hazardous, mountainous terrain, thick jungle foliage, and adverse weather conditions, Colonel Lownds' valiant combat leadership and indomitable command ability were the central instrument in achieving and maintaining the superb combat posture of the base. On 28 January 1968, when North Vietnamese divisions launched a coordinated attack on the Khe Sanh Combat Base with rockets, artillery, mortar, and machine-gun and small-arms fire, and with their main attack directed at Hill 861-A, Colonel Lownds' superb knowledge of and appreciation for the terrain and his aggressive utilization of all supporting arms minimized the effectiveness of the enemy attack and resulted in a large number of enemy casualties. During daily enemy rocket and artillery attacks, and on 23 February when the firing reached its peak with more than 1300 rounds impacting on the combat base, his superior tactical judgment, calm leadership, brave demeanor, and resolute endurance were an inspiration to all around him and were a prime factor in maintaining a high level of morale among his men. Giving no thought to his own safety, while exhibiting a compassionate concern for the welfare of his Marines, he gallantly and repeatedly exposed himself to hostile fire making daily visits to outlying units to observe tactical operations and to study conditions confronting his unit commanders. During the period 1 November 1967 to 31 March 1968, Colonel Lownds organized and directed Operation SCOTLAND, a highly effective search and destroy operation throughout the Khe Sanh tactical area of responsibility, which resulted in numerous enemy casualties, the capture of several enemy, and a large number of weapons confiscated. By his gallant leadership, distinguished personal bravery, and selfless devotion to duty throughout, Colonel Lownds upheld the highest traditions of the Marine Corps and the United States Naval Service.

LUCA, JOSEPH

Citation: For extraordinary heroism while serving as a Company Runner and Interpreter with Company F, Second Battalion, Seventh Marines, attached to the Third Battalion, Seventh Marines, First Marine Division (Reinforced) in Quang Ngai Province, Republic of Vietnam, on 5 March 1967. Company F was on a search and destroy mission when the lead elements crossed an open field and were taken under extremely heavy and accurate automatic weapons fire from cleverly concealed Viet Cong. Immediately, the point man was mortally wounded, and the remainder of the platoon drew up to a position on the secure side of a hedgerow that bordered the open area, to provide covering fire. Sergeant (then Corporal) Luca led the command group to the sound of the firing and, when he reached the hedgerow, joined in the firing at the suspected enemy positions. Realizing that he could more effectively give suppressive fire from the open field, he dashed through the hedgerow into the clearing, and from his new position took the enemy under fire and maintained his barely tenable position, bravely drawing all the enemy fire to himself, so that the wounded could be carried to the landing zone behind him. Then, when enemy fire suddenly ceased, the company moved out in pursuit. As the unit moved forward once again, a vicious stream of enemy automatic weapons fire caught the lead elements. The landing zone was saturated with enemy fire as the helicopters came in; however, Sergeant Luca calmly assisted in carrying the wounded to the helicopters. His uncommon resourcefulness and daring actions were inspirational to all who observed him. With complete disregard for his own safety, Sergeant Luca saved his comrades from further injury and possibly loss of life, thereby reflecting great credit upon himself and upholding the highest traditions of the Marine Corps and the United States Naval Service.

LUMBARD, DONALD W.

Citation: For extraordinary heroism while serving with Company B, First Amphibian Tractor Battalion, Third Marine Division during Operation MACON in Vietnam on 4 July 1966. Lance Corporal Lumbard was serving as Vehicle Commander of an amphibian tractor supporting a Marine infantry company during a search and clear operation in known enemy infested terrain when the lead element of the company came under extremely heavy small-arms and recoilless rifle fire in the vicinity north of An Hoa. One of the supporting tractors sustained severe hits and was disabled. Reacting immediately, Lance Corporal Lumbard maneuvered his vehicle alongside and, braving the withering fire, climbed aboard in a gallant attempt to aid his comrades. Finding the crew had been killed, he exhibited exceptional presence of mind in unloading the stricken vehicle's mortars and ammunition and distributing them to other units engaged in the vicious action. Undaunted by the increasingly heavy fire, he returned to the disabled vehicle and manned its machine gun, directing a devastating volume of fire at enemy positions until the ammunition was exhausted. He then raced to another damaged vehicle and used its machine gun to battle the Viet Cong. Then, turning the machine gun over to another Marine, he valiantly exposed himself to the hail of fire to distribute water, assist in the evacuation of the wounded and deliver supplies to units who were in dire need. Observing an unmanned machine gun, he was attempting to put it in action when he was painfully wounded by fragments from a recoillesss rifle round. Ignoring his pain, he administered first aid to two comrades wounded at the same time. Helping them aboard an amphibian tractor, he assisted the crew chief to maneuver the vehicle to a defilade position. When the vehicle carrying the wounded was hit, he reported the situation to the senior noncommissioned officer before being evacuated. Lance Corporal Lumbard's intrepid fighting spirit, inspiring courage and gallant concern for his comrades reflected great credit upon himself and the Marine Corps and upheld the highest traditions of the United States Naval Service.

*LUNSFORD, GLEN T.

Citation: For extraordinary heroism while serving as a Platoon Right Guide with Company D, First Battalion, Seventh Marines, First Marine Division (Reinforced), in the Republic of Vietnam on 3 February 1968. Upon the discovery of a large cave complex, at Phu Son (2), Sergeant Lunsford volunteered to accompany a reactionary force to destroy the tunnels. Locating several camouflaged underwater entrances to the cave, he placed a Marine near each of them to prevent the Viet Cong's escape. Unable to use explosives because of the necessity of obtaining prisoners, he supervised the excavation of an above ground entrance. Upon completing the new entrance, he threw a tear gas grenade into the opening, routing three Viet Cong who broke from the cave throwing grenades and were killed. Armed only with a pistol and a flashlight, he entered the tunnel and moved along a narrow passageway until he discovered a large room. Observing two Viet Cong trying to escape through an underwater passageway, he killed one and captured the other. Interrogation of the prisoner revealed that there were numerous enemy soldiers still in the cave complex. Realizing that the enemy was aware of the tunnel being searched and confined in a small area, Sergeant Lunsford nevertheless reentered the tunnel. As he neared a sharp bend in the tunnel, a Viet Cong, who was concealed around a corner, tossed a grenade which wounded him in both legs. Although painfully wounded, Sergeant Lunsford lunged forward and captured the Viet Cong as he attempted to escape. After bringing his prisoner to the top, he fearlessly reentered the tunnel with several comrades and searched the numerous small rooms and tunnels. His diligent efforts resulted in the capture of several weapons, supplies and valuable intelligence information. Sergeant Lunsford reflected great credit upon himself and the Marine Corps and upheld the highest traditions of the United States Naval Service.

*MACK, FRANCIS W.

Citation: For extraordinary heroism as a corpsman with Company F, Second Battalion, Fourth Marines in the Republic of Vietnam on 17 August 1966. When the lead platoon was suddenly taken under devastating enemy fire by automatic weapons and snipers from concealed positions during a reconnaissance-in-force operation in the Cam Lo River Valley, Quang Tri Province, Petty Officer Mack immediately began to administer aid to the wounded. Upon being informed that two seriously wounded Marines needed medical aid, but couldn't be evacuated due to intense and accurate enemy fire, he unhesitatingly moved over two hundred meters down the fire-swept road to reach the casualties. With bullets striking the ground near him, he nonetheless succeeded in administering lifesaving aid to the wounded men and remained with them until they were evacuated. Before moving back to a covered position in preparation for an air strike, Petty Officer Mack once again exposed himself to the intense enemy fire to assist a wounded Marine in the advance element who needed medical aid prior to being evacuated. While rendering first aid to the wounded man, Petty Officer Mack, himself, was mortally wounded. By his extraordinary initiative, inspiring valor and unswerving devotion to duty, he was directly responsible for saving the lives of three fellow servicemen. His heroic actions were in keeping with the highest traditions of the United States Naval Service.

MAC VANE, MATTHEW C.

Citation: For extraordinary heroism while serving as a Rifleman with Combined Action Company F, Headquarters Battalion, Third Marine Division (Reinforced), in the Republic of Vietnam on 14 August 1967. While deployed in its compound at Cam Hieu in Cam Lo District, Quang Tri Province, Corporal (then Lance Corporal) MacVane's platoon came under intense fire from an estimated company-sized North Vietnamese Army force. Utilizing satchel charges followed by small-arms fire, the determined enemy attempted for over an hour to penetrate the compound's defensive perimeter. Corporal MacVane constantly exposed himself to enemy fire to defend the perimeter and assist and encourage his companions. Fearlessly moving from one bunker to another, he ensured that all emplacements were manned while simultaneously delivering accurate fire against the enemy. When his ammunition was expended, he proceeded across the exposed compound to the ammunition bunker, armed himself with antitank assault weapons, and quickly returned to the perimeter and distributed them. Corporal MacVane again made his way to the ammunition bunker and, upon his return, with heavy enemy fire concentrating on him, commenced to distribute M-26 hand grenades to each position in the compound. Then, he resolutely continued to move along, encouraging the men and throwing hand grenades into the enemy positions. Subsequently, he obtained white phosphorous grenades from the ammunition supply and used these to protect the positions receiving the heaviest barrage of enemy fire. Until the enemy was forced to withdraw, he continued to move throughout the compound, throwing white phosphorous grenades into the midst of the enemy, encouraging his companions and aiding and comforting the wounded. His bravery and determination were instrumental in maintaining the security of the platoon's compound. By his fortitude, daring initiative, and selfless devotion to duty at great personal risk, Corporal MacVane upheld the highest traditions of the Marine Corps and the United States Naval Service.

MALONE, GEORGE M.

Citation: For extraordinary heroism while serving as a platoon commander with Company A, First Battalion, Ninth Marines, Third

Marine Division, in connection with operations against the enemy in the Republic of Vietnam. Early on the afternoon of 22 February 1969, Second Lieutenant Malone's platoon was moving as the lead element in a company-sized patrol north of the Ashau Valley in Quang Tri Province when it came under intense fire from a large North Vietnamese Army force well concealed in a heavily fortified bunker complex, and was pinned down. Reacting instantly, Second Lieutenant Malone completely disregarded his own safety as he repeatedly exposed himself to hostile fire while moving among his men to encourage them and maneuver them out of the fire-swept area. Seriously wounded by fragments from an enemy mortar round, he ignored his own painful injuries as he directed the fire of his machine gunners and grenadiers against the North Vietnamese emplacements. Retrieving the radio from his wounded radio operator, he then led a coordinated assault until his platoon was halted by intense enemy cross-fire of machine guns and mortar, rocket-propelled grenade, small-arms, and automatic weapons fire from bunkers and sniper positions in trees in the dense jungle canopy. With utter disregard for his own safety, he moved about the fire-swept area to transfer the casualties to covered positions and to reorganize his squads. Undaunted by the North Vietnamese rounds impacting around him, Second Lieutenant Malone boldly fired his light antitank assault weapon against an enemy bunker and hurled hand grenades as he fearlessly led four Marines on a daring charge against the hostile emplacement. Although he was again wounded and his four companions became casualties, he continued his attack and successfully destroyed the machine gun position, killing six North Vietnamese soldiers. Weakened by his serious injuries and rendered unable to move, he continued to urge his men forward to exploit their advantage and continue the attack. His heroic actions inspired the Marines to such aggressive action in a coordinated company attack that 105 North Vietnamese soldiers were killed and the large bunker complex was destroyed. By his courage, bold initiative, and unwavering devotion to duty, Second Lieutenant Malone upheld the highest traditions of the Marines Corps and the United States Naval Service.

MANN, BENNIE H., JR.

Citation: For extraordinary heroism as a Helicopter Aircraft Commander and Division Flight Leader with Marine Medium

Helicopter Squadron ONE HUNDRED SIXTY-THREE in Quang Bin Province, Republic of Vietnam, on 31 March 1965. Participating in a seventeen-aircraft flight transporting assault troops of the Fifth Vietnamese Airborne Battalion, Major Mann, along with the entire mission, was scheduled to make three assault landings into an area defended by an estimated force of two companies of insurgent communist (Viet Cong) guerrillas. During the first landing, his aircraft was hit in the engine compartment by intense enemy automatic weapons fire. Although he was experiencing aircraft power and control malfunctions, he continued to lead the attack a second and third time into ever increasing hostile fire. When, after lifting off from the third assault landing, he saw a downed aircraft and wounded crewmen under enemy attack in the landing zone, he unhesitatingly turned his aricraft around and braved the intense enemy onslaught for a fourth time in order to rescue the crew of a stricken helicopter. Displaying exceptional leadership and courage, he directed the rescue efforts, and when his crewmen and copilot were taken under fire by the nearby enemy, he fearlessly hovered his helicopter between the enemy and the crewmen in order to shield their rescue efforts. As a result of his courageous actions, inspiring leadership, and extraordinary airmanship, Major Mann contributed significantly to the successful assault mission and to saving the lives of several of his fellow Marines. His heroic conduct and selfless devotion to duty reflected great credit upon himself and the Marine Corps and were in keeping with the highest traditions of the United States Naval Service.

MARLANTES, KARL A.

Citation: For extraordinary heroism while serving as Executive Officer of Company C, First Battalion, Fourth Marines, Third Marine Division, in connection with operations against the enemy in the Republic of Vietnam. During the period 1 to 6 March 1969, Company C was engaged in a combat operation north of the Rockpile and sustained numerous casualties from North Vietnamese Army mortars, rocket-propelled grenades, small arms, and automatic weapons fire. While continuing to function effectively in his primary billet, First Lieutenant Marlantes skillfully combined and reorganized the remaining members of two platoons, and on 6 March initiated an aggressive assault up a hill, the top of which was controlled by a hostile unit occupying well-fortified bunkers. Under First Lieutenant Marlantes' dynamic leadership, the attack gained momentum which carried it up the slope and through several enemy emplacements before the surprised North Vietnamese force was able to muster determined resistance. Delivering a heavy volume of fire, the enemy temporarily pinned down the friendly unit. First Lieutenant Marlantes, completely disregarding his own safety, charged across the fire-swept terrain to storm four bunkers in succession, completely destroying them. While thus engaged, he was seriously wounded, but steadfastly refusing medical attention, continued to lead his men until the objective was secured, a perimeter defense established, and all other casualties medically evacuated. Then, aware that all experienced officers and noncommissioned officers had become casualties, he resolutely refused medical evacuation for himself. His heroic actions and resolute determination inspired all who observed him and were instrumental in a decisive rout of the North Vietnamese Army force with minimal friendly casualties. By his courage, aggressive fighting spirit, and unwavering devotion to duty in the face of grave personal danger, First Lieutenant Marlantes upheld the highest traditions of the Marine Corps and the United States Naval Service.

MARTIN, CECIL H.

Citation: For extraordinary heroism on the night of 21 November 1968 while serving with River Division 531 during riverine assault operations against enemy aggressor forces in the Mekong Delta region of the Republic of Vietnam. As Senior Boat Captain of a two-boat patrol, Petty Officer Martin was transiting from Rach Soi to Rach Gia, in conjunction with a concentrated patrol program adopted for the SEA LORDS interdiction campaign in the lower Delta, when his patrol came under heavy enemy attack on all sides. During the initial hail of fire, his cover boat received two direct rocket hits, wounding all personnel aboard and causing the craft to veer out of control and run aground directly in front of the enemy firing positions. Petty Officer Martin ordered his coxswain to reverse course and reenter the ambush area to rescue the cover boat's crew members. As his unit approached the stricken craft, Petty Officer Martin directed effective counterfire and, placing his boat between the beleaguered craft and the blazing enemy batteries, took command of the precarious rescue effort. While affording exemplary leadership and inspiration to the members of his surprised and battered patrol element, he directed the major fire-suppression efforts of his gunners, personally manning and firing a machine gun at crucial intervals. Additionally, Petty Officer Martin rendered first aid to casualties, extinguished a fire in the beached craft, advised his commanding officer in the Naval Operations Center of the seriousness of the situation, and coordinated the transfer of wounded personnel to his unit. Through his courageous and determined fighting spirit, he succeeded in safely extracting his men, undoubtedly saving numerous lives. His great personal valor in the face of heavy and sustained enemy fire was in keeping with the highest traditions of the United States Naval Service.

*MARTIN, RAYMOND C.

Citation: For extraordinary heroism while serving as a Squad Leader with Company F, Second Battalion, Ninth Marines, in the Republic of Vietnam on 18 March 1966. Suddenly engulfed by intense and devastating fire from small arms, automatic weapons, mortars, and recoilless rifles by an estimated reinforced Viet Cong battalion, the entire Marine company was pinned down and unable to advance. Facing the enemy on a one hundred eighty degree perimeter, the company decided to break the attack by splitting the Viet Cong positions in two. Displaying firm leadership and composure under fire, Sergeant Martin charged with his men over open fire-swept rice paddies to reach an enemy machine gun which his squad was employed to eliminate. He was seriously wounded during the final few meters of the attack, but ignoring his wounds he fought desperately to cover the remaining distance needed to close with the enemy position. He silenced the deadly hostile machine gun by hurling a hand grenade, and continuing the assault, he observed a fellow squad leader who had been hit by the machine gun just silenced. Finding him seriously wounded, Sergeant Martin was administering first aid when the company received a mortar concentration. As fragments began falling in his vicinity he placed his body over that of his fallen comrade, shielding him from further injury. In this position he was struck by fragments inflicting a mortal chest wound to which he succumbed a few hours later. Sergeant Martin's exceptional fortitude and composure in the face of enemy fire, coupled with superior professional skill and unswerving dedication to duty throughout, were an inspiration to all who observed him and upheld the highest traditions of the Marine Corps and the United States Naval Service. He gallantly gave his life in the cause of freedom.

MAYTON, JAMES A.

Citation: For extraordinary heroism on 21 May 1966, as a medical corpsman serving with Marine Observation Squadron TWO in the Republic of Vietnam as a member of the Squadron's Medical Evacuation Team. Receiving an emergency medical evacuation call from the Third Platoon, "A" Company, Ninth Marines, the Medical Evacuation Team immediately went to aid the platoon which was engaged in bitter combat, pinned down by a large well-armed North Vietnamese force, and therefore unable to assist their wounded comrades. As the medical evacuation helicopter landed in the zone, Petty Officer Mayton, without hesitation, leaped from the aircraft and, with intense enemy fire hitting all around him, raced back and forth carrying the wounded and dead to the aircraft. Again and again, during eight trips into zones around the scene of battle, he exposed himself fearlessly to enemy fire in order to rescue the wounded Marines. Due to his courageous and selfless actions, twenty-three casualties were evacuated under fire. Petty Officer Mayton's repeated voluntary actions in trying to save his wounded and dying comrades, at obvious risk to his own life, were in keeping with the highest traditions of the United States Naval Service.

MC AFEE, CARLOS K.

Citation: For extraordinary heroism while serving as Assistant Advisor to the Fifth Battalion, Vietnamese Marine Brigade in operations against the communist insurgents (Viet Cong) in the Republic of Vietnam on 12 June 1966. Captain McAfee was with the leading elements of the battalion when it became heavily engaged with a main force enemy unit. One rifle company and the Battalion Command Group were overwhelmed by an enemy assault, resulting in the deaths of the Battalion Commander, the Senior Battalion Advisor, the forward artillery observer, and many other Vietnamese officers and men. Captain McAfee, the only American remaining, was instrumental in reforming the shattered command and organizing the defense. He requested tactical air support, and with complete disregard for his own personal safety, stationed himself under the direct fire of the enemy in order to direct and adjust air strikes and artillery fire. Despite continued enemy fire of automatic weapons, machine guns, mortars and grenades, Captain McAfee directed the medical evacuation helicopters into his area to receive wounded. He moved continually between the helicopter landing area and the defense perimeter, directing the medical evacuation and adjusting air strikes and artillery support. After three hours of intense fighting, reinforcements arrived and were led by Captain McAfee on a counterattack. Through his valiant efforts, he prevented the possible annihilation of a Marine battalion by a numerically superior enemy force, and his courageous direction of the medical evacuation undoubtedly saved many lives. Captain McAfee's selfless devotion to duty, quick acceptance of responsibility, and great personal courage reflected credit upon himself and the Marine Corps and were in keeping with the highest traditions of the United States Naval Service.

MC CAULEY, BERTRAM W.

Citation: For extraordinary heroism as an Aircraft Commander with Marine Medium Helicopter Squadron TWO HUNDRED SIXTY-THREE during an emergency medical evacuation mission in the vicinity of Phu Tay, Quang Nam Province, Vietnam, on 5 September 1966. Disregarding the hail of automatic weapons fire from the enemy and the fact that he was unable to return the fire because of the proximity of friendly and Viet Cong forces in the area, Major McCauley was successful on two occasions in evacuating the critically wounded although his aircraft was so severely damaged that it was rendered unsafe for a return trip. To continue his mission, he obtained another helicopter. During his attempt to rescue more disabled Marines, the aircraft was damaged by an enemy hand grenade in the landing zone. He then elected to wave off and orbit until the Viet Cong fire could be neutralized. After being advised to lift off and depart, Major McCauley resolutely remained until the most critically wounded were loaded in his severely damaged and overloaded helicopter and proceeded to the nearest medical facility. Aware that approaching darkness would preclude a return trip before morning and that his aircraft was too badly crippled to risk a return trip, he volunteered to lead an additional section of aircraft into the rescue position. Through his skillful direction the remainder of the casualties were removed to safety. By his outstanding courage, superb leadership and selfless efforts in behalf of wounded men, Major McCauley upheld the highest traditions of the Marine Corps and the United States Naval Service.

*MC CORMICK, MICHAEL P.

Citation: For extraordinary heroism while serving as a Platoon Commander with Company D, First Battalion, Fourth Marines, Third Marine Division in the Republic of Vietnam on 20 March 1969. Second Lieutenant McCormick and a fire team from his platoon were helilifted into an area north of Khe Sanh as the assault element in an operation to secure Fire Support Base Argonne. Immediately upon disembarking from the aircraft, the entire team was pinned down by a heavy volume of fire from hostile soldiers occupying fortified bunkers overlooking the landing zone. Reacting fearlessly, Second Lieutenant McCormick moved across the fire-swept terrain from one man to another and, shouting words of encouragement, restored their confidence. Under cover of machine gun fire, he then initiated an aggressive assault upon the bunkers, and charging up the slope, he and his three-man team stormed and systematically destroyed three of the fortifications with hand grenades and close-range rifle fire, thereby providing security for the remaining Marines landing in the zone. Later that day, Second Lieutenant McCormick led one of his squads during a search and destroy operation in the surrounding area and encountered intense automatic weapons fire from a well-concealed emplacement. Repeated attempts by the Marines to recover their injured point man were thwarted by machine gun fire from concealed enemy soldiers. Unwilling to risk further Marine casualties, second Lieutenant McCormick directed his squad to provide protective fire and, with complete disregard for his own safety, maneuvered toward the casualty. He had almost attained his objective when he was mortally wounded by hostile fire. By his heroic actions, aggressive fighting spirit and unwavering devotion to duty, Second Lieutenant McCormick upheld the highest traditions of the Marine Corps and the United States Naval Service. He gallantly gave his life for his country.

MC DANIEL, EUGENE B.

Citation: For extraordinary heroism as a Prisoner of War (POW) in North Vietnam from 14 June to 29 June 1969. Due to an unsuccessful escape attempt by two of his fellow prisoners, his captors launched a vicious round of torture to single out the senior POW's who were to blame for the breakout. During these torture sessions a confession led to exposing him as the communications link between the senior ranking officer of the main prison camp and the adjacent annex detachment. He accepted the responsibility for the escape and fabricated a story of his own planned escape. After interrogation, the enemy severely tortured him in their attempt to obtain information about the organization and policies of the American POW's in the camp. Under the most adverse of conditions, he heroically resisted these cruelties and never divulged the information demanded by the North Vietnamese. His exemplary courage, maximum resistance, and aggressiveness in the face of the enemy reflected great credit upon himself and upheld the highest traditions of the Naval Service and the United States Armed Forces.

MC DANIEL, JAMES V.

Citation: For extraordinary heroism on 15 May 1975 as Platoon Commander, First Platoon, Company "G", Second Battalion, Ninth Marines while engaged in the recovery of SS MAYAGUEZ which had been seized in the Gulf of Thailand by units of the Cambodian Navy. Landing on Koh Tang Island in the first helicopter of the initial assault wave, Second Lieutenant McDaniel's helicopter team immediately came under intense enemy fire. Quickly organizing his small force, he attacked inland, securing a landing zone for subsequent waves. Given the mission of neutralizing an enemy automatic-weapons position, he organized an eight-man patrol. After moving thirty meters through dense undergrowth, the patrol came under a fierce enemy attack, instantly killing his point man and wounding five out of the eight Marines, including Second Lieutenant McDaniel. Painfully wounded and with complete disregard for his own safety, he moved to the front of his patrol, aiding the wounded Marines and directing fire into the enemy. Although in pain from multiple fragmentation wounds and under intense enemy fire, he personally carried two wounded Marines back to friendly lines. Only after ensuring that the wounded Marines were being treated did he accept medical aid and then immediately returned to his Platoon where he directed the defense in his area, routinely exposing himself to enemy fire for the remainder of the day. As the extraction of the Marine force began, he remained in the landing zone, personally ensuring all members of his Platoon were extracted. By his daring actions, inspiring leadership, and undaunted courage in the face of grave danger, Second Lieutenant McDaniel upheld the highest traditions of the Marine Corps and the United States Naval Service.

MC DONALD, THOMAS C.

Citation: For extraordinary heroism on the night of 28 March 1971 while serving as a pilot in Light Helicopter Squadron 167, Marine Aircraft Group Sixteen, First Marine Aircraft Wing during operations against enemy forces in the Republic of Vietnam. Assigned the mission of supporting a company-sized defense force which was heavily engaged in combat with two enemy battalions in a village southwest of Danang, Captain McDonald launched as helicopter aircraft commander and maneuvered beneath low cloud cover at search altitude until he located a large concentration of enemy soldiers. Unhesitatingly, he directed his spotlight upon the hostile force and immediately came under intense fire. Disregarding his own safety, he continued to illuminate the enemy position while simultaneously directing the fire of the supporting gunships. Following the destruction of the target, Captain McDonald once more orbited the area in search of enemy positions, skillfully darting into the clouds when hostile fire was concentrated on his helicopter. On two separate occasions he exposed himself to extremely heavy fire while illuminating targets and directing the fire of accompanying gunships. Throughout a period of approximately forty-five minutes, he directed the supporting aircraft in attacks which forced the enemy into a disorganized retreat. After refueling his helicopter, Captain McDonald returned to the scene of battle and trained his spotlight on enemy troops boarding six boats on a river shore. He then directed gunship attacks in destroying all six craft. By his superior airmanship, great personal courage, and inspiring leadership, Captain McDonald was instrumental in the decisive defeat of a sizeable enemy force. His performance was in keeping with the finest traditions of the Marine Corps and of the United States Naval Service.

MC EWEN, ROBERT M.

Citation: For extraordinary heroism on 30 March 1968 as a naval flight officer in Attack Squadron ONE HUNDRED SIXTY-FIVE, embarked in USS RANGER (CVA-61). Lieutenant Commander McEwen was the bombardier/navigator on a daring, single-airplane, night attack against the heavily defended and vital Hanoi port facility in North Vietnam. Although his aircraft developed difficulty with the inertial navigation system, Lieutenant Commander McEwen continued to navigate the aircraft to the target at an extremely low altitude and high speed over rough terrain in instrument flight conditions. While the pilot successfully evaded four surface-to-air missiles, intense radar-directed 57 and 85 millimeter antiaircraft fire, and constant tracking and barrage automatic-weapons fire, Lieutenant Commander McEwen calmly and professionally provided accurate navigation and attack parameters to the pilot, resulting in a devastating string of bombs dropped precisely on target. During retirement from the target area, he assisted his pilot in further evasive maneuvers to avoid heavy concentrations of automatic-weapons fire. Due to a low fuel state, the pilot had to rendezvous and refuel prior to completing recovery. Lieutenant Commander McEwen's heroic actions, professionalism, and fearless devotion to duty in the face of grave personal danger were in keeping with the highest traditions of the United States Naval Service.

MC HENRY, WILLIAM D.

Citation: For extraordinary heroism while serving with Headquarters and Service Company, First Battalion, Fifth Marines, First Marine Division (Reinforced), in the Republic of Vietnam on 1 February 1968. Corporal McHenry volunteered to accompany a thirty-man reaction force dispatched to aid a Marine unit which had been ambushed while attempting to reinforce the besieged Phu Loc District Headquarters. While en route to the Marine unit the reaction force was ambushed by a numerically superior enemy force, utilizing small-arms and automatic weapons fire. During the initial bursts of fire numerous casualties were sustained, including all the officers. Quickly assessing the situation, Corporal McHenry assumed command and began reorganizing the beleaguered reaction force. Undaunted by the intense enemy fire, he moved from position to position encouraging his men and directing their fire. Observing a wounded corpsman, he quickly rushed to the wounded man's aid and moved him to a position of relative safety. Ignoring the enemy rounds erupting around him, he administered first aid to other casualties and moved them to covered positions. Corporal McHenry, while attempting to rescue a wounded comrade in an open rice paddy, was wounded in the arm. Despite his wound and in great pain, he obtained a radio and requested artillery fire support. Directed to withdraw to allow artillery fire to be brought to bear on the enemy positions, he ordered his men to withdraw with the casualties and delivered accurate suppressive fire on the enemy to cover the movement of the Marines.

Ignoring Corporal McHenry's orders to leave him behind, two fellow Marines physically placed him aboard a vehicle and moved to a position of relative safety. By his bold initiative, intrepid fighting spirit, and loyal devotion to duty, Corporal McHenry reflected great credit upon himself and the Marine Corps and upheld the highest traditions of the United States Naval Service.

*MC KEEN, GERALD C.

Citation: For extraordinary heroism on 24 September 1966 as platoon corpsman, Company "G", Second Battalion, Seventh Marines, during Operation PRAIRIE in Quang Tri Province, Republic of Vietnam. While moving through an unfamiliar area, the company came under intense mortar, machine-gun and sniper fire from what was later estimated to be a North Vietnamese regiment. Although seriously wounded by a large piece of shrapnel, Hospitalman McKeen refused aid from his fellow corpsman and began crawling from one wounded man to another, rendering medical treatment. At one time, he crawled more than twenty meters under devastating fire to assist an exposed machine-gun team. While aiding the wounded Marines, Hospitalman McKeen received another severe wound which partially immobilized him. Once again he refused treatment, insisting that the other wounded be treated first. Many of these casualties were less seriously wounded than himself. Finally, after three hours, when his physical condition prevented him from continuing, Hospitalman McKeen crawled more than fifty meters back to the company command post where he succumbed to his wounds. By his inspiring and valiant efforts in behalf of his comrades, Hospitalman McKeen upheld the highest traditions of the United States Naval Service.

MC KEOWN, RONALD E.

Citation: For extraordinary heroism in action against the enemy as a pilot of jet aircraft while serving with Fighter Squadron ONE HUNDRED SIXTY-ONE embarked in USS MIDWAY (CVA-41). On 23 May 1972, in support of an air strike against the Haiphong petroleum products storage in North Vietnam, the Combat Air Patrol element, in which Lieutenant Commander McKeown participated as flight leader, was taken under attack by six enemy fighter aircraft. Demonstrating exceptional aeronautical skill, Lieutenant

Commander McKeown engaged the attackers in extremely low altitude aerial combat, accounting for the confirmed downing of one enemy aircraft. Continuing his expert maneuvering while negating several gun attacks by the enemy, Lieutenant Commander McKeown pressed an attack on an enemy fighter closing behind his wingman, resulting in a second confirmed downing of an enemy fighter aircraft. His superb airmanship and courage reflected great credit upon himself and were in keeping with the highest traditions of the United States Naval Service.

MC RAE, ARTHUR G.

Citation: For extraordinary heroism while serving as a Squad Leader in the Second Platoon, Company F, Second Battalion, Seventh Marines, attached to the Third Battalion, Seventh Marines in Quang Ngai Province, Republic of Vietnam, on 16 March 1967. Company F was conducting a search and destroy mission when suddenly the Second Platoon came under intense automatic-weapons and .50 caliber machine-gun fire from Viet Cong insurgents who were well concealed. Two Marines were instantly killed and four were seriously wounded in the initial erruption of fire. For over an hour, all attempts to relieve the beleaguered Marines proved futile as the enemy's vicious fire continued with devastating effect. Corporal McRae had, for over an hour, expertly supervised the fire of his squad when suddenly, fully realizing the personal risks involved, he left his firing position and boldly raced 150 meters aross the rice paddy to the aid of his fallen comrades. As he reached them, he immediately began to give them the sustaining support they so desperately needed. Courageously exhibiting outstanding professional skill, Corporal McRae aided a corpsman in the treatment of the wounded and simultaneously formulated his plan to lead the men to friendly lines. When preparations were made, he aggressively began to lead the men to safety. Air strikes and artillery barrages attempted to silence the enemy but they continued to fire, vainly trying to destroy the Marines that Corporal McRae was deliberately and fearlessly leading. Displaying exceptional leadership, resourcefulness and great professional skill, he succeeded in leading all the Marines to safety. Realizing that some weapons and equipment had been left in the open, he again exposed himself to the enemy's fire and returned into the rice paddy to gather equipment and weapons. By his outstanding courage, exceptional fortitude and valiant fighting spirit, in the face of almost certain death, Corporal McRae saved the lives of his comrades and upheld the highest traditions of the Marine Corps and the United States Naval Service.

*MC WHORTER, JAMES E.

Citation: For extraordinary heroism while serving as a Squad Leader with Company L, Third Battalion, Third Marines, Third Marine Division in connection with combat operations against the enemy in the Republic of Vietnam. On 22 August 1969, the Third Platoon of Company L was conducting a patrol in the northern sector of I Corps Tactical Zone. As the Marines proceeded toward their objective, they came under a heavy volume of small-arms and automatic-weapons fire from a large enemy force occupying a well-concealed bunker complex. Although painfully wounded during the initial moments of the fire fight, Lance Corporal McWhorter resolutely refused medical attention and skillfully deployed his squad into a more tactically advantageous location. Moving throughout the fire-swept terrain, he shouted instructions and encouraged his men as he ably directed their fire, enabling the more seriously-wounded Marines to be evacuated to a position of relative safety. When he observed three of his wounded companions lying dangerously exposed to the intense hostile fire, Lance Corporal McWhorter rushed across the hazardous area to the casualties. After evacuating two of the wounded Marines to a covered position, he attempted to rescue the third casualty but was mortally wounded by a burst of hostile rifle fire. His heroic and timely actions and sincere concern for the welfare of his fellowman inspired all who observed him and were instrumental in saving the lives of several Marines. By his courage, determination and selfless devotion to duty, Lance Corporal McWhorter contributed significantly to the subsequent defeat of the hostile force and upheld the highest traditions of the Marine Corps and of the United States Naval Service.

*MEIER, TERRANCE L.

Citation: For extraordinary heroism while serving as Platoon Sergeant of the Second Platoon, Company M, Third Battalion, Third Marines, Third Marine Division (Reinforced), in the vicinity of Ca Lu, Quang Tri Province, Republic of Vietnam, on 21 July 1967. The Second Platoon was moving along Vietnamese National Route 9, investigating a suspected enemy ambush site, when it was ambushed four miles west of Ca Lu. As the enemy fire increased, the point squad became separated from the remainder of the platoon by 150 meters. The platoon commander was wounded during the early stages of the encounter leaving Staff Sergeant Meier, who was with the rear elements, in command. While awaiting reinforcements and calling in artillery support he tried to lead the rear elements forward to the separated lead squad and the wounded commander, but was unsuccessful. Completely exposed to enemy fire, he courageously continued his efforts. Repeatedly he was driven back because of insufficient fire power and the numerically superior enemy. When the reinforcements with mounted weapons arrived, Staff Sergeant Meier organized and led them to evacuate the wounded and supply ammunition to the fighting Marines. While covering the evacuation of the casualties, he was mortally wounded by enemy fire and taken from the battle area. By his dauntless courage, initiative and selfless efforts in behalf of his fellow Marines, Staff Sergeant Meier served to inspire all who observed him and upheld the highest traditions of the Marine Corps and the United States Naval Service. He gallantly gave his life for his country.

*MENDEZ, ANGEL

Citation: For extraordinary heroism while serving as the Platoon Guide of the Third Platoon, Company F, Second Battalion, Seventh Marines in the Republic of Vietnam on 16 March 1967. During Operation DE SOTO in Quang Ngai Province, Company F was conducting a search and destroy mission when the rear elements of the company were taken under intense 50-caliber machine gun and automatic weapons fire from an estimated hard-core Viet Cong battalion. One half of the Second Platoon was pinned-down in an open rice paddy and all attempts to relieve the pressure on the beleaguered Marines had proven futile. Sergeant (then Corporal) Mendez, unhesitatingly volunteered to lead a squad into the face of the devastating and extremely accurate machine gun fire to assist the pinned-down Marines in returning to friendly lines with their two dead and two seriously wounded. The Viet Cong fire increased to a fever pitch as Sergeant Mendez calmly and courageously moved out onto a paddy dike, completely exposed to the intense fire, and commenced firing his M-79 at the enemy positions with deadly accuracy. He fired round after round as he stood, bravely defying the enemy, to give covering fire to his comrades. Sixty meters across the rice paddy from Sergeant Mendez, his Platoon Commander was seriously wounded and he fell, unable to move. Immediately Sergeant Mendez raced through the hail of bullets to his Platoon Commander's side. Shielding him with his body as he applied a dressing to the wound, he picked up the Lieutenant and started to carry him to friendly lines, which were more than seventy-five meters away. Exhibiting exceptional courage he moved toward the lines as the Viet Cong attempted to hit this double target. Twenty meters short of his goal, he was hit in the shoulder and two of his comrades ran out to assist him. Even though painfully wounded, Sergeant Mendez chose to be the rear man, refusing to relinquish his hold on his Lieutenant's legs as they carried him toward the hedgerow. He was shielding his Lieutenant with his own body when he was mortally wounded. By his dauntless courage, initiative and selfless efforts in behalf of another, Sergeant Mendez saved his platoon commander's life and upheld the highest traditions of the Marine Corps and the United States Naval Service. He gallantly gave his life for his country.

*MERCER, WILLIAM I.

Citation: For extraordinary heroism on 15 June 1968 while serving as Senior Corpsman of Company "M", Third Battalion, Fourth Marines, Third Marine Division in connection with operations against enemy aggressor forces in the Republic of Vietnam. While conducting a sector of the battalion defense perimeter, Company "M" became heavily engaged with a large North Vietnamese Army force near Khe Sanh, and sustained numerous casualties. Reacting instantly, Petty Officer Mercer began assisting the injured Marines to a covered area for treatment, ensuring their further movement to the battalion landing zone for medical evacuation. On many occasions, he unhesitatingly moved to the points of heaviest contact and maneuvered about the fire-swept terrain to treat men who lay wounded in their fighting holes or the perimeter. When a platoon was assigned the mission of searching the area forward of friendly positions, Petty Officer Mercer voluntarily accompanied this unit and subsequently came under accurate enemy sniper fire. Upon observing a seriously wounded Marine, he fearlessly left his covered position and maneuvered across the hazardous area to the side of his injured comrade. Completely disregarding his own safety, Petty Officer Mercer shielded the man with his own body as he administered first aid, and then carried him to a position of relative safety. Alertly observing another casualty lying in an area dangerously exposed to the intense fire, Petty Officer Mercer rushed to his aid, and again selflessly used his own body to protect the Marine from the hostile fire impacting around them. While administering medical treatment to his comrade, Petty Officer Mercer was fatally wounded by the North Vietnamese fire. By his daring initiative, exceptional valor, and inspiring actions, he was directly responsible for saving the lives of several wounded men. His selfless devotion to duty was in keeping with the highest traditions of the United States Naval Service.

*MEUSE, JOHN R.

Citation: For extraordinary heroism while serving as a Radio Operator with the First Squad, Second Platoon, Company E, Second Battalion, Third Marines, Third Marine Division (Reinforced) near Khe Sanh, Republic of Vietnam, on 3 May 1967. During the early morning hours Company E came under a heavy mortar barrage followed by an assault by a determined and well armed North Vietnamese force, overrunning their position and wounding Private First Class Meuse. When asked by his platoon commander for the situation, his radio transmissions indicated that he was severely wounded. With complete disregard for his own safety, he continued to report the situation for more than an hour. This accurate information on the disposition and nature of the enemy forces enabled the company commander to make essential decisions on the employment of his maneuvering elements and the coordination of supporting arms necessary to repulse the enemy attack and to inflict heavy casualties on the enemy. At about noon, when the area was recaptured, the body of Private First Class Meuse was found, his handset still in his hand and five enemy dead in front of his position. By his selfless refusal to leave his position when medical aid might have saved him, and by his skillful appraisal of the situation, he contributed materially to the success of the battle and upheld the highest traditions of the Marine Corps and the United States Naval Service. He gallantly gave his life for his country.

*MEYERKORD, HAROLD D.

Citation: For extraordinary heroism while serving with the Naval Advisory Group, United States Military Assistance Command,

Vietnam, and assigned as Naval Advisor to the River Force of the Vietnamese Navy. Directly involved in more than thirty combat operations against enemy aggressor forces, Lieutenant Meyerkord at all times served to inspire all who observed him by his superb leadership and cool courage while under enemy fire. On 30 November 1964, he was instrumental in turning defeat into victory when, under fire, he reconnoitered ahead of friendly forces and discovered that river craft could proceed no farther because of a Viet Cong canal block. He immediately proceeded to set up a shore command post, direct artillery fire, call for medical evacuation helicopters, and call for and direct air strikes. On 13 January 1965, he transferred from a command boat to a small boat, proceeded to a boat grounded in Viet Cong territory, administered first aid to the wounded, and returned to the command boat, all of which took place while he was exposed to constant enemy fire. On 24 January 1965, he assumed direction of a Vietnamese River Force flotilla when the Vietnamese Commander was wounded in an ambush. Later in the action, although wounded himself and facing heavy fire, he continued the fight for almost an hour, until victory was assured. In his final action, on 16 March 1965, Lieutenant Meyerkord lost his life while leading a river sortie into insurgent territory after he had again positioned himself in the leading boat in order to direct operations and set an example for the Vietnamese Naval personnel. Caught in a heavy ambush in which he was wounded by the first fusillade from the Viet Cong, he was reported to have returned their fire at pointblank range until he was again wounded, this time mortally. By his sustained leadership, initiative, and courage throughout these operations, Lieutenant Meyerkord contributed greatly to the United States effort in Vietnam and upheld the highest traditions of the United States Naval Service.

*MILIUS, PAUL L.

Citation: For extraordinary heroism on 27 February 1968 as an aircraft commander in Observation Squadron SIXTY-SEVEN. During a combat mission in Southeast Asia, Captain (then Commander) Milius' aircraft received multiple hits from 37mm antiaircraft-artillery fire during a run over the assigned target. Immediately, the aircraft burst into flames, several members of the crew received injuries, and dense smoke and fumes filled the fuselage. Remaining at the controls to insure stable flight, Captain Milius ordered his crew members to bail out. As a result of his action, seven of his nine crewmen were rescued within three hours of bail-out. Rescue flights, however, were unable to locate Captain Milius. His heroic efforts and inspiring devotion to duty were in keeping with the highest traditions of the United States Naval Service.

MILLER, CLEATUS A., JR.

Citation: For extraordinary heroism while serving as an Assistant Machine Gunner with Company K, Third Battalion, Seventh Marines, First Marine Division in connection with combat operations against the enemy in the Republic of Vietnam. On 25 October 1969, while Private First Class Miller's machine-gun team was moving as the point element down a narrow valley during a search and destroy operation in the Que Son District of Quang Nam Province, all members of the team were seriously wounded by a heavy volume of automatic weapons and sniper fire from enemy soldiers occupying well-concealed positions in the dense vegetation. Realizing the need for immediate action to prevent casualties among the men following the lead element, Private First Class Miller, whose right leg was immobile, resolutely dragged himself forward, grasped the machine gun, and, painfully crawling across the fire-swept terrain to an advantageous position, commenced delivering rapid bursts against the hostile emplacements. His valiant move placed him in full view of the enemy soldiers who immediately concentrated all their fire on him. Nevertheless, he steadfastly remained in his hazardous position and continued his determined efforts until, weakened by extreme pain and loss of blood, he lapsed into unconsciousness. His heroic and resolute actions inspired all who observed him and provided the time vitally necessary for the first squad to regroup and assault through the North Vietnamese Army emplacements. By his courage, aggressive fighting spirit, and unfaltering devotion to duty in the face of grave personal danger, Private First Class Miller upheld the highest traditions of the Marine Corps and of the United States Naval Service.

MITCHELL, ROBERT G.

Citation: For extraordinary heroism while serving as a Pilot with Marine Medium Helicopter Squadron 165, in connection with combat operations against the enemy in the Republic of Vietnam. On 29 November 1968, during Operation MEADE RIVER, Major Mitchell launched as Flight Leader of a section of four CH-46 transport helicopters assigned the emergency extraction of a reconnaissance team which was heavily engaged with a large hostile force south of Danang. Despite a heavy volume of enemy fire, he executed a successful landing, awaited the embarkation of the team and its dog, then, in a superb display of airmanship, skillfully executed maneuvers to avoid damage to his aircraft and passengers, and safely lifted from the zone. Shortly thereafter, he received a request to medically evacuate a severely wounded Marine from another reconnaissance team located in the vicinity. When he reached the fire-swept zone he boldly landed, awaited the embarkation of the injured Marine, and returned to Danang to deposit his passengers and pick up a relief unit. As he and other aircraft inserted the Marines in the dangerous zone, one helicopter was severely damaged and forced to execute an emergency landing. Major Mitchell landed his transport and embarked the crew of the downed helicopter. After unloading his passengers at Danang, he immediately flew a resupply of ammunition to a Marine unit which was in close contact with enemy soldiers. His heroic actions and determined efforts inspired all who observed him and were instrumental in saving the lives of numerous Marines. By his courage, superior aeronautical ability, and unwavering devotion to duty in the face of grave danger, Major Mitchell contributed significantly to the accomplishment of his unit's mission and upheld the highest traditions of the Marine Corps and the United States Naval Service.

MOE, ROBERT F.

Citation: For extraordinary heroism as Platoon Commander, Third Platoon, Company L, Third Battalion, Third Marine Division, in the Republic of Vietnam on 9 December 1965. The company was engaged in an operation to rescue the remnants of an Army of the Republic of Vietnam regiment which was overrun by the Viet Cong in Quang Tin Province. As it came under heavy small arms, automatic weapons, and accurate mortar fire on three sides from a numerically superior Viet Cong force of battalion size, Sergeant Moe, without hesitation, assaulted the objective, which contained approximately 100 Viet Cong. With full knowledge of the hazards involved and with complete disregard for his own safety, he repeatedly exposed himself to enemy fire while directing his platoon to a favorable position for the assault on the hill. Sergeant Moe secured the objective within thirty minutes of the battle, which lasted one hour and thirty-five minutes. In the face of continuing heavy enemy fire he led his platoon to a position where it could bring fire to bear on the enemy's flank. As a result of his professional abilities and stirring leadership, he penetrated and eliminated the enemy, who were in a position to attack the remaining forty or forty-five Vietnamese troops on Hill No. 43 approximately 300 meters north. By his daring actions and loyal devotion to duty in the face of personal risk, Sergeant Moe reflected great credit upon himself and the Marine Corps and upheld the finest traditions of the United States Naval Service.

MOFFIT, RICHARD E.

Citation: For extraordinary heroism while serving as a Fire Team Leader with Company G, Second Battalion, Twenty-sixth Marines, Third Marine Division (Reinforced) in Quang Tri Province, Republic of Vietnam, on 16 and 17 May 1967. Company G was conducting a search and destroy operation during Operation HICKORY, south of the Demilitarized Zone, when it came under devastating enemy mortar and automatic weapons fire from a deeply entrenched and heavily defended North Vietnamese Army force. Sergeant (then Corporal) Moffit's squad was assigned the mission of clearing the enemy from cleverly concealed positions in the outlying hedgerows. As he diligently maneuvered his squad toward the objective, they were pinned down by a heavy volume of machine-gun fire. Quickly assessing the situation and with complete disregard for his own safety, he courageously jumped to his feet and charged directly at the enemy position, firing as he went. Upon reaching the position, he fearlessly jumped into the fighting hole, and singlehandedly killed its two occupants. As the operation continued on 17 May 1967, the company again came under a heavy volume of automatic weapons fire which halted the forward elements. Once again he gallantly withstood the intense enemy fire as he singlehandedly charged toward the enemy position, throwing grenades to overwhelm and kill the enemy gun crew. By his intrepid fighting spirit, exceptional fortitude and gallant initiative, Sergeant Moffit served to inspire all who observed him and contributed in large measure to the success of his unit. His great personal valor reflected the highest credit upon himself and upheld the highest traditions of the Marine Corps and the United States Naval Service.

MONAHAN, FREDERICK G.

Citation: For extraordinary heroism while serving as an Intelligence Scout with Company E, Second Battalion, Third Marines, Ninth Marine Amphibious Brigade in connection with operations against the enemy in the Republic of Vietnam on 3 May 1967. During Operation BEACON STAR, while deployed on a hill complex south of Hill 881 in the vicinity of Khe Sanh, Lance Corporal Monahan's company came under intense mortar and automatic weapons fire and hand grenade attack from an estimated battalion of North Vietnamese Army forces. Lance Corporal Monahan positioned himself between the command post and the attacking enemy. After repeated vicious attacks, the enemy penetrated the perimeter and had advanced to within twenty meters of the command post when he boldly launched a fierce singlehanded assault with rifle fire and hand grenades. With complete disregard for his own safety, he fearlessly exposed himself to hostile fire to direct accurate rifle fire on the enemy. Although painfully wounded by grenade fragments, he repulsed repeated enemy assaults, killing the determined enemy soldiers in hand to hand combat as they attempted to overrun his position. With exceptional courage and fortitude, he kept the numerically superior North Vietnamese pinned down for more than two hours until reinforcements arrived at daylight. Steadfastly maintaining his position, he guided the relief force into position and skillfully directed their fire against the retreating enemy. By his intrepid fighting spirit, exceptional fortitude and gallant initiative, Lance Corporal Monahan served to inspire all who observed him and contributed in large measure to the success of his unit in repelling the attackers. His great personal valor reflected the highest credit upon himself and upheld the highest traditions of the Marine Corps and the United States Naval Service.

*MONAHON, ROBERT

Citation: For extraordinary heroism while serving as a Fire Team Leader with Company D, First Battalion, Ninth Marines, Third Marine Division (Reinforced) in operations against enemy forces in the Republic of Vietnam on 28 May 1967. During Operation PRAIRIE IV in Quang Tri Province, Lance Corporal Monahon's platoon was dispatched to reinforce a platoon heavily engaged with an estimated company size unit of North Vietnamese Army Regulars. Approaching to within 100 meters of the besieged platoon, his unit came under heavy automatic, small arms and mortar fire which seriously wounded the point man. Unhesitatingly and with complete disregard for his own safety, he ran more than thirty meters to the side of the wounded Marine and assisted him to safety. Upon returning to his position, he observed two wounded Marines lying in a path approximately seventy-five meters away. Although the enemy, in entrenched positions to the right of the path, was throwing satchel charges and grenades and delivering machine gun fire directly over the wounded men, Lance Corporal Monahon and a comrade volunteered to go to the aid of the men. Courageously moving forward, he dived for cover as he was hit by machine gun fire. Disregarding his painful wound, he continued forward, and upon reaching the wounded Marines' position found that one man had succumbed to his wounds. After quickly rendering first aid to the other Marine, he, exhibiting exceptional courage and fortitude, picked up a machine gun, rose to one knee and accurately fired a heavy volume of concentrated fire on the enemy bunker, killing three North Vietnamese and silencing their machine gun. During the vicious exchange of fire, Lance Corporal Monahon was mortally wounded. By his dauntless courage, bold initiative and selfless efforts in behalf of his fellow Marines, Lance Corporal Monahon served to inspire all who observed him and upheld the highest traditions of the Marine Corps and the United States Naval Service. He gallantly gave his life for his country.

MONTGOMERY, ROBIN L.

Citation: For extraordinary heroism while serving as Platoon Commander of the 81mm Mortar Platoon, First Battalion, Fifth Marines, First Marine Division in connection with combat operations against the enemy in the Republic of Vietnam. On 8 June 1969, while Second Lieutenant Montgomery was leading the advance party to a previously selected battalion command post site, the Marines were pinned down in an open rice paddy by a heavy volume of mortar, antitank rocket, and automatic weapons fire from enemy troops occupying well-fortified emplacements. Realizing the need for immediate action, Second Lieutenant Montgomery crawled close to the enemy lines and, pinpointing several principal sources of hostile fire, stood in full view of the enemy soldiers as he initiated an aggressive assault against the nearest maching-gun position, destroying it and silencing the fire from that sector. Although seriously wounded during this action, and suffering intense pain, he again braved the enemy fusilade to single-handedly destroy a machine-gun position occupied by several of the enemy. Weakened by loss of blood and the severity of his wounds, he was unable to continue his combat efforts. However, his heroic and determined actions so inspired his vastly outnumbered men that they surged forward and fought through the enemy lines. By his courage, aggressive fighting spirit and unfaltering devotion to duty in the face of grave personal danger, Second Lieutenant Montgomery contributed significantly to the defeat of the enemy force and upheld the highest traditions of the Marine Corps and of the United States Naval Service.

MOORE, FREDDIE L.

Citation: For extraordinary heroism on the early morning of 12 August 1969 as a squad leader with Company B, First Battalion, Seventh Marines, First Marine Division during operations against an armed enemy in the Republic of Vietnam. When several members of his platoon were pinned down by intense hostile fire following the initiation of an ambush against a large enemy force, Lance Corporal Moore, as leader of the remainder of the platoon members, deployed forward of the company position in an effort to reach the pinned-down platoon members. When his own unit was confronted with a heavy volume of hostile fire emanating from a tree line and throughout a rice paddy, Lance Corporal Moore observed two of his companions fall wounded in a position dangerously exposed to enemy fire. Quick to act, he rushed across the fire-swept area, carried his wounded companions to a place of relative safety, and administered medical aid until a corpsman arrived. Lance Corporal Moore then decided to initiate an aggressive assault against the entrenched enemy unit and, shouting instructions and encouragement to his men, succeeded in forcing the enemy troops to withdraw sufficiently to enable the remainder of the platoon to reach their trapped comrades. When the platoon sergeant was wounded, Lance Corporal Moore took charge of the platoon and continued to press the attack until the enemy force was in full retreat. By his courage, aggressive leadership, and inspiring devotion to duty, he contributed significantly to the defeat of the enemy and upheld the highest traditions of the Marine Corps and of the United States Naval Service.

*MOORE, RONALD A.

Citation: For extraordinary heroism while serving as a Fire Team Reconnaissance Patrol Leader with Company I, Third Battalion, Seventh Marines in Dai Loc District, Republic of Vietnam, on 19 July 1967. While on patrol, Lance Corporal Moore's Fire Team suddenly came under intense, point-blank enemy automatic weapons fire from a large force of well-concealed Viet Cong. The initial burst of fire killed the radioman, destroyed the radio and wounded three other members of his team, including Lance Corporal Moore. Despite his painful wound, he quickly returned fire and deployed his only effective rifleman. As the Viet Cong assaulted the decimated fire team, he quickly anticipated their tactics, shouted commands and encouragement to his rifleman, and together they repelled the assault. As the enemy regrouped, he ordered his rifleman to help their wounded comrades while he provided security on their vulnerable right flank. Compelled to drag himself across several yards of exposed ground being raked by unrelenting enemy fire and grenade explosions, Lance Corporal Moore established himself as a conspicuous target, delivered burst after burst of suppressive fire, and cut down four approaching enemy before he himself was mortally wounded. By his daring initiative, valiant fighting spirit and selfless devotion to duty in the face of insurmountable odds, Lance Corporal Moore was responsible in a great measure for saving the lives of his comrades and thereby upheld the highest traditions of the Marine Corps and the United States Naval Service. He gallantly gave his life for his country.

MOSHER, CHRISTOPHER K.

Citation: For extraordinary heroism while serving as a Forward Air Controller attached to Company K, Third Battalion, Fifth Marines, First Marine Division in connection with operations against the enemy in the Republic of Vietnam. On the morning of 13 May 1967, while moving to the support of another unit, Company K became pinned down by the concentrated machine gun and mortar fire from an estimated battalion of the North Vietnamese Army. Realizing the urgent need for supporting fire to relieve the pressure on the beleaguered unit, Lance Corporal Mosher unhesitatingly moved forward through the intense hostile fire in order to direct air strikes on the enemy positions. For five hours, he remained exposed to the enemy fire with complete disregard for his own safety while adjusting the air strikes and offering words of encouragement to wounded Marines. Utilizing his precise directions, the Marine aircraft delivered their ordnance with pinpoint accuracy. When Company M relieved his unit, Lance Corporal Mosher volunteered to remain at his positions to continue directing the air support and relay information on the enemy's location and strength to the air controllers attached to Company M. While briefing his counterparts, he was severely wounded in the back by enemy mortar fragments and was evacuated. His heroic efforts and superior skill contributed significantly to the accomplishments of his unit's mission. By his intrepid fighting spirit, uncommon courage, and selfless devotion to duty at great personal risk, Lance Corporal Mosher reflected great credit upon himself and upheld the highest traditions of the Marine Corps and of the United States Naval Service.

*MUIR, JOSEPH E.

Citation: For extraordinary heroism as Commanding Officer, Third Battalion, Third Marines, Third Marine Division during Operation STARLITE in Quang Ngai Province, South Vietnam, from 18 to 24 August 1965. With utter disregard for his own safety, Colonel Muir fearlessly exposed himself to intense enemy fire while leading his battalion in assault against insurgent communist (Viet Cong) forces. Though fully cognizant of the danger, he repeatedly positioned himself in the midst of the violent action. Upon encountering strong enemy resistance, he joined the assault companies in front line positions to personally direct their advance, and succeeded in conquering two of the more strongly defended hostile areas, resulting in 215 confirmed enemy dead. Despite an almost complete lack of sleep for three days, his tireless application of professional principles provided a major contribution to the success of the Operation. Colonel Muir's valiant conduct, inspiring leadership, and courageous fighting spirit reflected great credit upon himself and the Marine Corps and upheld the highest traditions of the United States Naval Service.

MULLOY, JAMES E., JR.

Citation: For extraordinary heroism while serving with Headquarters and Service Company, Third Battalion, Third Marines, during Operation STARLITE near Chu Lai, Republic of Vietnam, on 18 August 1965. While participating in a combat resupply mission in support of assault units of Regimental Landing Team Seven, Sergeant Mulloy was aboard an amphibious tractor when his armored column came under intense mortar, automatic weapons, small arms, and recoilless rifle fire from determined and well fortified insurgent communist (Viet Cong) forces. As he attempted to maneuver through the enemy fire his tractor became bogged down in a rice paddy. Quickly comprehending the gravity of the situation, he immediately responded to the challenge by providing the leadership and personal example of exceptional courage which helped to rally the Marines present to the defense of the stricken vehicle. He administered first aid to the wounded and inspired them with his calmness. Realizing that the armored tractor was especially vulnerable to attack due to limited observation from within, he left the tractor and assumed a position in the rice paddy. For twenty hours he conducted a virtual one-man defense. On several occasions Viet Cong guerrillas attempted to penetrate his position to get to the vehicle, but he repeatedly drove them back and inflicted extremely heavy casualties. When aid arrived the following morning he insured that all of the wounded were evacuated before seeking relief for himself. His courageous actions, inspiring leadership, and loyal devotion to duty without regard for his personal safety undoubtedly saved the lives of many of his fellow Marines. Sergeant Mulloy's heroic conduct throughout was in keeping with highest traditions of the United States Naval Service.

MURPHY, DAVID R.

Citation: For extraordinary heroism in action from 12 through 16 October 1966 while serving in a detachment of Helicopter Anti-Submarine Squadron SIX, temporarily embarked in USS INTREPID (CVS-11), flying as plane commander of an armored search and rescue helicopter during a series of related rescue missions in support of combat operations in Southeast Asia. Lieutenant Commander Murphy was vectored to an inland area of North Vietnam on two separate search and rescue flights in valiant attempts to rescue a downed Navy pilot. Although encountering intense enemy fire, he persisted in his determined attempts to locate and rescue the survivor. During the second search, his helicopter, while in a hover, was riddled by enemy automatic-weapons fire which completely disabled one of its engines. Lieutenant Commander Murphy successfully flew the aircraft out of range of the enemy's guns and retired toward the sea where, nearing the heavily-fortified coastline, a barrage of accurate enemy antiaircraft fire inflicted additional heavy damage to the already crippled helicopter and wounded all personnel. Nonetheless, he and his crew tenaciously nursed their helicopter through the enemy fire toward a United States destroyer, approximately fifteen miles from the enemy coastline. When the helicopter lost complete directional control as it neared the destroyer, Lieutenant Commander Murphy skillfully ditched the aircraft in an upright position, thereby preventing further injury to all personnel on board. By his outstanding courage, exceptional skill and fearless devotion to duty, he upheld the highest traditions of the United States Naval Service.

MURPHY, JAMES E.

Citation: For extraordinary heroism while serving as Air Liaison Officer of the Second Battalion, Fourth Marines, Third Marine Division (Reinforced), in the Republic of Vietnam on 26 October 1967. During a search and destroy operation near Con Thien, Captain Murphy was calling in close air support on a fanatical assault by North Vietnamese Army forces when he observed a helicopter shot down 150 meters in front of his position. As the helicopter burst into flames, the enemy troops surrounded the aircraft, and engaged the Marines in a fierce fire fight. With complete disregard for his own personal safety, he dashed alone from the Marine lines, through the enemy positions, to the burning aircraft. While under intense enemy fire, he dragged the two injured survivors to a defilade position. Armed only with a .45 caliber pistol, he shielded the wounded men with his body and attempted to hold off the onrushing enemy, calling in air strikes within 75 meters of his position. Although a rescue mission was attempted, it was beaten back with heavy casualties. For over an hour, Captain Murphy held off the frenzied enemy from his position with air strikes and his pistol. Through combined smoke and interlocking machine-gun fire, a helicopter succeeded in landing to extract the besieged men. After destroying his radio which was left behind he carried the two men aboard the aircraft. By his bold initiative, gallant fighting spirit and loyal devotion to duty, Captain Murphy was instrumental in saving two men from serious injury or possible death, reflecting great credit upon himself and the Marine Corps, and upholding the highest traditions of the United States Naval Service.

MURRAY, JOHN D.

Citation: For extraordinary heroism as the Commanding Officer, Company M, Third Battalion, Fifth Marines, First Marine Division (Reinforced), in the Quang Tin Province, Republic of Vietnam. On 4 September 1967 during Operation SWIFT, Captain (then First Lieutenant) Murray's company was moving to reinforce elements of the First Battalion when the lead platoon suddenly came under heavy small-arms and automatic weapons fire and mortar attack from a numerically superior and well-entrenched North Vietnamese Army force. Immediately assessing the situation, he deployed a reinforcing platoon forward, exposing himself so as to observe and control the fire and movement of all elements of his company. When the commander and key noncommissioned officers of the lead platoon became casualties, he quickly reorganized the unit, establishing strong defensive positions. Skillfully calling in close air support and accurate mortar and artillery fire, he forced the North Vietnamese to withdraw and launched an aggressive attack which took their positions. After recovering all the casualties, he arranged for their evacuation and consolidated his company position into a night defensive perimeter. On the nights of 6 and 10 September 1967, when companies of his battalion were surrounded and heavily engaged with the North Vietnamese, Captain Murray skillfully led his company to relieve the beleaguered companies. As a result of his bold initiative and aggressive fighting spirit, he undoubtedly saved many Marines from further injury, capture or possible death. By his superior professional skill, courageous leadership and selfless devotion to duty at great personal risk, Captain Murray was instrumental in the accomplishment of the hazardous missions and upheld the highest traditions of the Marine Corps and the United States Naval Service.

*MYERS, WILLIAM H.

Citation: For extraordinary heroism in action against elements of the North Vietnamese Army while serving as Assistant Gunner for the first machine-gun team of the Third Squad, Company D, First Battalion, Fifth Marines, in the Republic of Vietnam during Operation UNION on 12 May 1967. While moving with an aggressive attack by his unit in the vicinity of Que Son, the lead elements came under heavy automatic and semi-automatic small arms, grenade, and mortar fire. The platoon to which Private First Class Myers' gun team was attached maneuvered into position to provide flanking fire against the entrenched enemy soldiers. As his platoon was moving into position it came under intense small-arms fire from a range of about 200 meters. The gunner of the machine-gun team of which Private First Class Myers was a member was instantly killed. Unhesitatingly, Private First Class Myers picked up the gun and boldly advanced through withering fire across 150 meters of open rice paddy in order to place himself in a position to deliver enfilade fire upon the trench works. He skillfully placed his gun into action while bullets and grenades were tearing up the earth on all sides. His deadly fire and accurate aim caused numerous casualties and created untold confusion in the ranks of the enemy. When his ammunition was expended, he fearlessly returned across the open paddy to the body of his fallen gunner and recovered the machine-gun ammunition which the gunner had been carrying. In the face of almost certain death he again crossed the open paddy, returned to his position, and for the second time placed his gun into action. By this time his position had been pinpointed by enemy snipers to his right. With no regard for his own personal safety he continued to pour forth his endless stream of fire into the enemy positions. After approximately three minutes of steady firing, Private First Class Myers was hit by enemy fire and mortally wounded. His steadfast devotion to duty served as an inspiration to the entire company, which then rallied and drove the enemy from its almost impregnable position. Private First Class Myers' extraordinary courage and selfless devotion to duty reflected great credit upon himself and upheld the highest traditions of the Marine Corps and the United States Naval Service. He gallantly gave his life for his country.

NEIL, MICHAEL I.

Citation: For extraordinary heroism while serving as a Platoon Commander with Company D, First Battalion, Seventh Marines, First Marine Division (Reinforced), during operations against enemy forces in the Republic of Vietnam on 20 December 1967. Informed by a squad size ambush patrol that an estimated one hundred Viet Cong were moving toward its position at Phouc Ninh (2), in Quang Nam Province, First (then Second) Lieutenant Neil quickly organized a twelve-man reaction force and led his small unit to the assistance of the patrol. Disregarding the intense enemy fire, he led his men across 1,300 meters of thickly forested terrain to the Marine patrol which was heavily engaged with the enemy force. When the advance was halted by intense small-arms, automatic weapons and rifle grenade fire from the hostile positions, he, with complete disregard for his own safety, exposed himself to the devastating fire to hurl hand grenades and direct his men's fire which momentarily silenced the enemy weapons. Suddenly, the Marines came under mortar fire. Shouting words of encouragement to his men, he boldly moved through the hail of enemy fire, leading an assault against the enemy positions. Observing a wounded comrade in an exposed position he removed his armored vest and placed it over the casualty to protect him from further injury. Picking up the wounded man's M-79 Grenade Launcher, he delivered intense and accurate fire against the enemy. When the momentum of the attack decreased, he rallied his men and led a determined assault into the face of the enemy fire. Throwing hand grenades as he advanced, he destroyed a machine-gun emplacement and mortally wounded several enemy with his pistol. By his bold initiative, gallant fighting spirit and loyal devotion to duty, First Lieutenant Neil reflected great credit upon himself and the Marine Corps and upheld the highest traditions of the United States Naval Service.

NELSON, JAMES R.

Citation: For extraordinary heroism on 18 August 1968 while engaged in riverine assault operations against communist aggressor forces in the Republic of Vietnam. As Commander River Assault Division 112, consisting of twelve river assault craft, Lieutenant Nelson conducted operations along the Hai Muoi Tam Canal in Dinh Tuong Province. Shortly after noon, the assault boat column was attacked by what was later estimated to be a Viet Cong battalion. Lieutenant Nelson's command Monitor received two damaging rocket hits, at the outset, that sprayed him in the face with shrapnel and blinded him in his right eye. Ignoring the excruciating pain and the resultant loss of vision, he steadfastly remained at his station and continuously exposed himself to enemy fire by standing upright at his position on top of the boat, to gain the best possible view of enemy positions, in order to direct his assault boats in returning fire. Additionally, Lieutenant Nelson assumed complete control of his boat, shouting instructions to the coxswain while, at the same time, firing on the enemy positions himself with a grenade launcher. He then directed his units to lay down a steady barrage of fire which succeeded in suppressing the enemy's fire sufficiently to permit helicopter evacuation for the many casualties and the safe backloading of the remainder of the troops. Later that afternoon, Lieutenant Nelson was involved in a second intense ambush during which he again valiantly exposed himself to heavy enemy fire. As the infantry succeeded in securing this area, he maneuvered his craft into defensive positions and supervised evacuation of the wounded. Only after all wounded personnel had been evacuated and a relief officer was provided did Lieutenant Nelson submit to evacuation for badly-needed medical treatment. His superb leadership, courage under fire, and selfless devotion to duty were in keeping with the highest traditions of the United States Naval Service.

NOEL, THOMAS E.

Citation: For extraordinary heroism while serving as a Platoon Commander with Company C, First Battalion, Fourth Marines, Third Marine Division, in connection with combat operations against the enemy in the Republic of Vietnam. On 1 March 1969, Second Lieutenant Noel was directed to seize a hill near Ca Lu in Quang Tri Province, which was controlled by a North Vietnamese Army regiment occupying a well-fortified bunker complex. He quickly led his Marines up a slope, and as they neared the top the men came under hostile fire from small arms and automatic weapons. The unit became a lucrative target for sniper and mortar fire and was pinned down in a dangerously exposed position. Second Lieutenant Noel pinpointed major sources of enemy fire, then pulled the pins on two grenades which he clutched in his hands, and boldly raced toward the North Vietnamese Army bunkers. While charging the emplacements, he was repeatedly thrown to the ground by the concussion of mortars detonating nearby, but he steadfastly continued toward the enemy force. In a last desperate struggle, he reached his objective and threw his grenades through the apertures of two of the bunkers, killing all occupants. He fearlessly led his men in an aggressive attack on the remaining hostile positions, and during the ensuing fierce engagement he personally carried casualties to places of relative safety. Only after he had consolidated his position and ensured that all wounded Marines had been evacuated would he accept treatment for his injuries. His heroic efforts and selfless concern for his fellow men inspired all who observed him and were instrumental in his platoon accounting for twenty enemy soldiers killed. By his courage, aggressive fighting spirit, and unwavering devotion to duty in the face of grave personal danger, Second Lieutenant Noel contributed significantly to the accomplishment of his unit's mission and upheld the highest traditions of the Marine Corps and the United States Naval Service.

NOON, PATRICK J., JR.

Citation: For extraordinary heroism as Platoon Guide while serving with Company F, Second Battalion, Fourth Marines in the Thon Son Lam area, Republic of Vietnam, on 24 August 1966. At approximately 0200, Sergeant Noon volunteered, with other members of the Third Platoon, Company F, to relieve a platoon of Company B, which was trapped by enemy fire. Disregarding his own personal safety, he was one of the volunteers who descended into a natural bowl, three sides of which were controlled by the enemy, in a valiant effort to evacuate wounded Marines. Despite a barrage of enemy grenades, two wounded men were rescued. At 0600 the enemy attacked the Third Platoon from the front and left flank. The Platoon Commander was mortally wounded and the Platoon Sergeant was evacuated with severe wounds. Sergeant Noon took charge of the platoon and skillfully maneuvered it until the initiative was regained and the enemy beaten off. While going forward to recover the body of his Platoon Commander, he was hit by enemy fire, but disregarding his wound, he single-handedly brought the body back, then continued to direct supporting arms and encourage his men. Wounded a second time, he refused to be moved to the rear, and continued to direct the platoon until, weak from loss of blood, he was forced to turn the platoon over to the senior squad leader. By his inspiring leadership, aggressive fighting spirit and courageous initiative, Sergeant Noon contributed materially to breaking the enemy attack and upheld the highest traditions of the Marine Corps and the United States Naval Service.

*NORRIS, JAMES A.

Citation: For extraordinary heroism while serving as a Fire Team Leader with Company I, Third Battalion, Fifth Marines, First Marine Division in connection with combat operations against the enemy in the Republic of Vietnam. On 13 August 1969, while participating in a search and clear operation in Quang Nam Province, Lance Corporal Norris sighted four enemy soldiers in a camouflaged machine-gun emplacement. Reacting instantly, he shot one of the enemy and simultaneously shouted a warning to the Marines behind him to seek cover. Machine-gun fire immediately erupted from the hostile position, knocking Lance Corporal Norris to the ground and seriously wounding him. Undaunted by the intense enemy fire concentrated upon him, Lance Corporal Norris, despite his painful wounds, managed to get to his feet and wound two more of the enemy as he single-handedly assaulted the enemy emplacement. Struck to the ground a second time by the hostile machine-gun fire, he again regained his feet, advanced in the face of the hostile fire and succeeded in accounting for still another enemy casualty before he fell mortally wounded within ten meters of the enemy position. His resolute and heroic actions in drawing the hostile fire upon himself inspired his men to such aggressive action that his company proceeded to attack and capture the enemy machine-gun position and account for eight additional enemy casualties during the ensuing fire fight. By his indomitable courage, inspiring valor, and unswerving devotion to duty, Lance Corporal Norris upheld the highest traditions of the Marine Corps and of the United States Naval Service. He gallantly gave his life in the service of his country.

NORTON, JOHN J.

Citation: For extraordinary heroism while serving as Commanding Officer of Company E, Second Battalion, Fifth Marines, First Marine Division (Reinforced), in connection with operations in the Republic of Vietnam. On the night of 21 April 1968 during Operation BAXTER GARDEN, the battalion commander was conducting a command and staff conference to review the day's actions and make plans for the resumption of the attack the following morning. The meeting was held in the semidarkness of a small open area serving as the temporary battalion command post. As the meeting concluded, a trip wire attached to a hand grenade buried in the ground was accidentally pulled, activating the grenade. Instantly realizing the peril to the closely assembled group in the confined area, Captain Norton, completely ignoring the danger to his own life, unhesitatingly clutched the grenade to his chest, fell to the ground, and rolled on top of the grenade to shield other members of the command group from the expected blast. Lying motionless on the grenade, he calmly warned everyone to clear the area. When the device failed to detonate and engineers summoned to examine the grenade could not determine the exact condition of the firing device because of the position of Captain Norton's body on the grenade, he cleared the area of all personnel and courageously rolled away from the grenade. When the grenade failed to detonate, it was determined to have a faulty mechanism and was subsequently destroyed in place. By his courage, bold initiative, and selfless devotion to duty at the risk of his own life, Captain Norton upheld the highest traditions of the Marine Corps and the United States Naval Service.

NORWOOD, GEORGE O.

Citation: For extraordinary heroism while serving as a Fire Team Leader with Company G, Second Battalion, Seventh Marines in the Republic of Vietnam on 4 March 1966. During Operation UTAH, Corporal Norwood's unit was subjected to devastating fire from a hedgerow that concealed fortified machine gun bunkers and a trench line from which the Viet Cong were firing automatic weapons. Observing that his squad leader had been wounded, Corporal Norwood immediately assumed command of the squad and continued the assault on the enemy positions. Although two of his fellow Marines already had been killed attempting to destroy the machine gun position, he twice assaulted the bunker, firing his automatic weapon and throwing grenades. Each time he was forced to withdraw due to the withering fire from the trench line and nearby concealed automatic weapons. Undaunted, he made a third attempt and accurately hurled a grenade which neutralized the fire and enabled his squad to move forward and destroy the bunker. Although he was painfully wounded in the arm and face by enemy grenade fragments, he shunned evacuation and proceeded to position his men and direct fire which minimized the enemy counterattack which followed. By his uncommon courage in the face of almost certain death, intrepid fighting spirit and unfaltering dedication to duty throughout, Corporal Norwood upheld the highest traditions of the Marine Corps and the United States Naval Service.

OAKLEY, JOHN L.

Citation: For extraordinary heroism while serving as a Squad Leader with Company G, Second Battalion, Third Marines in the Republic of Vietnam on 22 August 1966. During Operation ALLEGHENY, Corporal Oakley's platoon was assigned the mission of relieving a platoon that had become temporarily pinned down by a numerically superior communist force. As the point element of the platoon, his squad was brought under intense hostile fire from an estimated sixty Viet Cong, well hidden in the underbrush and trees. As the platoon advanced, enemy fire increased in intensity and was reinforced by volleys of grenades from the front and both flanks, all of which were concentrated on Corporal Oakley's squad in the center of the formation. Suddenly, an automatic weapon opened up at point-blank range directly to his front, killing two Marines at his side. He nevertheless continued to advance in front of the platoon and assaulted the enemy position, firing his rifle at a dead run. Wounded and knocked down once by the heavy fire that was now converging on him, Corporal Oakley continued the assault, only to be wounded again by a hand grenade. Completely disregarding his wounds, he selflessly and heroically continued his single-handed effort until he had overrun the position and killed the defenders. As a result of his gallant conduct and disregard for his own safety, the momentum of the assault was maintained and the platoon was able successfully to relieve the pinned-down unit. By his initiative, inspiring leadership, and heroic devotion to duty, Corporal Oakley reflected great credit upon himself and the Marine Corps and upheld the highest traditions of the United States Naval Service.

O'CONNOR, MARTIN E.

Citation: For extraordinary heroism while serving as Senior Marine Advisor to Brigade B, Republic of Vietnam Marine Corps in connection with combat operations against the enemy in the Republic of Vietnam. On 5 November 1969, while Major O'Connor was aboard the command and control helicopter which was supporting Amphibious Task Force 211 during a combat operation in the U Minh Forest, a United States Army light observation aircraft was severely damaged by enemy fire and crash-landed in a rice paddy. When the helicopter in which Major O'Connor was riding landed in an adjacent rice paddy, it sustained damage from hostile fire. Nevertheless, Major O'Connor exited the aircraft and, making his way with a companion toward the downed helicopter, met the two occupants and assisted them back to the command and control helicopter. At that moment, another observation aircraft was downed approximately forty meters distant and again Major O'Connor left the relative security of his helicopter. Heedless of the enemy rounds impacting all around him, he waded across the rice paddy as hostile rockets set the stricken aircraft afire and caused secondary explosions. Although grenades were detonating within, Major O'Connor boarded and lowered the temporarily dazed and blinded observer to the ground and then dragged him through the enemy fusillade to the command and control helicopter. Subsequently, before the helicopter took off, he rescued one of the crewmen who was seriously wounded. Major O'Connor's heroic and determined actions inspired all who observed him and were instrumental in saving the lives of several United States Army personnel. By his courage, selfless concern for his fellowmen, and unwavering devotion to duty in the face of grave personal danger, he upheld the highest traditions of the Marine Corps and of the United States Naval Service.

O'KELLEY, JOHN W.

Citation: For extraordinary heroism on 26 May 1968 while serving with friendly forces engaged in armed conflict against communist insurgent (Viet Cong) forces in the Republic of Vietnam. Seaman O'Kelley's craft, Assault Support Patrol Boat (ASPB) 111-1, was engaged in minesweeping operations ahead of a column of River Assault Craft with embarked infantry personnel on the Ong Huong River of Kien Hoa Province when reconnaissance-by-fire delivered by ASPB 111-1 triggered a Viet Cong ambush from both sides of the narrow river. Sustaining recoilless-rifle and rocket hits in the first few minutes of the ambush, which killed the Boat Captain and the Coxwain, Seaman O'Kelley's boat went out of control and careened from bank to bank. Realizing the immediate peril to his boat and its surviving crew members, Seaman O'Kelley left his position of relative safety as a thirty-caliber machine gunner in the stern of the boat and dashed forward under a hail of enemy fire to attempt to bring the boat under control. Driven back by flames, and unable to enter the coxwain's flat because casualties inside were blocking the door, he crawled over the top of the boat to the canopy over the coxwain's flat. After cutting through the heavy canopy in the face of continuing hostile fire, Seaman O'Kelley entered the control area, restarted one of the stalled engines, and gained partial steering control. He then brought the boat alongside the Medical Aid Boat where he rendered assistance to critically wounded personnel and helped remove them for prompt evacuation by helicopter. Had Seaman O'Kelley not taken action instantly to regain control of his boat, the entire column of River Assault Craft could have been trapped in the ambush zone, and suffered heavy casualties and disruption of the entire operation. By his heroic actions and courage under fire, Seaman O'Kelley upheld the highest traditions of the United States Naval Service.

*ORLANDO, SAMUEL G.

Citation: For extraordinary heroism on 4 March 1966 while serving as a Corpsman in Company "H", Second Battalion, Seventh Marines, during Operation UTAH in the Republic of Vietnam. Upon learning that additional Corpsmen were needed when one of the platoons of his company was particularly hard hit by intense automatic weapons and heavy mortar fire and was sustaining heavy casualties, Orlando unhesitatingly left his position of relative safety and moved across a barren hill, in the face of intense fire, to the wounded Marines. Exercising outstanding professional skill and resourcefulness, he dressed many wounds and helped evacuate casualties, making several daring trips across the fire-swept area. During one of these trips, when he heard a call for more machine-gun ammunition, he quickly acquired the necessary rounds and carried them to the machine-gun position which was in critically short supply. Hearing the cries of a wounded Marine during an ensuing enemy counterattack, Orlando crawled forward in a courageous attempt to render aid, but was mortally wounded by enemy fire at the moment he reached his objective. In sacrificing his own life while saving the lives of many of his comrades, Orland displayed the highest degree of courage and self-sacrifice. His heroic and inspiring efforts were in keeping with the highest traditions of the United States Naval Service.

PALMER, FREDERICK F.

Citation: For extraordinary heroism in action as Commander, Attack Carrier Air Wing FOURTEEN, embarked in USS RANGER (CVA-61). During the devastatingly effective strike against the heavily defended Hai Phong petroleum and oil storage area in North Vietnam on 29 June 1966, Commander Palmer, as leader of the entire strike force, was responsible for the precise, well coordinated and imaginative plan which ultimately was responsible for the success of the entire mission. Knowingly placing himself in the middle of the strike force so that he could coordinate and evaluate the entire mission, he effected the rendezvous of the strike group of twenty-eight airplanes, directing them to the target with deliberate precision despite complete electronic and radar silence. At the target, he fired his rockets directly into fuel tanks causing a fireball which reached up to 1500 feet. Following his own attack, Commander Palmer, despite heavy enemy gunfire, turned back to the target to make the first essential evaluation of damage, noting that all ordnance had been accurately placed within the carefully prescribed target area and that the damage was extensive. His imaginative planning, skillful execution and outstanding courage in the face of extreme danger were in keeping with the highest traditions of the United States Naval Service.

PANIAN, THOMAS C.

Citation: For extraordinary heroism as Platoon Sergeant, First Platoon, Company I, Third Battalion, Fifth Marines, First Marine Division (Reinforced), in the Republic of Vietnam on 6 September 1967. During Operation SWIFT the company was engaged in search and destroy operations against the communist insurgent forces in Quang Tin Province. When the company came under heavy small-arms fire, automatic weapons and accurate mortar fire from a numerically superior North Vietnamese Army force of battalion size, the first platoon position on the left flank was hit by a devastating impact of eight automatic weapons, resulting in the death of the platoon commander; and half of the platoon were dead or wounded within the first five minutes of contact. Displaying outstanding professional ability, Sergeant Panian unhesitatingly deployed his platoon, organized a defense, and directed effective and accurate fire upon the enemy. Under his inspiring leadership, his platoon, during the subsequent eight hours of heavy contact, repulsed three more attacks on his position by an aggressive enemy, determined to overrun his defensive flank position. During this period, although wounded three times by enemy fire, he was able to evacuate his dead and wounded and reorganize his platoon with the rest of the company. After the company reconsolidated, Sergeant Panian was again successful in defending his flank position against another attack by an enemy of overwhelming odds. The following morning, despite his own wounds, he personally accounted for every man of his platoon, insured that the wounded were cared for, and then allowed himself to be evacuated. Sergeant Panian's bold initiative, valiant fighting spirit, and selfless devotion to duty were an inspiration to all who observed him and upheld the highest traditions of the Marine Corps and the United States Naval Service.

PARROTT, LEE R.

Citation: For extraordinary heroism while serving as Commander of the 81mm Mortar Platoon, Second Battalion, Third Marines, Third Marine Division during operations against enemy forces in the Republic of Vietnam on the early morning of 10 August 1969. When his platoon was subjected to a heavy ground attack by enemy troops who penetrated a section of the platoon's defensive position and wounded several Marines, Gunnery Sergeant Parrott rushed to the beleaguered sector and, opening fire with his rifle, succeeded in accounting for several enemy casualties. Despite the fierceness of the enemy fire attack, he reached the forward fighting positions, directed his men to secondary defensive positions, and then aided the wounded Marines to rear locations. All the while he continued firing at the invaders with his free arm while assisting the casualties with his other arm. As a result of his valiant and inspiring leadership in a potentially chaotic situation, the Marines effected a vigorous defense and repelled several ground attacks. Following the retreat of the defeated attackers, Gunnery Sergeant Parrott led his men outside the defensive perimeter to secure the area and to evacuate all casualties. While he was thus engaged, the area came under hostile mortar fire. Although wounded by one of the first mortars to explode in the area, Gunnery Sergeant Parrott skillfully adjusted supporting counter mortar fire on suspected enemy positions and continued to direct the removal of other casualties to a more tenable landing zone while he remained to provide rear-guard security. By his heroic actions, aggressive fighting spirit, and determined efforts in the face of seemingly overwhelming odds, he was directly instrumental in saving the lives of several fellow Marines, thereby upholding the highest traditions of the Marine Corps and the United States Naval Service.

PASKEVICH, ANTHONY, JR.

Citation: For extraordinary heroism while serving with Marine Observation Squadron Two, Marine Aircraft Group SIXTEEN, First Marine Aircraft Wing in connection with combat operations against the enemy in the Republic of Vietnam. On 17 March 1969, Captain (then First Lieutenant) Paskevich launched as the Pilot of an armed helicopter assigned the mission of supporting a Marine company which was heavily engaged in combat with a large North Vietnamese Army force near An Hoa in Quang Nam Province. Arriving over the designated location, he was informed that the unit on the ground had sustained several casualties and was pinned down in an open rice paddy by a heavy volume of automatic weapons fire. With skill and daring, Captain Paskevich commenced a series of rocket and machine gun attacks on enemy positions, flying dangerously low because of the deteriorating weather conditions. Observing that the ground unit was still unable to attain its objective because of the heavy volume of fire from the numerically superior enemy force and because it was encumbered by its casualties, Captain Paskevich landed his helicopter between the opposing units and succeeded in embarking a seriously wounded Marine. Skillfully evading the enemy fire, he then delivered the casualty to An Hoa. During the next four-hour period, he refueled and rearmed seven times as he repeatedly returned to the hazardous area to provide assistance for the beleaguered company. On three additional occasions, he landed his helicopter in the open area subjected to intense hostile fire, several rounds of which penetrated and extensively damaged his aircraft, to ensure the medical evacuation of critical casualties. Seemingly oblivious to the enemy fire directed against him, he repeatedly maneuvered over the enemy lines, destroying machine-gun and antiaircraft emplacements, thereby turning a potential disaster into a decisive Marine victory. Captain Paskevich's indomitable courage, bold initiative, and unfaltering devotion to duty in the face of grave personal danger were instrumental in saving the lives of four fellow Marines and were in keeping with the highest traditions of the Marine Corps and of the United States Naval Service.

PATE, JAMES W., JR.

Citation: For extraordinary heroism on 24 March 1968 as a pilot in Attack Squadron ONE HUNDRED SIXTY-FIVE, embarked in USS RANGER (CV-61). Lieutenant Pate served as the pilot of the first U. S. Navy A-6A night all-weather attack against the strategic and heavily defended Kinh No railroad yard, located on the vital northeast railroad of North Vietnam. Although encountering extremely intense enemy antiaircraft defenses, a barrage of four surface-to-air missiles, and a near miss that momentarily forced his aircraft into uncontrolled flight, Lieutenant Pate continued to press his attack and succeeded in dropping all weapons on target. During egress, Lieutenant Pate encountered a line of thunderstorms and heavy enemy defenses necessitating an aerial refueling in mid air to safely out-maneuver these obstacles and complete his return to his ship. His heroic actions, professional airmanship, and fearless devotion to duty in the face of grave personal risk were in keeping with the highest traditions of the United States Naval Service.

PECZELI, JOSEPH S.

Citation: For extraordinary heroism as Section Leader, First Section, Third Platoon, First Armored Amphibian Company, Eleventh Marines in Vietnam. The section was engaged in search and destroy operations in support of the Second Battalion, Fifth Marines against enemy forces near An Hoa in Quang Nam Province on 24 March 1967. While covering three LVTP5s and one LVTP6 tracked personnel carriers crossing open terrain, Gunnery Sergeant (then Staff Sergeant) Peczeli was in command of his vehicle when the enemy began a savage attack of small arms, automatic weapons, recoilless rifles, rockets and mortars from ambush against the vehicles and advanced elements of the Second Battalion, Fifth Marines. Disregarding his own personal safety, Gunnery Sergeant Peczeli, while on top of his vehicle, directed rapid and accurate fire into the heaviest enemy concentrations, which effectively suppressed the enemy and prevented heavy casualties to the adjacent friendly forces. Throughout the initial phase of this action he continued to direct his devastating fire to allow the accompanying infantry and vehicles to maneuver and bring their own fire power to bear on the enemy. Only when it was necessary for him to evacuate wounded infantrymen did he withdraw from the battle. Gunnery Sergeant Peczeli immediately returned to the ambush site, this time with his vehicles leading a Marine Company in an assault on the enemy's flank. Again exposed to heavy enemy fire, he closed to within 30 meters of the entrenched enemy, skillfully maneuvering his vehicle and directing effective fire toward the enemy. Although painfully wounded himself, he remained at his post, refusing medical aid and continuing his assault on the enemy. As a direct result of Gunnery Sergeant Peczeli's courageous aggressiveness and swift employment of his vehicle, the enemy ambush was defeated and undoubtedly the lives of many Marines were saved. By his daring actions, exceptional professional skill and loyal devotion to duty, Gunnery Sergeant Peczeli reflected great credit upon himself and the Marine corps and upheld the highest traditions of the United States Naval Service.

*PETERS, WILLIAM L., JR.

Citation: For extraordinary heroism while serving as a Pilot with Marine Medium Helicopter Squadron 165 in the Republic of Vietnam on 12 April 1969. First Lieutenant Peters launched as Wingman in a section of two Ch-46 transport helicopters assigned to helilift a reconnaissance team into hostile territory. After arriving over the designated location, the lead aircraft inserted the Marines without incident but, while lifting off, the aircraft came under a heavy volume of small arms and automatic weapons fire and sustained extensive damage. Observing that the reconnaissance team was pinned down where it had disembarked and that the Marines were surrounded by a numerically superior hostile force, First Lieutenant Peters circled the area while helicopter gunships and fixed wing aircraft bombed and strafed the enemy soldiers who clung tenaciously to their positions only 20 feet from the beleaguered unit. When the supporting aircraft had expended its ordnance, First Lieutenant Peters, fully aware of the possible consequences of his actions but concerned only with the welfare of the men on the ground, fearlessly elected to attempt the extraction and, as he approached the landing zone, became the target for intense automatic weapons fire. Although numerous rounds penetrated his helicopter, he landed in the fire-swept area and, with calm presence of mind, resolutely maintained his dangerously exposed position, despite a fanatical assault by two North Vietnamese Army soldiers who were killed by the reconnaissance team. Assuring that the ground unit was safely aboard, he then quickly lifted from the zone under an increasingly intense volume of fire from the frustrated enemy which damaged a vital control section of his helicopter. In a brilliant display of superb airmanship and unwavering devotion to duty, First Lieutenant Peters saved his fellow Marines from serious injury or possible death and thereby upheld the highest traditions of the Marine Corps and the United States Naval Service.

*PETERSON, DENNIE D.

Citation: For extraordinary heroism while serving as Artillery Forward Observer with the Second Battalion, Eleventh Marines and attached to Company I, Third Battalion, Fifth Marines, First Marine Division (Reinforced), in Quang Tin Province, Republic of Vietnam. On 6 September 1967, during Operation SWIFT, the advance of Company I was halted by devastating automatic weapons fire from a massed, entrenched North Vietnamese Army force. Fearlessly exposing himself to enemy fire, Second Lieutenant Peterson moved over the fire-swept terrain to a position from which he could bring supporting arms to bear on the determined enemy force. Courageously, he moved from one position to another to gain a better vantage point to adjust his fires. Fearing for the life of his radio operator, he took the radio, put it on his back, and moved into contested ground beyond the company perimeter to a position where he could better observe and continue to direct and adjust artillery. His prompt and accurate fires immediately inflicted heavy casualties on the enemy. Although he was drawing fire from at least five enemy automatic weapons and was painfully wounded, he remained in his unfavorable position for two hours adjusting artillery. After darkness fell and the enemy was soundly repulsed, he crawled back to his own lines, and despite his own wounds and the heavy volume of fire, assisted another wounded Marine into the perimeter. After being treated and with temporary discontinuation of artillery fires, Second Lieutenant Peterson organized groups of Marines and led them through the enemy lines on three occasions recovering casualties and carrying them to protected areas in the company area. Although he was wounded on four separate occasions, he disregarded his painful wounds and continued to direct and coordinate fire and aid wounded Marines at great personal risk. While being treated for his wounds, he was hit by a burst of automatic weapons fire and mortally wounded. By his calm courage, intrepid fighting spirit and dynamic leadership, Second Lieutenant Peterson served to inspire all who observed him and contributed materially to the accomplishment of his unit's mission. His great personal valor reflected the highest credit upon himself and enhanced the finest traditions of the Marine Corps and the United States Naval Service. He gallantly gave his life for his country.

PHELPS, JOHN G.

Citation: For extraordinary heroism as a Crew Chief of a UH-1E Helicopter attached to Marine Observation Squadron SIX, near Quang Ngai, Republic of Vietnam, on 19 August 1967. While conducting a regularly assigned mission, Lance Corporal Phelps' aircraft monitored a transmission giving the approximate location of four soldiers from a downed Army helicopter. The UH-1E diverted to the site and arrived to find the Army personnel in the midst of an estimated thirty to forty frenzied Viet Cong, who were bayoneting and beating them with rifle butts. As the UH-1E began a series of low level attacks, the Viet Cong scattered and withdrew to a tree line, firing frantically at the helicopter. Making another low level pass, they observed one soldier raise his hand in a gesture for help. Unhesitatingly, the UH-1E landed on the beach between the wounded men and the Viet Cong, who were now firing furiously at the aircraft. As the aircraft touched down, Lance Corporal Phelps laid down a heavy volume of fire to cover the gunner, who had leaped from the aircraft and raced to the wounded soldiers. When the gunner was unable to carry the man, because of his weight, Lance Corporal Phelps left his machine gun to help move the man. Observing the Viet Cong swarm around the helicopter, he ran back to his gun to provide protective fire, cutting down the enemy advance. Again observing problems being encountered in moving the third man, he handed his machine gun to one still conscious soldier, drew his pistol and raced to their aid. As the men moved with the wounded man, a lone Viet Cong, armed with a grenade, appeared from behind the UH-1E. Unhesitatingly, he released the wounded man, drew his pistol, and shot the Viet Cong. Once inside the helicopter, as it lifted for flight, Lance Corporal Phelps administered first aid to the wounded men until they reached a hospital. By his courageous actions, bold initiative, and unswerving devotion to duty, Lance Corporal Phelps was instrumental in saving the soldiers' lives. His great personal valor reflected great credit upon himself and the Marine Corps and enhanced the finest traditions of the United States Naval Service.

PHILLIPS, JOHN C.

Citation: For extraordinary heroism on 19 December 1968 while serving as a corpsman with Company C, First Battalion, Seventh Marines, First Marine Division, in connection with operations against enemy aggressor forces in the Republic of Vietnam. Shortly before noon, Hospitalman Phillips' unit was maneuvering to assist a friendly squad which was heavily engaged with a North Vietnamese Army platoon. As the Marines approached their beleaguered comrades, the Marine unit came under intense small-arms and automatic-weapons fire from a tree line. Observing the point man fall seriously wounded, Hospitalman Phillips unhesitatingly left his position of relative safety and, exposing himself to the intense enemy fire, rushed across the hazardous terrain to the side of the injured Marine. Ignoring the enemy rounds impacting about him, Hospitalman Phillips was skillfully treating the casualty's wounds when an enemy hand grenade landed in proximity to his patient. Completely disregarding his own safety, Hospitalman Phillips reacted instantly and threw his body across that of the wounded Marine, sustaining serious injuries to himself while absorbing the concussion and fragmentation from the exploding grenade. He ignored his own painful injuries to resume treating his wounded comrade, and continued his determined lifesaving efforts until both men were removed to a covered area. Cognizant of the seriousness of his companion's wounds, Hospitalman Phillips steadfastly refused medical attention for himself until the remaining corpsman had first treated the casualty. Hospitalman Phillips' heroic and decisive actions served to inspire all who observed him and were highly instrumental in saving the life of the injured Marine. By his courage, bold initiative, and selfless devotion to duty at great personal risk, Hospitalman Phillips upheld the highest traditions of the United States Naval Service.

PIATT, LOUIS R.

Citation: For extraordinary heroism while serving as a Platoon Commander with Company M, Third Battalion, Seventh Marines, First Marine Division, in connection with combat operations against the enemy in the Republic of Vietnam. On 23 February 1969, the Second Platoon of Company M was dispatched to the Bo Ban area of Hieu Duc District in Quang Nam Province to assist a squad from another platoon which had become heavily engaged with a well-entrenched North Vietnamese Army battalion. Having reached their objective, the Marines commenced a reconnaissance in force across a rice paddy covered with heavy grass and, led by Second Lieutenant Piatt, immediately were engaged in fierce hand-to-hand combat with hostile soldiers who had been concealed in the tall grass. As he led the Marines in a steady advance through the rice paddy, they killed twelve of the enemy. Mounting the second attack, the Marines sustained several casualties, and when a machine gunner was wounded, Second Lieutenant Piatt quickly seized the man's weapon and delivered rapid suppressive fire until he exhausted the ammunition, then utilized the light antitank assault weapon of another injured man and continued firing until assured that all casualties had been evacuated. Early the following morning, he rallied his men again and initiated a final, well-planned attack against the formidable North Vietnamese Army stronghold. In a splendid display of dynamic leadership, he led his men across the fire-swept terrain and seized the objective. His heroic and determined efforts inspired all who observed him and were instrumental in his platoon's accounting for thirty-six hostile soldiers killed and vast quantities of enemy weapons and equipment captured. By his courage, bold initiative, and unwavering devotion to duty in the face of grave personal danger, Second Lieutenant Piatt upheld the highest traditions of the Marine Corps and the United States Naval Service.

*PICHON, LOUIS A., JR.

Citation: For extraordinary heroism as Company Gunnery Sergeant with Company I, Third Battalion, Third Marine Division, in connection with operations against the enemy in the Republic of Vietnam on 24 March 1967. During a search and clear operation near Cam Lo in Quang Tri Province, Gunnery Sergeant Pichon was advancing with his company when it came under intense small arms and mortar fire from concealed North Vietnamese Army positions. Firing from a series of mutually supporting and well camouflaged bunkers, the enemy inflicted numerous casualties on the left flank platoon. Reacting instantly, Gunnery Sergeant Pichon unhesitatingly advanced to the area of heaviest fighting. With full knowledge of the hazards involved and with complete disregard for his own safety, he rallied the company's flank element and fearlessly charged the enemy bunkers until a heavy volume of grenades halted the advance. Armed only with a pistol and grenades, Gunnery Sergeant Pichon displayed dauntless courage by continuing the charge alone, despite intense hostile fire. Under continuous North Vietnamese fire, he silenced one enemy position and was advancing to a second when he became involved in a hand grenade duel with the enemy. As he lunged to pick up and return an enemy grenade thrown at him, he was mortally wounded by machine gun fire. His aggressive fighting spirit and gallant actions inspired his comrades to launch a determined assault, destroying the enemy positions and resulting in the successful accomplishment of his unit's mission. Gunnery Sergeant Pichon's exceptional leadership, uncommon courage in the face of almost certain death, and loyal devotion to duty reflected great credit upon himself and were in keeping with the highest traditions of the Marine Corps and of the United States Naval Service. He gallantly gave his life for his country.

PIERPAN, HERBERT E.

Citation: For extraordinary heroism in action while serving as Operations Officer of the First Battalion, Fourth Marines, Third Marine Division, in connection with combat operations against the enemy in the Republic of Vietnam from 20 to 22 March 1969. On 20 March 1969, Company D and elements of the First Battalion's command group were helilifted into Fire Support Base Argonne, located northwest of the Vandegrift Combat Base, to commence a sustained operation against North Vietnamese Army forces in the area. As the Marines landed they came under a heavy volume of mortar, small-arms, and automatic weapons fire, and their lead elements were pinned down by hostile soldiers occupying well-fortified bunkers overlooking the landing zone. Unhesitatingly maneuvering across the fire-swept area to a forward position, Major Pierpan shouted words of encouragement to his men, restoring their confidence and enabling them to provide a base of fire as he and a companion advanced toward the enemy strongholds. When his comrade was seriously wounded, Major Pierpan seized the man's weapon and boldly assaulted a bunker, killing two North Vietnamese soldiers. As he led continuing attacks against other enemy positions, he tossed a hand grenade through the aperture of a hostile emplacement and was wounded when a North Vietnamese soldier returned the grenade. Ignoring his painful injury, he resolutely continued his determined efforts until the bunker was destroyed. When his commanding officer was mortally wounded on the following morning, Major Pierpan unhesitatingly assumed command and, maneuvering his men with skill and daring, continued to lead the battalion against the enemy until he was relieved by a new commanding officer on 22 March. By his courage, dynamic leadership, and unwavering devotion to duty in the face of grave personal danger, Major Pierpan contributed significantly to the accomplishment of the battalion's mission and upheld the highest traditions of the Marine Corps and the United States Naval Service.

*PITTS, ROY E.

Citation: For extraordinary heroism while serving as a Grenadier with Company G, Second Battalion, Ninth Marines, Third Marine Division, in connection with combat operations against the enemy in the Republic of Vietnam. On 17 February 1969, Company G was conducting a reconnaissance in force twenty-five miles southeast of the Vandegrift Combat Base in Quang Tri Province when the lead platoon came under an intense volume of automatic weapons fire from a large hostile force well entrenched in a camouflaged bunker complex. Assigned to retrieve a Marine who was mortally wounded during the initial moments of the fire fight, Private First Class Pitt's point man maneuvered toward the fallen Marine, who was painfully wounded by enemy automatic weapons fire. After several attempts to aid the two Marines failed, Private First Class Pitts, reacting instantly and with complete disregard for his own safety, fearlessly left his covered position and commenced crawling across twenty meters of fire-swept terrain toward his wounded comrades. Reaching the critically injured point man and observing that he was bleeding profusely, Private First Class Pitts immediately administered emergency first aid to his companion. After skillfully applying a battle dressing to temporarily stop the bleeding, he began to drag the man toward a relatively safe area, offering him encouragement while simultaneously directing the covering fire of his squad. After pulling the Marine away from the area of heaviest contact, Private First Class Pitts was mortally wounded by enemy small-arms fire. His heroic and bold efforts inspired all who observed him and saved the life of his fellow Marine. By his courage, selfless concern for his fellowman, and unwavering devotion to duty in the face of grave personal danger, Private First Class Pitts upheld the highest traditions of the Marine Corps and the United States Naval Service. He gallantly gave his life for his country.

*POPP, JAMES A.

Citation: For extraordinary heroism while serving as a Grenadier with the Second Platoon, Company F, Second Battalion, Fourth Marines, Third Marine Division in the Republic of Vietnam on 8 April 1967. Private First Class Popp's squad was conducting a squad-size patrol against the Viet Cong forces in Quang Nam Province. While moving along a trail in search of the enemy, the squad was suddenly taken under a murderous volume of small-arms, hand grenade and 40 millimeter grenade fire. The heavy volume of fire rained in from three sides, killing or wounding several of his comrades. Seeing his comrades fall, and realizing that the remaining squad members needed covering fire in order to remove the casualties and select a defensive position, Private First Class Popp valiantly remained on the open trail and provided the necessary fire. Although wounded in the initial moments of the engagement, he completely disregarded his wounds and placed accurate and deadly 40 millimeter grenade fire on the enemy. His devastating fire immediately resulted in three enemy killed, sent many of them scurrying for cover and allowed several of the squad members to gain covered positions. The enemy was intent on annihilating the Marine squad and realized that Private First Class Popp was a deadly threat to the success of the entire enemy mission. The bulk of fire was immediately brought to bear on Private First Class Popp and he was struck a second time. Fearing for the safety of his comrades and critically wounded, he exhibited uncommon courage as he knelt in the withering fire and rained grenade after grenade on the enemy. He personally accounted for at least six Viet Cong killed and inflicted severe injuries on many others. He continued to fight, inspiring the men around him with his dynamic and courageous fighting spirit until he fell mortally wounded when struck for the third time. Private First Class Popp's actions in the face of insurmountable odds were responsible in great measure for saving four other Marines, though wounded, from death at the hands of the enemy and thereby upheld the highest traditions of the Marine Corps and the United States Naval Service. He gallantly gave his life for his country.

PORTER, ROBERT O.

Citation: For extraordinary heroism on 10 June 1970 while serving with River Division 513 as patrol officer of a two-boat patrol on the Giang Thanh River in the Republic of Vietnam. Having established a night waterborne guard post in support of interdiction operations, Chief Petty Officer Porter, after several hours of waiting, detected activity in the underbrush near his boat. Quickly alerting his crew to the imminent danger, he was concentrating on a muffled sound in the bushes when a hand grenade landed on the boat, and the bank of the river erupted in fire directed at his craft. Chief Petty Officer Porter instantly yelled "grenade" and then dashed through the intense enemy fire, picked up the grenade and hurled it back onto the beach. In a matter of seconds the grenade exploded, showering the boat with a deadly hail of shrapnel and wounding him in the face. Ignoring his wounds, Chief Petty Officer Porter directed accurate suppressive fire against the enemy positions until they were silenced. In risking his own life to protect the lives of his shipmates, he displayed the highest order of valor, dedication, and selflessness, thereby upholding the finest traditions of the United States Naval Service.

POULSON, LEROY N.

Citation: For extraordinary heroism while serving as a Gunner of a UH-1E Helicopter attached to Marine Observation Squadron SIX near Quang Ngai, Republic of Vietnam, on 19 August 1967. While conducting an assigned mission, Gunnery Sergeant Poulson's aircraft monitored an emergency transmission giving the approximate location of four Army personnel from a downed helicopter. The UH-1E crew diverted to the site and arrived to find the soldiers in the midst of an estimated 30 to 40 Viet Cong who were bayoneting and beating them with rifle butts. They began a series of low level machine-gun and rocket attacks, and the Viet Cong scattered and withdrew to a tree line. They made another low pass over the Army personnel and observed one man raise his arm in a gesture for help. Unhesitatingly, the UH-1E landed on the beach between the wounded men and the Viet Cong, who were now firing furiously at the aircraft. Gunnery Sergeant Poulson leaped out of the aircraft and raced to the side of the nearest soldier. Unassisted, and through a hail of enemy fire, he moved the man to the helicopter. With complete disregard for his personal safety and in the midst of heavy enemy fire, he ran to the second man, and because of his weight, was unable to move him. At this time the co-pilot joined him, and the two of them managed to get the man safely aboard the aircraft. The Viet Cong began to appear all around the aircraft as he made another attempt to rescue the third man. Because of the man's size, it took three crew members to move him. Upon placing the wounded man in the helicopter, Gunnery Sergeant Poulson made another attempt to rescue the fourth man. Upon reaching his side, under a heavy volume of fire, he discovered the man had succumbed to his wounds, and returned to the aircraft. As the aircraft lifted, he administered first aid to the wounded until they reached a medical facility. By his daring initiative, valiant fighting spirit and selfless devotion to duty in the face of insurmountable odds, Gunnery Sergeant Poulson was responsible for saving the lives of the Army personnel and thereby upheld the highest traditions of the Marine Corps and the United States Naval Service.

*POWELL, CHARLES T.

Citation: For extraordinary heroism while serving as a Platoon Guide with Company I, Third Battalion, Ninth Marines, Third Marine Division (Reinforced), in the Republic of Vietnam on 31 May

1968. While conducting a search and destroy operation north of Dong Ha in Quang Tri Province, elements of Company I suddenly came under a heavy volume of mortar, small-arms and automatic weapons fire from a numerically superior North Vietnamese Army force and were pinned down. Sergeant Powell unhesitatingly took charge of a fire team and led it in an aggressive assault against an enemy mortar position. Disregarding the rounds impacting near him, he boldly maneuvered to within 40 meters of the hostile emplacement and deployed the Marines for an assault. Despite the intense enemy fire, he fearlessly led the attack across the fire-swept terrain and, upon reaching the edge of the emplacement, mortally wounded two hostile soldiers and caused four others to flee in panic and confusion. While continuing their advance his men sustained two casualties from hostile small arms fire. Notwithstanding a critically low supply of ammunition, Sergeant Powell aggressively moved forward to an advantageous position and, while delivering accurate suppressive fire on the enemy, was seriously wounded. Ignoring his painful injury, he steadfastly remained in a dangerously exposed situation, providing covering fire while a corpsman administered first aid to his injured comrades. Upon silencing a hostile automatic weapon, he continued his resolute efforts, until he was mortally wounded. His bold initiative, aggressive fighting spirit and selfless devotion to duty inspired all who observed him, contributed immeasurably to the success of his unit's mission and upheld the highest traditions of the Marine Corps and the United States Naval Service. He gallantly gave his life for his country.

*POWELL, RICHARD L.

Citation: For extraordinary heroism on the morning of 29 August 1968 while serving as a corpsman with Company L, Third Battalion, Seventh Marines, First Marine Division, in connection with operations against enemy aggressor forces in the Republic of Vietnam. Hospitalman Powell's platoon was moving with Company M of the Third Battalion to establish a blocking position near Hill 55 southwest of Danang when the lead elements of the company received intense hostile sniper fire. As Hospitalman Powell's unit maneuvered across a large field in an attack on the enemy's flank, the Marines came under a heavy volume of automatic-weapons fire delivered from three sides by a large North Vietnamese Army force, and sustained numerous casualties. With complete disregard for his own safety, Hospitalman Powell unhesitatingly rushed forward and commenced treating the wounded men. During the ensuing fire fight, he fearlessly maneuvered about the fire-swept terrain from one injured man to another and, on several occasions, moved dangerously close to the hostile emplacements to assist casualties. Although struck by enemy machine-gun fire which immobilized one of his arms, he ignored his painful injuries as he steadfastly continued to render life-sustaining first aid to his fallen comrades. Observing a casualty who lay within fifteen meters of an enemy machine-gun position, Hospitalman Powell fearlessly advanced into the hazardous area and was mortally wounded by hostile fire while providing vital medical treatment to the injured Marine. By his outstanding initiative, personal valor, and sincere concern for the welfare of his comrades, Hospitalman Powell served to inspire all who observed him, succeeded in saving the lives of numerous Marines, and upheld the highest traditions of the United States Naval Service.

*POWERS, TRENT R.

Citation: For extraordinary heroism on 31 October 1965 while serving as a pilot of jet attack aircraft with Attack Squadron ONE HUNDRED SIXTY-FOUR, embarked in USS ORISKANY (CVA-34) during a combat mission over hostile territory in North Vietnam. Captain (then Lieutenant Commander) Powers was assigned the demanding and unusual task of leading a two-division, United States Air Force flight into an area heavily defended by antiaircraft artillery and surface-to-air missiles, with the mission of locating and destroying the missile installations. He planned the attack route and led the eight-plane group over more than six hundred miles of unfamiliar, cloud-shrouded, mountainous terrain, arriving in the target area precisely at a prebriefed time that had been selected to coincide with the strikes of two carrier air wings against a bridge. The target area was the scene of an intense air-to-ground battle, many surface-to-air missiles were being fired and heavy enemy antiaircraft fire was observed in all directions. With full knowledge of the serious hazards involved, Captain Powers courageously led the Air Force aircraft into battle. His bombs and those of the Air Force aircraft which he led inflicted severe damage to both missile sites. By his superior aeronautical skill and valiant determination, Captain Powers upheld the highest traditions of the United States Naval Service.

PRENDERGAST, FRANCIS S.

Citation: For extraordinary heroism on 9 March 1967, as a naval flight officer serving with Reconnaissance Attack Squadron THIRTEEN, on a combat mission over North Vietnam. After being shot down, pursued, and captured by a group of enemy militiamen and soldiers in the shallow, coastal waters off North Vietnam, Lieutenant (jg) Prendergast calmly and accurately assessed his dire situation and cunningly conserved his strength for a bold and extraordinarily heroic escape. Demonstrating the courage and alertness of a disciplined and well-trained fighting man, he seized upon a most dramatic escape opportunity which presented itself for, at the most, a few fleeting seconds. By his exceptionally prompt, daring and heroic action at this moment he succeeded in eluding his captors and was, shortly thereafter, picked up by a rescue helicopter. Lieutenant (jg) Prendergast's keen foresight, sound judgment and courageous conduct in the face of an armed enemy, were in keeping with the highest traditions of the United States Naval Service.

*QUICK, ROBERT L.

Citation: For extraordinary heroism while serving as a Rifleman with Company K, Third Battalion, Third Marines, Third Marine Division (Reinforced) in the Republic of Vietnam on 7 February 1968. While conducting a search and destroy operation south of Gio Linh, elements of Company K suddenly came under a heavy volume of fire from a numerically superior force. During the ensuing fire fight, Private Quick and four other men became temporarily separated from the remainder of the unit. Realizing the seriousness of the situation, he immediately moved to a dangerously exposed portion of his unit's position to provide security for his companions. Almost immediately an enemy hand grenade landed in the midst of the men. Reacting instantly, Private Quick fearlessly picked up the grenade and hurled it away from his comrades. Mortally wounded by the resulting explosion, his heroic action prevented serious injury or death to the men. His sincere concern for the welfare of his comrades was an inspiration to all who observed him. By his superb display of courage, daring initiative and selfless dedication to duty, Private Quick upheld the highest traditions of the Marine Corps and the United States Naval Service. He gallantly gave his life for his country.

*RALYA, WARREN H., JR.

Citation: For extraordinary heroism while serving as a Crew Chief with Company A, First Amphibian Tractor Battalion, Third Marine Division (Reinforced), in the Republic of Vietnam on 20 January 1968. Company A was participating in blocking operations in conjunction with the Junk Fleet and Vietnamese Popular Forces units along the Cua Viet River near the village of My Loc in Quang Tri Province. As Corporal Ralya's platoon was moving into its blocking position, it suddenly came under intense small-arms and automatic weapons fire and antitank grenade attack from a company-sized North Vietnamese Army ambush force, disabling the platoon's tractor and wounding several Marines. Immediately assessing the situation, Corporal Ralya, heedless of his own safety, unhesitatingly left the relative security of the amphibian tractor and advanced to the open ground on one side of the vehicle and courageously remained exposed to the intense hostile fire, while he delivered accurate M-79 grenade fire against the enemy, destroying two automatic weapons positions. Displaying exceptional combat skill and initiative he fearlessly moved to an open area in front of the tractor where his accurate fire destroyed the North Vietnamese antitank grenade launcher that had damaged his vehicle. With the amphibian tractor affording the only protection in the immediate area, he steadfastly remained in his exposed situation and delivered highly effective covering fire that enabled the wounded to be moved to safety behind the vehicle. Ignoring a painful injury and refusing to move to the protection of the vehicle, Corporal Ralya continued to fire his weapon until he was wounded a second time and knocked to the ground by the intense North Vietnamese fire. He had risen from the ground and continued to place accurate fire toward the enemy when he was hit for the third time. Refusing medical attention, he handed his weapon to another Marine and, armed with hand grenades, began to crawl toward the enemy positions. He had traveled only a short distance when he succumbed to his wounds. His determined fighting spirit, strong initiative and devotion to duty at great personal risk contributed substantially to the saving of his fellow Marines from further injury and possible death and were in keeping with the highest traditions of the Marine Corps and the United States Naval Service. He gallantly gave his life for his country.

*RASH, DONALD R.

Citation: For extraordinary heroism while serving as a rifleman with Company B, First Battalion, Twenty-sixth Marines, Third Marine Division, in connection with operations against the enemy in the Republic of Vietnam. On 30 March 1968, while conducting a reconnaissance in force near the Khe Sanh Combat Base, Company B suddenly came under a heavy volume of small-arms fire from a numerically superior North Vietnamese Army force occupying fortified positions. Although the majority of the hostile fire was directed at his squad, pinning down his companions, Private Rash disregarded his own safety as he unhesitatingly left a covered position and launched a determined assault against the enemy emplacements. Ignoring the hostile rounds impacting near him, he fearlessly advanced across the fire-swept terrain, boldly throwing hand grenades and delivering a heavy volume of rifle fire upon the enemy force. Although continuously exposed to the intense hostile fire, he resolutely continued his vicious attack until he had destroyed five enemy positions and killed numerous North Vietnamese soldiers. When his company was subsequently ordered to withdraw while under accurate enemy mortar fire, he steadfastly remained behind, and as he delivered suppressive fire to cover the evacuation of casualties he was mortally wounded. His bold initiative and resolute determination inspired all who observed him and were instrumental in his company accounting for 115 North Vietnamese soldiers confirmed killed. By his courage, intrepid fighting spirit, and selfless devotion to duty, Private Rash contributed immeasurably to the accomplishments of his unit's mission and sustained and enhanced the highest traditions of the Marine Corps and the United States Naval Service. He gallantly gave his life for his country.

*RAY, DARRELL T.

Citation: For extraordinary heroism as an automatic rifleman with the Second Platoon, Company C, Second Battalion, First Marines (Reinforced), Third Marine Division, in the Republic of Vietnam on 28 February 1966. Engaged in a sweep of the Phu Thu Peninsula near Phu Bai, the Second Battalion became heavily engaged with a hardcore Viet Cong battalion. Private Ray was assigned to one of the assault platoons with the mission of securing a complex bunker system located in a tree line. His squad was able to move through an intense hail of hostile fire up to a point approximately thirty meters from the tree line before being completely pinned down by a Viet Cong machine gun which was concentrating all its fire on the squad. Realizing that many of his fellow Marines would be killed if that machine gun position were not knocked out, Private Ray called to his squad to cover him. With complete disregard for his own safety and in the ultimate of sacrifice for the rest of the men in his squad, he jumped to his feet and personally assaulted the machine gun position, yelling and firing his automatic rifle. About ten meters from the machine gun bunker, he received three serious wounds that caused him to fall to the ground. Once again, with extreme personal courage and a high degree of valor, he struggled to his feet and moved the remaining distance to the bunker where he succeeded in silencing the deadly enemy machine gun. As a result of his extraordinary initiative and inspiring valor, Private Ray saved his comrades from injury and possible loss of life, and enabled his platoon to seize and hold this vital part of the battalion objective. His bravery and selfless devotion to duty upheld the highest traditions of the Marine Corps and the United States Naval Service. He gallantly gave his life for his country.

*REID, JOHN M.

Citation: For extraordinary heroism as a Rifle Squad Leader while serving with Company C, Battalion Landing Team 1/3 in the Republic of Vietnam on 10 May 1967. While participating in Operation BEAVER CAGE, Corporal Reid's platoon became heavily engaged in combat with a Viet Cong and North Vietnamese troop unit and was receiving casualties from enemy automatic weapons, small arms and mortar fire. One machine gun team was placed completely out of action by enemy mortars. Seeing that enemy fire had his platoon pinned down in exposed positions, he unhesitatingly moved across open ground to the machine gun, seized it and advanced another 20 to 30 meters. Being forced down several times during this maneuver, he reached his new position and delivered a heavy volume of accurate fire on the enemy positions, temporarily halting their fire, which allowed six other members of his squad to gain a covered position. Corporal Reid continued firing the machine gun from the exposed position in the rice paddy to thwart the advance of enemy troops attempting to overrun his platoon and endanger the Company's flank. While in his exposed position, Corporal Reid was wounded in the leg by rifle fire and as he moved forward to gain cover, he was hit again and mortally wounded. By his daring action and devotion to duty, Corporal Reid gave his life to save those of his fellow Marines, thereby upholding the highest traditions of the Marine Corps and the United States Naval Service. He gallantly gave his life for his country.

*REILLY, DONALD J.

Citation: For extraordinary heroism as a Helicopter Pilot in Marine Observation Squadron TWO in the Republic of Vietnam on 9 December 1965. With his squadron engaged in air support operations for Task Force Delta in Quang Tin Province, Major Reilly was designated as Tactical Aircraft Coordinator (Airborne). Reporting on station about 1800, he immediately answered an emergency request for support from a Marine company which was part of a mobile alert force that had been helicopter-lifted into a hostile area where it was heavily engaged by the Viet Cong using mortars, automatic weapons, and small arms. Although exposed to hostile rifle and machine-gun fire, he, with selfless determination and skill, fearlessly delivered devastating fire from low altitudes upon the Viet Cong who were encircling the company. Later, in response to a request for evacuation of eleven of the company wounded, he prepared to land. In darkness and under a 1200 foot overcast with three miles visibility he arranged for the company to guide him on the final approach with a flashlight. Directing his wingman to remain aloft and assist only if he were successful, he turned off aircraft lights and resolutely commenced his approach. Although encountering intense small-arms fire, he pressed on with determination and while slowing for landing, received a severe bullet wound. His copilot was unable to take over in time and the aircraft crashed on landing in the friendly zone. No further evacuations could be attempted due to enemy resistance until several hours later that night and by that time Major Reilly had succumbed to his grievous wound. His selfsacrificing action in the face of overwhelming odds sustained and enhanced the finest traditions of the Marine Corps and the United States Naval Service. He gallantly gave his life in the cause of freedom.

*REILLY, JAMES R.

Citation: For extraordinary heroism as a Machine Gunner with the Second Platoon, Company G, Second Battalion, Third Marines, Third Marine Division (Reinforced), Fleet Marine Force, in action against communist forces at Danang, Republic of Vietnam, on 17 March 1966. In the early morning hours of that day, Private First Class Reilly and a fellow Marine were vigilantly defending their two-man foxhole position on the unit's perimeter against repeated enemy small-arms and grenade attacks. Their position was of particular importance in that it blocked the possible approach of the enemy forces through a wooded draw. As Private First Class Reilly peered into the semidarkness he heard and saw an object, which he immediately recognized as a grenade, land about four feet from his position beyond the edge of the foxhole. The ground at this point sloped sharply toward his position and he realized instantly that the grenade would roll into the hole itself. With precious seconds already gone, Private First Class Reilly knew he could not retrieve the grenade and hurl it away in time. Without a moment's hesitation he called a warning to his comrade and, unmindful of his own personal safety, threw himself upon the deadly missile, absorbing the exploding charge in his own body and thereby saving his comrade from serious injury or possible death. Private First Class Reilly, by his superb courage and valiant spirit of selfsacrifice, reflected great credit upon himself and upheld the highest traditions of the Marine Corps and the United States Naval Service. He gallantly gave his life for his country.

*REIS, TIAGO

Citation: For extraordinary heroism while serving as a Fire Team Leader with Company F, Second Battalion, Fourth Marines, Third Marine Division (Reinforced), in the Republic of Vietnam on 21 September 1967. Corporal Reis was a member of a point squad which was participating in a search and destroy operation near Con Thien. The squad encountered a numerically superior unit of the North Vietnamese Army, which unleashed a murderous hail of automatic small-arms fire. The volume and accuracy of the enemy fire resulted in immediate and heavy casualties on the Marine squad and left Corporal Reis as the only member unwounded. With complete disregard for his own safety, he braved the continuing enemy fire and began dragging his wounded comrades from their exposed areas to sheltered positions. He quickly treated each man's wounds, comforted him and then courageously moved back into the vicious fire in search of other fallen comrades. On one trip he was struck by an enemy bullet, but paused only for a moment, and gallantly continued his rescue efforts. With all of the enemy fire directed at him, Corporal Reis exhibited uncommon courage as he worked feverishly to almost complete exhaustion, fearlessly exposed to the enemy fire and defying the enemy attempts to prevent him from aiding the wounded. Corporal Reis continued his courageous actions until he fell, mortally wounded, when struck a second time. By his intrepid fighting spirit, daring initiative and selfless efforts in behalf of his comrades, Corporal Reis upheld the highest traditions of the Marine Corps and the United States Naval Service. He gallantly gave his life for his country.

REYNOLDS, MARVIN D.

Citation: For extraordinary heroism on 17 July 1967 as a pilot in Attack Squadron ONE HUNDRED SIXTY-THREE, embarked in USS ORISKANY (CVA-34). As the leader of a section of A4E aircraft conducting a search and rescue mission for a pilot downed the previous day, thirty-two miles southwest of Hanoi, North Vietnam, Lieutenant Commander Reynolds proceeded seventy miles inland through darkness and heavy antiaircraft-artillery fire to the search area where he succeeded in establishing contact with the downed pilot. When the Search and Rescue Commander informed him that positive voice contact with the pilot must be established before the helicopter could cross the beach, Lieutenant Commander Reynolds reentered the area and established voice contact. Due to his low fuel state, he was forced to aerial refuel before returning to the scene, this time leading the rescue forces. Maneuvering so as to evade three surface-to-air missile launchings, he led the flight to the rescue scene. He attacked and silenced a large flak site endangering the helicopter. Lieutenant Commander Reynolds then made repeated, dangerously low passes over the pilot to ensure successful pickup. During egress, he successfully attacked and silenced one of the most menacing flak sites on the helicopter's egress route. By his courageous conduct, exceptional skill, and fearless devotion to duty, he was primarily responsible for the successful rescue of the downed pilot, thereby upholding the highest traditions of the United States Naval Service.

RHODES, FRANCIS E., JR.

Citation: For extraordinary heroism on 15 September 1967 during action against communist insurgent (Viet Cong) forces in the Mekong Delta region of the Republic of Vietnam. As Commander River Assault Squadron ELEVEN, Lieutenant Commander Rhodes was in command of twenty-three riverine assault craft, with elements of the 2nd Brigade, 9th United States Army Infantry Division embarked. While transiting the Rach Ba Rai River during combat riverine strike, search and destroy operations in the Cam Son Secret Zone, the entire task group came under heavy Viet Cong fire from fortified bunkers on both banks of the river, sustaining numerous personnel casualties and damage to several boats. Although momentarily stunned when two rockets knocked him and his crew to the deck, Lieutenant Commander Rhodes stationed himself in an exposed position on his command boat and, in the face of heavy, direct enemy fire from close range, quickly noted the condition and dispostion of his units, took personal command, by radio, of all units, and ordered them to regroup and return downstream out of the enemy's fortified area. After transferring casualties and reassigning personnel so that all boats were manned, Lieutenant Commander Rhodes again took his task group up the river and was subjected once more to heavy enemy fire. Hard hit for a second time by a large number of casualties, he nevertheless successfully landed embarked army units ashore in the assigned objective area, and set up a naval blockade of the river. In the face of enemy fire which could have resulted in a devastating defeat by the Viet Cong, Lieutenant Commander Rhodes made a most significant contribution to an operation that resulted in 213 Viet Cong killed in action, 66 probably killed, 600 bunkers destroyed, and a large quantity of war munitions captured. His heroic conduct and inspiring devotion to duty in the face of intense enemy opposition were in keeping with the highest traditions of the United States Naval Service.

RICHARDS, THOMAS A.

Citation: For extraordinary heroism on 5 and 6 June 1969 as a Fire Team Leader with Company H, Second Battalion, Ninth Marines, Third Marine Division during operations against an armed enemy in the Republic of Vietnam. When his platoon initiated contact with a company-sized hostile force occupying well-camouflaged positions on a cliff overlooking a trail, and were subjected to a heavy volume of fire, Corporal Richards, during the initial attack, skillfully regrouped his platoon and led his men in a counterattack, enabling them to establish a defensive perimeter. Throughout the night, he assisted in countering enemy attacks and in moving casualties to areas of relative safety. Although wounded by fragments of an enemy grenade, he steadfastly refused to be evacuated in order to remain with his men and continue the fight. Observing that a machine gun in his area was dangerously short of ammunition, he made several trips across the fire-swept zone to obtain and replenish ammunition for the weapon. When the machine gunner and assistant gunner sustained wounds, Corporal Richards unhesitatingly dashed to the gun position and, although exposed to the brunt of the enemy attack, concentrated a heavy volume of fire on the hostile troops, causing the attack to falter long enough for the Marines to repulse it. His gallant actions resulted in the death of eight enemy soldiers and prevented the Marine perimeter from being penetrated. Through his superb leadership, courage, initiative, and inspiring dedication, he contributed significantly to the defeat of the enemy and upheld the highest traditions of the Marine Corps and of the United States Naval Service.

RIENSCHE, HAROLD A.

Citation: For extraordinary heroism while serving as Maintenance Chief with Company B, Third Tank Battalion, Third Marine Division in the Republic of Vietnam on 24 March 1969. Staff Sergeant Riensche and his four-man crew were embarked aboard an M51 Tank Retriever assigned the recovery of a disabled tank located near Dong Ha, when their vehicle detonated a mine and sustained extensive damage. While repairing the retriever, the Marines came under a heavy volume of automatic weapons fire from a North Vietnamese Army platoon occupying well-concealed emplacements in the tall elephant grass nearby. In the initial burst of fire which came from all sides, two of Staff Sergeant Riensche's crew were killed and two wounded, leaving him the sole defender of the retriever. Although in a dangerously exposed position, he commenced returning fire with a mounted .50 caliber machine gun. When a hostile round rendered the weapon inoperable, he moved across the top of the tracked vehicle to an M-60 machine gun, removed it from its mount and, standing in full view of the enemy, continued firing at the advancing North Vietnamese. When the barrel vibrated loose and fell from his weapon, Staff Sergeant Riensche caught the red hot cylinder in mid air and, while reinserting it, sustained serious burns to his hands. Ignoring his painful injury, he resolutely resumed firing all around his vehicle until the machine gun malfunctioned. While attempting to correct the difficulty, he observed a hostile soldier who had maneuvered to a point next to the recovery vehicle and quickly killed the man with his .45 caliber pistol. Unable to pinpoint the location of each North Vietnamese soldier in the gathering darkness, he then commenced throwing hand grenades in all directions, forcing the enemy to withdraw. Following their retreat with grenade launcher fire, Staff Sergeant Riensche, although still a very vulnerable target and vastly outnumbered, tenaciously manned his hazardous position and continued firing on possible hostile emplacements until a friendly tank arrived to render assistance. His heroic and decisive action inspired all who observed him and saved the lives of two fellow Marines. By his courage, aggressive fighting spirit and selfless devotion to duty in the face of grave personal danger, Staff Sergeant Riensche upheld the highest traditions of the Marine Corps and the United States Naval Service.

RIPLEY, JOHN W.

Citation: For extraordinary heroism on 2 April 1972 while serving as the Senior Marine Advisor to the THIRD Vietnamese Marine Corps Infantry Battalion in the Republic of Vietnam. Upon receipt of a report that a rapidly moving, mechanized, North Vietnamese army force, estimated at reinforced divisional strength, was attacking south along Route #1, the THIRD Vietnamese Marine Infantry Battalion was positioned to defend a key village and the surrounding area. It became imperative that a vital river bridge be destroyed if the overall security of the northern provinces of Military Region ONE was to be maintained. Advancing to the bridge to personally supervise this most dangerous but vitally important assignment, Captain Ripley located a large amount of explosives which had been prepositioned there earlier, access to which was blocked by a chain-link fence. In order to reposition the approximately 500 pounds of explosives, Captain Ripley was obliged to reach up and hand-walk along the beams while his body dangled beneath the bridge. On five separate occasions, in the face of constant enemy fire, he moved to points along the bridge and, with the aid of another advisor who pushed the explosives to him, securely emplaced them. He then detonated the charges and destroyed the bridge, thereby stopping the enemy assault. By his heroic actions and extraordinary courage, Captain Ripley undoubtedly was instrumental in saving an untold number of lives. His inspiring efforts reflected great credit upon himself, the Marine Corps, and the United States Naval Service.

RIVERA, JOSE L.

Citation: For extraordinary heroism while serving as a Fire Team Leader with Company L, Third Battalion, Fifth Marines, First Marine Division in connection with combat operations against the enemy in the Republic of Vietnam. On the night of 26 March 1969, Lance Corporal Rivera and six other Marines from Company L were occupying a listening post approximately 100 yards forward of the company perimeter in Quang Nam Province. Suddenly, the Marines came under a heavy ground attack by a numerically superior enemy force. Lance Corporal Rivera was attempting to alert the company by radio when a hostile hand grenade landed in his position. Without hesitation, he covered the grenade with his helmet and two protective vests and, shouting a warning to his comrades, smothered the explosion with his own body. Although suffering from multiple fragmentation wounds, he ignored his painful injuries and commenced delivering accurate fire at the assaulting enemy, resolutely refusing to leave his position until his comrades had reached friendly lines. His heroic and timely actions and sincere concern for the welfare of his fellowmen inspired all who observed him and were instrumental in saving the lives of several Marines. By his courage, aggressive determination and unswerving devotion to duty in the face of extreme personal danger, Lance Corporal Rivera contributed significantly to the subsequent defeat of the enemy force and upheld the highest traditions of the Marine Corps and of the United States Naval Service.

*RIVERS, JETTIE, JR.

Citation: For extraordinary heroism as Company First Sergeant while serving with Company D, First Battalion, Ninth Marines in the Republic of Vietnam on 14 and 15 May 1967. While engaged in search-and-destroy operations against units of the North Vietnamese Army, Company D became engaged with an estimated reinforced enemy company and Second Lieutenant (then First Sergeant) Rivers, a member of the company command group, was wounded. Realizing that the enemy had forced a gap between the command group and one platoon and the two rear platoons, he immediately informed the company commander. At dusk the enemy fire and mortar barrages intensified, and as casualties mounted, the two separate elements set up a hasty perimeter of defense. Second Lieutenant Rivers expertly directed his men's fire, placed personnel in strategic positions, and personally participated in repelling the enemy assault. Observing a number of enemy soldiers maneuvering toward the perimeter, he mustered a small force of Marines and personally led them to meet the enemy, killing several of the enemy soldiers. When evacuation of the wounded was completed, Second Lieutenant Rivers requested permission to take the point in an attempt to link up the smaller element with the other two platoons. A short distance from the perimeter, the group encountered withering machine-gun fire which instantly killed the platoon sergeant and seriously wounded the platoon leader. Second Lieutenant Rivers immediately took command of the situation, aiding the wounded and personally pinning down the enemy machine gun while the casualties were removed. Now under complete darkness and subject to continuous enemy crossfire and sporadic mortar barrages, Second Lieutenant Rivers assisted in joining the two units. Discovering that all of the platoon leaders had become casualties, he assisted the company commander in setting up an effective perimeter and personally supervised the medical evacuation preparations. Presently a deadly mortar barrage precipitated an all-out enemy assault on the company. Second Lieutenant Rivers was everywhere — encouraging the men, directing fire, assisting the wounded, and distributing ammunition to critical positions. Wounded himself, he continued this pace until late in the afternoon when relief arrived. By his initiative, devotion to duty, and aggressive leadership, he served to inspire all who observed him and was instrumental in saving the lives of many Marines. His great personal valor reflected great credit upon himself, the Marine Corps and the United States Naval Service.

ROBERSON, JAMES J.

Citation: For extraordinary heroism while serving with the First Armored Amphibian Company, Eleventh Marines, attached to the Second Battalion, Fifth Marines, First Marine Division in Vietnam on 24 March 1967, during Operation NEW CASTLE in the Quang Nam Province. Second Lieutenant Roberson was Officer-in-Charge of two armored amphibian vehicles engaged in a search and destroy mission, and while advancing across open terrain in an armored amphibian accompanied by three other tracked vehicles, his vehicle came under a heavy volume of small arms, automatic weapons and accurate mortar fire from an estimated battalion sized enemy force strategically positioned in an inverted U-shaped ambush. Aware that the leading elements of the company were pinned down by the intense fire, Second Lieutenant Roberson, exposing himself to enemy fire, unhesitatingly directed his vehicles into the center of the attack delivering accurate 105 millimeter and .50 caliber machine gun fire into the enemy positions. Continuing his advance over 800 meters of fire-swept terrain, he was knocked from his vehicle twice, sustaining painful fragment wounds by the increasing Viet Cong fire being delivered from all three sides. Despite his painful wounds he remounted his vehicle and calmly continued the movement until he reached the company's forward positions. He then increased the volume of fire from his vehicles attempting to gain fire superiority from the enemy, and again disregarding his wounds and exposing himself to the intense enemy fire, he dismounted to assist in loading the wounded aboard his vehicle for evacuation. He then transported the wounded to a medical facility, resupplied his ammunition and returned to the ambush area in support of another company as it enveloped the enemy. Although receiving intense Viet Cong rocket, recoilless rifle and mortar fire, Second Lieutenant Roberson again fearlessly positioned himself on top of his vehicle as he led the attack on the enemy's flank, closing to within forty meters of the Viet Cong while coordinating the delivery of small arms and automatic weapons fire. Due to his aggressive and courageous actions, the enemy ambush was repulsed, numerous enemy weapons were destroyed and approximately forty Viet Cong killed. Demonstrating sincere concern for the welfare of the wounded, Second Lieutenant Roberson again refused medical attention and remained in the area until the units of the battalion had regrouped and all the wounded were safely evacuated. By his daring actions, exceptional professional skill and loyal devotion to duty, he undoubtedly saved the lives of many Marines, reflected great credit upon himself and the Marine Corps, and upheld the highest traditions of the United States Naval Service.

DAVID B. ROBINSON

Citation: For extraordinary heroism while serving as Commanding Officer of the patrol gunboat, USS CANON (PG-90), during operations against enemy forces in the Republic of Vietnam on 11 August 1970. While Lieutenant Commander Robinson was directing his ship's harassment and interdiction fire as the craft proceeded up the Bo De River, the ship suddenly came under intense enemy automatic weapons, rocket and small arms attack from an estimated forty-man force located in well-concealed positions in a mangrove swamp on both banks of the river. During the initial hail of enemy fire, Lieutenant Commander Robinson sustained a broken leg and numerous shrapnel wounds when a rocket exploded on the port side of the flying bridge. Despite his serious wounds and loss of blood, he continued to direct his ship's fire until the enemy attack was suppressed. Refusing medical evacuation, Lieutenant Commander Robinson submitted to first-aid treatment and then requested that he be strapped in a strecher and placed in an upright position so that he could continue to direct the actions of his ship until it cleared the enemy ambush site. Only after the ship was anchored at an advanced tactical support base and he was assured that his ship and crew were capable of continuing their assigned mission, did he allow himself to be medically evacuated. By his extraordinary courage, resolute fighting spirit and inspiring personal example in the face of a fierce enemy attack, Lieutenant Commander Robinson upheld the finest traditions of the United States Naval Service.

*RODRIGUES, JOE G., JR.

Citation: For extraordinary heroism while serving as a Platoon Sergeant with Company L, Third Battalion, Fourth Marines, Third Marine Division in connection with combat operations against the enemy in the Republic of Vietnam from 22 February to 3 March 1969. On 26 February, while Company L was patrolling in support of Fire Base Pete north of the Rockpile in Quang Tri Province, Sergeant Rodrigues' platoon became heavily engaged with a large North Vietnamese Army force and, during the ensuing fierce fire fights, sustained several casualties. Fearlessly maneuvering across the fire-swept terrain, Sergeant Rodrigues directed the suppressive fire of his men and skillfully deployed them away from the hazardous area to rejoin the main body of the company. On the afternoon of 28 February his platoon commander was mortally wounded. Unhesitatingly assuming command, Sergeant Rodrigues completely disregarded his own safety as he moved about the hazardous area, reorganizing his men and restoring their confidence and effectiveness as an aggressive fighting unit. Maneuvering them to a more tenable position, he then established a night defensive perimeter. During the early morning hours of 3 March, his sector of the perimeter was breached by a North Vietnamese Army unit, accompanied by sappers, and in the initial moments of the vicious attack numerous Marines were seriously wounded. Reacting instantly, Sergeant Rodrigues ignored the hostile fire and rushed to the point of heaviest contact and, moving from one position to another, assisted the injured men to locations of relative safety. After repeatedly crossing the fire-swept terrain to aid the casualties, he observed two wounded Marines lying in positions dangerously exposed to the enemy fire and unhesitatingly placed himself between the injured men and the North Vietnamese Army soldiers and provided covering fire for his comrades. Although struck several times by small arms fire, he valiantly continued his determined efforts to protect his comrades until he succumbed to his wounds. By his inspiring courage, aggressive fighting spirit and unwavering devotion to duty, Sergeant Rodrigues upheld the highest traditions of the Marine Corps and the United States Naval Service. He gallantly gave his life for his country.

ROGERS, GERALD W.

Citation: For extraordinary heroism on 30 March 1968 as a pilot in Attack Squadron ONE HUNDRED SIXTY-FIVE, embarked in USS RANGER (CVA-61). Lieutenant Commander Rogers was the pilot of a daring, single-airplane, night attack against the heavily defended and vital Hanoi port facility in North Vietnam. Although his aircraft developed difficulty with the inertial navigation system, Lieutenant Commander Rogers pressed on to the target at an extremely low altitude and high speed in instrument flight conditions. He successfully evaded four surface-to-air missiles, intense radar-directed 57 and 85 millimeter antiaircraft fire, and constant tracking and barrage automatic-weapons fire to drop a devastating string of bombs on target. During retirement from the target area, he encountered heavy automatic-weapons fire necessitating further evasive maneuvers. Due to his low fuel state following these maneuvers, he had to rendezvous with the tanker and refuel in order to complete his recovery. Lieutenant Commander Rogers' heroic actions, professional airmanship, and fearless devotion to duty in the face of grave personal danger were in keeping with the highest traditions of the United States Naval Service.

ROGERS, RAYMOND G., JR.

Citation: For extraordinary heroism while serving as First Sergeant, Company I, Third Battalion, Ninth Marines, Third Marine Division

(Reinforced) in Quang Tri Province, Republic of Vietnam, on 30 March 1967. While on Operation PRAIRIE III, northwest of Cam Lo, near the Demilitarized Zone, the command post group with two squads and a sixty-millimeter mortar section were preparing night positions on Hill 70 when they were hit with a vicious mortar barrage followed by an intense and vicious ground assault by an estimated reinforced North Vietnamese Army company. Seeing his company commander's position occupied by the enemy, he single-handedly charged through heavy automatic weapons fire and grenades to assist him. Upon reaching the position, he found his company commander mortally wounded and engaged the numerically superior enemy force, killing several. In this instant he was severely wounded by rifle fire, but despite his painful injuries, he continued to deliver accurate and effective fire upon the enemy. Seeing the weapons platoon commander go down, he crawled to him, administered first aid and, at the injured man's request, propped him into a firing position. Being the senior Marine present, he assumed command of his remaining forces and crawled through a widely exposed area to radio and re-establish contact with the battalion. While attempting to call in artillery fire on his own position, a Huey Gunship came into the area. He established contact with the gunship and directed fire on the enemy, but the enemy hordes kept coming into his positions. Although seriously wounded, he led six seriously wounded survivors to a covered position and established a hasty defense. As a result of his professionalism, courageous leadership and stirring example, the fanatic enemy assaults were stopped, and he and his forces accounted for sixty-two enemy soldiers killed. By his daring initiative, valiant fighting spirit and selfless devotion to duty in the face of grave personal risk, First Sergeant Rogers served to inspire all who observed him and upheld the highest traditions of the Marine Corps and the United States Naval Service.

ROLAND, JOHN R., JR.

Citation: For extraordinary heroism on 28 January 1969 while serving as Officer in Charge of Patrol Craft Fast (PCF) 35 during combat operations against communist aggressor forces in Kien Hoa Province, Republic of Vietnam. Accompanied by PCF-100, Lieutenant (jg) Roland conducted a daring daylight probe into a narrow canal off the Ham Luong River, deep into enemy-held territory. After completing a devastatingly effective gunfire mission,

*RUDD, DONALD L.

Citation: For extraordinary heroism on 3 March 1969 while serving as Senior Corpsman with Company L, Third Battalion, Fourth Marine Regiment, Third Marine Division, Fleet Marine Force, during combat operations against enemy forces north of Khe Sanh, Quang Tri Province, Republic of Vietnam. With his unit sustaining several casualties when a reinforced enemy squad penetrated the friendly lines and engaged the Marines throughout the perimeter, Petty Officer Rudd immediately went to the assistance of the injured Marines in the face of heavy hostile fire, administered lifesaving first aid, and removed the wounded to positions of relative safety. On several occasions, to insure the safety of his charges, he was forced to use protective fire, at close quarters, against the attackers. When he observed a seriously wounded Marine who was pinned down by enemy fire, Petty Officer Rudd rushed to the side of the victim and protected him with his own body while administering medical aid. In an attempt to silence the hostile fire, Petty Officer Rudd again picked up a weapon to deliver fire against the enemy position, still shielding his patient. While engaged in this action, he was fatally wounded by small-arms fire. By his great personal valor and self-sacrificing efforts, Petty Officer Rudd was directly responsible for saving the lives of at least five Marines. His inspiring and steadfast devotion to duty was in keeping with the highest traditions of the United States Naval Service.

Petty Officer Rudd's citation, (between pp 278-279) and that of Cdr. Shepherd, (between pp 310-311) were missing from the original set of documents and were obtained after this book was printed and folded but not yet bound. The unnumbered pages were inserted prior to binding at an opportunity in the process as close to their proper alphabetical position as possible. *NOTE:* The addidtion of these two citations alters the Awards Statistics (Part III, page 357). U.S. Navy (Awards) should read 123, Total Awards should read 487.

both boats were caught in a deadly cross-fire from a numerically-superior Viet Cong force entrenched in both banks of the canal. PCF-100 sustained two serious B-41 rocket hits which wounded the Officer in Charge and one crew member, and knocked them over the side. The helmsman of PCF-100, blinded by heavy smoke, was unaware of this situation and proceeded out of the canal. Upon observing the situation, and realizing the grave danger of the two stricken men, Lieutenant (jg) Roland unhesitatingly placed his boat between the two men and the bank in an effort to protect them from further injury. Due to the severity, volume, and accuracy of the enemy fire, he found it necessary to make several passes before stopping and pulling his two wounded comrades aboard PCF-35. Lieutenant (jg) Roland's rescue efforts were undaunted by the fact that his boat had received a direct hit from a rocket-propelled grenade round; he directed the operation to a successful climax despite the intense enemy opposition. Through his inspiring personal leadership, his composure under extremely heavy fire, and his disregard for his own personal safety, he was instrumental in saving the lives of his two stricken comrades. By his daring action and loyal devotion to duty in the face of extreme personal risk, Lieutenant (jg) Roland upheld the highest traditions of the United States Naval Service.

ROLLER, ROBERT T.

Citation: For extraordinary heroism as a Squad Leader with Company F, Second Battalion, Fifth Marines in the Republic of Vietnam on 13 October 1966. During a search and clear operation near the Demilitarized Zone in Quang Tri Province, the lead elements of the company were attacked by enemy sniper fire. Sergeant Roller's platoon was deployed to pursue and eliminate the snipers. They were hit by extremely heavy automatic weapons fire and grenades from a large enemy force concealed in a well camouflaged trench line. Although painfully wounded in the hand and leg from the initial burst of fire, he quickly gave first aid to the other wounded Marines and organized the evacuation of his fallen comrades, at the same time directing a heavy volume of fire on the enemy position. He also assisted in bringing in medical evacuation helicopters for the more critically wounded. Disregarding his wounds, he refused evacuation and rejoined his platoon to rally the men and charge the heavily fortified enemy position. With only a pistol, Sergeant Roller led the assault, shouting encouragement to his men, and was wounded again.

His aggressive and heroic actions in the face of grave personal danger inspired his men to overrun the enemy, routing them from their position and causing them to leave seven of their dead and numerous weapons behind. By his daring initiative, inspiring leadership and indomitable fighting spirit, Sergeant Roller upheld the highest traditions of the Marine Corps and the United States Naval Service.

ROLLINGS, WAYNE E.

Citation: For extraordinary heroism on 18 September 1969 as a patrol leader with the First Reconnaissance Company, First Reconnaissance Battalion, First Marine Division during operations against enemy forces in the Republic of Vietnam. While First Lieutenant Rollings was leading a long-range reconnaissance patrol deep into enemy-controlled territory in Quang Nam Province, the point man spotted twelve enemy soldiers in almost hidden emplacements and immediately fired at the hostile troops. Observing that the point man's weapon had become inoperable, First Lieutenant Rollings dashed across the fire-swept terrain and positioned himself between the point man and the enemy. Although small-arms fire tore his clothing and ripped his gas mask, and fragments of an enemy grenade struck him in the face and legs, First Lieutenant Rollings continued to deliver suppressive fire, accounting for several enemy casualties and forcing the remainder of the hostile troops to withdraw. Assuming the dangerous point position, and once again faced with intense enemy fire, he charged up an enemy-held knoll in a fiercely determined assault, resulting in the complete routing of the enemy. Despite the pain of his injuries, First Lieutenant Rollings continued to expose himself to fire from the retreating enemy while he skillfully directed air strikes upon all possible routes of egress. By his courage, dynamic leadership, and unfaltering devotion to duty, he contributed significantly to the accomplishment of his patrol's mission and upheld the highest traditions of the Marine Corps and of the United States Naval Service.

ROMINE, RICHARD E.

Citation: For extraordinary heroism as Helicopter Pilot, Troop Commander, and Tactical Air Controller with Marine Medium Helicopter Squadron 165 in the Republic of Vietnam on 3 and 4 June 1967. When his transport helicopter was hit during an emergency retraction of a besieged combat team from an enemy-surrounded bomb crater, Lieutenant Colonel (then Major) Romine displayed exceptional aeronautical skill in maneuvering his crippled aircraft away from enemy concentrations prior to crash landing into the mountain forest. Directing his crew to bring all the battle equipment that they could carry, he fought and led them through the almost impassable and enemy-populated forest back to the besieged forces position. With darkness closing, illumination flares were requested and adjusted to pinpoint accuracy. He exposed the advancing enemy, brought them under fire, and prevented surprise attacks. Awake throughout the cold, rainy night, Lieutenant Colonel Romine resumed calling in air strikes at dawn. Without thought of personal risk, he exposed himself along the barren crater rim to direct the strikes within ten meters of his position. Faultlessly, for twenty-four torturous hours, he gallantly controlled air operations and directed his nearly decimated ground forces against insistent, overwhelming enemy attacks until their guns were silent, the enemy beaten, and the trapped men were helicopter-lifted to safety. Lieutenant Colonel Romine's dynamic leadership, indomitable fighting spirit, and relentless exposure to the enemy to control ground and air operations that saved the lives of his men, reflected great credit upon himself and the Marine Corps and were in keeping with the highest traditions of the United States Naval Service.

*ROSENBERGER, ROGER D.

Citation: For extraordinary heroism while serving as a Rifleman with Company M, Third Battalion, Third Marines, Third Marine Division in connection with combat operations against the enemy in the Republic of Vietnam. On 17 June 1969, Company M was participating in Operation VIRGINIA RIDGE approximately seven miles north of the Dong Ha Combat Base in Quang Tri Province. As the Marines crossed a large open field, the point element came under a heavy volume of small arms, automatic weapons, machine gun, and rocket-propelled grenade fire from enemy forces well-concealed in a hedgerow. Observing that his companions were pinned down by the intense hostile fire, Private First Class Rosenberger unhesitatingly rushed across the fire-swept terrain to attack the most forward enemy position. Although seriously wounded and knocked to the ground by the explosion of a hostile hand grenade, he resolutely regained his footing and continued his aggressive assault against the enemy

281

emplacement, temporarily suppressing the enemy fire. As the enemy soldiers began to retreat, one of them threw a second hand grenade at Private First Class Rosenberger, mortally wounding him. His heroic actions and sincere concern for the welfare of his fellowman inspired all who observed him and were instrumental in saving the lives of several Marines. By his courage, determination and selfless devotion to duty, Private First Class Rosenberger contributed significantly to the subsequent defeat of the hostile force and upheld the highest traditions of the Marine Corps and of the United States Naval Service.

ROSS, DAVID L.

Citation: For extraordinary heroism while serving as a Pilot with Marine Observation Squadron TWO, in the Republic of Vietnam, on 4 September 1967. Major Ross was assigned to a single armed UH-1E providing escort for a UH-34 helicopter flying medical evacuation mission in support of elements of the First Battalion, Fifth Marine Regiment, which had come under heavy attack from a large enemy force. As the UH-34 made its approach, Major Ross commenced firing runs, hoping to suppress the enemy fire. Despite this, the UH-34 was hit several times and was forced to shut down in the zone. Major Ross' UH-1E was also hit and he was able to accomplish a successful autorotation into the same zone as the UH-34. Once on the ground, he made his way across this area, which was now under heavy fire, to the command post and discovered that the situation was extremely grave, with the Company Commander fatally injured and many troops wounded. Major Ross made radio contact with a flight of armed UH-1Es orbiting overhead and a Marine C-1C, which was controlling air strikes to the southwest, briefed them regarding the situation on the ground and directed their attacks to the eastern side of the perimeter. The command post was in a location directly susceptible to enemy fire but commanded an excellent view of both friendly and enemy positions on the northern and eastern sides of the perimeter. With complete disregard for his own safety, Major Ross maintained his vulnerable position throughout the ensuing action. With the help of friendly air forces, the ground defense was able to hold its own, until the enemy obviously decided on a full scale assault. Due to the close proximity of the enemy, Major Ross could not use his fixed-wing support, so instead, he directed the armed UH-1Es on target. He continuously exposed himself to hostile fire in order to determine its exact location and insure accurate counterfire. Occasionally these strikes came within 50 meters of the friendly perimeter. When aid finally arrived, Major Ross refused evacuation for himself, until all injured personnel and helicopter crews were out. His courage and devotion to duty were an inspiration to all who observed him, undoubtedly prevented the company from being overrun and were in keeping with the highest traditions of the Marine Corps and the United States Naval Service.

*RUSHER, ROBERT C.

Citation: For extraordinary heroism while serving as a Squad Leader with Combined Action Platoon Hotel-6, Third Combined Action Group, Nuoc Ngot Village, Phu Loc District, Thua Thien Province, Republic of Vietnam. During the early morning hours of 7 January 1968, Corporal Rusher's compound came under heavy enemy mortar, rocket, and ground attack including sappers and enemy troops attempting to gain entry into the compound. Corporal Rusher fearlessly and courageously rallied his men and began delivering accurate fire on the enemy soldiers who were returning fire and detonating satchel charges. During the heat of the battle, two enemy soldiers, firing small arms and carrying a satchel charge, dashed toward Corporal Rusher and a fellow Marine. With deliberate and exacting fire, Corporal Rusher killed both, but not before the enemy soldiers were successful in hurling their satchel charges at him and his comrade. Displaying extraordinary heroism, Corporal Rusher placed himself between the impending blast and his comrade, thereby protecting his fellow Marine with his own body. As the charge detonated, Corporal Rusher absorbed the full brunt of the explosion and was mortally wounded. By his dauntless courage, intrepid fighting spirit and grave concern for another, he served to inspire all who observed him and upheld the highest traditions of the Marine Corps and the United States Naval Service. He gallantly gave his life for his country.

RUSSELL, TIMOTHY W.

Citation: For extraordinary heroism while serving as a Squad Leader with Company D, First Battalion, Fourth Marines, Third Marine Division (Reinforced), in connection with operations against the enemy in the Republic of Vietnam. During the early morning hours on 2 February 1968, the Cam Lo District Headquarters came under heavy artillery, mortar and recoilless rifle fire followed by a well coordinated ground attack by a numerically superior enemy force. Although bleeding profusely from multiple fragmentation wounds to his arms and legs and temporarily rendered unconscious from the explosion of an enemy rocket round during the initial moments of the attack, Corporal Russell refused immediate medical attention for himself in order to control and direct the fire of his men against the assaulting force. Displaying exceptional courage and bold initiative, he completely ignored the danger to his life as he repeatedly exposed himself to hostile fire in order to pinpoint enemy positions for his unit and deliver effective rifle fire against the attackers. Exhibiting outstanding leadership and composure during the five-hour engagement, he steadfastly refused medical aid and evacuation for himself and continued to move throughout the fire-swept area, skillfully directing the fire of his squad and encouraging his men. Although the enemy penetrated a portion of the compound's eastern perimeter, which threatened the Marine defenses, and reinforcements were required to prevent the attackers from overruning the northern perimeter, Corporal Russell ably directed his squad members to counter the hostile force and, as a result, forced the enemy to break contact and withdraw, undoubtedly preventing his sector of the perimeter from being penetrated. His dauntless courage and bold initiative inspired all who observed him and were instrumental in repulsing the attackers, accounting for numerous casualties and the capture of thirty-eight soldiers and confiscation of numerous weapons and items of equipment. By his aggressive fighting spirit, resolute determination and selfless devotion to duty at great personal risk, Corporal Russell upheld the highest traditions of the Marine Corps and the United States Naval Service.

RUSSELL, WILLIAM E.

Citation: For extraordinary heroism while serving as Commanding Officer of Company E, Second Battalion, Third Marines, in connection with operations against the enemy in the Republic of Vietnam. On 28 May 1968, Captain Russell was assigned the mission of leading his company and a tank platoon to a ridgeline position in Quang Tri Province to relieve a unit which had been heavily engaged with the enemy the previous night. Under his superb leadership, his unit maneuvered to the ridgeline and killed sixty-five enemy soldiers while advancing under fire. Upon arriving at the besieged Marines' position and despite strong enemy resistance, Captain Russell rallied his forces and, after evacuating the casualties, consolidated the perimeter and coordinated his units' defensive actions. On the night of 30 May when his position was attacked by a reinforced North Vietnamese battalion, he directed well coordinated and highly accurate air strikes and artillery fire around his perimeter, killing ninety-six enemy soldiers and forcing the hostile force to discontinue the attack and withdraw from the area. Although sustaining painful fragmentation wounds from the enemy mortar fire, Captain Russell refused medical assistance and continued to direct supporting fire against the retreating enemy throughout the night. Early the following morning, a relief force maneuvering along the ridgeline to his position came under heavy enemy fire and was pinned down. Disregarding his own safety, he quickly adjusted fire on the enemy positions, killing forty-four North Vietnamese soldiers and enabling the Marines to reach the relative safety of the company perimeter. Assuming command of the relieving company when its commanding officer was wounded, Captain Russell, even though wounded a second time, continued to direct the actions of his men throughout the night. He accepted medical evacuation the following day only when assured that the vital position was secure. His sustained heroism in the face of a numerically superior, determined enemy force inspired all who observed him and contributed immeasurably to the accomplishment of his unit's mission. By his intrepid fighting spirit, superb leadership, and selfless devotion to duty at great personal risk, Captain Russell upheld the highest traditions of the Marine Corps and the United States Naval Service.

RUSTH, JOHN E.

Citation: For extraordinary heroism while serving as a Fire Team Leader with Company C, First Battalion, Fifth Marines, First Marine Division (Reinforced), in the Republic of Vietnam on 10 May 1967. During Operation UNION, Corporal (then Lance Corporal) Rusth was moving with the lead elements of his company, as they secured the crest of Hill 110 in Suoi Cho Valley, advancing against an estimated battalion of North Vietnamese Army regulars. Accompanied by other elements of his company, he was leading his fire team to secure the military crest on the northeastern slope, when they came under intense enemy fire from positions concealed in hedgerows, tree lines and cane fields at the base of the hill, sustaining numerous casualties.

Immediately assessing the situation, Corporal Rusth moved among the wounded to ensure that all had received proper care, while he steadfastly remained exposed to hostile fire on the bare hillside. He displayed outstanding leadership, courage, and tactical skill, as he aggressively led his men in the grenade and bayonet assault down the hill against the North Vietnamese positions, routing the enemy and forcing it to flee to alternate ground. Corporal Rusth, completely disregarding his own safety, fearlessly moved down the hillside on nine occasions to assist casualties up the slope to safety. Although painfully wounded in his thigh from an enemy round when he began his tenth trip to rescue a wounded Marine, he quickly bound his injury and, displaying exceptional physical stamina and courage, assisted the stricken man to safety before collapsing from the effects of his painful wound and heat exhaustion. By his prompt and courageous action, he was instrumental in saving several Marines from further injury or possible death and contributed significantly to the successful accomplishment of his unit's mission. By his bold initiative and unswerving dedication to duty at great personal risk, Corporal Rusth inspired all who observed him and upheld the highest traditions of the Marine Corps and the United States Naval Service.

SADLER, CHARLES D.

Citation: For extraordinary heroism as a Machine Gun Team Leader with the Third Platoon, Company A, First Battalion, Ninth Marines in Vietnam on 21 May 1966. Corporal Sadler's platoon participated in a helilift to a position in order to block the withdrawal of a large enemy force operating in the area. When the helicopters landed in an open rice paddy, the area was immediately subjected to intense mortar and automatic weapons fire from Viet Cong positioned on all sides of the landing zone. More than twenty Marine casualties were inflicted in the first few minutes of the savage action. With exceptional composure and presence of mind in the tense situation, Corporal Sadler quickly took charge of his team and began returning fire, fearlessly exposing himself to the enemy to accomplish his task. When supplies of ammunition were depleted, he directed Marines around him to retrieve that which had been carried by the casualties, and twice he braved the withering fire to recover ammunition from wounded men who were lying in the exposed rice paddy. On one occasion he spotted a Viet Cong running from a tree line with a machine gun and reacting instantly, Corporal Sadler stood in the midst of the grazing fire and fired his machine gun from an offhand position, felling the enemy. Finding that only five other Marines in his immediate vicinity were not dead or wounded, he organized the small group and on two separate occasions attempted to mount an assault against the nearest Viet Cong position. Realizing the futility of further attempts, he judiciously directed the men to dig in and save two magazines of ammunition, ordered all rocket misfires to be stacked in the position for last second detonation, and instructed his men to stand by for a probably physical assault by the enemy. His daring initiative and relentless fighting spirit served to inspire and encourage all who observed him, and were instrumental in preventing the enemy from overrunning the position. His resolute effort contributed in large measure to the eventual entrapment of the enemy force, resulting in fifty-three Viet Cong killed and seventeen weapons captured. By his extraordinary courage in the face of extreme danger, bold initiative, and unwavering dedication to duty throughout, Corporal Sadler upheld the highest traditions of the Marine Corps and the United States Naval Service.

*SAMPSON, GERALD H.

Citation: For extraordinary heroism while serving as Commanding Officer of Company B, First Battalion, Third Marines, Third Marine Division in connection with combat operations against the enemy in the Republic of Vietnam. In the early morning hours of 28 August 1969, Company B, occupying a night defensive position deep in hostile territory northwest of Cam Lo, was assaulted by a large North Vietnamese Army force employing automatic weapons and rocket-propelled grenades. In the initial onslaught, the second platoon commander was wounded and his sector of the perimeter was in grave danger of being breached by the enemy. With complete disregard for his own safety, Captain Sampson moved across the fire-swept terrain to the point of heaviest contact, rallied the beleaguered Marines, and began to direct their fire against the advancing North Vietnamese. During the fierce fire fight, he continually moved from one fighting position to another, instructing and encouraging his men and ensuring that the wounded received immediate treatment. While maneuvering across an exposed area on the foremost edge of the perimeter, Captain Sampson was mortally wounded by enemy fire. His unflagging determination and bold fighting spirit inspired his men to heroic efforts and were instrumental in turning a critical situation into an overwhelming Marine victory. By his leadership, extraordinary courage and selfless devotion to duty, Captain Sampson upheld the highest traditions of the Marine Corps and of the United States Naval Service.

*SANDERS, THOMAS

Citation: For extraordinary heroism as a Machine Gun Squad Leader with Company C, Battalion Landing Team ONE THREE, in the Republic of Vietnam on 10 May 1967. While participating in Operation BEAVER CAGE, in Tinh, Quang Nam Province, Corporal Sanders enabled his platoon to move from positions exposed to heavy automatic and small arms fire, to a protected trench line, by advancing himself to an exposed position with his squad's machine gun when all other members of the squad became casualties. He then placed a heavy volume of accurate fire on Viet Cong and North Vietnamese Army troops causing them to cease fire. When the enemy troops advanced to the cover of the trench line, in which other members of his platoon were located, he placed himself between the enemy and friendly troops. As the enemy approached to within six meters in front of him, Corporal Sanders delivered machine gun fire down the long axis of the trench line killing approximately two of them and wounding three others before he was killed by enemy fire. As a result of his heroic conduct and fearless devotion to duty, his actions enabled nine Marines, some of whom were wounded, to gain cover in the trench line and to gain positions where grenades and M-79 fire could be delivered on the enemy. By his outstanding courage, exceptional fortitude and valiant fighting spirit, Corporal Sanders served to inspire all who observed him and upheld the highest traditions of the Marine Corps and the United States Naval Service. He gallantly gave his life for his country.

*SARGENT, GEORGE T., JR.

Citation: For extraordinary heroism while serving as Commanding Officer of the First Battalion, Fourth Marines, Third Marine Division, in connection with operations against the enemy in the Republic of Vietnam. On 20 March 1969, Lieutenant Colonel Sargent was in command of a heliborne attack against enemy positions in Quang Nam Province during Operation PURPLE MARTIN when the lead helicopter came under a heavy volume of North Vietnamese Army fire, causing it to crash in the landing zone. Directing the debarkation of the battalion at a smaller zone on the slope of a hill below the designated area, Lieutenant Colonel Sargent took command of the lead company, and after starting up the hill, the Marines encountered a hostile force occupying a well-fortified position. As he led his men in an aggressive assault against the enemy emplacements, Lieutenant Colonel Sargent observed a machine gun which was pinning down a portion of his unit. Fearlessly moving across the fire-swept terrain toward the North Vietnamese emplacement, he boldly hurled several hand grenades, which killed two hostile soldiers and destroyed the enemy weapon. Skillfully maneuvering his men, he secured the slope of the hill, and early the following morning, despite a fragmentation wound sustained during the previous day's engagement, commenced the final assault against the enemy soldiers. During the ensuing fire fight, the Marines were subjected to intense North Vietnamese mortar and small-arms fire and rocket propelled grenades. Ignoring the hostile rounds impacting near him, Lieutenant Colonel Sargent remained with the forward units, effectively controlling the actions of his men and exploiting every enemy contact to the maximum extent until he was mortally wounded. His timely actions and aggressive leadership inspired all who observed him and were instrumental in the accomplishment of his unit's mission. By his courage, intrepid fighting spirit, and unwavering devotion to duty, Lieutenant Colonel Sargent upheld the highest traditions of the Marine Corps and the United States Naval Service. He gallantly gave his life for his country.

*SCHLEY, ROBERT J.

Citation: For extraordinary heroism while serving as a Machine Gun Team Leader with Company M, Third Battalion, Third Marines, Third Marine Division in the vicinity of Khe Sanh, Quang Tri Province, Republic of Vietnam, on 30 April 1967. During a search and destroy mission, Company M was assigned the mission of seizing and securing Hill 881, a strategic area commanding the approaches into the Khe Sanh complex. While advancing on the numerically stronger, well-trained and equipped enemy in fortified positions, Corporal Schley's squad was taken under a heavy volume of intense and accurate enemy fire. Realizing the necessity of immediate counter action to suppress enemy fire, he unhesitatingly advanced to position himself and his machine gun team where they could deliver the most effective fire on the enemy. Due to his accurate and well controlled fire,

Corporal Schley was able to inflict numerous casualties upon the enemy. As the intensity of the conflict increased and the ammunition depleted, he exposed himself to intense enemy fire to resupply the gun. Painfully wounded in the shoulder during this task, he refused medical attention and evacuation to return to his machine gun and continue firing. Wounded a second time and finding himself the only member of his team able to fight, he bravely continued to man his weapon until he succumbed to his wounds. By his dauntless courage, initiative and indomitable fighting spirit, he served to inspire all who observed him and upheld the highest traditions of the Marine Corps and the United States Naval Service. He gallantly gave his life for his country.

SCHREIBER, KLAUS D.

Citation: For extraordinary heroism as a Patrol Leader with Company C, First Reconnaissance Battalion, First Marine Division (Reinforced), in Thu Thien Province, Republic of Vietnam, on 14 October 1967. While he was leading a twelve-man reconnaissance patrol, north of Danang, First Lieutenant (then Second Lieutenant) Schreiber's patrol came under a devastating machine-gun and automatic weapons attack from a numerically superior enemy force. The initial burst of fire killed two men and wounded another. He repeatedly exposed himself to the heavy enemy fire to position his men on line and direct their fire. With complete disregard for his own safety, he crawled forward, through the intense enemy fire to bring back a fellow comrade who was mortally wounded. When his radio operator was wounded, First Lieutenant Schreiber took over the radio and established communications and tended the wounded man. Hearing the cries of the frenzied Viet Cong, he ordered his men to deliver full automatic fire into the oncoming enemy hordes. Observing that he was in the most advantageous position to throw hand grenades, he ordered his men to pass their grenades to him, and standing upright, in full view of the enemy, hurled grenade after grenade into the frenzied enemy charge. Again, with complete disregard for his own safety, he stood up to pinpoint his position, amidst the enemy fire, enabling aircraft to bombard the enemy positions. He called in napalm and strafing runs to within 25 meters of his position in an attempt to neutralize the enemy force, which was trying to penetrate his defensive position. For eight more hours, he directed earth-shattering air support around his position, and the explosions from their ordnance hurled his men to the ground. As the aircraft ordnance rocked the enemy positions, an attempt was made for medical evacuation of the casualties, but because of intense ground fire, he was forced to expose himself to enemy fire to warn off approaching aircraft. As a company-sized reaction force pushed forward into his position, he directed their fire and advance upon the enemy positions. By his bold initiative, gallant fighting spirit and loyal devotion to duty, First Lieutenant Schreiber was instrumental in defeating an estimated battalion of North Vietnamese regulars, reflecting great credit upon himself and the Marine Corps and upholding the finest traditions of the United States Naval Service.

SCHUNCK, HENRY M.

Citation: For extraordinary heroism while serving as a Field Artillery Batteryman with Battery D, Second Battalion, Thirteenth Marines, First Marine Division (Reinforced), in connection with operations against the enemy in the Republic of Vietnam. On 10 May 1968, Corporal Schunck was a member of a detachment of two howitzers at the United States Army Special Forces camp at Ngok Tavak in Quang Tin Province. In the early morning hours, the camp was attacked by a reinforced North Vietnamese Army battalion which attempted to overrun the hill-top position. Corporal Schunck unhesitatingly left his covered post adjacent to the command bunker and moved under intense fire to the 4.2-inch mortar emplacement in the center of the compound. Although wounded in the leg by grenade fragments en route, he resolutely continued to the mortar position and attempted to deliver mortar fire singlehandedly. Suddenly, he was attacked by a North Vietnamese soldier armed with a flamethrower. Reacting instantly, Corporal Schunck mortally wounded the enemy with accurate rifle fire and then left the mortar emplacement to assist a comrade who had been wounded while attempting to reach the mortar. After moving the casualty to a covered position, he shifted to the 81mm mortar, and with the aid of a companion, directed a heavy volume of fire against the attackers, inflicting several casualties as they launched a concentrated attack on his position. Although wounded a second time by grenade fragments, he selflessly disregarded his painful injuries in order to continue bringing effective fire to bear against the hostile force until his supply of ammunition was expended. Leaving the emplacement, he moved along his unit's defenses, distributing ammunition and moving casualties to the Fire Direction Center bunker for treatment. Throughout the remainder of the engagement, until the enemy had been repulsed, he continued to move along the defensive lines, encouraging and directing his companions. Then, weakened from his wounds and near exhaustion, he accepted evacuation. By his uncommon courage, unfaltering determination, and selfless devotion to duty at great personal risk, Corporal Schunck upheld the highest traditions of the Marine Corps and the United States Naval Service.

SCOTT, DONALD W.

Citation: For extraordinary heroism while serving with Company D, First Battalion, Twenty-sixth Marines, Third Marine Division, Fleet Marine Force, in the Republic of Vietnam on 18 September 1966. As the company approached the village of Gia Binh, the point was taken under attack and sustained many casualties; the platoon commander was killed. After surveying the situation, Sergeant Scott reacted quickly and alertly and without regard for his own personal safety as he moved forward to aid the fallen men. Subjected to intense fire from enemy automatic small-arms directed upon the wounded men, Sergeant Scott, on six separate occasions, courageously worked his way up through the hail of enemy fire and retrieved his dead and wounded comrades. When he himself was painfully wounded, he refused medical attention and went back to retrieve the last of his dead men. On his last trip into the village he was again wounded, but continued on beyond the point required by duty and succeeded in recovering the body of a fellow Marine. Through his daring and courageous actions in the face of almost certain death, and while seriously wounded, Sergeant Scott personally saved the lives of three Marines, and recovered the bodies of three of his fallen comrades. By his daring initiative, valiant fighting spirit and selfless devotion to duty, Sergeant Scott reflected great credit upon himself and the Marine Corps and upheld the highest traditions of the United States Naval Service.

SEE, ROGER D.

Citation: For extraordinary heroism in action as a Patrol Leader with Company A, Third Reconnaissance Battalion, Third Marine Division during combat operations against the enemy in the Republic of Vietnam. On 8 June 1969, while his six-man reconnaissance team was establishing an observation post, Corporal See observed two enemy soldiers in proximity to the Marine position and took them under fire. During the exchange of fire both enemy soldiers were wounded, one of whom was captured by Corporal See. With the enemy force now in close pursuit, Corporal See picked up the wounded prisoner and began carrying him to the helicopter extraction site. During this action, he was wounded in the thigh, but managed to regain his feet and continue toward the extraction site. When another Marine coming to his assistance was seriously wounded, Corporal See remained in a dangerously exposed position to treat his companion's wounds and to administer mouth-to-mouth resuscitation in a futile effort to save the man's life. After his comrade succumbed to his wounds, Corporal See seized the grenade launcher the Marine had been carrying and delivered covering fire for his men. When he had expended all the grenades, he utilized his rifle and a weapon dropped by an enemy soldier until he had fired every round available, and then painfully maneuvered to join his team on the hill. As the unit attempted to attain the crest, the Marines were subjected to intense fire from a bunker position. Corporal See crawled across an exposed area and silenced the fire by dropping a fragmentation grenade through an aperture at the top of the position. When an extraction helicopter arrived on station and approached for a landing, intensified fire from hostile positions around the hill forced the pilot to lift off. Until the early morning hours of the following day when a successful extraction became possible, Corporal See, despite the pain of his wound, continually patrolled the defensive perimeter to encourage his men, ascertain their welfare and direct their fire. By his courage, valiant leadership, and unfaltering devotion to duty in the face of seemingly overwhelming odds, he contributed significantly to the accomplishment of his unit's intelligence mission and upheld the highest traditions of the Marine Corps and the United States Naval Service.

SEXTON, CHARLES T.

Citation: For extraordinary heroism while serving as a Radio Operator with the Third Force Reconnaissance Company, Third Marine Amphibious Force in connection with combat operations against the enemy in the Republic of Vietnam. On 5 February 1970, Corporal Sexton was a member of a six-man reconnaissance team which was patrolling deep in the A Shau Valley when it came under a heavy volume of small arms and automatic weapons fire from approximately fifty enemy soldiers occupying well-concealed emplacements in the dense elephant grass. During the initial moments of the attack, three Marines were mortally wounded and two were seriously wounded. After a rapid assessment of the precarious situation, Corporal Sexton directed the fire of his two wounded companions and moved about the fire-swept area to collect hand grenades and ammunition from his fallen comrades. Utilizing his radio, he then reported the situation to his commanding officer and requested assistance. For the next several hours, while the enemy attempted to encircle and overrun his position, Corporal Sexton repeatedly adjusted helicopter and fixed-wing air strikes on the hostile unit, hurled hand grenades, shouted encouragement to his wounded companions, and simultaneously furnished a running commentary to his company commander until a reaction force arrived to lend support. His heroic and determined actions were an inspiration to all who served with him and undoubtedly saved his fellow Marines from further serious injury or even death. By his courage, superb leadership, and valiant devotion to duty in the face of grave personal danger, Corporal Sexton upheld the highest traditions of the Marine Corps and the United States Naval Service.

SEXTON, HARRY E.

Citation: For extraordinary heroism while serving as Commanding Officer of Marine Light Helicopter Squadron 367, Marine Aircraft Group Sixteen, First Marine Aircraft Wing in connection with combat operations against the enemy in the Republic of Vietnam. On 11 September 1970, Lieutenant Colonel Sexton launched as Flight Leader of a flight of nine helicopters assigned the mission of inserting a friendly force into a mountainous area deep in enemy-controlled territory which was heavily defended by enemy antiaircraft weapons. Shortly after arriving over the designated area, the entire flight came under an extremely heavy volume of enemy fire, damaging each of the gunships and the lead transport. Lieutenant Colonel Sexton maneuvered his aircraft on repeated rocket and strafing runs and led his flight in delivering such devastatingly effective strikes upon the hostile positions that the enemy fire was suppressed sufficiently to enable the friendly force to be safely inserted. By 13 September, the ground unit had sustained approximately twenty casualties while heavily engaged with a North Vietnamese Army force and requested an emergency extraction. Returning to the beleaguered unit,

Lieutenant Colonel Sexton braved the intense hostile fire as he skillfully coordinated the extraction efforts of twenty-two Marine and United States Army and Air Force aircraft which resulted in the safe medical evacuation of all of the casualties and the extraction of the crew of one of the transports which was forced to land in a nearby open area when severely damaged by enemy fire. When it became apparent the following day that the ground force required an immediate extraction, Lieutenant Colonel Sexton expertly directed the laying down of smoke screens and the rocket and strafing runs of his gunship helicopters, thereby enabling the transports to enter the dangerous area and safely extract the friendly force. Although his helicopter was seriously damaged by hostile fire, he resolutely remained in the battle area until his extraction mission was completed and then skillfully maneuvered his crippled aircraft to safety. By his dauntless courage, superb airmanship, and unwavering devotion to duty in the face of great personal danger, Lieutenant Colonel Sexton upheld the highest traditions of the Marine Corps and of the United States Naval Service.

SEXTON, MERLYN A.

Citation: For extraordinary heroism while serving as Commanding Officer, Company I, Third Battalion, Fourth Marines, Third Marine Division, in connection with operations against the enemy in the Republic of Vietnam from 19 June to 8 July 1968. Captain Sexton was assigned to defend a ridgeline overlooking National Route One approximately 2,000 meters southeast of the Khe Sanh Combat Base. Despite sporadic mortar and artillery attacks, he established a strong perimeter, developed a fire plan, and conducted offensive patrols throughout the surrounding area. On the night of 30 June, when his position came under attack by a numerically superior North Vietnamese Army force supported by rocket, artillery, and mortar fire, Captain Sexton quickly directed well coordinated supporting arms fire against the hostile positions and consolidated his perimeter. When the enemy penetrated a sector of the protective wire, he fearlessly moved to the point of heaviest contact, rallied his men, and directed their fire against the enemy. Disregarding his own safety, he skillfully adjusted highly accurate artillery fire around the perimeter, forcing the hostile force to break contact and withdraw. Throughout the night, Captain Sexton continued to direct supporting arms fire against the retreating enemy and, on the following morning, dispatched patrols to search out and destroy hidden hostile positions. During the day, he adjusted air strikes by helicopter gunships and fixed-wing aircraft against the enemy's withdrawal routes until assured that his vital position was secure. His sustained heroism in the face of a numerically superior, determined North Vietnamese Army force inspired all who observed him and contributed immeasurably to his unit accounting for 212 North Vietnamese soldiers confirmed killed and 77 weapons seized. By his courage, intrepid fighting spirit, and unwavering devotion to duty at great personal risk, Captain Sexton upheld the highest traditions of the Marine Corps and the United States Naval Service.

*SHERMAN, ANDREW M.

Citation: For extraordinary heroism as Platoon Commander, Second Platoon, Company E, Second Battalion, Fourth Marines, northwest of Cam Lo in Quang Tri Province, Republic of Vietnam, on 8 August 1966. In carrying out its assigned mission of assisting in the evacuation of a reconnaissance team which was surrounded by North Vietnamese, Second Lieutenant Sherman's platoon was attacked on two sides in great strength and rapidly encircled; heavy automatic weapons fire and grenades inflicted fifty percent casualties upon them. With the North Vietnamese force threatening to overrun the position, Second Lieutenant Sherman, with complete disregard for his own safety, moved about through extremely heavy rifle and automatic weapons fire in full view of the enemy, directing the fire fight and giving encouragement to his men. The viciousness of the assault by the North Vietnamese pushed the defenders into tenuous secondary positions. Second Lieutenant Sherman, undeterred by the five-to-one odds, rallied his remaining men and led a counterattack back across forty meters of open, fire-swept terrain, and regained the original positions. By this time, the force had suffered sixty percent casualties and the situation was deteriorating rapidly. Repeated attempts at evacuation were thwarted by the loss of four helicopters. Second Lieutenant Sherman bravely continued to move from position to position deploying his weapon, and shouting orders and words of encouragement until he was mortally wounded. By his valiant leadership, outstanding courage, and stirring example in the face of tremendous odds, he inspired his men and gave them the spirit to repulse the enemy and crush the attack. His steadfast devotion to duty was in keeping with the highest traditions of the Marine Corps and the United States Naval Service. He gallantly gave his life for his country.

*SIPPLE, CONRAD A.

Citation: For extraordinary heroism as a Squad Leader with Company C, Second Battalion, Fourth Marines, in the Republic of Vietnam, on 5 March 1966. The company was engaged in operations against insurgent communist forces in the vicinity of An Tuyet, Quang Ngai Province, when Corporal Sipple's platoon came under extremely heavy small-arms and automatic weapons fire from Viet Cong forces entrenched on a commanding ridgeline. Numerous casualties were inflicted on the platoon and many fell in areas exposed to annihilating fire. With full knowledge of the hazards involved and with complete disregard for his own safety, Corporal Sipple braved the fierce, hostile fire repeatedly to assist in the evacuation of wounded Marines. Oblivious to the unrelenting fusillade of automatic weapons fire, he braved the storm alone on two occasions to assist wounded comrades to safety. On two other occasions he returned into the vicious enemy fire to assist others in the evacuation of seriously wounded comrades who had to be carried bodily from the extremely hazardous area. On his fourth sally into the furious hail of enemy fire he was mortally wounded. Through his outstanding initiative and inspiring valor in the face of great personal risk he saved his comrades from further injury or possible loss of life. He gallantly gave his life in the cause of freedom.

*SIROUSA, MICHAEL A.

Citation: For extraordinary heroism while serving as a Squad Leader with Company C, First Battalion, Seventh Marines, First Marine Division in connection with combat operations against the enemy in the Republic of Vietnam. On 12 February 1970, Company C was moving as a reaction force to support another Marine unit which was heavily engaged in combat with a hostile force in Quang Nam Province. While moving across a stream, the point squad came under intense small arms and automatic weapons fire from an enemy unit well entrenched on the opposite bank, wounding several Marines and pinning the squad down on a sandbar in the middle of the stream. Reacting instantly, Private First Class Sirousa skillfully maneuvered his squad to firing positions along the river bank and directed the delivery of maximum fire at the enemy positions. Realizing that the amount of fire delivered by Marines along the bank was insufficient to suppress the hostile fire, he gathered as many hand grenades as he could carry and rushed across the stream in a valiant one-man assault on the enemy positions. Firing his rifle and hurling hand grenades, he continued his gallant efforts, despite the concentration of hostile fire directed at him, until he was mortally wounded. His dauntless fighting spirit inspired all who observed him and was greatly instrumental in the defeat of the enemy. By his courage, bold initiative, and unwavering devotion to duty, Private First Class Sirousa upheld the highest traditions of the Marine Corps and the United States Naval Service. He gallantly gave his life in the service of his country.

*SKIBBE, DAVID W.

Citation: For extraordinary heroism while serving as a Platoon Commander with Company C, First Reconnaissance Battalion, First Marine Division in connection with combat operations against the enemy in the Republic of Vietnam. On 2 March 1970, while Second Lieutenant Skibbe was leading a patrol deep in enemy-controlled territory, the team came under a heavy volume of fire from a large hostile force. During the initial moments of the engagement, Second Lieutenant Skibbe observed a wounded man fall in a forward position, and unhesitatingly placed himself between the casualty and enemy soldiers to deliver intense covering fire which forced the enemy momentarily to break contact and enabled the Marines to move the wounded man to a more secure location. While the radio operator was requesting fixed-wing air support, the enemy launched a ground assault in an attempt to overrun the Marine position. Despite the hostile rounds impacting around him, Second Lieutenant Skibbe exposed himself to the enemy fire to direct the defensive activities of his men and, while thus engaged, was severely wounded in the ankle. Although suffering intense pain and unable to walk, he nevertheless skillfully directed the bombing and strafing runs of supporting aircraft with such accuracy that the hostile soldiers broke contact and retreated, thereby enabling a medical evacuation helicopter to come to a safe hover overhead. As Second Lieutenant Skibbe was being hoisted toward the aircraft, the hoist apparatus sustained a malfunction, and he was mortally injured when he fell to the ground. His heroic and determined actions throughout this mission contributed significantly to the defeat of the numerically superior enemy force. By his courage, valiant leadership, and unwavering devotion to duty in the face of grave personal danger, Second Lieutenant Skibbe upheld the highest traditions of the Marine Corps and of the United States Naval Service. He gallantly gave his life in the service of his country.

SKWERES, JEFF C.

Citation: For extraordinary heroism while serving with Marine Medium Helicopter Squadron 364, Marine Aircraft Group Sixteen, First Marine Aircraft Wing in connection with combat operations against the enemy in the Republic of Vietnam. On the evening of 1 June 1970, Corporal Skweres launched as an Aerial Gunner aboard a transport helicopter assigned the medical evacuation of several Marine casualties who had been extensively wounded by enemy mines. Arriving over the designated location, he observed that, when the tall elephant grass was parted by the downdraft from the rotar blades, the entire field was literally seeded with mines. Despite this extreme hazard, Corporal Skweres unhesitatingly volunteered to execute a bold and imaginative plan whereby he would be lowered on the hoist, wait on the spot while a wounded man was lifted to the aircraft and then board the hoist to be moved to where the next casualty lay. For approximately an hour, Corporal Skweres valiantly moved from one stricken man to another in performing his rescue mission. With the fall of darkness, it was necessary to utilize the exterior lights to aid in his examination of the casualties and he thus became a vulnerable target for automatic weapons and rocket propelled grenade fire which enemy soldiers delivered from several different directions. Undaunted by this additional adversity, he steadfastly continued his determined efforts with calm deliberation until all casualties had been embarked and the transport helicopter was directed toward the nearest medical facilities at Danang. By his courage, inspiring initiative, and unfaltering devotion to duty in the face of grave personal danger, Corporal Skweres was instrumental in accomplishing an extremely dangerous lifesaving mission and upheld the highest traditions of the Marine Corps and of the United States Naval Service.

SLATER, ALBERT C., JR.

Citation: For extraordinary heroism as Commanding Officer, Company A, First Battalion, Ninth Marines, during Operation BUFFALO in the Republic of Vietnam on 6-7 July 1967. In command of both Companies A and C, he moved his forces into a strategic position north of Con Thien. Shortly before dark, the companies came under extremely heavy barrages of enemy artillery and mortars. During the barrages, Captain Slater fearlessly maneuvered his command into a perimeter where it could counter the attack he was certain would come. With full knowledge of the hazards involved, he ignored the heavy barrages of enemy artillery and personally checked each position to insure that they were secure. When the attack came, by an estimated two battalions of the North Vietnamese Army, Captain Slater unhesitatingly moved to an exposed position where he could properly control the situation. He repeatedly exposed himself to the withering enemy fire in order to better observe the air and artillery support he coordinated for his now surrounded command. For six hours, Captain Slater, with complete disregard for his own personal safety and with full composure and presence of mind, moved from one exposed position to another, giving encouragement and directing the men of his command. He aggressively employed all available fire and personally led his men in hand-to-hand combat through extremely dense underbrush which reduced the action to a man-to-man struggle. Throughout the entire night, Captain Slater, although constantly exposed to enemy artillery, mortars, grenades, and small-arms fire, was always at a strategic point of contact directing his unit and encouraging his men. By his courage, tenacity, and outstanding leadership, Captain Slater brought stability to an otherwise untenable situation, which resulted in at least two hundred North Vietnamese regulars killed with small losses to his command. Captain Slater's daring actions and loyal devotion to duty in the face of great personal risk reflected great credit upon himself and the Marine Corps and upheld the highest traditions of the United States Naval Service.

SLATER, ROBERT M. S.

Citation: For extraordinary heroism as a Staff Advisor in the Republic of Vietnam from 5 to 11 January 1968. Lieutenant Slater, at the risk of his life, above and beyond the call of duty, volunteered to undertake a hazardous mission into enemy territory to gather vital intelligence. On 6 January he was inserted for the first time and successfully brought back essential intelligence. Due to the success of his first mission, he volunteered to go back a second time for additional information. With full knowledge of the continuing possibility of imminent capture or death, he returned again into enemy territory and brought back a great amount of invaluable intelligence. With great courage, he returned for a third and final mission. Although his chances for survival were slim he again successfully brought back the vitally needed intelligence. Lieutenant Slater's extraordinary heroism resulted in extremely heavy materiel damage and personnel casualties to the enemy and led to the saving of many American and South Vietnamese lives, both military and civilian. His courageous actions and loyal devotion to duty were in keeping with the highest traditions of the Marine Corps and the United States Naval Service.

*SLEIGH, DUNCAN B.

Citation: For extraordinary heroism as a platoon commander in Company M, Third Battalion, Seventh Marines, in Quang Nam Province, Republic of Vietnam, on 6 November 1968. The company advanced in a sweep operation south of Hill 55 where it encountered a large North Vietnamese Army force and sustained heavy casualties at the first bitter engagement. The well entrenched enemy kept the company pinned down with rocket propelled grenades and heavy small-arms and automatic-weapons fire, making evacuation of casualties a hazardous chore. As the company pressed the attack, the wounded and dead were moved toward the rear where Second Lieutenant Sleigh was directing the establishment of a landing zone. Taking charge of the critical situation, Second Lieutenant Sleigh strategically deployed his men to return suppressive fire and at the same time maintained control of the evacuation. Two helicopter landings were attempted, and on the second effort a rocket propelled grenade landed near the wounded who were being treated. Observing the danger to the wounded, Second Lieutenant Sleigh crawled to one casualty and lay huddled over him as a shield when another rocket propelled grenade landed less than a meter away, instantly killing Second Lieutenant Sleigh. He thus absorbed most of the shock with his body, not only saving the life of one Marine, but also preventing injury to others near him. His valiant leadership and courageous fighting spirit inspired all the men of the company who observed his last brave act. Second Lieutenant Sleigh's heroism reflected great credit upon himself and the Marine Corps and upheld the highest traditions of the United States Naval Service. He gallantly gave his life for his country.

SLIBY, DENNIS M.

Citation: For extraordinary heroism while serving as a Fire Team Leader with Company A, First Battalion, Fifth Marines, First Marine Division (Reinforced), in connection with operations against the enemy in the Republic of Vietnam. On 30 March 1968, during Operation HOUSTON, Corporal Sliby's company deployed into defensive positions around several vital bridges in the Phu Bai area. Early the following morning, the company command post, located at the Troui River Bridge in Phu Loc District, came under a heavy mortar and rocket attack followed by a ground assault by two North Vietnamese army companies. Without hesitation, Corporal Sliby rallied his fire team and directed a heavy volume of accurate fire against the enemy. In the ensuing attack, he aggressively maneuvered his men from one position to another in an effort to seize a bunker which had been overrun by the enemy. As he was moving his team into a position to deliver fire into the emplacement, the enemy threw a grenade which landed among his men. With complete disregard for his own life, Corporal Sliby covered the grenade with his body, shielding his companions from the blast. Even though critically wounded, he shouted words of encouragement to his men and directed them into a secure position before crawling, unassisted, to the platoon command post for aid. His timely and selfless actions inspired all who observed him and undoubtedly saved the lives of his men. By his extraordinary courage, bold initiative, and unwavering devotion to duty at great personal risk, Corporal Sliby upheld the highest traditions of the Marine Corps and the United States Naval Service.

SMITH, CHESTER B.

Citation: For extraordinary heroism in action against communist insurgent forces in the Republic of Vietnam, while serving with River Patrol Section 531 on 11 December 1966. As Patrol Officer on a PBR combat patrol on the Mekong River, Petty Officer Smith pursued a sampan, with three Viet Cong aboard, into a narrow canal where the sampan's occupants, aided by eight other Viet Cong along the canal banks, opened fire on the patrol boat. Petty Officer Smith promptly directed his crew in returning suppressive fire which accounted for eight Viet Cong killed. Bringing in his cover boat from the main river, Petty Officer Smith reentered the canal where he came upon a company-size Viet Cong force preparing to board forty sampans. The enemy opened fire on the patrol boats, but were completely repulsed and demoralized by Petty Officer Smith's sudden attack, causing them to retreat in confusion. At least two of the enemy were confirmed as killed. While still returning the heavy fire the Viet Cong were directing at him, Petty Officer Smith systematically destroyed their water transport and equipment. After extracting his patrol to rearm, he reentered the canal for a third time and personally directed his machine gunners in silencing six enemy weapons positions. Petty Officer Smith then vectored a U. S. Navy helicopter in a rocket run on a cleverly camouflaged bunker. A large secondary explosion resulted, completely destroying an enemy ammunition cache. When the overall four-hour engagement had ended, Petty Officer Smith's PBR's had accounted for fifteen enemy confirmed killed, twenty-eight enemy sampans sunk, twelve damaged, three captured, and an enemy ammunition cache destroyed. His daringly aggressive actions, outstanding initiative, extraordinary courage, and gallant leadership were in keeping with the highest traditions of the United States Naval Service.

*SMITH, HOMER L.

Citation: For extraordinary heroism on 19 and 20 May 1967, while serving as Commanding Officer of Attack Squadron TWO HUNDRED TWELVE, embarked in USS BON HOMME RICHARD (CVA-31), during aerial attacks on two strategically important and heavily defended thermal power plants in Hanoi and Bac Giang, North Vietnam. As strike leader in each of these actions against the enemy, Captain (then Commander) Smith was faced with adverse weather and difficult terrain, formidable opposition from the enemy, and the necessity for violent, evasive maneuvering. Despite these obstacles, he expertly led his strike groups in executing brilliantly successful attacks which subsequently hindered the enemy in his efforts to make war. By his heroic actions, superb airmanship, and inspiring devotion to duty throughout, Captain Smith reflected great credit upon himself and his squadron, and upheld the highest traditions of the United States Naval Service.

SMITH, RAY L.

Citation: For extraordinary heroism during the period 30 March to 1 April 1972 while serving as advisor to a Vietnamese Command group numbering approximately 250 Vietnamese Marines located on a small hilltop outpost in the Republic of Vietnam. With the Command Group repulsing several savage enemy assaults, and subjected to a continuing hail of fire from an attacking force estimated to be of two-battalion strength, Captain Smith repeatedly exposed himself to the heavy fire while directing friendly air support. When adverse weather conditions precluded further close air support, he attempted to lead the group, now reduced to only 28 Vietnamese Marines, to the safety of friendly lines. An enemy soldier opened fire upon the Marines at the precise moment that they had balked when encountering an outer defensive ring of barbed wire. Captain Smith returned accurate fire, disposing of the attacker, and then threw himself backwards on top of the booby-trap-infested wire barrier. Swiftly, the remaining Marines moved over the crushed wire, stepping on Captain Smith's prostrate body, until all had passed safely through the barrier. Although suffering severe cuts and bruises, Captain Smith succeeded in leading the Marines to the safety of friendly lines. His great personal valor and unrelenting devotion to duty reflected the highest credit upon himself, the Marine Corps and the United States Naval Service.

*SNYDER, STEPHEN F.

Citation: For extraordinary heroism as Platoon Commander, Third Platoon, Company F, Second Battalion, Fourth Marines, in the Thon Son Lam area, Quang Tri Province, Republic of Vietnam, on 23 and 24 August 1966. Volunteering to attempt to relieve a trapped platoon, Second Lieutenant Snyder unhesitatingly led his platoon in a daring night march through unfamiliar, dense, enemy-infested jungle terrain. Upon arrival at the besieged platoon's position, he fearlessly took a small group into the trap to assist in evacuating wounded from the enemy-dominated location. Though met with a deadly hail of enemy grenades and small-arms fire, he managed to direct the evacuation of two wounded under the cover of darkness. For the next two hours, with complete disregard for his own safety, he selflessly exposed himself to intense fire while he directed suppressive fires which delayed the enemy assault. When the North Vietnamese finally attacked at dawn, Second Lieutenant Snyder heroically led his platoon in a determined counterattack in an effort to protect the trapped men. Undeterred by the murderous enemy grenade barrages and automatic weapons and sniper fire, he courageously led his men forward until he was mortally wounded. Second Lieutenant Snyder's stirring example, exceptional leadership, and marked courage were the determining factor in breaking the enemy assault and saved the lives of the trapped Marines. His great personal valor reflected great credit upon himself and was in keeping with the highest traditions of the Marine Corps and the United States Naval Service.

*SOLIZ, THOMAS

Citation: For extraordinary heroism while serving as a Radio Operator with Company A, First Amphibian Tractor Battalion, Third Marine Division (Reinforced), in Quang Tri Province in the Republic of Vietnam on 6 September 1967. While on patrol, the Third Platoon of Company A was suddenly attacked by a numerically superior North Vietnamese Army force. Observing his Platoon Commander wounded and the platoon sustaining heavy casualties from a withering enemy fire of automatic, small-arms and antitank weapons, Corporal Soliz, with complete disregard for his own safety, ran about twenty-five meters through extremely heavy fire to climb aboard an amphibian tractor to man a machine gun. Knowing the safety of the platoon and outcome of the battle depended on his platoon gaining fire superiority, he unhesitatingly proceeded to place a heavy volume of well-aimed fire on the enemy which enabled the platoon to gain fire superiority, deploy to better defensive positions and evacuate several seriously wounded Marines to amphibian tractors where they could be treated. As he was delivering his devastating fire into the enemy, he was severely wounded by enemy fire which rendered him unconscious. Before assistance could arrive, Corporal Soliz was hit again and mortally wounded. Corporal Soliz's concern for the other members of his platoon coupled with his keen professional skill and unfaltering dedication to duty were in keeping with the highest traditions of the Marine Corps and the United States Naval Service. He gallantly gave his life for his country.

SOTOMAYOR, MIGUEL A. RIVERA

Citation: For extraordinary heroism while serving as a Grenadier with Company F, Second Battalion, Ninth Marines, Third Marine Division (Reinforced), in Quang Tri Province, Republic of Vietnam, on 29 July 1967. While moving in a battalion-sized operation in connection with Operation KINGFISHER, the entire battalion was attacked by a large element of the North Vietnamese army and began receiving a heavy barrage of mortar, rocket and automatic weapons fire. The Third Platoon of Company F, called to the front of the battle, was pinned down in a heavy cross fire from enemy machine guns. Receiving a call for his support, Corporal Rivera Sotomayor responded immediately, though he had been painfully wounded in the arm by shrapnel earlier in the battle. Rushing out into the direct line of enemy fire, with utter disregard for his own safety, he fired his complete supply of ammunition. His firing was so effective that it completely silenced the enemy machine guns and allowed his platoon to move from its pinned down position to establish an effective base of fire against the enemy. With his ammunition expended, Corporal Rivera Sotomayor observed a machine-gun team whose members were too seriously wounded to fire their gun. Running across the opening in which he was standing, through intensifying enemy automatic rifle fire, he quickly loaded it and again, with no thought of his intense pain or severe wound, stood up with the gun and fired several rounds. Observing that the enemy was shifting positions, he grabbed a rifle and struggling into the open from his covered position, he fired a complete magazine of ammunition. Returning as quickly as possible for another magazine, he had to be restrained by a corpsman from going out again. By his daring actions and loyal devotion to duty in the face of personal risk, Corporal Rivera Sotomayor upheld the highest traditions of the Marine Corps and the United States Naval Service.

*SPARK, MICHAEL M.

Citation: For extraordinary heroism while serving as Commanding Officer, Third Marines, Third Marine Division (Reinforced), Fleet Marine Force, in connection with operations against enemy forces in the Republic of Vietnam on 15 January 1969. During a multi-battalion search and clear operation in the vicinity of An Hoa, Colonel Spark exhibited outstanding courage and presence of mind in the midst of violent combat action. While commanding a bold, highly imaginative, mobile operation in the mountainous terrain, Colonel Spark directed an assault against heavily fortified enemy positions. After ensuring that his men were properly positioned, Colonel Spark went airborne, by the use of a helicopter, to observe and direct the operation. During the process of the operation, it was necessary for the helicopter to descend, and as the helicopter hovered over the landing zone, which had been hastily cut out of the jungle, the enemy took the aircraft under automatic-weapons fire. Despite the enemy fire, he defiantly continued the personal direction of his men until finally the helicopter was hit and caused to crash. As the helicopter impacted, the enemy continued firing upon it, killing all the occupants. Throughout the entire operation, Colonel Spark placed requirements for full and direct support of his combat elements above any concern for his own personal safety. He spent the majority of his time with his forward-most units in order to effectively control the action. This enabled him to maximize exploitation of many situations, and served as an inspiration to the officers and enlisted Marines of his command. By his intrepid fighting spirit, daring initiative, and unswerving dedication to duty, Colonel Spark upheld the highest traditions of the Marine Corps and the United States Naval Service. He gallantly gave his life for his country.

SPARKS, NEIL R., JR.

Citation: For extraordinary heroism in aerial flight on 17 July 1967 as aircraft commander of an armored helicopter in Helicopter Anti-Submarine Squadron TWO, during a search and rescue mission over North Vietnam. Lieutenant Sparks courageously penetrated the coastal defenses of North Vietnam to rescue a downed naval aviator in a heavily defended area thirty miles south of Hanoi. Although the helicopter was hit by intense and accurate enemy fire, disabling the radios, automatic stabilization equipment, and airspeed indicator, he skillfully hovered for twenty minutes until the survivor was safely hoisted aboard. Under intense antiaircraft fire, Lieutenant Sparks, through adept maneuvering, prevented further damage to the helicopter during the flight back to the coastline. Two and one-half hours after penetrating the coastal defense over North Vietnam, and having traveled two hundred miles over heavily-fortified hostile territory, he brought his crew and the downed aviator to safety. By his courageous actions, exceptional skill and fearless devotion to duty, Lieutenant Sparks prevented the capture by hostile forces of a fellow aviator, thereby upholding the highest traditions of the United States Naval Service.

SPEER, PAUL H.

Citation: For extraordinary heroism on 19 May 1967 as a pilot in Fighter Squadron TWO ONE ONE, embarked in USS BON HOMME RICHARD (CVA-31). As the flight leader of six F8 aircraft assigned to escort and provide target combat air patrol for two A4 aircraft during a strike against a thermal power plant in North Vietnam, Commander Speer demonstrated outstanding leadership and airmanship in the planning and execution of the defense of the strike group. Encountering an intense barrage of about twenty-five surface-to-air missiles, and under attack from enemy MIGs, he pressed on toward the target, maintaining flight discipline and integrity. Despite increasingly heavy and accurate antiaircraft fire, his flight successfully defended the bombers who scored direct hits on the target, causing extensive damage. During retirement from the target area, Commander Speer sighted a MIG closing dangerously to attack the A4s. Through his skillful execution of tactical maneuvers, he was able to fire two sidewinders at the MIG, causing it to dive into the ground and explode on impact. Continuing the retirement, his flight downed two other enemy aircraft with sidewinders and damaged another by 20mm cannon fire. By his superior airmanship, leadership and sound tactical judgment, Commander Speer contributed greatly to the successful execution of this mission, thereby upholding the highest traditions of the United States Naval Service.

*SPICER, JONATHAN N.

Citation: For extraordinary heroism while serving with Company C, Third Medical Battalion, Third Marine Division in the Republic of Vietnam on 8 March 1968. During an intense enemy rocket, mortar and artillery attack against the Khe Sanh Combat Base, Private Spicer unhesitatingly volunteered to serve as a stretcher bearer and assisted in embarking the numerous casualties aboard transport helicopters for evacuation. Completely disregarding his own safety, he continued to expedite the loading of the wounded aboard the aircraft, despite the increasing intensity of the attack, and was the last man to seek shelter in a bunker at the edge of the air strip. Observing a mortar round exploding near an evacuation helicopter loaded with casualties, he unhesitatingly left his position of relative safety to assist the wounded who were unable to move from their exposed position. Moments later, another round exploded within a few feet of Private Spicer, seriously wounding him, as he shielded a Marine from the blast with his own body. Unable to walk, he warned his comrades to remain in their protective positions while he attempted to crawl from the hazardous area to safety by himself. His selfless actions undoubtedly prevented serious injury or possible death to his fellow Marines and were an inspiration to all who observed him. By his dauntless courage, unfaltering determination and selfless devotion to duty at great risk, Private Spicer upheld the highest traditions of the Marine Corps and the United States Naval Service.

*SRSEN, STEVE A.

Citation: For extraordinary heroism as a Rifleman while serving with Company A, First Battalion, Third Marines in the Republic of Vietnam on 27 January 1967. Private First Class Srsen was with the First Platoon, Company A, when it was engaged in action as a reaction force assigned to link up with a reconnaissance patrol. Early the next morning following the linkup, Private First Class Srsen's squad came under heavy small-arms fire and grenade attack. When an enemy grenade landed in his squad's position, Private First Class Srsen warned three other members of the squad, allowing them to take cover and escape injury. Wounded in his right side and leg from the grenade, Private First Class Srsen, after being treated by a corpsman requested permission to return to his position in the perimeter. Approximately thirty minutes later another enemy grenade landed close to another Marine and Private First Class Srsen gallantly pushed him to the ground, thereby saving his life. Mortally wounded by the exploding grenade, Private First Class Srsen, by his dauntless courage and grave concern for another had risked his life to save that of a fellow Marine, thereby upholding the highest traditions of the Marine Corps and the United States Naval Service. He gallantly gave his life for his country.

STAHL, MYKLE E.

Citation: For extraordinary heroism as Platoon Sergeant, 4.2 Mortar Platoon attached to Company "K," Third Battalion, Twenty-Sixth Marines, Third Marine Division (-) (Reinforced), Fleet Marine Force, Pacific, in connection with combat operations against the enemy in the Republic of Vietnam on 21 January 1968. While maintaining a combat outpost on hill 861, the Company came under enemy mortar, rocket, and ground attack. After the defensive positions on the southwest side of the hill were penetrated by enemy sappers, Captain (then Sergeant) Stahl, although having received shrapnel wounds, led eight Marines from the 4.2 Mortar Section and advanced up the trenchline to make contact with the Third Platoon. Realizing that by now the enemy forces were manning the bunkers in the trenchline, he launched a one man assault while other Marines provided a base of fire, thus enabling several wounded Marines to be evacuated. As he advanced further up the trenchline, Captain Stahl encountered three enemy soldiers who tried to capture him. Although receiving bayonet wounds and having his M-16 rifle malfunction during the struggle, he killed two of the enemy soldiers while another Marine fatally wounded the third. Captain Stahl then picked up an AKA-47 assault rifle and continued up the trenchline and assaulted the third bunker, killing three and capturing three enemy soldiers. Linking up with the Third Platoon, the trenchline was consolidated and evacuation of wounded Marines was completed. Captain Stahl then moved to a .50 caliber machine gun and, although wounded for the third time, continued directing suppressive fire into the attacking enemy forces. By his bold courage and steadfast dedication, Captain Stahl reflected great credit upon himself, the Marine Corps, and the United States Naval Service.

STARRETT, EDWARD F.

Citation: For extraordinary heroism while serving as a Mortar Gunner with Company G, Second Battalion, Fifth Marines, First Marine Division in connection with combat operations against the enemy in the Republic of Vietnam. During the early morning hours of 9 December 1970, while occupying a position in defense of a hamlet in Que Son District of Quang Nam Province, a unit of Marines and Regional Forces soldiers came under ground attack by a large North Vietnamese Army force supported by intense mortar and rocket-propelled grenade fire. During the initial moments of the assault, Lance Corporal Starrett was wounded when an enemy mortar damaged the bunker in which he was located. Although momentarily stunned, he recovered quickly and ran across the fire-swept terrain to his mortar position. As he commenced firing illumination rounds, a grenade landed in the pit he occupied, but he escaped further injury by quickly diving out of the emplacement. Returning to his gun, he found it inoperable and also observed that some of the hostile soldiers had penetrated the defensive perimeter. Observing one of the enemy preparing to hurl a hand grenade at the communications center, he prevented this action with an accurate burst of fire. Lance Corporal Starrett then commenced firing at the advancing enemy soldiers and immediately became a target for enemy grenades. Although wounded again, he continued his vigorous defense of the position, accounting for two more hostile soldiers and preventing further penetration at that point. Later, he stood in full view of the enemy, and seemingly oblivious to the grenades detonating around him, fired round after round into the attacking unit. Sustaining numerous casualties, the enemy was forced to retreat. By his courage, aggressive fighting spirit,

SHEPHERD, BURTON H.

Citation: For extraordinary heroism in aerial flight on 26 October 1967 as Commander, Attack Carrier Air Wing SIXTEEN, embarked in USS ORISKANY (CVA-34). As the strike leader of an eighteen-plane strike group launched against the strategically located and heavily defended Hanoi thermal power plant in North Vietnam, Commander Shepherd, although hampered by adverse weather conditions en route, maintained the precise timing necessary to properly execute the intricate strike plan. Skillfully maneuvering to avoid the numerous tracking missiles and intense and accurate barrages of 57mm and 85mm flak, he led the strike group to the optimum roll-in point and then aggressively pressed home his attack, releasing all bombs on target. Egressing from the target area in a hail of enemy fire, he retired to the relative safety of the karst hills and checked in his strike group. After proceeding expeditiously to the coast to refuel, Commander Shepherd returned to an area south of the target to search for one of his missing strike pilots. Continuing the search for more than an hour over enemy terrain in the face of the most concentrated enemy fire in North Vietnam, he finally returned to the coast after reaching a low fuel state. By his aggressive leadership, professional airmanship, and determination, Commander Shepherd contributed in large measure to the destruction of this major target, and upheld the highest traditions of the United States Naval Service.

Petty Officer Rudd's citation, (between pp 278-279) and that of Cdr. Shepherd, (between pp 310-311) were missing from the original set of documents and were obtained after this book was printed and folded but not yet bound. The unnumbered pages were inserted prior to binding at an opportunity in the process as close to their proper alphabetical position as possible. *NOTE:* The addidtion of these two citations alters the Awards Statistics (Part III, page 357). U.S. Navy (Awards) should read 123, Total Awards should read 487.

and unfaltering devotion to duty in the face of grave personal danger, Lance Corporal Starrett was greatly instrumental in repelling a determined enemy force and upheld the highest traditions of the Marine Corps and of the United States Naval Service.

STAYTON, NORMAN B.

Citation: For extraordinary heroism on 26 March 1971 while serving as second gunner in the lead aircraft of a light fire team from Helicopter Attack (Light) Squadron THREE, flying convoy escort along the Can Gao Canal, Kien Giang Province, Republic of Vietnam. Petty Officer (then Airman) Stayton was participating with his fire team in providing overhead cover for a boat convoy when one of the boats carrying 9,000 gallons of explosive jet fuel struck a mine, detonating the fuel. Two enemy rockets then struck the boat, following which burning fuel spewed across the water. When he observed a wounded man struggling to shore to escape the flames and the hail of enemy bullets hitting the water, Petty Officer Stayton alerted his pilot, took the initiative and dived from the hovering helicopter into the burning canal to carry a life preserver to the survivor. Although immediately wounded in the leg, Petty Officer Stayton nonetheless succeeded in reaching the victim, who had sustained serious burns and was in a state of shock, and shielded him with his own body while attempting to tow him to the recovery site. Thwarted in five attempts to reach the hovering helicopter because of the current, the enemy fire, and the helicopter rotor downwash, Petty Officer Stayton, although close to complete exhaustion, managed to wave his arms and get the attention of a river assault craft which proceeded to rescue both men. By his valiant and persevering efforts in the face of intense enemy fire and almost insurmountable circumstances, Petty Officer Stayton was directly instrumental in the rescue of a seriously wounded fellow serviceman. His heroic actions were in keeping with the highest traditions of the United States Naval Service.

*ST. CLAIR, CLARENCE H., JR.

Citation: For extraordinary heroism while serving as a Squad Leader with Company K, Third Battalion, Seventh Marines, First Marine Division in connection with combat operations against the enemy in the Republic of Vietnam. On 28 August 1969, while Company K was conducting a search and destroy operation in Quang

Nam Province, the lead platoon was pinned down by small arms, automatic weapons, and antiaircraft fire from enemy soldiers concealed in well-camouflaged emplacements. Directed to assist the pinned-down element, Corporal St. Clair deployed his men to the point of heaviest contact and instantly came under intense fire. Observing two principal sources of hostile fire, he directed two of his fire teams to provide covering fire while he maneuvered his third team toward the enemy emplacements. While crawling toward their objective, the men were seriously wounded by enemy grenades. Quick to act, Corporal St. Clair began crawling through the enemy cross fire toward the first objective and had advanced only five meters when he was severely injured by the detonation of another grenade. Recovering quickly, he pressed his advance until he was close enough to the enemy bunker to hurl a grenade through its aperture, destroying the position and its occupants. Although suffering intense pain, he valiantly continued in the direction of the second objective and, while thus engaged, was mortally wounded. By his courage, aggressive fighting spirit and unwavering devotion to duty in the face of grave personal danger, Corporal St. Clair contributed significantly to the accomplishment of his unit's mission and upheld the highest traditions of the Marine Corps and of the United States Naval Service.

*STEWART, MICHAEL E.

Citation: For extraordinary heroism in action while serving as an Anti-tank Assaultman with the Second Platoon, Company A, First Battalion, Ninth Marines, on 13 May 1967 in Quang Tri Province, Republic of Vietnam. During a search and clear operation in the village of Phu An, Lance Corporal Stewart's company came under heavy small arms, machine gun and mortar fire from a well entrenched North Vietnamese Regular force, estimated at company strength. At the outset, several Marines were killed and others wounded in an area affording them little or no cover from the deadly accurate fire which felled them. Realizing that these Marines could not return unassisted to safety, Lance Corporal Stewart unhesitatingly, with full knowledge of the hazards involved and of the great risk of his own life, left his relatively safe position and crawled alone over fifty meters through open area to were the wounded lay helpless. One man was shot in the face and could not see. With uncommon calmness and bravery and while constantly exposing himself to the withering fire which continued to deplete his company's ranks, he calmed the man and guided him through the hail of bullets to safety. Again, ignoring the deadly accurate fire which had halted his company's advance, he returned to the field where others lay wounded. While dragging a second casualty to the rear, the man was again wounded. Lance Corporal Stewart steadfastly refused to leave the twice wounded Marine. As he daringly continued through the enemy fire toward safety, he was mortally wounded. Through his valiant spirit of self-sacrifice in the face of great personal risk, Lance Corporal Stewart saved one Marine from almost certain death and gave his own life helping another. His bold initiative, unswerving devotion to duty and courageous efforts inspired all who observed him and were in keeping with the highest traditions of the Marine Corps and the United States Naval Service. He gallantly gave his life for his country.

STOCKMAN, ROBERT D.

Citation: For extraordinary heroism while serving as a Scout Dog Handler with the Third Military Police Battalion, Force Logistic Command in connection with combat operations against the enemy in the Republic of Vietnam. On 14 January 1970, Sergeant Stockman accompanied a platoon on a mission to search a designated village for North Vietnamese Army soldiers and equipment. As the platoon neared its objective, the lead element was pinned down by a heavy volume of automatic weapons and rocket-propelled grenade fire from an enemy company occupying a well-fortified bunker complex. After rapidly assessing the situation, Sergeant Stockman tied his dog in a covered location, rushed across fifty meters of open area, and charged the nearest hostile emplacement, silencing the fire from that sector. Directing a companion to provide covering fire, Sergeant Stockman and another Marine maneuvered across the fire-swept terrain and attacked and destroyed the remaining bunker. At this time, the platoon came under intense fire from two other directions. Observing a wounded man fall in an open area, Sergeant Stockman unhesitatingly ran to his side, picked him up, and carried him to a covered location. When a medical transportation helicopter approached a pick-up site, the hostile fire immediately increased in intensity, delaying the landing. Seizing the initiative, Sergeant Stockman rallied the other members of the platoon and led an aggressive assault on the enemy force which forced it into a disorganized retreat, leaving behind two mortally wounded soldiers. By his courage, aggressive fighting spirit, and inspiring devotion to duty in the face of grave personal danger, Sergeant Stockman contributed significantly to the defeat of a numerically superior enemy force and upheld the highest traditions of the Marine Corps and of the United States Naval Service.

STONE, GUY E.

Citation: For extraordinary heroism on 27 January 1970 during operations against the enemy in the Republic of Vietnam. Engaged in clearing a graveyard of booby traps for a detachment of Underwater Demolition Team TWELVE during a bunker-destruction sweep near the Vinh Dien River, Chief Petty Officer Stone suddenly discovered eight of the enemy hidden in the grass. The hostile troops opened fire with automatic weapons and began hurling hand grenades. Yelling a warning to the other members of his team, Chief Petty Officer Stone, without a weapon at that moment, took cover behind a mound and proceeded to direct the fire of his companions. Subsequently, in the face of the hostile fire, he raced to within fifteen feet of the enemy and hurled three grenades into their midst. Observing two of the enemy soldiers retreating, he again exposed himself to the hostile fire to borrow a weapon from a team member and shoot the fleeing soldiers, accounting for a total of six enemy dead and two captured. Chief Petty Officer Stone's instinctive reactions saved two United States and two Vietnamese Naval personnel in his team from certain death. His exceptionally courageous and heroic actions and selfless efforts on behalf of his team memebers were in keeping with the highest traditions of the United States Naval Service.

STRODE, GERALD M.

Citation: For extraordinary heroism on 4 September 1967, while serving as a corpsman with the First Platoon, Company B, First Battalion, Fifth Marines, First Marine Division (Reinforced), FMF, in connection with operations against North Vietnamese Army forces in the Republic of Vietnam. At this time, Company B was engaged in Operation SWIFT in Quang Ngai Province, and came under heavy small-arms, automatic-weapons, and mortar fire from an estimated regimental-sized North Vietnamese Army force. Without hesitation, Petty Officer Strode moved to the point of initial contact, undaunted by the heavy volume of fire, and began administering first aid to the casualties. In order to protect his wounded comrades, he utilized a pistol and hand grenades effectively in their defense. Although wounded, he then engaged in hand-to-hand combat until the enemy withdrew. Starting once again to treat the wounded, Petty Officer Strode carried his injured comrades to a protected area about seventy-five meters away. When he returned to the line, he worked continuously through the night with the casualties until he was relieved by the company corpsman the next morning, caring for his own wounds and allowing himself to be evacuated only when all other casualties had been evacuated. By his swift actions, professional skill, and cool demeanor under fire, he inspired the men of his platoon and undoubtedly saved many lives, thereby upholding the highest traditions of the United States Naval Service.

STUCKEY, JAMES L.

Citation: For extraordinary heroism as a Fire Team Leader with Company C, First Battalion, Ninth Marines, Third Marine Division (Reinforced), in Quang Tri Province, Republic of Vietnam on 6 July 1967. While in a defensive position and surrounded by a large North Vietnamese Army force, Corporal (then Lance Corporal) Stuckey's fire team occupied a strategic point on the company's right flank. During one heavy attack, three enemy grenades landed in the fire team's position. Completely disregarding his own safety, Corporal Stuckey unhesitatingly picked up the grenades and hurled them back toward the enemy. As he was throwing the third grenade, it exploded severing his right hand. Despite the painful wound, he steadfastly refused to abandon his position, and courageously continued to fight and encourage his men. Although he evacuated one of his wounded men, Corporal Stuckey refused to seek aid for himself and staunchly repulsed the furious onslaught throughout the night, accepting treatment only when the enemy had withdrawn the following morning. His valiant leadership and courageous fighting spirit served to inspire the men in his platoon to heroic endeavor in repelling the enemy, and reflected the highest credit upon himself and the Marine Corps. By his heroic conduct and fearless devotion to duty, Corporal Stuckey upheld the highest traditions of the United States Naval Service.

SULLIVAN, DANIEL F., JR.

Citation: For extraordinary heroism while serving as a Machine Gun Team Leader with Company L, Third Battalion, Fourth Marines, in the Republic of Vietnam. On the night of 11 April 1966, Corporal Sullivan and his team were assigned to set up an ambush outside the hamlet of Nam Pho Ha in Phu Loc District in conjunction with Operation GOLDEN FLEECE II. Several Viet Cong were allowed to proceed within five feet of the Marines' machine gun before they were brought under fire. As two of the enemy fell in front of the machine gun, a grenade was thrown into Corporal Sullivan's position. With complete disregard for his own life, he leaped on the grenade and covered it with his body. Rolling onto his back and still clutching the sputtering grenade to his body, he hurled it upward and away from the Marines. Before it touched the ground, the grenade exploded harmlessly about six feet in front of the position. His valiant effort doubtlessly saved his three comrades from death or severe injury. By his gallant concern for his fellow Marines in the face of almost certain death, Corporal Sullivan upheld the highest traditions of the Marine Corps and the United States Naval Service.

SULLIVAN, GEORGE R.

Citation: For extraordinary heroism while serving as a Platoon Commander with Company L, Third Battalion, Fourth Marines, Third Marine Division in Vietnam on 17 March 1967 during Operation PRAIRIE II. While on a search and clear mission in the vicinity of Dong Ha in the Quang Tri Province, Second Lieutenant Sullivan's platoon was approaching a suspected Viet Cong controlled village when it came under intense small arms and automatic weapons fire from a well concealed enemy force of estimated battalion size. After skillfully employing his men in order to bring a heavy volume of fire on the enemy positions, Second Lieutenant Sullivan observed an enemy automatic weapon to his front and realizing the necessity of neutralizing the well-fortified position, he courageously moved across open fire-swept terrain to within ten meters of the Viet Cong emplacement and silenced the enemy weapon with a grenade. After he had directed a machine gun team into a forward position to deliver suppressive fire at the enemy, he observed that the team's weapon had malfunctioned. Unhesitatingly he moved through concentrated enemy fire to the team's location and cleared the weapon. Meanwhile, another machine gun team had begun moving their weapon forward, but both Marines were wounded and fell in an area exposed to enemy fire. Courageously, Second Lieutenant Sullivan again disregarded the heavy enemy fire and unmindful of his own personal safety, moved to their position and carried them to a defiladed area, undoubtedly saving their lives. Later, while moving among his men, encouraging them and directing their fire, he was painfully wounded in his shoulder, arm and both legs. Although unable to move, he continued to direct the actions of his platoon while requesting air support, medical evacuation for the wounded and a resupply of ammunition, and only after reinforcements had arrived, under the cover of darkness, did he allow himself to be evacuated. By his intrepid fighting spirit, selfless courage, bold initiative and unswerving devotion to duty at great personal risk, Second Lieutenant Sullivan reflected great credit upon himself, and upheld the highest traditions of the Marine Corps and the United States Naval Service.

TAFT, DAVID A.

Citation: For extraordinary heroism on 27 August 1967 while serving as a surgeon with the First Medical Battalion (Reinforced), First Marine Division (Reinforced), FMF near Danang, Republic of Vietnam, in direct support of combat operations against communist insurgent (Viet Cong) forces. When a seriously wounded casualty with an "armed" 2.75in rocket imbedded in his left leg was brought by helicopter to the First Medical Battalion, Lieutenant Commander Taft carefully diagnosed the case, concluding that surgical amputation was imperative and time was of the essence. Anticipating that the rocket might detonate at any moment, he immediately supervised the patient's emergency treatment and transfer to the operating room, setting an outstanding example of calmness and courage. He assisted with the administration of spinal anesthetic which necessitated manipulating and positioning the victim several times. Lieutenant Commander Taft cleared the operating room of all personnel with the exception of the patient, himself, and a Navy Hospital Corpsman, and then, with complete disregard for his own safety, coolly and competently performed the necessary surgery. By his expeditious treatment of the patient, his superior professional skill, and his unfaltering devotion to duty, Lieutenant Commander Taft undoubtedly saved the injured man's life, and was instrumental in removing the threat of death or injury from other personnel in the vicinity of the operating room, thereby upholding the highest traditions of the United States Naval Service.

*TAYLOR, JESSE J.

Citation: For extraordinary heroism in aerial flight as a pilot in Carrier Air Wing SIXTEEN, embarked in USS ORISKANY (CVA-34), during a rescue combat air patrol over hostile territory in North Vietnam on 17 November 1965. Although his aircraft was severely damaged by heavy enemy ground fire while he was attempting to locate a downed pilot, Lieutenant Commander Taylor persisted in his efforts until he had definitely ascertained the location of his fellow airman. He then proceeded to attack enemy gun sites which threatened the approach of the rescue helicopter. Only after his aircraft caught fire and a crash was imminent did Lieutenant Commander Taylor cease his efforts. With his aircraft burning and heavily damaged, he succeeded in reaching the coast of the Gulf of Tonkin in an attempt to ditch but did not survive the crash of his crippled aircraft. In sacrificing his life in an effort to save the life of a fellow airman, Lieutenant Commander Taylor displayed the highest degree of courage and self-sacrifice. His actions were in keeping with the finest traditions of the United States Naval Service.

THATCHER, CHARLES D.

Citation: For extraordinary heroism as a Tank Commander with Company A, Third Tank Battalion, Third Marine Division, in connection with operations against the enemy in the Republic of Vietnam on 8 May 1967. While operating in support of the First Battalion, Fourth Marines, Lance Corporal Thatcher's tank was hit and heavily damaged by enemy fire during a savage mortar and infantry attack on the battalion's positions at Gio Linh by a 400-man North Vietnamese Army force. During the initial enemy antitank rocket assault, two of his crewmen were killed and one wounded. Although painfully wounded in the back and neck, he courageously reentered the burning tank to remove the dead and wounded and administered first aid to the surviving crewman. For one hour, while awaiting reinforcements, he cared for his wounded companion while fighting off repeated enemy assaults. When he was assured that his comrade had been moved to a secure area, he resolutely returned to his tank and boldly engaged the North Vietnamese alone with his .30-caliber machine gun, inflicting heavy casualties on the enemy. Having expended his maching gun ammunition, he left his disabled tank, retrieved a rifle from a dead infantryman, and continued to deliver a heavy volume of accurate fire on the enemy. Realizing that the infantrymen were dangerously low on small-arms ammunition, he completely disregarded his own safety to carry resupplies to their fighting holes while under intense hostile fire. With three tanks disabled by the enemy fire, Lance Corporal Thatcher reacted instantly when he observed a North Vietnamese soldier about to fire a rocket at one of the operative tanks. Displaying bold initiative, he killed the enemy as he rushed the tank with his rocket launcher. Throughout the vicious fire fight, he repeatedly risked his own life to assist his wounded companions and provide continuous covering fire. His daring and heroic actions were instrumental in repulsing the North Vietnamese attack. Lance Corporal Thatcher's uncommon courage, inspiring leadership, and unwavering devotion to duty in the face of enemy fire reflected great credit upon himself and were in keeping with the highest traditions of the Marine Corps and of the United States Naval Service.

*THOMAS, MICHAEL H.

Citation: For extraordinary heroism while serving as a Platoon Commander with Company I, Third Battalion, Twenty-sixth Marines, Third Marine Division (Reinforced), in connection with operations against the enemy in the Republic of Vietnam on 20 January 1968. While leading his men in a coordinated attack with an adjacent platoon along a parallel ridge line in the vicinity of Hill 881 South, Lieutenant Thomas' platoon was taken under intense enemy automatic weapons fire from an estimated battalion-sized enemy force. The hostile fire wounded several Marines. As a medical evacuation helicopter endeavored to land to extract the wounded, it was taken under intense enemy machine-gun fire and crashed. Quickly assessing the situation, Lieutenant Thomas organized a rescue team and accompanied his men to the crash site to supervise rescue operations. Learning that the adjacent platoon was pinned down by enemy fire and that the platoon commander and others were wounded, he maneuvered his unit through the intense enemy fire across 500 meters of open terrain to reinforce the beleaguered platoon. Consolidating his force, he repeatedly exposed himself to enemy fire as he moved from one position to another encouraging and directing his men's fire. Discovering that eight men were missing, he organized and personally led a search party into the fire swept area, successfully locating five of the wounded and moved them to positions of relative safety. Although wounded as he was carrying a sixth Marine to safety, he refused medical assistance and elected to continue his rescue efforts. Despite his painful wound and near exhaustion, he again moved into the hazardous area in an attempt to rescue the two remaining casualties who were lying in a dangerously exposed area, when he was mortally wounded. By his bold initiative, gallant fighting spirit and loyal devotion to duty, Lieutenant Thomas was instrumental in saving several Marines from further injury or possible death, thereby reflecting great credit upon himself and the Marine Corps and upholding the highest traditions of the United States Naval Service. He gallantly gave his life for his country.

THOMAS, ROBERT J.

Citation: For extraordinary heroism on 23 March 1969 while serving with SEAL Team Detachment ALFA, Seventh Platoon, during combat operations against communist aggressor forces in the Republic of Vietnam. Embarked in a Seawolf helicopter on a visual reconnaissance and strike mission on Da Dung Mountain near the Cambodian border when the aircraft was struck by enemy ground fire and crashed in an exposed rice paddy, Petty Officer Thomas was thrown from the wreckage, sustaining multiple injuries. Fighting off the stunning effects of shock, he immediately moved to the aid of the helicopter crewmen who were still in the burning aircraft. Despite the intense flames and the heavy gunfire from both the mountain and a nearby tree line, Petty Officer Thomas managed to remove one of the crewmen to safety and, with the aid of another man who had been dropped onto the site by an accompanying helicopter, succeeded in freeing the trapped pilot from the flaming cockpit. Petty Officer Thomas then made a gallant attempt to rescue the two remaining men trapped beneath the twisted metal, discontinuing his efforts only when driven back by the exploding bullets and rockets of the burning helicopter. After moving the two previously rescued men to a greater distance from the crash site, Petty Officer Thomas realized that Viet Cong troops were steadily advancing on his position. He selflessly threw himself upon the body of one of the wounded men and began returning the enemy fire. His deadly accuracy accounted for at least one enemy dead and held the aggressors at bay until an Army rescue helicopter landed. By his valiant efforts and selfless devotion to duty while under hostile fire, Petty Officer Thomas upheld the highest traditions of the United States Naval Service.

THOMPSON, BROCK I.

Citation: For extraordinary heroism while serving as Fire Team Leader, Second Squad, Third Platoon, Company E, Second Battalion, Seventh Marine Division (Reinforced), in the Republic of Vietnam on 19 October 1967. The Second Squad was acting as security for Bridge 11 on Highway 1, in Quang Nam Province, when it came under an extremely heavy barrage of grenades and withering small-arms and automatic weapons fire from a numerically superior Viet Cong force of estimated platoon size. Instantly maneuvering himself to a position from where he could observe the enemy entering the perimeter, Corporal Thompson opened fire, mortally wounding one of the enemy. Learning that his Squad Leader was seriously wounded, he immediately took command of the situation and moved to consolidate the surviving members of the squad and to direct fire upon the enemy. As the enemy advanced, a grenade landed between Corporal Thompson and a member of his fire team. With complete disregard for his own safety, Corporal Thompson unhesitatingly picked up the grenade, turned to place his body between the certain devastating blast and his fellow Marines, and attempted to throw the grenade. The grenade exploded critically wounding him. Despite his severe injury, he displayed magnificent determination and courage, and, refusing medical attention, he continued to direct and control the remaining members of the squad in organizing the successful defense of the position until additional friendly forces arrived. Only after all other wounded members of the squad had been treated, did he allow himself to be cared for and evacuated. Corporal Thompson's courageous actions and inspiring leadership upheld the highest traditions of the Marine Corps and the United States Naval Service.

THOMPSON, CLINTON W.

Citation: For extraordinary heroism on 13 and 14 March 1969 as a squad leader/platoon sergeant in Company M, Third Battalion, Fourth Marines, Third Marine Division during operations against an armed enemy eleven miles north of Khe Sanh, Quang Tri Province, Republic of Vietnam. When his platoon was pinned down by extremely intense hostile fire during an assault on a well-entrenched enemy position consisting of reinforced bunkers, Corporal Thompson maneuvered through the barrage of hostile fire, located the exact positions of the enemy emplacements, and launched a single-handed assault on the enemy bunkers, using fragmentation grenades to destroy the positions and utilizing the rest of the squad in providing an effective base of fire. During a period of over one-half hour, he made repeated trips down an exposed slope to replenish his supply of grenades. During his daring assault, he destroyed three enemy bunkers, along with their occupants, following which the remainder of his platoon was able to maneuver around the enemy and secure the objective. On the following day, when the enemy counterattacked the company's position, concentrating on Corporal Thompson's platoon and forcing his men to withdraw, Corporal Thompson assumed the billet of platoon sergeant when that leader was wounded, rallied his men and led the assault to recapture the position, following the removal of the wounded to a safe area. It was during this period that an enemy bunker began to deliver fire on Corporal Thompson and his men. Once again, he personally assaulted the position with grenades, destroying the bunker and three occupants. He then organized his platoon and instilled in his men the courage and aggressiveness needed to seize the objective and subsequently hold it under a heavy enemy counterattack. Corporal Thompson's outstanding personal valor, leadership, and dedication were in keeping with the highest traditions of the Marine Corps and of the United States Naval Service.

*THOMPSON, JERRALD R.

Citation: For extraordinary heroism as a squad leader serving with the First Platoon, Company C, First Reconnaissance Battalion, First Marine Division (Reinforced) in the Republic of Vietnam on 16 June 1966. While occupying an observation post at 0100 on Hill 488, Quang Tin Province, deep in enemy controlled territory, the platoon of 18 men was subjected to an intense assault by a North Vietnamese unit estimated at battalion size. Corporal Thompson immediately ordered his squad to withdraw to a predetermined defensive perimeter. Braving a hail of small arms fire, automatic weapons, and mortar fire, the small bank of courageous Marines fought their way to the relative safety of the defensive position. In the course of this action, Corporal Thompson was painfully wounded by an enemy hand grenade and was unable to proceed. Armed with only a knife, he engaged the enemy in hand-to-hand combat and killed two before he fell, mortally wounded. By his indomitable fighting spirit in the face of seemingly insurmountable odds he was instrumental in the defense of his platoon's position. Corporal Thompson's courageous action under hostile fire reflected great credit upon himself and the Marine Corps and upheld the highest traditions of the United States Naval Service. He gallantly gave his life in the cause of freedom.

THOMPSON, JOHN C.

Citation: For extraordinary heroism with Marine Medium Helicopter Squadron THREE HUNDRED SIXTY-FOUR in support of the Republic of Vietnam against the insurgent communist guerrilla forces (Viet Cong) on 30 April 1964. During this action, Sergeant Thompson was assigned as loadmaster to service a flight of eighteen helicopters ordered to effect the evacuation of an outpost which was totally surrounded by the insurgent communist guerrillas. He arrived in the zone on the first aircraft and remained at his post until all the trapped personnel had been safely evacuated. As each aircraft approached for landing, he willingly stood up, exposing himself to heavy fire being placed on the landing zone and guided the aircraft to a safe landing by use of hand and arm signals. During intervals between landing helicopters, he armed himself with hand grenades and employed them in the defense of the landing zone. When the final aircraft arrived there were six persons, including Sergeant Thompson, left to be evacuated. As the pre-established number of five passengers was loaded, he gallantly offered to remain alone in the face of certain death in order to keep the load of the helicopter at a safe weight for take-off and to cover it with fire during its withdrawal. The pilot ordered him aboard and as the helicopter was taking off and he was pulled in, the passengers and crew fired over his body at the attacking enemy. His great personal valor and fearless devotion to duty reflected great credit upon himself and the Marine Corps and were in keeping with the highest traditions of the United States Naval Service.

THOMPSON, ROBERT H.

Citation: For extraordinary heroism while serving as the Commanding Officer, First Battalion, Fifth Marines, First Marine Division (Reinforced), in the Republic of Vietnam, from 12 February to 3 March 1968, while participating in Operation HUE CITY, Lieutenant Colonel (then Major) Thompson aggressively led his battalion in intense fighting against well entrenched North Vietnamese forces within the Citadel. On 13 February, he deployed elements of his unit across the Perfume River to reduce enemy resistance in the southeast corner of the walled city. Almost immediately, small-arms, automatic weapons, and rocket fire from a large North Vietnamese force slowed his advance. Ignoring the intense enemy fire, he moved to an exposed vantage point where he rapidly assessed the situation and unhesitatingly moved across the fire-swept front of his battalion, directing the efforts of the company commanders and shouting words of encouragement to individual Marines, inspiring them to resume the momentum of the attack. Ordered to commence an attack northwest of the city on 28 February, Colonel Thompson fearlessly moved his command group with the attacking companies, repeatedly moving to the areas of heaviest contact in order to personally assist his unit commanders and influence the course of the engagement. When an attached company engaged a well entrenched North Vietnamese force on 1 March, Colonel Thompson accompanied a reinforcing unit dispatched to establish a blocking position to prevent the enemy's escape. Located with the lead elements, he personally coordinated supporting arms fire with the movement of the advancing Marines as they overwhelmed the enemy and accomplished the mission. By his intrepid fighting spirit, inspiring leadership, and selfless devotion to duty at great personal risk, Colonel Thompson upheld the highest traditions of the Marine Corps and the United States Naval Service.

THORYK, BARRY L.

Citation: For extraordinary heroism while serving as a Machine Gun Section Leader with Company A, First Battalion, Ninth Marines, Third Marine Division, in connection with operations against the enemy in the Republic of Vietnam. On 4 April 1968, Corporal Thoryk was participating in a company assault on Hill 471 near Khe Sanh, when his platoon came under an enemy grenade attack and intense automatic-weapons fire. Although he sustained multiple fragmentation wounds in the initial moments of the attack, Corporal Thoryk refused medical aid and singlehandedly launched an aggressive assault against an enemy machine gun position, killing three of its defenders. Having expended his ammunition, he quickly obtained an enemy weapon and delivered fire at two enemy soldiers, killing them as they ran from their position. With complete disregard for his safety, Corporal Thoryk continued to maneuver forward, retrieving enemy hand grenades and throwing them at several hostile positions as he advanced. His courageous actions and steadfast determination were instrumental in seizing the enemy-occupied hill and inspired all who observed him. By his intrepid fighting spirit, bold initiative, and selfless devotion to duty, Corporal Thoryk upheld the highest traditions of the Marine Corps and the United States Naval Service.

*THOUVENELL, ARMAND R.

Citation: For extraordinary heroism while serving as a Machine Gun Team Leader with Company M, Third Battalion, Fourth Marines, Third Marine Division (Reinforced) in the Republic of Vietnam on 29 May 1967. While engaged in Operation PRAIRIE IV, one fire team and one machine gun team were sent to reconnoiter two enemy bunkers. Almost immediately they became pinned down in a deadly machine gun crossfire from the two enemy positions. As casualties mounted, the machine gun ran low on ammunition, and the enemy was close enough to throw hand grenades into their position. Private First Class Thouvenell, a machine gun team leader from a different squad, unhesitatingly collected nine hundred rounds of ammunition and ran to the beleaguered unit. In order to accomplish this task, he had to run directly in front of the two bunkers, in the open and fully exposed to the enemy's devastating fire. When the team was ordered to pull back, he stayed behind to give covering fire, enabling the other members of the team to return to safety. As he exposed himself to the heavy enemy fire to effectively cover their withdrawal, he was mortally wounded. By his daring initiative, valiant fighting spirit and selfless devotion to duty in the face of insurmountable odds, Private First Class Thouvenell was responsible in great measure for saving many of his comrades and thereby upheld the highest traditions of the Marine Corps and the United States Naval Service. He gallantly gave his life for his country.

*TIMMONS, JAMES M.

Citation: For extraordinary heroism while serving as a Messenger with Company M, Third Battalion, Seventh Marines, First Marine Division, in connection with operations against the enemy in the Republic of Vietnam. On 6 November 1968, Company M was conducting a reconnaissance in force near Hill 55 in Quang Nam Province when the Marines came under intense small arms, automatic weapons, and rocket-propelled grenade fire from a North Vietnamese

Army regiment occupying fortified positions. Sighting several Marines lying wounded in an area exposed to a heavy volume of fire, Private Timmons boldly traversed the fire-swept terrain and assisted a wounded comrade to a position of relative safety. Ignoring the hostile rounds impacting near him, he fearlessly returned to the hazardous area on two more occasions and assisted injured companions to the designated landing zone. As the evacuation helicopter attempted to land, the aircraft was forced from the zone by intense hostile machine-gun fire. On the second attempt, the aircraft again drew a heavy volume of small arms and rocket-propelled grenade fire which impacted near the casualties. Reacting instantly, Private Timmons courageously placed his body across that of a wounded Marine, shielding him from the North Vietnamese fire. While engaged in this selfless task, Private Timmons was mortally wounded. His daring initiative and sincere concern for the welfare of his comrade saved the life of a fellow Marine and contributed significantly to the accomplishment of his unit's mission. By his courage, resolute determination, and unwavering devotion to duty, Private Timmons upheld the highest traditions of the Marine Corps and the United States Naval Service. He gallantly gave his life for his country.

TONKYN, MICHAEL S.

Citation: For extraordinary heroism while serving as a Squad Leader with Company C, First Battalion, Fifth Marines, First Marine Division, in connection with combat operations against the enemy in the Republic of Vietnam. During the early morning hours of 11 June 1969, while Company C was providing battalion security northwest of An Hoa in Quang Nam Province, the Marines came under a heavy volume of mortar, rocket, and small-arms fire from an estimated three North Vietnamese Army companies. In the initial moments of the ensuing fierce engagement, ten well-armed hostile soldiers infiltrated the company perimeter and took cover in a trenchline approximately twenty meters behind Lance Corporal Tonkyn's platoon. Reacting instantly, Lance Corporal Tonkyn and a companion crawled across the unprotected area to throw grenades and deliver rifle fire upon the invaders. When his comrade was seriously wounded and fell into the hostile trenchline, Lance Corporal Tonkyn leaped into the emplacement and dragged the injured Marine to a safe location. Then, determined to dislodge or kill the North Vietnamese soldiers, he returned to the enemy emplacement to continue his efforts. On four occasions, Lance Corporal Tonkyn maneuvered across the fire-swept terrain to procure additional hand grenades, and boldly raced along the position firing his rifle and throwing grenades, personally accounting for six hostile soldiers killed. His exceptional display of valor instilled confidence and aggressiveness in other Marines, who subsequently came to his assistance and eliminated the remainder of the enemy unit, thereby preventing the destruction of friendly mortar positions. By his courage, aggressive fighting spirit, and unwavering devotion to duty in the face of grave personal danger, Lance Corporal Tonkyn contributed significantly to the accomplishment of his unit's mission and upheld the highest traditions of the Marine Corps and the United States Naval Service.

*TRENT, WILLIAM D.

Citation: For extraordinary heroism while serving as a Machine Gun Squad Leader with Company M, Third Battalion, Fifth Marines, First Marine Division (Reinforced), in connection with operations against the enemy in the Republic of Vietnam. On 9 May 1968, when Company M encountered a large North Vietnamese Army force in Quang Nam Province, Corporal Trent's platoon, serving as the forward element, came under heavy enemy automatic weapons and small-arms fire. Reacting instantly, he skillfully maneuvered his machine gun teams toward the enemy positions, despite the continuing hostile fire. When both the gunner and assistant gunner of one of the teams became casualties, Corporal Trent, undaunted by the enemy fire erupting around him, manned the machine gun and continued to advance against the enemy. Disregarding his own safety, he delivered effective fire into a fortified position, silencing the automatic weapon. Shifting his fire to another target of opportunity, he quickly annihilated a second enemy position. He then observed two North Vietnamese soldiers moving to occupy the first gun position. Instantly, he seized his machine gun and a belt of ammunition and courageously advanced against the enemy occupied position, firing his weapon as he maneuvered forward. Moving to within a few feet of the pinned down enemy, he killed both hostile soldiers. Quickly emplacing his machine gun in the fortified position, he began firing into the enemy's flank. Although mortally wounded by an enemy hand grenade, he remained at his exposed position until elements of his platoon were able to maneuver forward. By his bold initiative, intrepid fighting spirit and selfless devotion to duty, Corporal Trent inspired all who observed him and upheld the highest traditions of the Marine Corps and the United States Naval Service. He gallantly gave his life for his country.

*TRUETT, QUINCY H.

Citation: For extraordinary heroism on the night of 20 January 1969 while serving with River Division 551, engaged in armed conflict against North Vietnamese and Viet Cong communist aggressor forces on the Kinh Dong Tien Canal in the Republic of Vietnam. As Patrol Officer of two River Patrol Boats (PBR's) in company with an Armored Troop Carrier (ATC) and two other PBR's, Chief Petty Officer Truett was aboard the fourth boat in the column when the entire unit came under intense enemy fire. PBR 8137, the boat ahead of Chief Petty Officer Truett, was taken under extremely heavy fire and began to burn, forcing the five occupants aboard into the water. Observing the men struggling to reach the safety of a ditch, Chief Petty Officer Truett ordered his PBR into the area of the burning craft to recover the men in the water. Without regard for his own personal safety, he deliberately exposed himself to the blistering enemy fire, positioning himself on the bow of his boat to provide covering fire and to assist the men from the water. Because of several bright fires from grass huts burning along the canal bank, Chief Petty Officer Truett was completely visible to the enemy during the entire rescue. Mortally wounded after he had helped rescue the last man from the water, Chief Petty Officer Truett, by his outstanding valor, concern for his shipmates' safety, and inspiring devotion to duty, contributed directly to the safe recovery of the crew of PBR 8137. His selfless efforts were in keeping with the highest traditions of the United States Naval Service.

*TYCZ, JAMES N.

Citation: For extraordinary heroism while serving with the First Platoon, Company A, Third Reconnaissance Battalion, near Khe Sanh in the Republic of Vietnam on 9 May 1967. Sergeant Tycz was the patrol leader of a seven-man reconnaissance patrol deep in enemy-controlled territory. Shortly after midnight a North Vietnamese Army unit, estimated to be about 30-50 men, was heard moving toward the patrol's position. Sergeant Tycz cautioned his men to remain silent so as not to be detected; however, several of the enemy troops walked into the patrol's position and started to unsling their weapons after sighting the patrol. One of the Marines quickly took two of the enemy under fire, killing them instantly. Alerted to their location, the enemy immediately began delivering a heavy volume of small-arms fire into the patrol's perimeter. One patrol member was killed instantly and another was wounded. Sergeant Tycz quickly deployed the remainder of his patrol and fearlessly moved among his men directing their fire and shouting words of encouragement despite the heavy volume of enemy fire being poured into his perimeter. Within a few minutes the assistant patrol leader was seriously wounded, as was the corpsman attached to the patrol and the second radio operator. Sergeant Tycz moved to a radio and began calling in artillery fire on the enemy positions. When an armed enemy hand grenade landed near one of the seriously wounded Marines, Sergeant Tycz courageously and with complete disregard for his own personal safety moved forward, picked up the grenade and attempted to throw it back at the enemy. The grenade exploded after traveling only a short distance, and he fell, critically wounded. Throughout the encounter, Sergeant Tycz set an example of calmness and coolness under fire that was an inspiration to the remainder of his patrol. By his unselfish act of courage, he risked his life to save his comrades from injury and possible loss of life and thereby upheld the highest traditions of the Marine Corps and the United States Naval Service.

*TYRONE, WILLIE D.

Citation: For extraordinary heroism as Assistant Advisor to the Vietnamese 39th Ranger Battalion while serving with Advisory Team Seven of the U.S. Military Assistance Command, Vietnam, on the night of 30-31 May 1965. When the battalion was subjected to heavy small-arms, mortar and 57-mm recoilless rifle fire, Staff Sergeant Tyrone, with complete disregard for his own safety, moved about to point out targets and improve the position. Although painfully wounded in the shoulder, he refused evacuation, and when the Battalion Commander and Battalion S-3 were also wounded, and the Battalion Advisor killed, creating a critical command situation, Staff Sergeant Tyrone, in spite of his wound, assumed the advisory responsibility alone. He maintained radio contact throughout the night and continually encouraged his comrades by his words and valiant example. When the Viet Cong launched a strong counterattack early in the morning, he was mortally wounded, but continued to inspire his comrades by firing his weapon, killing at least an additional ten of the enemy before he died. Staff Sergeant Tyrone's conspicuous gallantry, willing self-sacrifice and extraordinary bravery, reflected great credit upon himself and the Marine Corps and were in keeping with the highest traditions of the United States Naval Service. He gallantly gave his life in the cause of freedom.

UNDERWOOD, DAVID F.

Citation: For extraordinary heroism while serving as a Pilot with Marine Medium Helicopter Squadron 163 in connection with operations against the enemy in the Republic of Vietnam. On the afternoon of 16 February 1968, Captain Underwood launched as Section Leader of a flight of two UH-34 helicopters in support of the emergency extraction of an eight-man reconnaissance team which was heavily engaged with a numerically superior North Vietnamese Army force six miles northwest of Dong Ha. When the initial extraction attempt by another helicopter was prevented due to intense enemy ground fire, Captain Underwood immediately commenced a low-altitude approach to the besieged unit, which had sustained three serious casualties. Nearing the landing zone, his aircraft suddenly came under a heavy volume of enemy automatic-weapons fire from all sides. With complete disregard for his own safety, he fearlessly continued his approach and landed in the hazardous area. Realizing that a second landing in the area would be extremely hazardous due to hostile fire and reduced visibility, he unhesitatingly elected to embark the entire team. Ignoring the intense enemy fire striking his aircraft, he courageously remained in the fire-swept area and calmly directed the fire of his gunners, enabling five of the Marines to embark. Forced to lift from the zone due to the increasing intensity of the hostile fire, which impacted in the helicopter's cockpit and resulted in extensive damage to vital aircraft components, he skillfully maneuvered his damaged aircraft back to Dong Ha. His superior aeronautical ability, resolute determination, and sincere concern for the welfare of his comrades saved the lives of several Marines and inspired all who served with him. By his courage, intrepid fighting spirit, and selfless devotion to duty in the face of extreme personal danger, Captain Underwood upheld the highest traditions of the Marine Corps and the United States Naval Service.

*VALDEZ, PHIL I.

Citation: For conspicuous gallantry and intrepidity in action on the morning of 29 January 1967, while serving with Company B, First Battalion, First Marines, in the vicinity of Danang, Republic of Vietnam. As corpsman with the third platoon, Petty Officer (then Hospitalman) Valdez participated in a helilift with his platoon in support of Company H of the Second Battalion. Immediately upon landing, the platoon came under heavy enemy fire and sustained several wounded while maneuvering forward. Without hesitation, Petty Officer Valdez ran over seventy-five yards of open terrain, under constant enemy fire, to aid a fallen Marine. He then moved the wounded man to a safe area and, quickly and competently, rendered medical assistance. Again exposing himself to enemy fire, Petty Officer Valdez moved across approximately fifty yards of open ground to another Marine. While treating the second Marine, he positioned himself between the man and the hostile fire. It was at this time that Petty Officer Valdez was mortally wounded by enemy small-arms fire. Through his heroic actions and selfless devotion to duty, he was responsible for saving the lives of two Marines. His inspiring efforts were in keeping with the highest traditions of the United States Naval Service.

VAMPATELLA, PHILIP V.

Citation: For extraordinary heroism on 21 June 1966 as pilot of a jet fighter aircraft in Fighter Squadron TWO HUNDRED ELEVEN, embarked in USS HANCOCK (CVA-19). Although his aircraft was critically low on fuel and had already been severely damaged by hostile antiaircraft fire, Lieutenant (jg) Vampatella, upon learning that two of his squadron mates were being attacked by four North Vietnamese MIG-17 jet fighters, reversed his course and returned deep into enemy territory to render assistance. Engaging two of the MIG fighters in low-altitude, aerial combat, he succeeded in maneuvering his crippled aircraft into position to fire a missile and shoot down one of the enemy fighters. Only then did he disengage from the aerial battle and proceed to the coast, arriving with less than five minutes of fuel remaining. After skillfully and calmly executing an in-flight refueling from a waiting aerial tanker, he returned his crippled fighter to the HANCOCK. Lieutenant (jg) Vampatella's superb airmanship, outstanding courage, and inspiring devotion to duty in the face of enemy antiaircraft fire and aerial opposition were in keeping with the highest traditions of the United States Naval Service.

VANCOR, NORMAN W.

Citation: For extraordinary heroism while serving as a Radio Operator with Company C, Third Reconnaissance Battalion, Third Marine Division, in connection with combat operations against the enemy in the Republic of Vietnam. On the morning of 7 May 1969, while Lance Corporal Vancor's five-man reconnaissance team was observing hostile movement in an area northwest of the Dong Ha Combat Base, the Marines came under a heavy volume of enemy small-arms fire and sustained two casualties. The team leader directed a withdrawal toward a pre-selected helicopter landing zone three hundred meters distant and as the men proceeded toward the designated location they again came under intense small-arms fire from North Vietnamese Army soldiers, mortally wounding two Marines and seriously injuring two others. Apparently believing that they had annihilated the friendly team, the enemy soldiers left their concealed positions and advanced toward the casualties. Lance Corporal Vancor, the only uninjured member of the reconnaissance patrol, boldly engaged the North Vietnamese, killing one and forcing the others to withdraw into the underbrush. He then administered first aid to his companions and contacted nearby aircraft to brief them on the current situation. Realizing that the critical conditions of the two men would not permit awaiting arrival of a reaction force, he made two hazardous trips along an unprotected ridgeline through two hundred meters of extremely hostile territory, successfully carrying his injured comrades to the landing site. Undaunted by intense enemy fire, he guided the aircraft into the position and directed the safe extraction of his patrol. His heroic actions and calm presence of mind during a critical situation inspired all who observed him and saved the lives of two Marines. By his courage, selfless concern for his fellowmen, and unwavering devotion to duty in the face of grave personal danger, Lance Corporal Vancor upheld the highest traditions of the Marine Corps and the United States Naval Service.

VAN KIET, NGUYEN

Citation: For extraordinary heroism while serving with friendly forces engaged in armed conflict against the North Vietnamese and Viet Cong communist aggressors in the Republic of Vietnam. On 13 April 1972, Petty Officer Kiet participated in an unprecedented recovery operation for a downed United States aviator behind enemy lines in Quang Tri Province, Republic of Vietnam. He courageously volunteered to accompany a United States SEAL Advisor in an extremely hazardous attempt to reach the aviator, who was physically unable to move toward friendly positions. Using a sampan and traveling throughout the night, they silently made their way deep into enemy territory, past numerous major enemy positions, locating the pilot at dawn. Once, after being spotted by a North Vietnamese patrol, he calmly continued to keep the enemy confused as the small party successfully evaded the patrol. Later, they were suddenly taken under heavy machine gun fire. Thinking first of the pilot, he quickly pulled the sampan to safety behind a bank and camouflaged it while air strikes were called on the enemy position. Due to Petty Officer Kiet's coolness under extremely dangerous conditions and his outstanding courage and professionalism, an American aviator was recovered after an eleven-day ordeal behind enemy lines. His self-discipline, personal courage, and dynamic fighting spirit were an inspiration to all; thereby reflecting great credit upon himself and the Naval Service.

*VASQUEZ, JESUS R.

Citation: For extraordinary heroism while serving as an Explosive Ordnance Disposal Technician with the Ammunition Company, Supply Battalion, First Force Service Regiment/Force Logistic Command in connection with operations against the enemy in the Republic of Vietnam on 30 January 1968. During a mortar and rocket attack at the Khe Sanh Combat Base, several rounds landed in the ammunition supply point, igniting a stack of ammunition. Sergeant Vasquez, unhesitatingly rushed to the burning munitions and assisted in fighting the fire. Observing an 81mm mortar round burning and aware of the proximity of his comrades and the possibility of detonation, he lifted the round in an attempt to throw it into a deep crater where its lethal effects would be absorbed should it detonate. In his attempt to throw the round, it exploded, mortally wounding him. By his bold initiative, gallant fighting spirit and loyal devotion to duty, he was instrumental in saving his comrades from further injury or possible death by absorbing most of the impact with his own body. His great personal valor reflected great credit upon himself and enhanced the finest traditions of the Marine Corps and the United States Naval Service. He gallantly gave his life for his country.

VERHEYN, DAVID A.

Citation: For extraordinary heroism while serving as a Team Leader with the Second Platoon, Company A, First Reconnaissance Battalion, First Marine Division in connection with operations in the Republic of Vietnam. On the night of 3 February 1967, while on an eleven-man reconnaissance patrol deep in enemy controlled territory, Lance Corporal Verheyn's unit was attacked by an estimated sixty Viet Cong. In the initial moments of the fire fight, the Patrol Leader and Assistant Patrol Leader were killed. Displaying outstanding initiative and presence of mind, he assumed command of the patrol, organized defensive positions and directed the fire of his men. Despite the intense fire, Lance Corporal Veheyn disregarded his personal safety to move from position to position, administering medical aid to his wounded companions. Subsequently, he was wounded by fragments from a Viet Cong grenade while he was directing fire at the enemy and shouting words of encouragement to his men. Ignoring his painful wounds, Lance Corporal Verheyn attempted to repair two radios which had been damaged by enemy fire in order to establish communications with higher headquarters. As the volume of fire momentarily decreased, he moved the wounded to a position of safety and prevented the Viet Cong from capturing their weapons. After distributing ammunition and improving the patrol's defensive positions, Lance Corporal Verheyn remained alert throughout the night for the possibility of another Viet Cong attack. At daylight, he used smoke grenades to signal relief helicopters and skillfully directed the aircraft into the landing zone. Assured that all of his patrol members were safely loaded aboard the helicopter, he searched the vacated positions, making sure that there were no weapons left behind. Lance Corporal Verheyn's inspiring leadership, steadfast courage, bold initiative, and unswerving devotion to duty under extremely hazardous conditions undoubtedly saved numerous Marine lives, reflected great credit upon himself, and upheld the highest traditions of the Marine Corps and of the United States Naval Service.

WALKER, JAMES R.

Citation: For extraordinary heroism on 14 September 1968 while serving with Helicopter Attack (Light) Squadron THREE, Detachment THREE, during operations against enemy aggressor forces in the Republic of Vietnam. As the Fire Team Leader of a Light

Helicopter Fire Team which was called in to support United States naval forces that were under heavy attack on the Mekong River, Lieutenant Walker, upon arrival at the scene of the enemy ambush, immediately commenced his attacks against the entrenched hostile emplacements on both sides of the river. After diverting the intense enemy fire from the badly-damaged ships to himself and his fire team, he continued to press his attacks and was able to suppress much of the Viet Cong fire. With his ammunition expended, Lieutenant Walker was preparing to leave the scene of action to rearm when he was informed of the need of an immediate medical evacuation of a critically-wounded crewman aboard a severely-damaged lighter. Realizing that no medical-evacuation aircraft could approach the crippled ship due to the heavy fire, Lieutenant Walker courageously volunteered to attempt the evacuation, in the face of the withering hail of bullets, and with full knowledge that the ship had no landing capabilities for his aircraft. He hovered his aircraft over the bow of the moving ship and successfully completed the evacuation of the injured man under the most hazardous conditions. He then flew the casualty to awaiting medical attention at Vinh Long Airfield and quickly rearmed, returning to the scene of contact to press his attacks on the enemy positions. Forced to rearm once again at Vinh Long, Lieutenant Walker again returned to the ambush scene and succeeded in breaking the fiercely-resisting insurgents and suppressing all their fire. Through his tenacious and courageous attacks, he turned a well-planned enemy ambush on United States naval forces into a disastrous enemy rout. Lieutenant Walker's composure under fire, outstanding professionalism, and valorous dedication were in keeping with the highest traditions of the United States Naval Service.

WALLACE, ERNIE W.

Citation: For extraordinary heroism while serving as a machine gunner with Company H, Second Battalion, Fourth Marines, Third Marine Division (Reinforced), during Operation STARLITE against insurgent communist (Viet Cong) forces in the Republic of Vietnam on 18 August 1965. While the platoon to which he was attached was temporarily pinned down by intense mortar, automatic weapons, and small arms fire, Corporal Wallace and one rifle squad took cover in a trench. Realizing that the enemy was closing in on the squad in the trench line, he fearlessly moved into an exposed position and, firing his machine gun from the offhand and assault positions at close range,

335

delivered such devastating fire into the stunned adversary that he personally accounted for twenty-five dead enemy, allowing the squad he was with to maneuver to a more advantageous area. Throughout the rest of the day he was seemingly inexhaustible in his efforts. Time and again he fearlessly exposed himself, as he dashed out into the open to provide cover by fire for the evacuation of wounded Marines in exposed areas. On one such occasion the bipod was shot from his weapon; however, he was not deterred as he continued to fire, accounting for the killing of fifteen more of the enemy. His outstanding performance of duty undoubtedly saved many Marine lives and materially aided the company in turning the tide of battle into a virtual annihilation of a numerically superior foe. Corporal Wallace's extraordinary heroism and inspiring dedication to duty reflected great credit upon himself and the Marine Corps and were in keeping with the highest traditions of the United States Naval Service.

*WARD, JAMES "C"

Citation: For extraordinary heroism while serving as a Weapons Squad Leader with Company D, First Battalion, Fifth Marines, First Marine Division, in connection with combat operations against the enemy in the Republic of Vietnam. On 9 May 1969, Corporal Ward's platoon was returning from a combat patrol when the lead element came under a heavy volume of hostile fire from a numerically superior force occupying well-concealed emplacements. Reacting instantly, Corporal Ward skillfully deployed his squad into effective fighting positions and directed counterfire on the enemy unit. Alertly observing that one of his fire teams had been pinned down in a dangerously exposed position and had sustained two serious casualties, he unhesitatingly mustered four companions and was boldly leading them across the fire-swept terrain when a grenade launcher round carried in the belt of a Marine manuevering close beside him was detonated by enemy fire. Although partially blinded by the concussion of the grenade, Corporal Ward, concerned only for the safety of his injured comrades, resolutely continued his determined efforts to reach the fire team. With his light antitank assault weapon he quickly destroyed an enemy emplacement, which was the principal source of hostile fire, and reaching the side of one of his wounded men, he quickly administered first aid. After speaking words of encouragement to his comrade to restore his confidence, he moved through the hazardous area to the side of the second injured Marine.

Unable to drag the casualty to a place of relative safety and undaunted by the closeness of enemy gun emplacements, Corporal Ward was boldly attempting to lift the wounded Marine onto his shoulders when he was mortally injured by enemy fire. By his courage, selfless concern for his comrades, and unwavering devotion to duty, Corporal Ward upheld the highest traditions of the Marine Corps and the United States Naval Service. He gallantly gave his life for his country.

WARREN, ROGER O.

Citation: For extraordinary heroism while serving as a Machine Gunner with Company F, Second Battalion, Fifth Marines, First Marine Division (Reinforced), in action against the enemy in the Republic of Vietnam. On 3 February 1968, during Operation HUE CITY, Corporal Warren's platoon was taken under intense enemy automatic weapons and rocket fire as they attempted to assault the city's Treasury Building. As the unit entered a large courtyard, one Marine was seriously wounded by a sudden burst of hostile fire and was unable to move from his exposed position. Corporal Warren, who had been wounded earlier, ignored his own painful injuries and courageously ran into the open courtyard under intense enemy fire and placed his body between the casualty and the hostile fire. Disregarding his own personal safety, he commenced firing his machine gun from the hip at suspected enemy positions until he depleted his supply of ammunition. Quickly reloading his weapon, he once again placed fire on the enemy allowing the casualty to be evacuated. On 5 February, as he was delivering a heavy volume of suppressive fire on the enemy from the second story window of a building, he was suddenly hurled through the wall into the adjoining room by two enemy rocket rounds. Wounded in both legs and temporarily stunned by the force of the explosion, he was carried downstairs and placed with six other casualties awaiting treatment. Realizing the heavy enemy fire was preventing expeditious evacuation of the casualties, he exposed himself to the intense enemy fire and brought accurate M-16 fire to bear on the enemy. Assured that the more severe casualties had been evacuated, he allowed himself to be evacuated and helped carry a wounded comrade to the aid station. Despite his several wounds, he refused medical evacuation and elected to return to his unit due to the shortage of qualified machine gunners. Upon returning to his unit Corporal Warren directed intense fire on the enemy positions. He gallantly continued to perform his duties until the seriousness of his wounds caused him to be evacuated on 10 February 1968. By his intrepid fighting spirit, exceptional fortitude, bold initiative and devotion to his fellow Marines, Corporal Warren reflected great credit upon himself and the Marine Corps and upheld the highest traditions of the United States Naval Service.

*WEBB, BRUCE D.

Citation: For extraordinary heroism as Commanding Officer of Company I, Third Battalion, Third Marines, Third Marine Division (Reinforced), in the Republic of Vietnam on 18 August 1965. Captain Webb's company was engaged in search and destroy operations against the communist insurgent forces in Quang Ngai Province when two of his platoons came under heavy small arms, automatic weapons and mortar fire from a Viet Cong force of battalion size. Without hesitation he moved immediately to the point of crisis in order to maintain his company's momentum in attacking the enemy and to supervise the maneuver of his command. With full knowledge of the hazards involved and with complete disregard for his own safety, he repeatedly exposed himself to enemy fire while directing the operation of his forces. Observing that the aggressive actions of the enemy threatened an adjacent unit, he requested permission to move his company into the adjoining zone of action and to attack the Viet Cong forces in the flank. In the face of heavy enemy fire he led his company across an open field to assault the enemy. As the attack progressed, the enemy fire increased in volume and accuracy, but he continued to set an example of calmness and courage. Moving from position to position, he inspired his men with his dynamic leadership and courageous fighting spirit until he fell, mortally wounded by an enemy hand grenade. As a result of his professional ability and stirring example the enemy positions were destroyed and over forty enemy killed. Captain Webb's inspiring professional ability and courageous devotion to duty reflected great credit upon himself and the Marine Corps and were in keeping with the highest traditions of the United States Naval Service. He gallantly gave his life in the cause of freedom.

WEBB, JAMES H., JR.

Citation: For extraordinary heroism while serving as a Platoon Commander with Company D, First Battalion, Fifth Marines, First Marine Division in connection with combat operations against the enemy in the Republic of Vietnam. On 10 July 1969, while participating in a company-sized search and destroy operation deep in hostile territory, First Lieutenant Webb's platoon discovered a well-camouflaged bunker complex which appeared to be unoccupied. Deploying his men into defensive positions, First Lieutenant Webb was advancing to the first bunker when three enemy soliders armed with hand grenades jumped out. Reacting instantly, he grabbed the closest man and, brandishing his .45 caliber pistol at the others, apprehended all three of the soldiers. Accompanied by one of his men, he then approached the second bunker and called for the enemy to surrender. When the hostile soldiers failed to answer him and threw a grenade which detonated dangerously close to him, First Lieutenant Webb detonated a claymore mine in the bunker aperture, accounting for two enemy casualties and disclosing the entrance to a tunnel. Despite the smoke and debris from the explosion and the possibility of enemy soldiers hiding in the tunnel, he then conducted a thorough search which yielded several items of equipment and numerous documents containing valuable intelligence data. Continuing the assault, he approached a third bunker and was preparing to fire into it when the enemy threw another grenade. Observing the grenade land dangerously close to his companion, First Lieutenant Webb simultaneously fired his weapon at the enemy, pushed the Marine away from the grenade, and shielded him from the explosion with his own body. Although sustaining painful fragmentation wounds from the explosion, he managed to throw a grenade into the aperture and completely destroy the remaining bunker. By his courage, aggressive leadership, and selfless devotion to duty, First Lieutenant Webb upheld the highest traditions of the Marine Corps and of the United States Naval Service.

WEISE, WILLIAM

Citation: For extraordinary heroism while serving as Commanding Officer, Second Battalion, Fourth Marines, Ninth Marine Amphibious Brigade, in the Republic of Vietnam from 30 April to 2 May 1968. Colonel Weise exhibited exceptional valor and courage while leading his battalion against an estimated 2,000 North Vietnamese Army regulars entrenched in a well fortified bunker complex and supported by artillery fire. Initially having only a small portion of the battalion's combat elements available to engage the enemy, he skillfully utilized and coordinated effective air strikes and artillery fire upon the hostile force, maintaining constant pressure on the enemy and thus denying him freedom of maneuverability. As additional elements arrived, Colonel Weise integrated his forces and initiated assaults which eliminated successive enemy strong points. His masterful tactical employment of forces, combined with his personal direction of the ground forces, provided the inspiration required to mount repeated attacks in the face of seemingly overwhelming odds, despite the unit's depletion due to previous heavy combat commitments. When the enemy launched several counterattacks against his units, he continually moved among his men, rallying them and inspiring confidence in his unit leaders and among individual Marines while reorganizing and maintaining maximum combat effectiveness within each element. On the third day of battle, while personally leading in a fierce assault on the enemy's furthermost portion of the heavily defended objective, Colonel Weise was seriously wounded, but actively directed the orderly withdrawal of his forces to supporting positions. Steadfastly maintaining control of his battalion, he tenaciously continued to direct the evacuation of casualties to the secondary positions until he collapsed from his critical wound. During this period, the battalion accounted for hundreds of North Vietnamese casualties and four enemy prisoners. By his dynamic leadership, unfaltering courage and selfless devotion to duty throughout, Colonel Weise inspired all who served with him and upheld the highest traditions of the Marine Corps and the United States Naval Service.

WESELESKEY, ALLEN E.

Citation: For extraordinary heroism on 9 March 1968 while serving as an Attack Helicopter Fire Team Leader with Helicopter Attack (Light) Squadron THREE in the Mekong Delta region of the Republic of Vietnam. While attempting to rescue two United States Army advisors who had been critically wounded when their Vietnamese battalions engaged communist insurgent (Viet Cong) forces, Lieutenant Commander Weseleskey and his helicopter fire team were caught in an intense cross fire during the attempt to land. Signaled to abort and clear the area, by ground troops, the fire team departed the zone, machine guns blazing. When his wingman's aircraft commander and gunner were wounded, Lieutenant Commander Weseleskey ordered them to return to base while he remained on station to complete the mission alone. Witnessing a Vietnamese aircraft receive several hits which forced it to depart station,

Lieutenant Commander Weseleskey renewed his determination to complete a successful rescue of the Americans. Joined by an Army AH-1G gunship to cover his attempt, he led his crew into the combat zone, again receiving intense enemy automatic-weapons and .50 caliber fire. He landed his helicopter on target, in an extremely confined zone, and brought aboard the two critically wounded U.S. Army advisors and a seriously wounded Vietnamese soldier. Lifting his heavily laden helicopter out of the zone, Lieutenant Commander Weseleskey maintained absolute control of his aircraft despite adverse flying conditions. By his professional leadership and courageous fighting spirit, he served to inspire his crew to perform to their utmost capability, thus ensuring the success of the mission. His heroic actions were in keeping with the highest traditions of the United States Naval Service.

WESTIN, BRIAN E.

Citation: For extraordinary heroism on 27 April 1966 while serving as a Bombardier/Navigator in Attack Squadron EIGHTY-FIVE during a combat mission over North Vietnam. When his pilot was seriously wounded and partially incapacitated during a daylight bombing run, Lieutenant (jg) Westin, by calmly coaxing and physically assisting him in the control of the aircraft, succeeded in reaching the open sea where he made sure that the semiconscious pilot ejected safely before he, himself, exited the plane. The first to be picked up by rescue helicopter, Lieutenant (jg) Westin directed the crew to the estimated position of his pilot. When the latter was unable to enter the rescue sling because of his injuries, Lieutenant (jg) Westin re-entered the water to assist him despite the fact that a shark was spotted near the bleeding victim. Following the rescue of the pilot, and before his own retrieval, the hoisting device aboard the helicopter malfunctioned. Realizing the urgency of immediate medical attention for the now unconscious pilot, Lieutenant (jg) Westin waved the helicopter off and remained in the shark-infested water until the arrival of a second rescue helicopter five minutes later. Through his quick thinking, cool courage, and selflessness in the face of grave personal risk, he was directly responsible for saving the life of his pilot. His heroic efforts were in keeping with the highest traditions of the United States Naval Service.

WESTPHAL, WARREN R.

Citation: For extraordinary heroism on 24 November 1968 while serving with River Division 572 during combat operations against enemy aggressor forces on the Mekong River in the Republic of Vietnam. As Patrol Officer for River Patrol Boats (PBRs) 138 and 55, Petty Officer Westphal was conducting a routine mission on a narrow branch of the Mekong River when his patrol encountered a communist battalion crossing southward. The enemy force took the two PBRs under increasingly intense fire from at least twenty positions. Realizing that they were caught in the kill zone of a hostile force vastly larger than their own, the patrol boat crewmen accelerated to full speed and headed for the open river. Suddenly a rocket detonated directly in front of the lead boat, PBR 138, in which Petty Officer Westphal was embarked, seriously wounding the forward machine gunner. Believing that PBR 55 was in more serious trouble, Petty Officer Westphal gave the order to turn toward it and then personally manned the forward gun battery in PBR 138 until his craft received three additional hits which wounded the entire crew, including himself, flooded the boat, and rendered its weapons useless. After transferring two seriously-injured crew members to PBR 55, and ordering the cover boat to proceed out of the canal, he beached his own craft on the far bank and personally provided medical assistance for another injured man. Petty Officer Westphal's crew received no additional enemy opposition, and he was then able to request a medical evacuation helicopter and vector outside assistance to engage the retreating enemy. By his exemplary courage and outstanding professional ability, he prevented a large enemy force from crossing the river, and was directly responsible for saving the lives of eleven of his comrades. Petty Officer Westphal's heroic actions in the face of almost overwhelming enemy opposition were in keeping with the highest traditions of the United States Naval Service.

WIANT, JEFFRIE E., JR.

Citation: For extraordinary heroism on 30 August 1968 as pilot of a search and rescue helicopter, serving with Detachment 110, Helicopter Combat Support Squadron SEVEN, embarked in USS STERETT (DLG-31). Lieutenant (jg) Wiant launched from STERETT to attempt recovery of a Navy attack pilot downed near Vinh, North

Vietnam, in an area requiring a circuitous flight of approximately fifty miles over enemy territory. Despite heavy antiaircraft fire, combined with small-arms fire en route to and in the rescue area, he skillfully and expeditiously maneuvered his aircraft over the downed pilot and commenced a pickup. Although his aircraft was hit several times while in hover, he steadfastly remained in position until the airman was hoisted aboard. Lieutenant (jg) Wiant's courage and calm professionalism while piloting his helicopter through a veritable hail of antiaircraft fire were key factors in the successful accomplishment of his mission. His superb aerial skill, valor, and devotion to duty reflected great credit upon himself and were in keeping with the highest traditions of the United States Naval Service.

WIDGER, ROBERT I.

Citation: For extraordinary heroism on 7 June 1969 as a Machine Gun Squad Leader in Company K, Third Battalion, First Marines, First Marine Division in connection with combat operations against an armed enemy in the Republic of Vietnam. When his platoon commander and platoon sergeant were seriously wounded, along with several other Marines, during a ground attack by a numerically superior hostile force which penetrated the defensive perimeter, Corporal Widger immediately assumed command of the platoon and repeatedly exposed himself to the enemy fire while directing the fire of his men and coordinating the defensive actions. On one occasion, he manned a machine gun and accounted for several enemy casualties. On still another occasion, when his weapon malfunctioned, he succeeded in eliminating an attacking enemy soldier in hand-to-hand combat. With several wounded Marines lying in dangerously exposed positions, Corporal Widger moved across the fire-swept terrain to his fallen comrades, administered first aid, and moved them to covered positions. Under his decisive leadership, the enemy attack was repelled and the hostile troops were driven from within the perimeter. He then provided cover while the medical evacuation helicopters extracted the wounded. By his heroic and inspiring actions, Corporal Widger contributed greatly to the success of his platoon in accounting for numerous enemy casualties and in capturing large quantities of weapons and ammunition. His outstanding courage, initiative, and devotion to duty in the face of great personal danger were in keeping with the highest traditions of the Marine Corps and of the United States Naval Service.

*WILHELM, MACK H.

Citation: For extraordinary heroism on 19 February 1969 as a corpsman serving with Company D, First Battalion, Ninth Marines, Third Marine Division in connection with combat operations against the enemy in the Republic of Vietnam. When his company came under a heavy volume of fire from an enemy force occupying a well-concealed bunker complex at the crest of a hill in the northern section of the I Corps Tactical Zone, Petty Officer Wilhelm observed a seriously wounded Marine lying dangerously exposed to the intense hostile fire, and quickly raced across the fire-swept terrain to the side of the casualty. Although Petty Officer Wilhelm was painfully wounded in the shoulder, he skillfully administered emergency first aid to his companion, picked him up and, shielding him with his own body, commenced to carry him to a sheltered position. Once again wounded, this time in the leg, Petty Officer Wilhelm nonetheless managed to evacuate his patient to a relatively safe location. He then returned through the hail of fire to the side of another critically wounded Marine and was in the process of examining the casualty when he, himself, was mortally wounded by a burst of enemy rifle fire. By his daring initiative, outstanding courage, and selfless dedication, Petty Officer Wilhelm was directly instrumental in saving the life of a fellow serviceman. His heroic and determined efforts were in keeping with the highest traditions of the United States Naval Service.

*WILLEFORD, FRANKLIN P.

Citation: For extraordinary heroism on 14 December 1968 while serving as a Platoon Corpsman in Company C, First Battalion, Fifth Marines, First Marine Division, in Quang Nam Province, Republic of Vietnam. As Hospitalman Willeford's platoon was participating in a company-sized sweep through an area, the lead element came under intensive automatic-weapons fire which wounded and trapped one Marine in very close proximity to one of the enemy bunkers. Seeing his comrade fall and subsequently receive another hit from a grenade, Hospitalman Willeford unhesitatingly left his position of relative security and moved forward to the side of the mortally-wounded Marine. Hidden from the enemy positions by the tall grass in the area, he found the Marine bleeding severely and in no condition to be moved. Hospitalman Willeford raised himself up and into the grazing zone of hostile fire in order to administer a heart massage and mouth-to-mouth resuscitation, continuing his desperate attempts to save the Marine until all hope of life had expired. Only then did he begin the slow return through the fire-swept zone to the trench line, bringing with him the body of his comrade. As his platoon again started through the area, the enemy opened up with intensive small-arms and automatic-weapons fire, wounding and trapping the three lead Marines. When two Marines started to move out of the trench line to retrieve the casualties, one was mortally wounded and the other critically wounded. Disregarding the intense danger, Hospitalman Willeford again moved forward to aid his fellowman. Finding the first Marine mortally wounded, and realizing the impossibility of trying to move him back to a secure area, Hospitalman Willeford stayed with the Marine, rendering what aid and comfort he could, until the Marine succumbed to his injuries. After he had informed the remainder of the platoon that the Marine had died, he proceeded deeper into the fire zone toward the second Marine, and drew fire from an enemy bunker a short distance from the wounded man. With full knowledge that the enemy was now concentrating their fire upon him, Hospitalman Willeford forged his way through the tall grass to the wounded Marines's side and began administering aid. While treating the fallen Marine, Hospitalman Willeford was also struck and mortally wounded. His courageous actions were an inspiration to all who observed him and were in keeping with the highest traditions of the United States Naval Service.

WILLIAMS, JAMES E.

Citation: For extraordinary heroism on 15 January 1967 while serving with River Section 531 and friendly foreign forces during combat operations against communist insurgent (Viet Cong) forces on the Mekong River in the Republic of Vietnam. As Patrol Officer of a combat River Patrol Boat (PBR) patrol, Petty Officer Williams interdicted a major enemy supply movement across the Nam Thon branch of the Mekong River. He directed his units to the suspected crossing area, and was immediately taken under intense hostile fire from fortified positions and from along the river banks. After coordinating Vietnamese artillery support and U. S. Air Force air strikes, Petty Officer Williams courageously led his three PBR's back into the hazardous river to investigate and destroy the enemy sampans and supplies. Blistering fire was again unleashed upon his forces. Frequently exposing himself to enemy fire, he directed his units in silencing several automatic-weapons positions, and directed one PBR to investigate several sampans which could be seen, while the other PBR's provided cover fire. Almost immediately, the enemy renewed their fire in an effort to force the PBR's away from the sampans. Petty Officer Williams ordered the destruction of the sampan and the extraction of all his units. During the fierce firefight following the temporary immobilization of one of the units, Petty Officer Williams was wounded. Despite his painful injuries, he was able to lead his patrol back through the heavy enemy fire. His patrol had successfully interdicted a crossing attempt of three heavy-weapons companies totalling nearly four hundred men, had accounted for sixteen enemy killed in action, twenty wounded, the destruction of nine enemy sampans and junks, seven enemy structures, and 2400 pounds of enemy rice. By his outstanding display of decisive leadership, his unlimited courage in the face of heavy enemy fire, and his utmost devotion to duty, Petty Officer Williams upheld the highest traditions of the United States Naval Service.

WILLIAMS, LLOYD T., JR.

Citation: For extraordinary heroism on 28 April 1969 while serving as a crew chief and door gunner with Helicopter Attack (Light) Squadron THREE, Detachment THREE, during a strike mission against enemy sampans in the Republic of Vietnam. When the wing-aircraft was struck by ground fire and crashed, and his own aircraft was also struck and forced to land, Petty Officer Williams calmly directed the preparations for the forced landing while continuing to return the enemy fire. After his aircraft had landed and the crew had abandoned it, he advanced toward the enemy under heavy fire and established a defensive position on the path leading to the enemy positions. Observing a crew member from the crashed wing-aircraft moving in the midst of the wreckage, Petty Officer Williams exposed himself to the blistering fire and ran across an open field to rescue the casualty. After carrying the severely injured man back across the open field to an area near the defensive perimeter, Petty Officer Williams returned to the wreckage in an attempt to find others from its crew. Obliged to suppress enemy fire in order to conduct his search, he persisted in his rescue attempts, despite the heat from the fire and the dangers of the exploding ammunition, until his ammunition was exhausted. Petty Officer Williams then ran to the defensive perimeter to report that the enemy had started using mortars, and proceeded to assist a casualty aboard a rescue helicopter before boarding the craft himself to render first aid to the other wounded. Petty Officer Williams' determined efforts, his indomitable courage under fire, and his inspiring devotion to duty were in keeping with the highest traditions of the United States Naval Service.

WILLIAMS, ROBERT S.

Citation: For extraordinary heroism as Platoon Commander, First Platoon, Company I, Third Battalion, Fifth Marines, First Marine Division in the Cam Lo District, Republic of Vietnam on 24 and 25 July 1966. As Company I moved onto Hill 362, First Lieutenant (then Second Lieutenant) Williams' platoon overran the forward security elements of an estimated battalion of the North Vietnamese Army. While in conflict with the security elements the Second Platoon bypassed the First Platoon and came under devastating preplanned fire by the enemy's main force, suffering many casualties. Realizing the graveness of the situation and being constantly exposed to intense enemy fire, First Lieutenant Williams led his platoon in the same frontal assault. Inspired by his courageous leadership and apparent calm in the face of overwhelming odds, the First Platoon gained the time and terrain to cover the rescue of the Second Platoon's wounded. When the numerically stronger force counterattacked, First Lieutenant Williams took command of the two platoons and formed them into a right perimeter for a better defense. Fearing that wounded had been left behind, he went out of the perimeter alone to search for them. There were bursts of automatic weapons fire, and the covering force began receiving withering assault fire from the advancing enemy. Artillery fire was called in to within seventy-five yards of the forward positions to avoid being completely overrun. Returning to the perimeter, First Lieutenant Williams emerged from the tall grass and reported he could not find any more wounded. Throughout the remainder of that day and the next, First Lieutenant Williams, constantly exposed to enemy fire, moved from position to position encouraging his men and directing their fire. Then early in the evening of 24 July, being too engrossed in his duties to seek cover, he was painfully wounded in the leg by a mortar attack; but he refused treatment until his troops had been cared for and continued moving from position to position bolstering morale and the fighting efficiency of his unit. First Lieutenant Williams' extreme valor, undying devotion to duty, and initiative at the risk of his own life, saved the lives of many Marines and upheld the highest traditions of the Marine Corps and the United States Naval Service.

WILSON, WILLIS C.

Citation: For extraordinary heroism as a Platoon Commander with Company B, First Battalion, Third Marines in connection with operations against communist forces in the Republic of Vietnam on 2 April 1966. During Operation ORANGE, Lieutenant Wilson's platoon became heavily engaged with the enemy near the hamlet of Lap Thuan. Intense enemy mortar fire, close-range small-arms fire, and barbed wire obstacles covered by automatic weapons prevented the forward movement of the platoon. Although painfully wounded during the initial mortar barrage, Lieutenant Wilson courageously moved up and down his platoon's positions, directing his men and judiciously ordering the deployed squads to bypass the barbed wire in an attempt to eliminate the Viet Cong threat. When his platoon sergeant was wounded and became entangled in the barbed wire, Lieutenant Wilson, with complete disregard for his own safety, started across seventy-five meters of open terrain in an attempt to retrieve the mortally wounded man, who was still being hit by small-arms fire. Before he could reach the sergeant's position, Lieutenant Wilson was caught in the hail of small-arms fire and seriously wounded in the shoulder. Although thwarted in the rescue effort, he competently resumed direction of the platoon and established a strong base of fire to provide cover for a deployed squad. When a radio operator was wounded in a sudden flurry of Viet Cong fire, Lieutenant Wilson again braved the withering fire to assist the man. For the third time, he was hit, sustaining a serious wound in the chest from small-arms fire. With extraordinary determination and presence of mind, he continued to maintain direction of his platoon. Increasing the rate of fire from his base squads, he launched an attack by the enveloping squad which finally silenced the Viet Cong fire. By his exceptional valor despite his suffering from multiple wounds, daring initiative and unswerving dedication to duty throughout, Lieutenant Wilson upheld the highest traditions of the Marine Corps and the United States Naval Service.

*WIRICK, WILLIAM C.

Citation: For extraordinary heroism while serving as a Mortar Section Leader with Company I, Third Battalion, Twenty-sixth

Marines, Ninth Marine Amphibious Brigade in connection with combat operations against the enemy in the Republic of Vietnam. On the night of 8 December 1968, while Corporal Wirick's platoon was maneuvering across a large open rice paddy, the Marines were pinned down by a heavy volume of automatic weapons fire from a hostile force occupying well-fortified emplacements, and were then subjected to intense sniper fire from enemy soldiers located in elevated positions. Although seriously wounded during the initial moments of the fierce fire fight, Corporal Wirick ignored his painful injury and maneuvered boldly across the fire-swept terrain, supervising the evacuation of other casualties. Observing that another wounded and helpless companion had become a vulnerable target for sniper fire, Corporal Wirick unhesitatingly threw himself across his companion and, with his own body, absorbed the primary effects of several sniper rounds. His heroic action and selfless concern for his fellowman inspired all who observed him and saved the life of another Marine. By his courage, bold initiative and unwavering devotion to duty in the face of grave personal danger, Corporal Wirick upheld the highest traditions of the Marine Corps and of the United States Naval Service. He gallantly gave his life in the service of his country.

WOODS, LLOYD

Citation: For extraordinary heroism while serving as a Radio Operator with Company F, Second Battalion, Fifth Marines, First Marine Division (Reinforced) in Quang Tin Province, Republic of Vietnam, on 2 June 1967. During Operation UNION II, Corporal Woods' company came under intense enemy automatic weapons, small arms and mortar fire which temporarily pinned down the first platoon in an exposed rice paddy. In the initial burst of fire, the platoon sustained numerous casualties, including the platoon commander. Upon observing his wounded commander lying exposed to the intense enemy fire, he unhesitatingly ran through the heavy volume of fire to his side, placed him on his shoulder and carried him to a position of relative safety. Then, rallying four companions, he again moved across the open rice paddy to evacuate another wounded Marine who was lying in close proximity to an enemy machine gun position. Upon reaching the wounded man and realizing it was impossible to move him because of the enemy machine gun fire, he boldly maneuvered into the tree line towards the enemy position, and singlehandedly assaulted the gun, killing the gunner and capturing his weapon. He then boldly leaped into the adjacent emplacement and, in fierce hand-to-hand combat, killed that gunner and commenced to fire the enemy machine gun against other hostile positions, providing cover while his companions evacuated the wounded man. As a result of Corporal Woods' courageous actions, his unit was able to regroup and succeeded in evacuating its casualties to positions of safety. By his intrepid fighting spirit, exceptional fortitude and gallant initiative, Corporal Woods inspired all who observed him and upheld the highest traditions of the Marine Corps and the United States Naval Service.

WORK, WARREN A., JR.

Citation: For extraordinary heroism on 8 April 1967 while serving as a corpsman with Company F, Second Battalion, Fourth Marines, Third Marine Division in connection with combat operations against insurgent communist (Viet Cong) forces in the Republic of Vietnam. While on a security patrol in Quang Nam Province, Petty Officer Work's reinforced squad came under intense small-arms fire and grenade attack from a numerically superior enemy force. With his squad pinned down, and the machine gunner hit during the initial burst of fire, Petty Officer Work rushed across an exposed area to render medical assistance to the fallen Marine. As he was approaching, he observed two enemy soldiers firing their weapons as they maneuvered toward the wounded machine gunner. Aware of the extreme danger to his patient, Petty Officer Work directed fire at the enemy soldiers and killed them before treating and comforting the wounded man. After encouraging and aiding the mounting number of casualties, he found that one of the injured was too seriously wounded to move. Petty Officer Work administered first aid to the Marine and hid him in the dense underbrush to await later evacuation. While the enemy was regrouping for another attack, Petty Officer Work, singlehandedly assisted his seriously wounded patrol leader to the security of the platoon's perimeter, solacing him and caring for his wounds. By his steadfast determination and deep compassion for his comrades, Petty Officer Work was instrumental in saving several Marine lives. His extraordinary courage, bold initiative, and inspiring devotion to duty in the face of enemy fire were in keeping with the highest traditions of the United States Naval Service.

WYNN, EDWARD H.

Citation: For extraordinary heroism while serving as a Platoon Radio Operator with Company E, Second Battalion, Fourth Marines, Ninth Marine Amphibious Brigade, in connection with operations against the enemy in the Republic of Vietnam. On the morning of 25 May 1968, Company E was assaulting two North Vietnamese Army companies occupying well-fortified positions near the village of Nhi Ha (2) in Quang Tri Province when the point platoon became pinned down by intense small arms, automatic weapons, and mortar fire. Realizing that the heavy volume of fire was preventing his platoon from reinforcing the lead elements, Private First Class Wynn fearlessly exposed himself to the furious hostile fire and commenced delivering suppressive fire upon the enemy emplacements. Observing a corpsman attempting to assist a wounded Marine to a covered location, he unhesitatingly maneuvered across the fire-swept terrain to a more advantageous firing position and directed devastating covering fire which enabled the injured man to be moved to an area of relative safety. Although seriously wounded by intense grenade fire, Private First Class Wynn steadfastly refused medical treatment and continued his determined efforts against the enemy. Alertly observing three hostile soldiers approaching a tank from the rear, he courageously assaulted the enemy attackers, wounding two and capturing the third soldier. Ignoring the hostile rounds impacting near him, Private First Class Wynn rapidly returned to his platoon with the prisoner and, fearlessly traversing the dangerously exposed area on two additional occasions, recovered the two remaining injured North Vietnamese and delivered them to his unit. Although weak from his wounds, he resolutely resumed his fighting position and assisted his comrades until all of the other casualties were medically evacuated. By his intrepid fighting spirit, exceptional fortitude and gallant initiative, Private First Class Wynn served to inspire all who observed him and contributed in large measure to the success of his unit in assaulting the enemy. His great personal valor reflected the highest credit upon himself and enhanced the finest traditions of the Marine Corps and the United States Naval Service.

*YARBER, VERNON L.

Citation: For extraordinary heroism while serving as a Squad Leader with Company L, Third Battalion, Third Marines, Third

Marine Division in connection with combat operations against the enemy in the Republic of Vietnam. On the night of 26 August 1968, Corporal Yarber was occupying a listening post in front of his company's defensive position near the Rockpile in Quang Tri Province when the Marines came under a heavy volume of enemy mortar fire. Realizing the seriousness of the situation, he rapidly maneuvered his men to a relatively safe position from which to more effectively observe the surrounding area. Following the mortar attack, Corporal Yarber alertly detected a reinforced North Vietnamese Army platoon moving toward the Marine perimeter and, immediately directing his radio operator to inform his commanding officer of the impending attack, boldly led his small force in delivering a heavy volume of fire upon the hostile soldiers. When ordered to return to the perimeter, he unhesitatingly ordered his men to depart the listening post and, disregarding his own safety, fearlessly remained behind as he provided effective covering fire for his comrades. As the last man departed, Corporal Yarber attempted to withdraw from his isolated position and was mortally wounded. His daring initiative and heroic efforts inspired all who observed him and were instrumental in preventing a surprise attack on his company. By his courage, sincere concern for the welfare of his comrades, and steadfast devotion to duty, Corporal Yarber contributed significantly to the accomplishment of his unit's mission and upheld the highest traditions of the Marine Corps and the United States Naval Service. He gallantly gave his life for his country.

*YATES, JOHN CHARLES

Citation: For extraordinary heroism while serving as the Communications Chief of Company B, First Amphibian Tractor Battalion, Third Marine Division in connection with operations against the enemy in the Republic of Vietnam. On the morning of 17 October 1968, Second Lieutenant Yates, then a Staff Sergeant, was participating in the transportation of Marines by amphibian tractor during operations north of the Cua Viet River in Quang Tri Province. When informed that one of the vehicles had detonated a hostile antitank mine, immobilizing the tractor and trapping the driver inside, he unhesitatingly ran to the disabled and flaming vehicle. Undaunted by the danger of potential explosions from fire he observed within the tractor, he completely disregarded his own safety as he fearlessly climbed on top of the vehicle. While he was preparing to enter the tractor through the crew chief's hatch to rescue the driver, the fuel cells within the vehicle exploded and fatally injured Second Lieutenant Yates. By his courage, bold initiative and unwavering devotion to duty, Second Lieutenant Yates inspired all who observed him and upheld the highest traditions of the Marine Corps and of the United States Naval Service. He gallantly gave his life in the service of his country.

YORDY, CHARLES R.

Citation: For extraordinary heroism while serving with Company K, Third Battalion, Twenty-seventh Marines, First Marine Division (Reinforced), in connection with operations against the enemy in the Republic of Vietnam. On 24 May 1968 during Operation ALLEN BROOK in Quang Nam Province, Private Yordy's platoon was assigned the mission of enveloping an enemy village in order to relieve the pressure on an adjacent platoon which was pinned down by the heavy volume of fire from well fortified hostile positions. As the Marines moved up on the flank of the enemy, the unit came under intense automatic weapons fire from several North Vietnamese bunkers and spider holes, pinning down the platoon and inflicting numerous casualties, including the platoon commander who fell directly in front of an enemy machine-gun emplacement. Unhesitatingly and with complete disregard for his personal safety, Private Yordy rushed across the hazardous area firing his M-16 rifle from the hip and succeeded in reaching the side of the injured officer. Picking up the wounded man's M-79 grenade launcher and ignoring the enemy rounds striking around him, he fired directly into the aperture of the bunker silencing the hostile fire. Observing another enemy bunker nearby which had pinned down his companions, he crawled to the emplacement and destroyed it with several hand grenades. As the platoon began to withdraw, Private Yordy selflessly remained behind and covered the withdrawal of his unit by throwing hand grenades and firing his grenade launcher at the hostile position, abandoning his precarious position only when he was assured that his fellow Marines had reached relative safety. Throughout the battle, his heroic actions and presence of mind were an inspiration to all who observed him and were responsible for the successful extraction of his unit, undoubtedly saving the lives of many of his comrades. By his courage, aggressive fighting spirit, and selfless devotion to duty in the face of great personal danger, Private Yordy upheld the highest traditions of the Marine Corps and the United States Naval Service.

YOUNG, WILLIAM D.

Citation: For extraordinary heroism on the night of 6 August and early morning of 7 August 1972 while serving with Helicopter Combat Support Squadron SEVEN, Detachment 110, embarked in USS SARATOGA (CVA-60). As copilot of a combat rescue helicopter during nearly five hours of a coordinated search and rescue effort for a United States Navy pilot downed in North Vietnam, Lieutenant Young, in the face of intense enemy fire, rendered valuable assistance in carrying out a low-level flight with the helicopter's landing lights turned on in order to facilitate the search. Although his aircraft was repeatedly hit by enemy ground fire, he continued the search until the downed airman was visually located and picked up. Lieutenant Young then flew back to the safety of SARATOGA at treetop level with his crippled aircraft. By his skilled airmanship, courage, and devotion to duty, he contributed materially to the success of an extremely hazardous rescue mission and upheld the highest traditions of the United States Naval Service.

YOUNG, WILLIAM H.

Citation: For extraordinary heroism while serving as a Radio Operator with Company A, First Battalion, Third Marines, Third Marine Division in connection with combat operations against the enemy in the Republic of Vietnam. On the afternoon of 7 March 1968, while advancing toward the village of Phu Tai in Quang Tri Province, Company A came under intense automatic weapons and mortar fire from a numerically superior North Vietnamese Army force concealed in fortified bunkers. Although the Marines were pinned down in an open rice paddy, where any movement away from the protection afforded by the small dikes might mean almost certain death or serious injury, Corporal Young ignored the rounds impacting near him and fearlessly moved to positions from which he could effectively control air strikes on the enemy emplacements. When friendly casualties increased, he again disregarded his own safety as he unhesitatingly maneuvered forward and directed the evacuation of the wounded to a helicopter landing zone which he had established. During a subsequent assault on the village, he repeatedly exposed himself to intense hostile fire in order to coordinate and control the fire of supporting helicopter gunships. As the Marines moved through the hazardous area, an enemy soldier suddenly ran out of a nearby bunker and prepared to fire directly at the advancing command group. Shouting a warning to his comrades, Corporal Young boldly assaulted the North Vietnamese, killing him with accurate pistol fire. Although he was later wounded in the chest and leg by sniper fire and moved to a covered position, he ignored his painful injuries and continued to coordinate vital air support for approximately three hours. His heroic and selfless actions inspired all who observed him. By his courage, intrepid fighting spirit, and unwavering devotion to duty in the face of great personal danger, Corporal Young contributed immeasurably to the defeat of the enemy and upheld the highest traditions of the Marine Corps and the United States Naval Service.

ZACHARIAS, JERROLD M.

Citation: For extraordinary heroism on 24 February 1968 as a pilot in Attack Squadron SEVENTY-FIVE, embarked in USS KITTY HAWK (CVA-63), and launched from USS ENTERPRISE (CVA(N)-65) in a joint attack with Attack Squadron THIRTY-FIVE. Commander Zacharias participated in a coordinated, night, low-level strike against the heavily defended port facilities within the city of Hanoi, North Vietnam. Soon after launching, he developed serious systems difficulties in his aircraft. Through the professionalism and determination of Commander Zacharias and his bombardier/navigator, this discrepancy was overcome and they rejoined the flight to continue the attack. En route to, and in the target area, extremely heavy and accurate antiaircraft fire was encountered and the aircraft received a hit in the left wing. Notwithstanding this battle damage, Commander Zacharias aggressively piloted his aircraft to the target through multiple surface-to-air missile attacks which he successfully evaded through extremely low-altitude maneuvering. He then delivered his ordnance directly on the target area. During egress from the target area, he again came under an intense attack from surface-to-air missiles and was forced to maneuver violently at very low altitude. One missile was seen to explode aft and below his aircraft, buffeting it violently. By his daring action, exceptional skill, and loyal devotion to duty in the face of intense enemy opposition, Commander Zacharias upheld the highest traditions of the United States Naval Service.

ZINSER, HARRY J.

Citation: For extraordinary heroism in action on the night of 6 August and early morning of 7 August 1972 while serving with Helicopter Combat Support Squadron SEVEN, Detachment 110, embarked in USS SARATOGA (CVA-60). As pilot in command of a combat rescue helicopter during nearly five hours of a coordinated search and rescue effort for a United States Navy pilot downed in North Vietnam, Lieutenant Zinser, in the face of intense enemy fire, commenced a low-level flight and turned on his landing lights in order to facilitate the search. Although his aircraft was repeatedly hit by enemy ground fire, he continued the search until the downed pilot was visually located. Lieutenant Zinser then carried out a skillful landing, picked up the downed airman and succeeded in flying his crippled aircraft at treetop level back to the safety of SARATOGA. By his outstanding aeronautical skill, courageous leadership, and inspiring dedication, Lieutenant Zinser reflected great credit upon himself and the Marine Corps and upheld the highest traditions of the United States Naval Service.

PART III

AWARDS OF THE NAVY CROSS

VIETNAM — 1964 - 1973

U.S. MARINE CORPS
   TOTAL AWARDS — VIETNAM ERA 362
      (Second Awards - First Award Korea - 2)
      (Second Awards - First Award Vietnam - 2)

U.S. NAVY 121
      (USS LIBERTY - Eastern Mediterranean - 2)

U.S. ARMY 1

REPUBLIC of VIETNAM NAVY 1

                         TOTAL AWARDS   485

PART IV

NAVY CROSS INDEX